THE CHANGING LANDSCAPE OF MILTON KEYNES

by

R.A. CROFT and D.C. MYNARD

With Contributions by

Margaret Gelling, R.J. Ivens, R.J. Zeepvat and R.J. Williams.

The Buckinghamshire Archaeological Society
Monograph Series No 5

Series Editor: J. Chenevix Trench

Published by Buckinghamshire Archaeological Society
The Museum, Church Street, Aylesbury

ISBN 0 949003 12 3

© Buckinghamshire Archaeological Society 1993
All rights reserved

Cover illustration based upon Robert Morden's eighteenth-century map of Buckinghamshire, with aerial photographs of (*top left*) the Toot, Shenley Church End, and (*bottom right*) Bancroft Villa, surrounded by modern development.

ACKNOWLEDGEMENT

The Buckinghamshire Archaeological Society and the Milton Keynes Archaeology Unit gratefully acknowledge the total funding by Milton Keynes Development Corporation of the publication of this volume

Typeset in Linotype Times by: Mike Kelly Photosetting
'Avalon', Hartham Lane, Biddestone, Chippenham, Wiltshire, from Author's discs.

Printed and Bound by Longdunn Press Limited, Bristol, Avon

CONTENTS

List of figures iv
List of tables v
List of plates vi

ACKNOWLEDGEMENTS ix

INTRODUCTION xi

GEOLOGY AND TOPOGRAPHY R.J. Zeepvat 1

PREHISTORIC LANDSCAPE R.J. Williams 5

ROMAN LANDSCAPE R.J. Zeepvat 11

SAXON LANDSCAPE 15

MEDIEVAL LANDSCAPE 19
Boundaries 19
Parishes 21
Villages 21
Manors 21
Roads and trackways 25
Castles 26
Markets 28
Mills 28
Moats 30
Fisheries 31
Field systems 32
Woods and parks 33
Religious houses 34

POST-MEDIEVAL LANDSCAPE R.J. Zeepvat 37

PLACE-NAMES OF THE MILTON KEYNES AREA M. Gelling 45

PARISH ESSAYS

Bletchley 51
Bow Brickhill R.J. Zeepvat 61
Bradwell 71
Bradwell Abbey 83
Great Linford 91
Loughton 111
Milton Keynes 121
The Shenleys R.J. Ivens 131
Simpson 145
Stantonbury 153
Tattenhoe R.J. Ivens 159
Walton 165
Willen 171
Wolverton 179
The Woolstones 195
Woughton on the Green 201

BIBLIOGRAPHY 209

LIST OF FIGURES

1 Location map showing the area before the construction of Milton Keynes. xii
2 Surface geology and drainage. 2
3 Distribution map of Palaeolithic to Bronze Age sites. 6
4 Distribution map of Iron Age sites. 9
5 Reconstruction of the Iron Age settlement at Pennyland. 10
6 Distribution map of Roman sites. 12
7 Reconstruction of Bancroft villa, c.AD.350 13
8 Distribution map of Saxon sites. 16
9 Relationship of Roman and Saxon sites to medieval boundaries. 17
10 Medieval landscape features. 20
11 Boundaries of the Saxon Hundreds and parishes. 22
12 Reconstruction of Great Linford post-mill. 29
13 Distribution of post-medieval industrial sites. 38
14 Bletchley parish in 1967, showing major archaeological sites. 52
15 The estate of Browne Willis in Eaton and Fenny Stratford, 1718. 53
16 The fishpond at Water Hall, based on 1881 OS map. 55
17 Guild of St Margaret and St Katherine the Virgin, Fenny Stratford; reconstruction of medieval framework. 58
18 Bow Brickhill parish in 1967, showing major archaeological sites. 62
19 Bow Brickhill; reconstruction of 1791 enclosure map. 65
20 Caldecotte village earthworks and moated site. 67
21 Bow Brickhill parish; medieval field system. 68
22 Reconstruction of Caldecotte watermill 70
23 Bradwell parish in 1967, showing major archaeological sites. 72
24 Bradwell; earthworks of the medieval manor and the motte-and-bailey castle. 74
25 Bradwell: the estate map of William Bailey, 1792. 74
26 Bradwell medieval field system. 77
27 Bradwell; reconstruction of tithe award map, 1839. 78
28 Bradwell Abbey parish in 1967, showing major archaeological sites. 84
29 Bradwell Abbey; the earthworks and a reconstruction of the plan of the priory buildings. . . . 85
30 Bradwell Abbey medieval field system. 87
31 Bradwell Abbey; the estate of the Earl of Dartmouth, 1797. 89
32 Great Linford parish in 1967, showing major archaeological sites. 92
33 Great Linford village earthworks. 94
34 Great Linford; probable extent of the village by the early fourteenth century. 97
35 Great Linford village in 1641, based on the estate map. 98
36 Great Linford; reconstruction of the 1641 estate map. 100
37 Great Linford; reconstruction of the 1678 estate map. 102
38 Great Linford medieval field system. 105
39 Loughton parish in 1967, showing major archaeological sites. 112
40 Loughton village earthworks. 113
41 Loughton moat and fishponds. 115
42 Loughton medieval field system. 118
43 Loughton; reconstruction of the 1769 tithe map. 119
44 Milton Keynes parish in 1967, showing major archaeological sites. 122
45 Milton Keynes; reconstruction of the 1685 estate map. 124
46 Milton Keynes village earthworks. 126
47 Milton Keynes village in 1685, reconstructed from the estate map. 127
48 22 Milton Keynes Village; reconstruction of medieval framework. 128
49 Milton Keynes parish medieval field system. 129
50 Shenley Brook End in 1967, showing major archaeological sites. 132
51 Shenley Church End in 1967, showing major archaeological sites. 133
52 Shenley Church End earthworks. 135
53 Shenley Brook End earthworks. 138
54 Shenley Church End medieval field system. 142
55 Shenley Brook End medieval field system. 143
56 Simpson parish in 1967, showing major archaeological sites. 146

iv

57	Simpson; earthworks of manor, moat and fishponds.	147
58	Simpson; reconstruction of manor and mill sites, from the 1781 estate map.	149
59	Simpson medieval field system.	151
60	Stantonbury parish in 1967, showing major archaeological sites.	154
61	Stantonbury medieval field system.	156
62	Tattenhoe parish in 1967, showing major archaeological sites.	160
63	Tattenhoe; earthworks of medieval village and moated site.	161
64	Tattenhoe medieval field system.	164
65	Walton parish in 1967, showing major archaeological sites.	166
66	Walton village earthworks.	167
67	Walton medieval field system.	169
68	Willen parish in 1967, showing major archaeological sites.	172
69	Willen village earthworks.	173
70	Willen Mill in 1822.	174
71	Willen; cottages in Mill Lane, 1822.	175
72	Willen medieval field system.	176
73	Willen; reconstruction of 1690 estate map	177
74	Wolverton parish in 1967, showing major archaeological sites.	180
75	Wolverton village earthworks.	184
76	Wolverton; reconstruction of the 1742 estate map.	188
77	Wolverton medieval field system.	190
78	The Woolstones in 1967, showing major archaeological sites.	196
79	Great Woolstone; village, moat and fishpond earthworks.	197
80	Little Woolstone; earthworks of moated site.	199
81	The Woolstones medieval field system.	200
82	Woughton on the Green in 1967, showing major archaeological sites.	202
83	Woughton on the Green village earthworks.	203
84	Woughton on the Green medieval field system.	206

TABLES

1	List of mills mentioned in the Domesday survey.	28
2	Continuity of field names in Bradwell parish.	80
3	Medieval field names in Walton parish.	169

LARGE FORMAT MAPS
(in wallet inside back cover)

- L1 Bletchley; Browne Willis estate map, 1718.
- L2 Bletchley tithe map, 1813.
- L3 Great Linford estate map, 1641.
- L4 Great Linford estate map, 1678.
- L5 Loughton enclosure map, 1769.
- L6 Milton Keynes estate map, 1782.
- L7 Shenley Brook End estate map, 1698.
- L8 Simpson estate map, 1781.
- L9 Tattenhoe; Selby estate map, 1801.
- L10 Willen; estate of Richard Busby, 1822.
- L11 Salden estate map, 1599.

PLATES

1	Late Bronze/early Iron Age roundhouse, Blue Bridge.	8
2	Secklow Hundred meeting mound, after landscaping.	18
3	Bradwell village, from the south-west.	23
4	Bradwell Bury earthworks, from the north.	24
5	Loughton Manor farm house, 1987.	25
6	Shenley Toot motte and bailey earthworks, from the south.	27
7	Bradwell windmill.	29
8	Caldecotte moat from the north-east, before backfilling.	30
9	Bradwell Abbey; the large fishpond after cleaning, 1975.	31
10	Ridge-and-furrow in Great Linford parish, c.1975.	32
11	Shenley township boundary, visible as a soil-mark, 1980.	33
12	Snelshall Priory earthworks, 1975.	34
13	Wood Farm, Great Linford, 1974.	39
14	Canal basin, Great Linford, c.1880	40
15	Arch of medieval North Bridge, Newport Pagnell.	40
16	Wolverton; industrial housing and railway works, c.1960.	42
17	Water Hall, Bletchley, 1710–60.	56
18	Construction of Caldecotte Lake, 1981.	69
19	Bradwell village; Vicarage Road in the nineteenth century.	76
20	Bradwell Abbey from the south, c.1969	90
21	Great Linford manor, almshouses and church, 1980.	96
22	Cottages at Granes End, Great Linford, c.1900.	108
23	'Ye Olde Wharf Inn' and entrance to Newport Pagnell Canal, Great Linford.	108
24	Loughton moat, fishponds and associated earthworks.	114
25	Milton Keynes village, from the south-east, c.1960.	123
26	Moated grange, Shenley Church End.	136
27	Westbury-by-Shenley village earthworks, from the east.	140
28	Simpson manor, moat and fishponds earthworks, from the south.	148
29	Stantonbury village earthworks and church, c.1950.	155
30	Tattenhoe village earthworks, c.1965.	162
31	Tattenhoe village earthworks, 1979.	163
32	Walton Hall and Walton church, from south-west, 1968.	168
33	Stony Stratford and Watling Street, 1979.	182
34	Wolverton village earthworks, church and motte.	185
35	Wolverton; village earthworks around Manor Farm.	187
36	Woughton; earthworks east of Woughton House, c.1960.	204
37	Woughton; earthworks on and east of the green, c.1960.	205

Copyright: Aerofilms 3, 16, 25; Cambridge University 4, 20, 24, 27, 35 37; Mansell Collection 14; Ministry of Defence 8, 30, 34, 36; RCHM 31; all others Milton Keynes Archaeology Unit.

Plates 17, 19 and 23 are reproduced by kind permission of Sir Philip Duncombe, Northamptonshire Record Office, and Mrs Elsie Tompkins respectively.

It was – and is – a rather featureless but pleasant bit of England. The villages, with unromantic disyllabic names – Simpson, Broughton, Woughton, Woolstones, Willen – seemed each to be just over a mile from the next. Each clustered around a cross-road and an inn; each had its parsonage and church, its two or three farmhouses, its individual life.

This description of part of Milton Keynes was written by Joan Evans, a former president of the Society of Antiquaries, who spent part of her childhood in Milton Keynes village. In these few words she captured the heart of the Milton Keynes landscape as it was before the development of the City. This volume aims to broaden that picture and look at the evolution of this northern part of Buckinghamshire.

ACKNOWLEDGEMENTS

Firstly, the authors would like to thank Milton Keynes Development Corporation for totally financing the work detailed in this volume. Acknowledgements are also due to the many former colleagues in all departments of the former Development Corporation, particularly the Estates Department, for their assistance.

A number of Unit staff were involved in the fieldwork projects comprising this survey, in particular; Norman Adams, Dave Bent, Julie Bradley, Chris Hooper, Tristram Land, Bruce Induni, Tony Johnston, John Small, Paul Smith and Bob Zeepvat. One earthwork survey, that of the deserted village of Westbury-by-Shenley, was carried out for the Unit by a team of surveyors from the Royal Commission for Historical Monuments, led by Robert Wilson-North.

Most of the documentary research was carried out by Elizabeth Baines, Bob Croft, Dennis Mynard and Jonathan Sharp, and we are indebted to David Hall and the late Gerald Elvey and Jack Seymour for help with difficult translation and transcription.

Typing of this volume was undertaken by Leena Lindholm-White and Emma Jones, while much of the in-house editing was the work of Bob Zeepvat, who was primarily responsible for seeing the volume into print.

For permission to copy maps we are indebted to the late Mrs Betty Elvey of the Buckinghamshire Archaeological Society, to the County Archivists of Bedfordshire, Buckinghamshire, Leicestershire and Northamptonshire, and to Mrs Stoddart, formerly of Westbury Farm, Shenley Brook End. Several members of staff painstakingly traced the maps, including Barbara Hurman, Brendan Murphy and John Small. The cover and all of the figures in this publication have been prepared by Bob Zeepvat, except for; Brian Giggins (Figs 5, 22, 48), Tora Hylton (Figs 4, 8), Derek Mynard (7), and Paul Woodfield (17).

Finally we would like to acknowledge the many farmers in Milton Keynes, both landowners and tenants, who readily gave permission for access to their land to Unit surveyors.

INTRODUCTION

There are few areas in the country which have been the subject of such an intensive programme of field survey, excavation and back-up documentary research as that chosen for the site of Milton Keynes (Fig. 1).

The Milton Keynes project is unique in that approximately 9000 hectares (22,000 acres) of the rural south-east Midlands are affected by the development of the city, and in that an archaeological team has been employed during the first twenty years of the development to record the archaeological landscape that has been destroyed in the process.

The Milton Keynes Archaeology Unit was established by Milton Keynes Development Corporation in 1971. The Unit's brief was not only to excavate and record sites threatened by development, but also to advise on the preservation, use and management of those sites which could be retained within the landscape of the new city.

From 1971 until 1991, when the Unit ceased fieldwork, it is unlikely that any major and possibly very few minor sites that were disturbed by development escaped notice. The results of the project illustrate the variety and survival of the rich archaeological heritage in this part of England.

At the time the Unit was established, several sites in the area were protected by scheduling under the Ancient Monuments Act, but most were only partly scheduled and others omitted. Over the years the Unit has ensured that further sites have been scheduled, and that others have been more completely scheduled by the Department of the Environment. Most of these sites are now preserved as part of the City's archaeological heritage, while the few that have been affected by development have been excavated.

An extensive archive of historical information has been compiled by the Unit for each parish, and this has provided information to enable the planners to retain and enhance the local environment. For example, the re-use of former field names and local family names for areas and roads in the city has been actively encouraged by the Unit, and many old names survive on the modern map.

In 1971, archaeological landscape surveys were not as fashionable as they are today. However, the importance of recording all landscape features within each parish was recognised and undertaken by the Unit. As rescue excavation was regarded by the funding authorities to be the Unit's priority, resources for survey work were slender.

As the historic landscape was disappearing at an alarming rate it was decided to record the physical remains of the field systems on the ground whilst they survived, and to combine the results with other evidence from air photographs, early maps and other documentary evidence at a later date. Along with this, most earthwork sites in the city were surveyed, and are published together with the ridge-and-furrow surveys in this volume. Copies of all the known historic maps of the area are held within the Unit's archive, and many are also published here.

This volume was initially conceived in 1972 as a survey of the medieval sites and landscapes in the city. In 1975 Elizabeth Baines joined the Unit as its Historian, and carried out documentary research into sites which had been excavated at Great Linford, Bradwell, Woughton and Walton. From 1978 to 1986 Bob Croft continued and expanded this research, and produced the first drafts of much of this monograph. These have since been substantially rewritten by D.C. Mynard, who also wrote the parish essays for Bradwell, Bradwell Abbey, Great Linford and Stantonbury. The parish essay for Bow Brickhill has been written by Bob Zeepvat, who also wrote the Roman and post-Medieval sections, and a note on the geology of the area. Essays on Tattenhoe and the Shenleys were written by Richard Ivens, and the prehistoric section was contributed by Bob Williams.

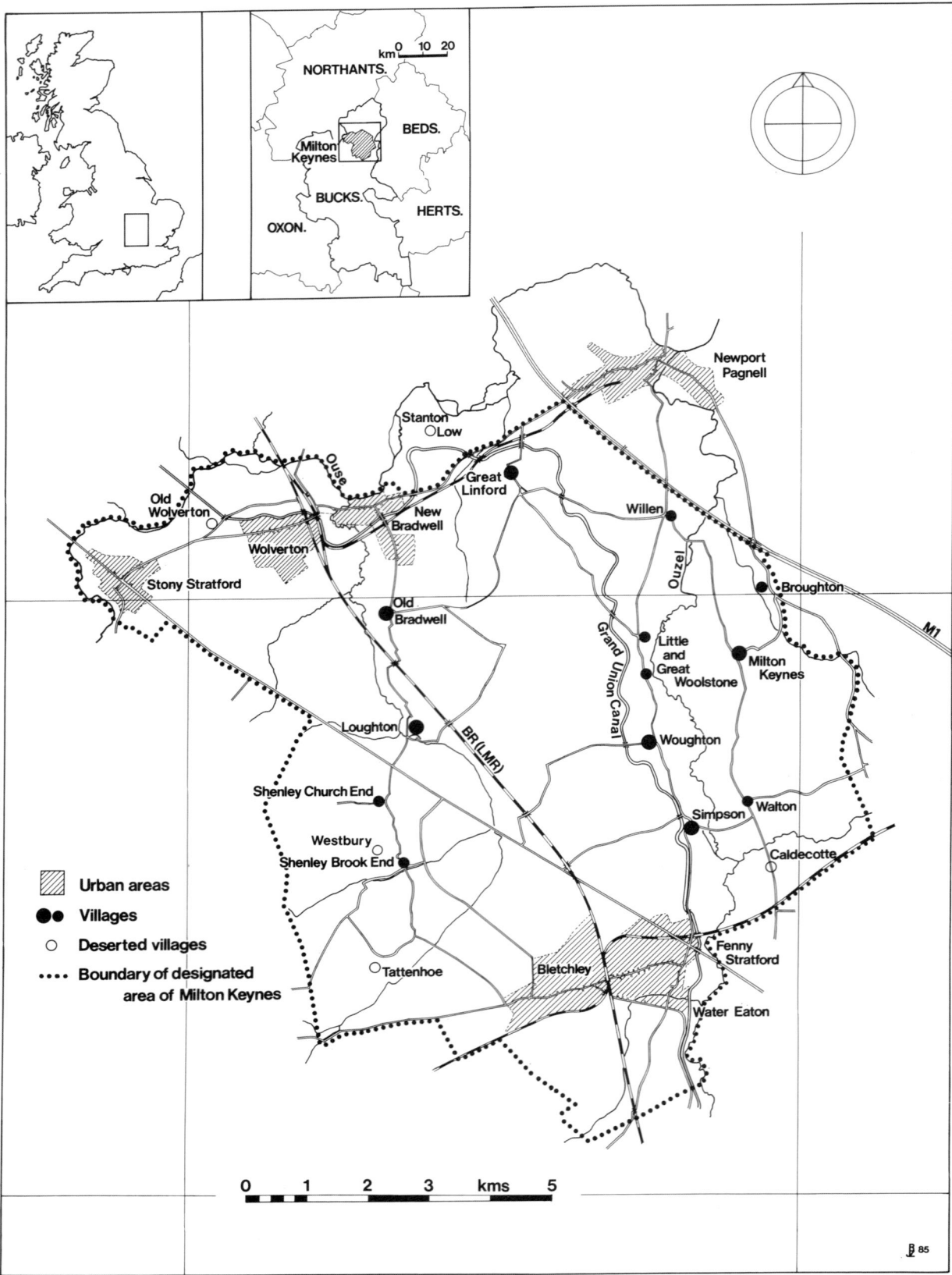

Figure 1: Location map showing the area before the construction of Milton Keynes.

xii

GEOLOGY AND TOPOGRAPHY

R.J. Zeepvat

Broadly speaking, the area now occupied by Milton Keynes (Fig. 2) forms a part of the Oxford Clay vale of the East Midlands, wherein the strata dip south-south-eastwards towards the Lower Greensand escarpment. The processes of glacial erosion and deposition have much modified the topography and soils. What follows here is a brief, simplified description of the structural geology and topography of the area; all the relevant detailed information is contained in the report of a survey conducted by the Institute of Geological Sciences (Horton, Shepherd-Thorn and Thurrell, 1974).

Structurally, the geological sequence in the Milton Keynes area is represented primarily by rocks of the later Jurassic period, beginning with the mudstone and limestones of the Upper Lias, which outcrop on the edges of the Great Ouse floodplain. The slopes overlooking this flood plain also reveal the deposits overlying the Upper Lias, a succession of mudstone, silts and limestones which together form the Inferior and Great Oolite Series. Most notable among these for their influence on the future human development of the landscape are the Blisworth and Cornbrash limestone beds.

Moving south-eastwards, much of the higher ground now occupied by Central Milton Keynes is underlain by beds of Oxford Clay, which outcrop extensively on the west side of the Ouzel floodplain, on the slopes overlooking Bradwell Brook, and in the Bletchley and Whaddon areas. Further outcrops of these beds occur east of Fenny Stratford, where the Oxford clays, capped by the Woburn sands beds, help to form the Lower Greensand escarpment, which rises to a height of 154 m OD at Little Brickhill.

More than half of the Milton Keynes area is covered by Pleistocene and Recent deposits, primarily glacial in origin. The high ground separating the river Ouzel and the Bradwell Brook consists of a sheet of Boulder clay, rising to a height of about 90 m OD, the erosional remnant of a sheet which once probably covered the whole area. Extensive glacial sand and gravel deposits can also be found along the Ouse valley between Stony Stratford and Great Linford, at Walton, and around Fenny Stratford.

Recent alluvial deposits have mainly developed along the valleys of the two major rivers and their tributaries, in the form of terrace gravels and alluvium. The first of these rivers is the Great Ouse, which flows in a north-easterly direction, and meanders in a broad flood plain between Stony Stratford and Newport Pagnell, forming the northern boundary of the new city. The second, the river Ouzel (or Lovat) also follows a broad flood plain in a northerly direction, meeting the Ouse at Newport Pagnell, from whence the latter continues north-eastwards to the Wash. The Ouse floodplain falls at an average gradient of 1:1500, from 65 m OD at Passenham to 53 m OD at its confluence with the Ouzel at Newport Pagnell, while the latter falls more steeply from 71 m OD at Stoke Hammond, a gradient of 1:900. The lesser tributaries, of which the most prominent is Bradwell (or Loughton) Brook, descend steeply from the Boulder-clay-capped uplands, broadening to the narrow flood plains which mark their confluence with the major rivers. Deposits of head are found on the slopes of many of these smaller valleys, and mantling the Oxford clay slopes below the Lower Greensand escarpment. Small outcrops of calcareous tufa are also present, particularly in the Haversham area.

Given the above structural components, the Milton Keynes area can best be considered as an area of more or less dissected boulder-clay plateau having a gently rolling topography, with streams falling fairly steeply to the Ouse and Ouzel flood plains, across slopes cut chiefly into Oxford Clay. Rocky outcrops, primarily formed by Blisworth and Cornbrash limestones, are mainly confined to the areas bordering the Ouse valley. Soils in the area are generally heavy, owing to the predominance of underlying Oxford and Boulder clays, though lighter soils are found in the areas with gravel subsoil. Despite the presence of many small streams flowing down from the Boulder clay uplands, drainage is generally poor, as the clay soils tend to retain water, and this is perhaps one of the major factors which led the Ministry of Agriculture to give a Grade III classification to over 80% of the area (Ministry of Agriculture, Fisheries and Food, 1961). Poor drainage is not limited to the upland areas alone, as both the

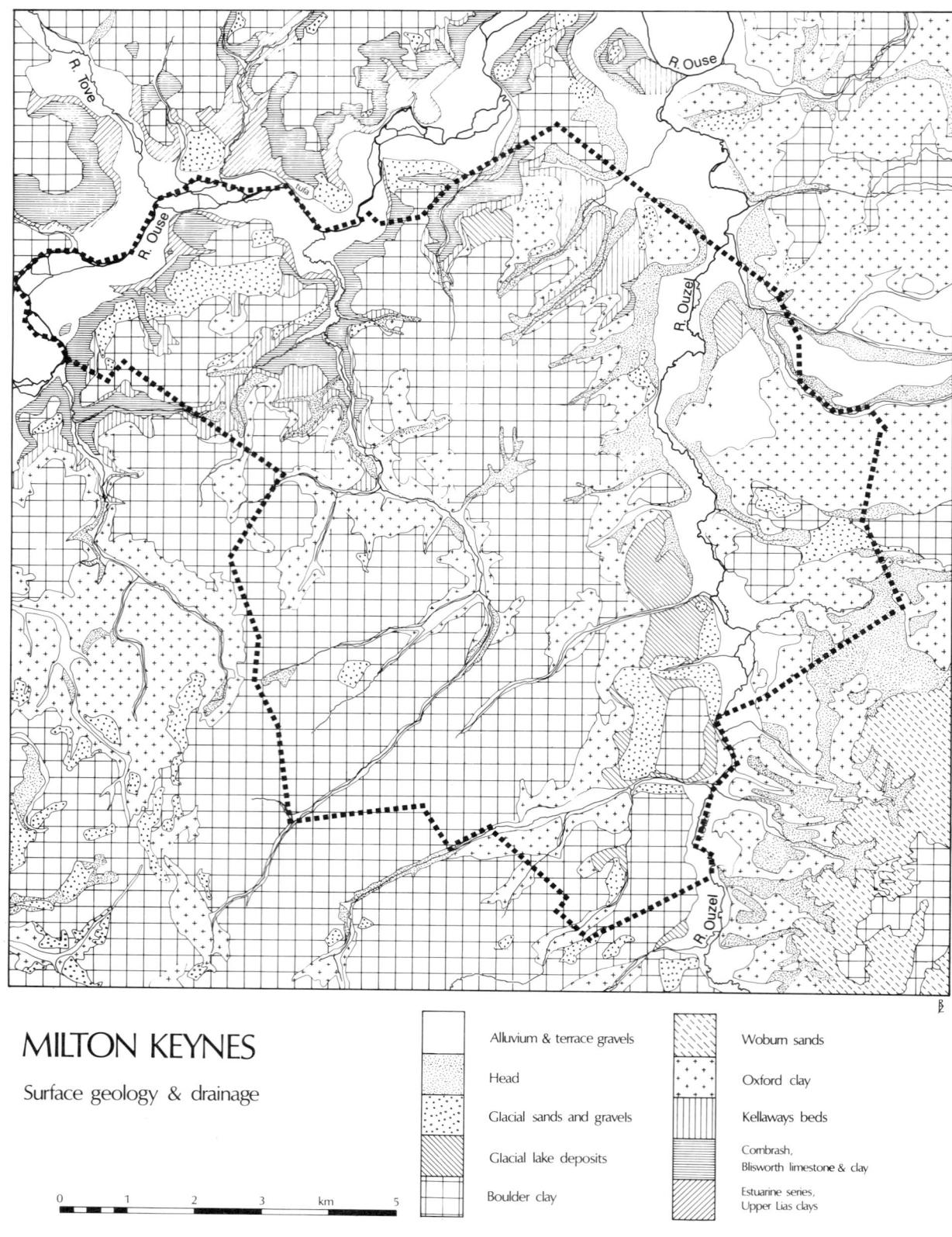

Figure 2. Surface Geology and Drainage.

Ouse and Ouzel valleys have been prone to serious flooding until comparatively recent times.

The differing geology described above is reflected in the contrasting building materials used in the villages of Milton Keynes. In the north the local limestone was the major material for houses and walls, whereas buildings in the southern part of the city used timber framing with panels infilled with wattle and daub and, more recently, brick. The principal roofing material for the village houses was thatch, with tile used for the more important buildings. It is interesting to note that there is little evidence of the use of stone slates, which were used in the Roman period.

The North Buckinghamshire countryside was similar to other parts of the rural south Midlands. It was the product of a slow process of development and change of the landscape, much of which can never be recorded. This volume presents random glimpses of the past landscapes of the area and our efforts to record and interpret them.

PREHISTORIC LANDSCAPE

R.J. Williams

Any detailed reconstruction of the palaeoenvironment of Milton Keynes before the first millennium BC is severely limited by a lack of environmental samples. Even where early sites have been excavated, conditions have often been unsuitable for the preservation of pollen, snails and waterlogged remains and even the evidence from carbonised seeds and charcoal is of limited use.

Palaeolithic activity in Milton Keynes (Fig. 3) is almost entirely represented by chance finds of several flint hand-axes (Millard 1965: Green 1971) mainly made during the 1920s in gravel pits in the Bletchley area. Of the fourteen examples studied by Millard, only one is a typical Middle Acheulian type, the remainder having closer affinities to the later Levallois style.

More extensive Pleistocene deposits have been located in recent years in the Ouzel Valley, principally at Hartigans gravel pit (MK3), Cotton Valley (MK21) and Caldecotte Lake (MK10). No trace of human activity has been recorded, but significant amounts of Pleistocene faunal remains have been found. These include numerous fragments of *Elephas antiquus* tusks and teeth, a scapula of a mammoth (*Elephas primigenius*) as well as *Equus* and *Bos primigenius* bones.

Unfortunately there is no correlation between the distribution of palaeolithic artefacts and the faunal remains in the area, as all have resulted from chance discoveries, so it has not been possible to identify any pattern of activity for this period.

Evidence of the Mesolithic landscape (Fig. 3) is almost as scarce as that for the Palaeolithic period. Significant quantities of Mesolithic flints, including microliths and large numbers of narrow blades, have been found in both the Ouse Valley and its tributaries, the River Ouzel and Loughton Brook. At Bancroft (MK105 and MK360) the presence of many worked flints and tools of both Mesolithic and Neolithic origin in an assemblage of over six hundred flints recovered from excavations and fieldwalking on the Iron Age and Roman sites demonstrates continuity of occupation in a preferred valley location from a very early period.

Another large concentration of worked flints, (MK326) consisting of a typical earlier Mesolithic 'narrow blade' industry, has been exposed during ploughing on the west side of the River Ouzel at Little Woolstone (Williams 1980).

Fieldwork during the construction of the Caldecotte Lake has also revealed at least two scatters (MK353) of Mesolithic flints, one of which included a scalene triangle microlith. Both were located at the interface of the gravel terrace and the overlying thick alluvial layer covering the valley floor (Williams forthcoming). The presence of fragments of bone, burnt stones and numerous flint cores indicates that this may have been a short-lived settlement on the river margin.

The discovery of at least two tranchet axes, one over 2 km from the River Ouzel at Pennyland (MK250), and one nearer the river at Walton (MK147), may indicate Mesolithic penetration into the woodland and perhaps the beginnings of woodland clearance on the heavier clay soils away from the river valleys.

It is only in the Neolithic period with the gradual introduction of a more sedentary lifestyle, based upon the rearing of domestic animals and the cultivation of early forms of cereal, that more evidence of the prehistoric landscape and the pattern of human activity begins to emerge. The distribution of artefacts, mainly in the form of flint tools of Neolithic type (Fig. 3), indicates that settlement before the Bronze Age was still primarily riverine in character. However, the discovery of 'settlement' sites at Stacey Bushes (MK228), Heelands (MK342) and Secklow (MK300) suggests the beginnings of movement away from the valley floors onto the higher more intractable claylands. This movement, requiring the exploitation of an entirely different ecosystem, would have been combined with the continued clearance of the primary forest which still covered much of Milton Keynes at this period. Many Neolithic axes, of both polished and flaked form, have been recorded as isolated finds (Adkins and Mynard 1978), often some distance from the watercourses, although unfortunately none have yet been found in association with any other contemporary artefacts.

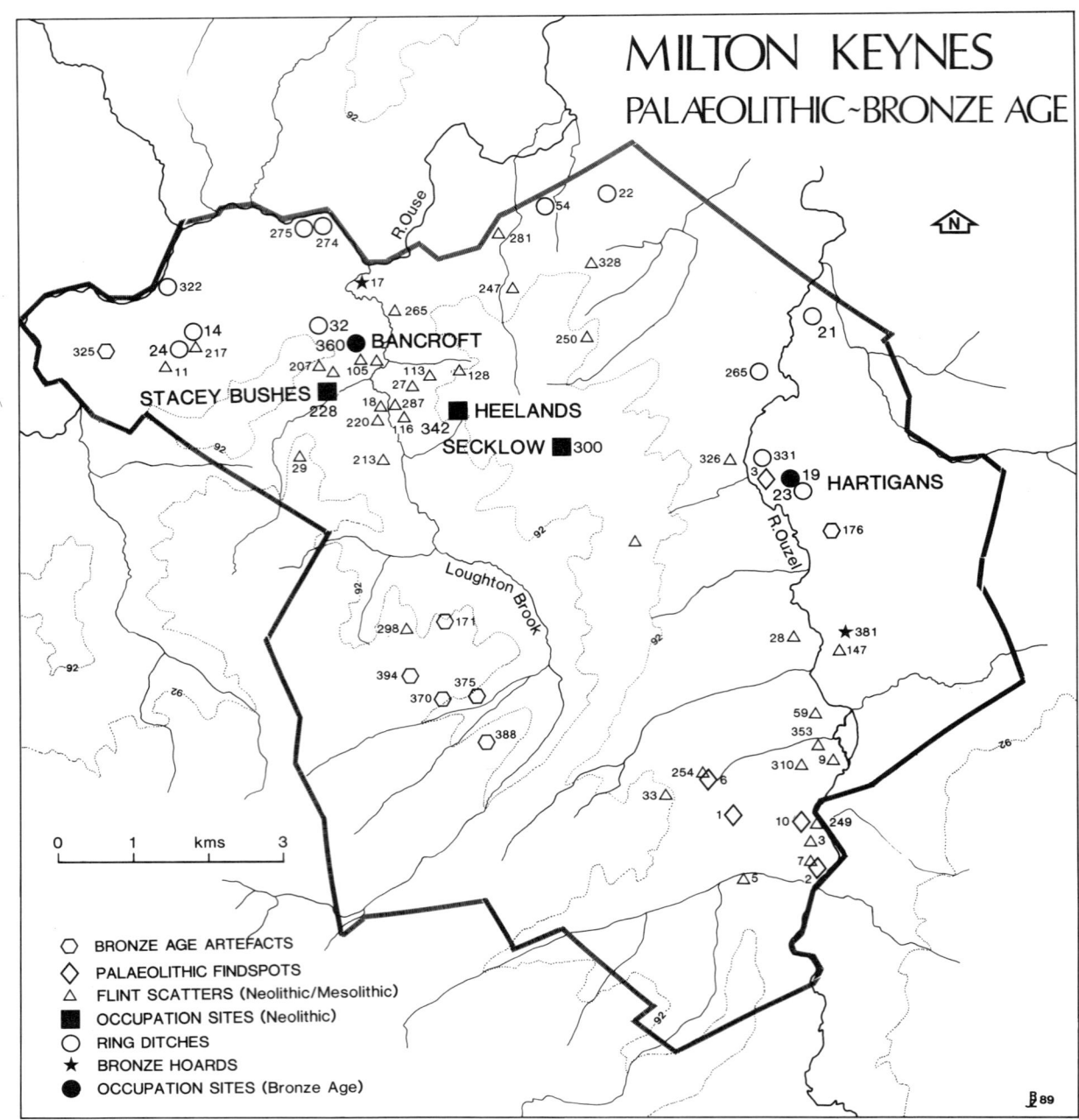

Figure 3: Distribution map of Palaeolithic to Bronze Age sites.

The excavation of the small late Neolithic settlement at Stacey Bushes (Green and Sofranoff 1985) revealed a number of amorphous pits dug into the cornbrash limestone bedrock. These have been interpreted as either 'borrow' pits for clay, or as sumps, helping to drain adjacent structures. The environmental evidence from them indicates that some tree clearance had taken place, but perhaps the most significant discovery was the presence of two distinctive forms of pottery, namely Grooved Ware and Grimston style. This variety of pottery styles may imply that at least two discrete human communities coexisted in the Upper Ouse Valley (*ibid.*, 29). However, it is uncertain whether they represent distinct communities exploiting different parts of the ecosystem, or separate strata within a social hierarchy.

Both the Heelands (MK342) and the Secklow (MK300) sites are of considerable interest in that they are also of later Neolithic date, and also consisted of small amorphous pits (Williams 1981). Unfortunately no examination of the environmental remains from these sites has yet been undertaken, but their importance lies in their location on the heavy Boulder clay, which further reinforces the suggestion of woodland clearance, or at the very least seasonal penetration into areas away from the river courses.

Because of the complete absence of pollen samples from the Milton Keynes area, there is no evidence for climatic change or the 'elm decline' which is known to have occurred at this period. However, it has been argued elsewhere (Rackham 1986, 72) that most of the original tree cover or 'wildwood' was removed in the Neolithic period, and that during the Bronze Age and certainly by the Iron Age much of this part of England was cleared.

Evidence for earlier and middle Bronze Age activity in Milton Keynes (Fig. 3) has almost entirely come from the excavation (Green 1974) of four 'ring ditches', at Warren Farm (MK14), Little Pond Ground (MK24), Milton Keynes (MK23) and Cotton Valley (MK21). Whilst the ring ditch at Little Pond Ground contained a primary Beaker burial dated to 1720 ± 80 bc, the other three ring ditches date from the second half of the second millennium BC, and contained a wide range of Bronze Age urns. Although the evidence from these sites relates mainly to the sepulchral practices of the period, there is some evidence for both earlier and contemporary settlement around the Warren Farm ring ditch, and later activity adjacent to the Milton Keynes burial. Environmental evidence has also indicated that the burials were sited in an open grassland environment which supported a pastoral economy.

The excavation of these four burials has provided the basis for a pioneering study relating burial, territories and population (Green 1974, 129–136) in the area. Dr Green concluded that the excavated ring ditches may have had a much closer relationship to the contemporary settlements (which are still very scarce), than has generally been accepted. Furthermore, his analysis indicates that the physical construction of barrows in any one area was quite within the capacity of the local population, but that perhaps no more than two per cent of the community actually ever received barrow burial.

In recent years increasing numbers of isolated Bronze Age artefacts have been found by metal detector users. These include a socketed axe from Stony Stratford (MK325), a palstave from Shenley (MK370) and a very rare form of tanged bronze arrowhead also from Shenley (MK375). A probable dispersed hoard (MK381), consisting of parts of two spearheads, a pin and a broken socketed axe, was found during building work at Walton. Previous to this the only other hoard (MK17) was found in 1849 during the construction of the 'County Arms' public house in New Bradwell (Kennett 1969). This consisted of a sword of Ewart Park type, two spearheads, a palstave and twelve socketed axes, which are now in Northampton Museum.

Unfortunately, as with earlier periods the recorded distribution of Bronze Age artefacts in Milton Keynes relates more to areas that have been intensively investigated (in this case by metal detectorists) than to the overall distribution of such artefacts in the new city area.

It is only in the later Bronze Age period that any significant traces of occupation are found in Milton Keynes. At Blue Bridge, adjacent to the site of the Roman mausoleum (MK360), was excavated the remains of a very large circular building (Plate 1), 18.50 m in diameter, constructed of three rings of substantial posts (Williams 1986, Zeepvat and Williams forthcoming). Although the Carbon–14 results are indicative of a very early Iron Age date, the pottery from the building is of a very distinctive late Bronze Age form, similar to that from a number of pits post-dating the construction of the Milton Keynes ring ditch (MK23) and from a field scatter at Weston Underwood, to the north of the city. The building itself is one of the largest of its kind yet discovered in Britain, and fits into the late Bronze Age and early Iron Age tradition of very large circular timber houses. Its size and isolation may indicate that it fulfilled a communal function, since several large extended families could have lived within it in reasonable comfort.

Plate 1: Late Bronze/early Iron Age roundhouse, Blue Bridge. *(MKAU)*

A hierarchical structure in society (Green 1974) continued and eventually developed into the later Iron Age tribal society. The discovery, south of Milton Keynes village (MK176), of a very rare form of Late Bronze Age coil-ended gold bracelet which would have been owned by a 'wealthy' member of society is clear evidence of this social hierarchy, and is also a good example of how high-value items continued to be traded over long distances.

In direct contrast to the earlier prehistoric periods, evidence for Iron Age occupation in Milton Keynes provides the most complete example of prehistoric settlement distribution (Fig. 4) within the area. As with the earlier period the settlements still exhibit a broadly riverine distribution, avoiding the heavy Boulder clay plateau between the Ouzel and Loughton Brook Valleys. However, the seven main sites located do display a greater range of topographic settings than might be expected within a comparatively small area. These range from Furzton (MK158) on a flood plain, Hartigans (MK19) and Caldecotte (MK282) on gravel terraces, Wavendon Gate (MK145) on a 'head' deposit overlooking Caldecotte Brook, Pennyland (MK250) and Bancroft (MK360) on more elevated situations, the former over 2 km from the river Ouzel, and Westbury (MK636) in an inhospitable location on the heavy clay soils overlooking Shenley Brook. To some extent this diversity is a reflection of the spread, during the later part of the Iron Age in the case of the Westbury and Furzton sites, onto more marginal tracts of land. This occurred as a result of an increase in population, the use of new forms of cereal including Bread Wheat, and the ability to cultivate heavier clays. The latter was made possible by the introduction of heavier iron-bladed ploughs.

The Furzton site provides a good example of how a community managed to adapt itself to a particular environmental niche. The settlement is dominated by a large rectangular ditched stock enclosure, and all the available environmental data (Williams and Hart forthcoming) points to a predominantly cattle-based economy utilizing the adjacent flood plain. The use of stock enclosures, and to a lesser extent droveways, is a commonly-noted phenomenon on local Iron Age sites, occurring at Bancroft, Pennyland, Hartigans and possibly Caldecotte.

Pennyland in particular (Williams 1993) has provided a useful insight into the economy of a middle Iron Age site. Here cattle rearing predominated, while the relative lack of pigs and wild animal bone suggests a lack of either rough ground or woodland in the vicinity. The discovery of numerous grain storage pits indicates that cereal

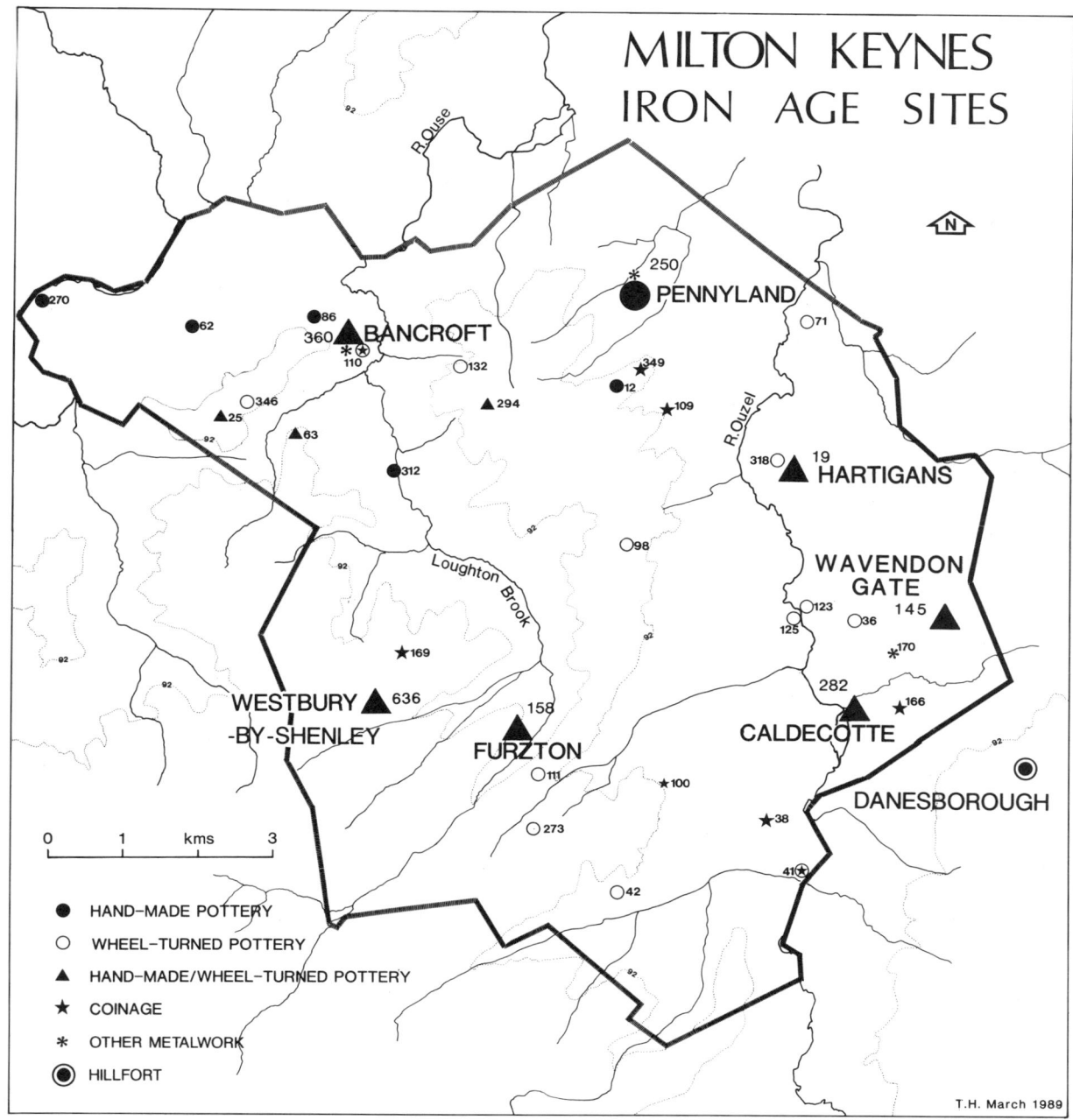

Figure 4: Distribution map of Iron Age sites.

Figure 5: Reconstruction of part of the Iron Age settlement at Pennyland. (*Brian Giggins*)

cultivation was taking place on a significant scale, while the evidence from seed remains suggests that spelt wheat formed the staple diet, supplemented by a limited number of cultivated vegetables. From this evidence it appears that, while the cultivation of cereals made a significant contribution to the local economy in this period, animal husbandry was equally important (Fig.5).

Bancroft (Zeepvat and Williams forthcoming) provides the best example of settlement continuity in the region, from the late Bronze Age to the early Saxon period. All the available evidence indicates that it was able to exploit an almost ideal agricultural habitat, enabling it to develop into a higher-than-average-status settlement. This is reflected in the quality of burial goods accompanying the 'Belgic' cremation burials of the final inhabitants of the hilltop site, before the construction of the villa in the nearby valley location in the later first century AD.

Although the number and distribution of Iron Age sites is impressive for such a small geographical area, it is still impossible to show how they related to one another, or to demonstrate whether any division of land had occurred by the later Iron Age period. The establishment of a local tribal centre on the Woburn Sands Heights at Danesborough may indicate that, even before the Roman invasion, society was becoming more structured.

ROMAN LANDSCAPE

R.J. Zeepvat

During the later part of the Iron Age, the Milton Keynes area, in common with much of south-eastern Britain, was settled by migrants from northern France and the Low Countries. By the time of the Roman invasion in 55BC, the tribe occupying the area had become part of a tribal confederation, the *Catuvellauni*, possibly named after its leader, Cassivellaunus. The territory of the Catuvellauni is believed to have extended northwards from the Thames to the Nene, and westwards from the rivers Lea and Cam to the Cherwell (Branigan 1987, 1–32). The local tribal centre appears to have been the hillfort or *oppidum* at Danesborough, one kilometre south-east of the city, on the Woburn Sands Heights.

Following the Conquest in AD43, and throughout the Roman period, the political situation in the region seems to have remained unaltered. The *civitas Catuvellaunorum*, with its tribal capital at *Verulamium*, covered much the same area as the former tribal area, while the local tribal centre at Danesborough was replaced by the small town of *Magiovinium*, three kilometres to the south-west.

The transition from the late Iron Age to the Roman period cannot be discerned readily in the archaeological record in Milton Keynes. A few sites, such as Furzton and Pennyland, appear to have been deserted in the mid first century AD, but others, including Westbury, Caldecotte and Wavendon Gate remained in use beyond the Conquest, while at Bancroft the Iron Age farmstead metamorphosed, albeit with a slight shift in location (*c*.300 m), into a Roman villa. Similar shifts in position, but not in character, have also been noted at Hartigans (Williams 1993) and Wavendon Gate (Williams *et al.*, forthcoming).

The archaeological evidence relating to the Roman period in Milton Keynes has been presented and discussed in some detail elsewhere (Mynard 1987: Zeepvat 1991); what follows is a synopsis of these publications.

One major change to the landscape and the economy during the Roman period was the establishment of towns, which provided focal points for the communities in the surrounding areas, as social and administrative centres, as well as markets for local produce. The local centre for the Milton Keynes area was *Magiovinium*, a small town covering some 7.5 hectares, close to the Watling Street crossing of the Ouzel, south-east of Fenny Stratford. As with many other Roman towns, *Magiovinium* was established close to the local tribal centre, next to a fort dating from the Conquest (Woodfield 1977), and served both the local area and travellers on Watling Street. Little is known of the town's history, and the site is a scheduled ancient monument, but extensive suburbs have been excavated to the south-east along Watling Street (Neal 1987).

The other noticeable change to the landscape following the Conquest was the construction of a comprehensive major road network, initially for military and administrative purposes. One of these major routes, Watling Street (now city grid road V4, formerly the A5) crosses Milton Keynes on a north-west to south-east alignment. Other known Roman routes of a lesser nature in the area include the Fenny Stratford to Thornborough road (B4034) and a road, discovered in 1980, leading northwards from *Magiovinium*, probably continuing to the Roman town at Irchester, Northants. In addition there must have been a network of trackways serving the many villas and farmsteads in the area. One such was excavated at Bancroft, probably linking the villa with Watling Street (Zeepvat and Williams, forthcoming).

The pattern of rural settlement in the area during the Roman period is of a mixed agrarian economy, exploiting the available resources by means of a variety of different-sized units (Fig. 6). These varied from small farmsteads of 'native' type, such as Woughton (MK297) and Wood Corner (MK64), through small farms with Roman-style buildings, such as Wymbush (MK211), to small but substantial 'villa' establishments (Fig. 7), as excavated at Bancroft (MK105) and Stantonbury (MK301). It is interesting to note that sites of the latter category did not reach the same standards of wealth as villas in the Chilterns, to the south, or in Northamptonshire, to the north of the Ouse. This probably reflects the lack of growth of *Magiovinium*, which remained a small town, albeit with linear suburbs extending to the south-east along Watling Street, throughout the Roman period. Settle-

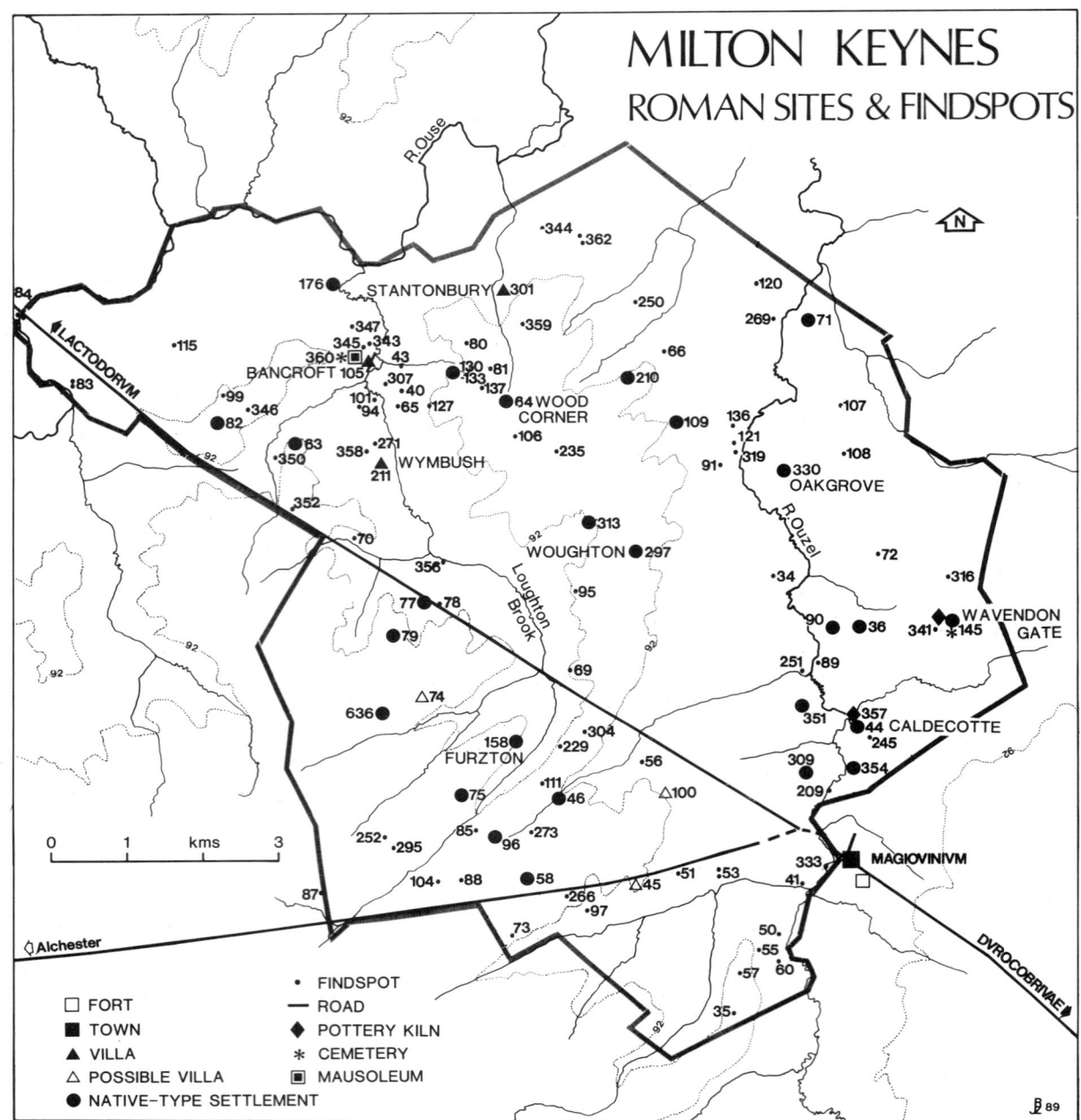

Figure 6: Distribution map of Roman sites.

Figure 7: Reconstruction of the house and garden at Bancroft villa, c.AD 350. (*Derek Mynard*)

ments, probably of the 'native' type, are also believed to have existed at Campbell Park (MK109) and Wavendon Gate (MK145), as excavations at both sites produced large quantities of pottery, metalwork and domestic refuse of Roman date. However, evidence for contemporary buildings was not found in either excavation.

From the available environmental evidence it can be seen that agriculture in the area was mixed. Cattle or oxen were the most common animals kept, followed by sheep and goats, pigs, horses and domestic fowl. Sufficient feed was available for the wintering of grazing animals, which were kept for hides and other by-products as well as meat. In cereal cultivation spelt wheat predominated, while free-threshing and emmer wheats and barley were also grown, as was flax, which like barley was introduced in the Roman period. Vegetables too made their debut at this time, including cabbage, carrot, celery and coriander, parsnips, summer savory and turnips. In favourable areas fruit trees were grown, including apple, pear, plum and damson, cherry, mulberry, chestnut and walnut. Much of the evidence for fruit and vegetable cultivation was recovered from waterlogged deposits in two second-century walled garden areas at Bancroft.

Given the lack of raw materials and fuel supplies, it comes as no surprise that few traces of Roman industrial activity have come to light in Milton Keynes. The major industry in the area was the production of pottery and tile. Pottery kilns have been excavated at Caldecotte (MK44, MK357) and Wavendon Gate, while pottery production on a much larger scale was carried out at Emberton, Warrington, Harrold, Bromham and Bozeat in the Ouse Valley, and at Great Houghton on the Nene, taking advantage of the easily obtainable clays in the river valleys.

The only other industrial activity of which traces have been found in the area is metalworking. Evidence of smithing was recovered from *Magiovinium*, probably catering for travellers on Watling Street as well as local demand (Neal 1987). From the villa establishments at Bancroft and Stanton Low, on the Ouse (Woodfield 1989), sufficient quantities of slag and scrap iron, and in the latter case an anvil, were recovered to suggest a permanent smithy. The discovery at Caldecotte of a hearth and crucibles suggested the existence of a bronze-working industry, probably producing a variety of toilet instruments (Zeepvat *et al.*, forthcoming).

It is possible for the first time in this period to make some assessment of the population in the Milton Keynes area. Using the generally accepted estimates based on heads per square kilometre (Jones 1979) and settlement size and density (Taylor 1975), the rural Roman population of the area now occupied by Milton Keynes would have been between 900 and 1350, with a further 750–1500 people living in *Magiovinium*.

SAXON LANDSCAPE

The general historical model for the development of the post-Roman landscape suggests that in the fifth century Germanic settlers gradually migrated into southern and eastern Britain. It is clear that settlement of the area in the Roman period was extensive, so it is likely that any Saxon people entering the area would have found the remains of a well-managed agrarian landscape. Saxon sites and findspots in the city area are detailed in Fig. 8.

It is likely that rough pasture, scrubland and even woodland had regenerated over some of the former arable lands of the villa estates. The place-name evidence in the Shenley (Bright clearing) and Bletchley (Blaecc's clearing) areas tends to confirm the wooded nature of these areas in the seventh and eighth centuries. (Gelling, below).

The evidence for continuity of settlement sites from Roman into the pagan-Saxon period is minimal, and even sites such as Bancroft (MK360) appear to be abandoned in the fifth or sixth centuries. That there was continuity of land use is assumed, but direct continuity of settlement sites is difficult to prove from the evidence available. The major Saxon sites are shown in relation to Roman 'villas' and to later villages and parishes listed in the Domesday survey in Fig. 9.

The evidence for pagan-Saxon settlement in the city area is relatively good in comparison with the rest of the southern Midlands. Excavations of the Saxon farmsteads at Pennyland (MK568) and Hartigans gravel pit (MK508) have revealed little evidence of Roman occupation at either site (Williams 1993), even though both settlements were first occupied during the Iron Age period. Both were abandoned in the first century BC, and remained unoccupied until the fifth or sixth century AD. Work at both sites in conjunction with excavations at Great Linford Church and a watching brief at Milton Keynes village has also led to suggestions that the settlements were moved during the middle Saxon period. In each case the new location may have formed the nucleus of a new late Saxon settlement, around which the villages of Great Linford and Milton Keynes developed. The analysis of the excavated evidence from both these sites has added valuable information on the nature of settlement size, building construction and most importantly the contemporary environment in the Saxon period.

Fieldwork and excavation in the Shenleys have recovered a considerable number of Saxon artefacts. These seem to be concentrated around three foci: Shenley Church End itself, the deserted medieval village of Westbury, and a third site in the south of Shenley Brook End parish. Perhaps the most noteworthy of these finds was the small burial group of the later seventh century discovered during the course of excavations at Westbury. It is important to stress that the apparent concentration of Saxon artefacts in this part of the city is due more to the level of archaeological activity than to any actual preference on the part of the Saxon inhabitants.

The known early or middle Saxon settlements are rarely in the same location as the villages of the later Saxon period. Admittedly not all village sites have been available for excavation, because the disturbance of the existing village cores has been minimal during the construction of Milton Keynes. In any case, most infilling or other development has been watched, and only at Bradwell and Great Linford has early to middle Saxon pottery been found within the modern village. The date of the establishment of most of the villages in the area, on the basis of the available ceramic evidence, seems to be in the tenth to eleventh century.

The establishment of the villages must have been roughly contemporary with the formalisation of the parish boundaries. It is tempting to imagine that many of the parish boundaries are those of former Roman or Saxon estates, although the distribution of Roman or middle Saxon sites within them does little to support this theory. Many of the parish boundaries follow those of the furlongs of the field systems, implying that that they were agreed between the people of adjoining parishes at a time when the fields were being laid out. That the villages were established within a landscape which had been farmed for almost a thousand years is certain, but to what extent it was already subdivided and how much of the former Roman or early Saxon field systems survived is unknown.

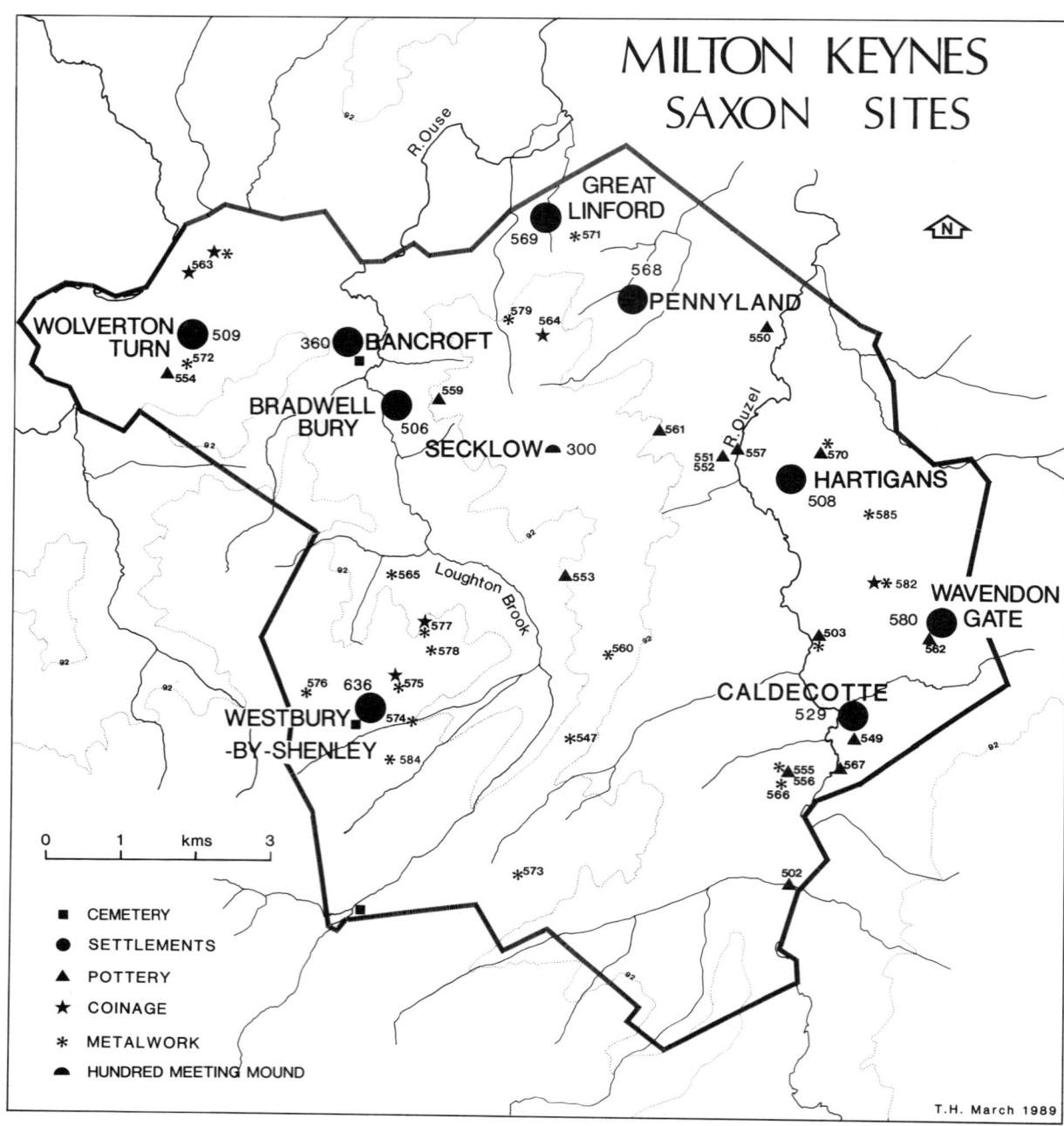

Figure 8: Distribution map of Saxon sites.

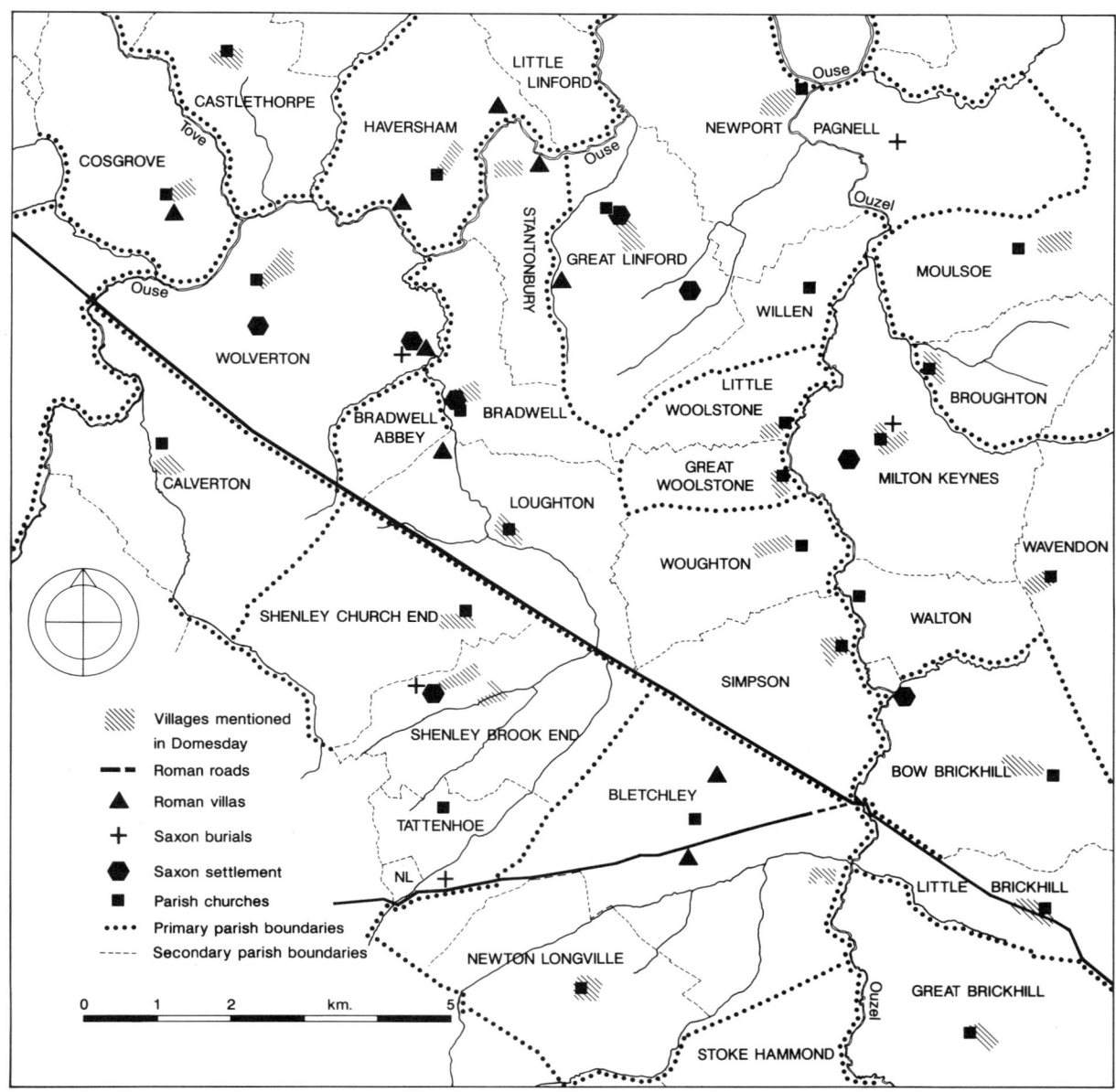

Figure 9: Relationship of Roman and Saxon sites to medieval boundaries.

The natural boundaries that followed watercourses or other topographical features must have been used from the earliest times, and those that were laid out at right angles to these early boundaries may be of the same date or not much later. The line of the Roman Watling Street, which was used as a boundary between parishes right across the city area, can also be considered as indicating an early date. In contrast, many boundaries zigzagged around the furlong boundaries within established field systems, and are therefore more recent, in some cases possibly representing subdivision of larger blocks of land.

If these later 'secondary' boundaries are removed (Fig. 9) the city area can be seen to contain eight major land units and small parts of two others. However, the distribution of known Roman or early to middle Saxon sites within these areas is not such that one can safely argue that they represent estates of those periods.

The only recognised earthwork which survives from the late Saxon landscape is the meeting mound of the Secklow Hundred (MK300). Situated at the junction of Bradwell, Great Linford and Little Woolstone parishes, it was still recognisable in 1641, when it was recorded on a map of Great Linford (BAS 632/43) as 'Selly Hill'. Excavation has confirmed that the mound was turf-built, approximately 25 m in diameter and 0.35 m high, and post-Roman in date, containing medieval pottery in the primary silting of its ditches (Adkins and Petchey, 1984). The mound has now been reconstructed (Plate 2), and forms part of the public garden at the rear of the City Centre Library.

It is likely that all the parish churches in Milton Keynes were proprietary churches, established by the Saxon landlords to serve their manors. None of the local churches are mentioned in the Domesday survey, but this is true for almost the whole of Buckinghamshire, including the important seventh-century church at Wing. None of the churches in the city fall into the category of early churches known as *Minster Churches*, the nearest being probably at North Crawley, to the north of the city area.

Excavation at several churches in Milton Keynes has shown that they existed on their present sites before the Norman conquest. Only at Milton Keynes village is there any suggestion that the village church may not be on the original site. The finding in 1967 of seven christian burials (MK501) of late Saxon date (Mynard 1968, 13) some 150 m to the south-west of the church, and the discovery in May 1992 that these burials were part of an extensive cemetery, suggest that this cemetery may have belonged to an earlier church which was nearer to it than the present parish church, which dates from the fourteenth century (Woodfield 1986, 83).

Plate 2: Secklow Hundred meeting mound, after landscaping. *(MKAU)*

MEDIEVAL LANDSCAPE

INTRODUCTION

All the villages in the city area (Fig. 10) have their origins in the late Saxon or early medieval period. Most flourished but others declined, leaving grass-covered house sites and crofts as reminders of their former size. Despite these changes the overall settlement pattern has changed little over the centuries. Whether the villages and their parishes were established over a short period of time or they represent a gradual development of settlement is uncertain.

The Ouse valley villages of Wolverton, Great Linford and Newport Pagnell all occupied prominent locations overlooking the river valley. In contrast, Stantonbury was sited adjacent to the flood plain, near a bridging point. It is interesting to note that the latter was abandoned in the fifteenth century, whereas the former three continued in occupation; perhaps this is a comment on the suitability of its location.

In this part of Buckinghamshire, Linford is the only instance of a parish name being the same on both sides of a major river boundary. The boundaries between Great and Little Linford and the parishes to the east and west intersect on the Ouse at the same points, which may indicate that the original Linford land unit existed on both sides of the river. The elements of the name *Linforde* are thought to mean 'lime tree causeway' (Gelling, below).

In the Ouzel valley, villages on the west side of the river were fairly regularly spaced at about 1.5 km to 2 km intervals, and were usually sited a short distance from the river on land above the flood plain. On the opposite side of the valley the villages were irregularly spaced, and were situated on higher ground, usually further from the river.

The parishes of Bradwell, Loughton, The Shenleys and Tattenhoe all occupy higher clayland areas away from the river valleys. Bradwell and Loughton were both situated in the Bradwell Brook valley, and part of Little Loughton was so close to the brook that the southern end of the green and adjacent cottages were often flooded.

These villages are both roughly circular in shape, the road system forming the boundary of the village core, resulting in the centre of the village being an open area, perhaps originally green-like, but gradually built on in the later medieval and post-medieval period.

The villages of Shenley Church End, Bletchley, and the hamlet of Shenley Brook End were, as their names suggest, originally located in a wooded area. The suffix *-ley* or *-leah* is usually taken as meaning a clearing within woodland. *Shenley* may be derived from two elements meaning 'bright clearing'. This area continues to be the most wooded part of Milton Keynes, with woods at Howe Park, Shenley and Oakhill. The settlement pattern was essentially of the nucleated type, with each village centred around two or three discrete farmsteads. The deserted villages of Tattenhoe and Westbury were also in this wooded part of the city area.

There are three examples where individual manors within a parish each acquired parish or village status in the twelfth or thirteenth century, resulting in both villages having the same name but with the prefix 'Great' or 'Little' being added.

BOUNDARIES

The origin of the parish boundaries has already been discussed in the essay on the Saxon landscape. Parish and manor boundaries were often the same, unless the parish had more than one manor. Some parishes, such as Bletchley and Shenley, were subdivided into townships, the boundaries of which may have been the same as those of the manors.

The parishes of Bradwell, Broughton, Great Linford, Milton Keynes, Simpson, Stantonbury, Tattenhoe, Little Woolstone, Great Woolstone, Wolverton and Woughton on the Green each contained a single settlement focus. The remaining parishes contained several settlements, probably as a result of different land holdings developing into independent manors. These 'multi-settlement' parishes were BLETCHLEY, which included

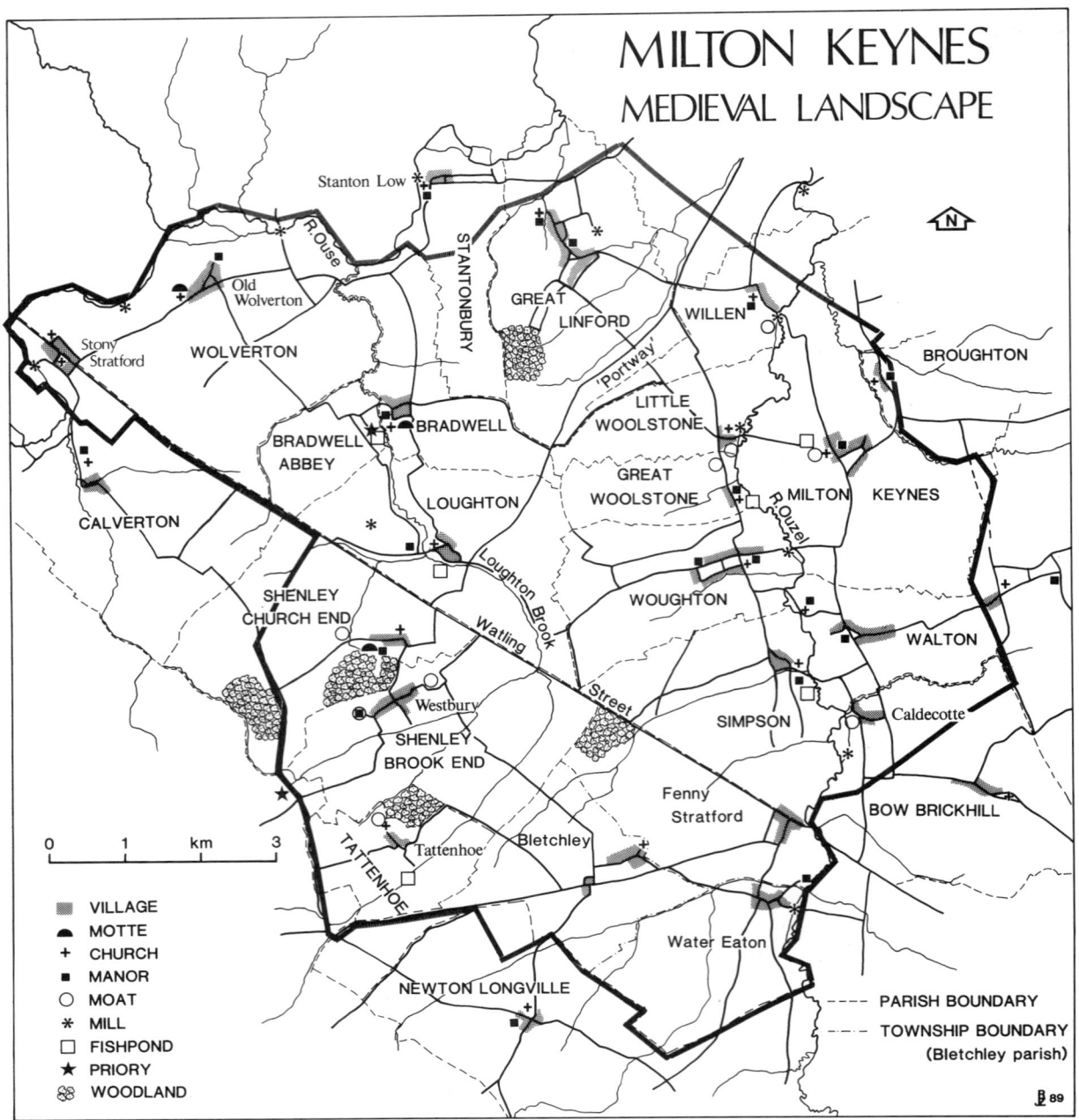

Figure 10: Medieval landscape features.

Bletchley, Fenny Stratford and Eaton; BOW BRICKHILL, which included Bow Brickhill and Caldecotte; CALVERTON, which included Lower Weald, Middle Weald, Upper Weald and Stony Stratford; LOUGHTON, which included Great and Little Loughton; SHENLEY, which included Brook End, Church End, East Green and Westbury, and WILLEN, which included Willen and Caldecote.

Watling Street appears to have defined a marked change in the settlement pattern of the medieval villages, since those parishes on the south side of it (Calverton, Shenley and Bletchley) were multi-settlement. Bletchley and Shenley parishes were subdivided into townships each with their own boundaries and field systems, but there is no evidence for Calverton having had separate field systems associated with the hamlets of Upper, Lower or Middle Weald.

HUNDREDS

Parishes were grouped together to form hundreds, which were administrative units mid-way between the manor and the county. The main role of the hundreds was to provide court facilities for the vills (villages), to decide local taxation and examine any serious offences which may have occurred (Gelling 1978, 191–214).

Most of the parishes in Milton Keynes fell within the Saxon hundred of Secklow (Fig. 11), apart from those on the east side of the Ouzel which were in the Moulsoe hundred, and part of Shenley Brook End which was in the Mursley hundred.

The men of the Hundred met together at specific meeting places to conduct the administrative and legal business related to their hundred. A number of such meeting places, often sited on an existing mound, earthwork or local landmark are known throughout the country. Meeting mounds were frequently on the boundaries of manors or estates, usually in an area of no-mans land.

The Secklow Hundred was said by Browne Willis (BL Add. Mss 5839) to have taken its name from "an hillock at the top of Linford ground leading into Bradwell Field". This mound was recorded on the 1641 estate map of Great Linford as *Selly Hill*, and was situated at the crossroads on the edge of Bradwell and Great Linford, in Bradwell parish. The mound was the meeting place of the Secklow hundred from Saxon times through to the thirteenth century, when the three hundreds of Secklow, Bunsty and Moulsoe were amalgamated to form the hundred of Newport. The mound is described in the Saxon landscape essay.

The hundred boundaries normally followed parish boundaries, the only exception being around Shenley Brook End, where the township boundary between Brook End and Church End was also the hundred boundary between Secklow and Cottesloe.

VILLAGES

Geographers such as Roberts (1982) have attempted to classify village plans into basic types. The problem with this approach is that it tends to examine village plans as they were at particular points in time, and does not take into consideration the changing nature of the village plan. The plan of a village is largely dictated by its topographical location. Villages were rarely sited at the centre of their parish, but at preferred locations adjacent to water sources and at road junctions.

In Milton Keynes, eighteen of the twenty medieval villages were located at crossroads, and two at 'T' junctions. The latter, Caldecotte and Shenley Brook End, were outlying manors that became hamlets. Most villages tended to have a strong linear element to their plan, favouring development along the more important of the roads that ran through them. Several had triangular greens in the angle of converging roads and only four, Bradwell, (Plate 3). Great Linford, Westbury and Woughton on the Green, had large greens.

All the medieval villages in Milton Keynes contain earthworks of some form but only four villages, Caldecotte, Tattenhoe, Westbury and Wolverton, can be termed 'deserted'. The plans of these villages have been recovered by careful survey of their earthworks and the study of aerial photographs. Excavation at several sites has provided positive dating evidence for desertion, whereas documentary evidence often records only the process of shrinkage and decay.

MANORS AND MANOR HOUSES

The earliest references to the villages in the area occur in the Domesday Survey of 1086. At that time the manors were listed under each owner by 'vills', which developed into the villages that survived into the pre-city landscape. The identification of a Saxon or medieval manor with a modern site bearing the same name is only possible if the descent (details of the ownership) can be confirmed by continuous documentary evidence.

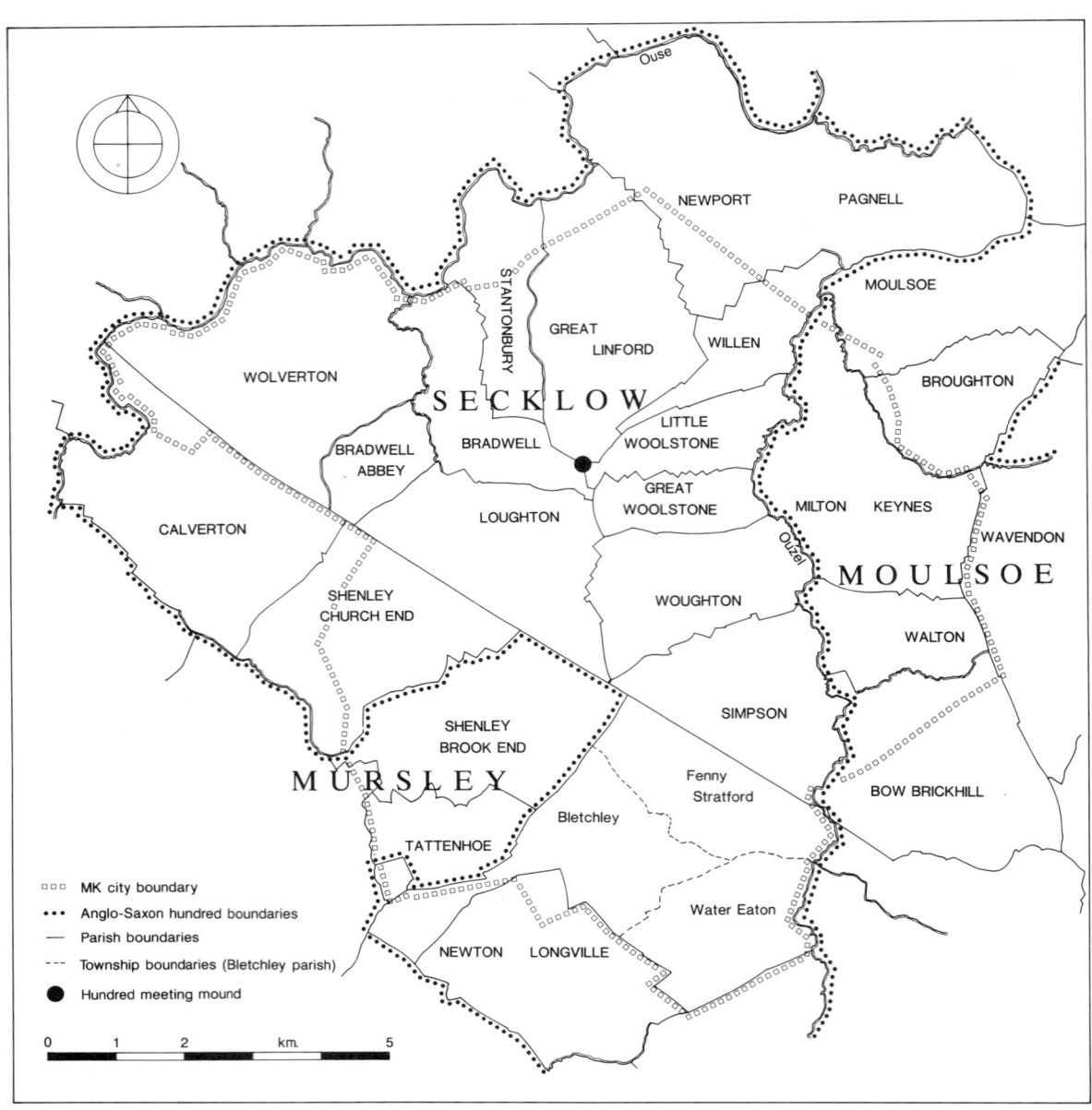

Figure 11: Boundaries of the Saxon Hundreds and parishes.

Plate 3: Bradwell village, from the south-west. *(Aerofilms)*

Plate 4: Bradwell Bury earthworks, from the north. *(Cambridge University Collection of Air Photographs: copyright reserved)*

Plate 5: Loughton Manor farm house, 1987. *(MKAU)*

The manor was the local administrative unit, and from the twelfth century onwards documents survive recording the important role it played in medieval society. The manor courts created their own legislation, and details of their business and the offenders appearing before them were recorded. The court records or rolls survive for several local manors, providing an insight into the local population that cannot be obtained by excavation.

In some of the smaller parishes such as Willen only one manor is known, but in larger parishes there were several, and occasionally the bounds of individual manors can be traced from cartographic evidence. It is often assumed that each manor had a manor house with a resident lord, but this was not necessarily the case. Several manors were often held by one lord, who would reside at one and have a bailiff or reeve to manage the others.

At Bradwell, excavation of the manorial site, Bradwell Bury (Plate 4), revealed traces of sixth to seventh-century occupation (Mynard 1976), and confirmed that the site was first occupied in the ninth or tenth century with timber buildings, which were replaced with a stone house in the thirteenth century.

Within the city only one medieval manor-house survives as a standing building. This is 'Manor Farmhouse' at Little Loughton (Plate 5), which is of late fifteenth-century date. At Milton Keynes village the cottage known as '22 Milton Keynes' dates from the early fourteenth century and was the 'cadet' manor house, the home of the bailiff of the estate of the lord of the manor, Philip de Aylesbury, who resided at another of his manors in Bradwell. This is the oldest known domestic building in the city (Woodfield 1986, 84).

ROADS AND TRACKWAYS

The oldest roads in the area are those which are known to be of Roman date. These are Watling Street, running north-west to south-east through the city, the road from Fenny Stratford to Buckingham, a route running from *Magiovinium* northwards along the east side of the Ouzel valley to Irchester, Northants., and a route running north-east from the Shenleys through Loughton and Great Linford parishes towards the crossing of the Ouse at Newport Pagnell.

Several other Roman roads suggested by the Viatores (Viatores 1964) have since been shown to be non-existent, or mis-interpretations of features such as headlands and banks associated with medieval field systems (Mynard 1987, 11).

The medieval roads and ways within the city area either connected the villages with each other, or were minor routes linking the villages with their fields. Roads ran from the villages to the market towns of Fenny Stratford, Newport Pagnell and Stony Stratford, and the name for these roads, *Portway*, occurs in all of the parishes through which they pass.

In the river valleys, the villages on opposite sides of the river were linked by roads which generally crossed the river at mill sites. Several medieval bridge sites are known within the city. One at the north end of Bradwell parish (SP 824415) where the road crossed Bradwell Brook was called the *Stanbruge* in the thirteenth century (Jenkins 1952, No. 129). Another is known to have been built over the Ouse at the north end of Great Linford parish where it joined Newport Pagnell and Little Linford, probably in the area of the existing Little Linford Lane bridge. The only surviving part of a medieval bridge that can be seen in the area is at Newport Pagnell, where one arch of a bridge remains on the south side of the Ouse in Ousebank gardens.

Roads which cut across the ridge and furrow of the medieval furlongs are clearly later then the field systems. However, without them many villages would appear to have no direct link with adjoining settlements. One explanation may be that in the early medieval period people varied their route depending on the time of the year, and on whether the fields they were crossing were under cultivation or lying fallow. Another factor that must be taken into account is that much early enclosure took place in the area, and that a lot of previously ploughed fields became pasture during the medieval period, allowing the establishment of a route. Therefore if a road crosses ridge and furrow it should not always be considered to be post-medieval in date.

Whilst the Roman Watling Street formed an important parish boundary through the area, it is interesting that none of the primary villages were actually sited on it. Both Fenny Stratford and Stony Stratford were established as market towns on the Watling Street, at fording points across the Ouzel and Ouse respectively. Bridges carrying the Watling Street across the two main rivers are first noted in the medieval period. That at Fenny Stratford was some 200 m downstream of its present location, on the site of the Roman river crossing, and was rebuilt in a direct line with Watling Street in the early eighteenth century. Its location and the alignment of its approach roads are indicated by a 'kink' in the parish boundary. At Stony Stratford, it is assumed that the existing bridge is on the same site as earlier bridges and fords.

An important route running along the Ouse Valley, almost directly along the main limestone outcrop on the south side of the river, was the road linking Newport Pagnell with Stony Stratford, which formed part of the route linking Cambridge and Bedford with Buckingham and Oxford.

To the north-east of the city area a road ran south-east from Newport Pagnell and passed through Woburn, before joining the Watling Street at Hockliffe. This was an important route enabling travellers to Northampton and the north to avoid the river crossings at Stony Stratford and Fenny Stratford, the latter often being virtually impassable in winter months.

As well as the roads detailed above, there were many minor routes linking the villages in the area. Whenever these have been located by excavation they have proved to be no more than tracks, reinforced here and there with random cobbling. The best-surfaced roads were found in the villages, where extensive use was made of cobbles and limestone, depending on availability.

CASTLES

Milton Keynes contains three motte-and-bailey castles; one at Shenley Church End, another at Wolverton, and a smaller example at Bradwell. Their presence in the landscape as overgrown grassy mounds provides the visitor with few clues as to their original character or function. No traces of buildings survive on these sites and their construction is not recorded in any surviving documents.

Motte-and-bailey castles consisted of earth-built mounds normally topped with a timber tower, standing within a flat open 'bailey', enclosed by a wall or palisade and outer ditch. This area would have contained a few timber buildings. Many motte-and-bailey castles were constructed during the turbulent years of the Anarchy, in the reign of King Stephen (1135–1153). The conflict at this time was between supporters of the King and those of the Empress Matilda, but fighting between the two sides was a rare event, commonly taking the form of sieges of major castles around the country.

The fact that three castles were erected within a distance of three kilometres or so of each other is presumably a reflection of the strategic importance of the area around Bradwell, Wolverton and Shenley. The Watling Street and the east-west road from Bedford to Oxford were important routes during this period, and their domination by the holders of the Wolverton and Shenley castles would have been desirable.

Plate 6: Shenley Toot motte and bailey earthworks, from the south. *(MKAU)*

The castle at Shenley (Plate 6), probably constructed by Hugh, Earl of Chester in the later years of the eleventh century, would have been in existence during the period of the Anarchy, and probably functioned as an important local base for the supporters of the King.

Wolverton was the head of the barony of Wolverton, which derived from the Domesday holding of Manno the Breton. At the start of the war the castle there was held for the King by Meinfelin, who held the barony of Wolverton for fifteen knights fees and the service of defending the castle of Northampton. The castle, probably commenced by Manno, survived as the main seat of his son Meinfelin, who was to hold the offices of Sheriff of Bedfordshire and Buckinghamshire in 1125. In such a position he would have been involved with the general upheavals which Chibnall (1979) refers to as being widespread during the period 1135–53. Meinfelin was succeeded by his son Hamon in about 1155, but no records survive to confirm whether any parts of the castle were in existence at that time.

The small earthwork castle at Bradwell (Plate 3) is the least well-preserved of the three. Its origins are thought to be directly related to the Anarchy. Lands in Bradwell were held by William Bayeux of the honour of Wallingford, which was held by Brian Fitz Count, a personal friend of the empress Matilda. No doubt Fitz Count encouraged William de Bayeux to build the castle at Bradwell in order to keep favour with Matilda.

There were three other local castles during this period, at Castlethorpe, Lavendon and Newport Pagnell. The most substantial was at Lavendon, and was held by John de Bidun during the war, but whether his loyalty lay with Matilda or with Stephen is not recorded. At Newport Pagnell the castle was situated at the confluence of the Ouzel in what is now the old cemetery. A thirteenth-century deed in the Snelshall Cartulary (Jenkins 1953, No. 182) refers to a house in the *vetere mota*, meaning 'old moat'. The date of this reference suggests that it is more likely to refer to the defensive ditch around a castle mound than to a homestead moat.

The castle at Castlethorpe was within Hanslope manor, and was called 'Handslope Castle'. It was built in the early twelfth century by the lord of Hanslope, William Maudit, who was a supporter of the empress Matilda. This castle was taken and destroyed by Fawkes de Breaute in 1215. The substantial earthworks, a scheduled ancient monument, can be seen to the west of the parish church at Castlethorpe.

MARKETS

Bedford and Northampton were the major market towns serving the Milton Keynes area. The smaller towns such as Newport Pagnell or Olney and Hanslope were little more than large villages, but their importance lay in their right to hold a market and fair.

The principal market town in the area was Newport Pagnell which was established early in the tenth century (Baines 1986). Stony Stratford and Fenny Stratford, situated on the Watling Street, were market towns which were established in the late twelfth and early thirteenth century as new towns to satisfy the local need for additional markets. A market is first recorded in Stony Stratford in 1199, and in Fenny Stratford in 1204.

As well as being the centres for markets and fairs, towns were also the main focus for the foundation of Guild premises such as the Guild of St Margaret and St Katherine at Fenny Stratford, and the Guild of St Margaret and St Thomas at Stony Stratford. The latter town was one of the resting places of the funeral cortege of Queen Eleanor *en route* to London, and a cross was erected to commemorate this event at the northern end of the High Street. This cross, which was destroyed during the Civil War, was no doubt similar in style to the one at Geddington, Northants.

Both Fenny Stratford and Stony Stratford prospered with the growth of coaching traffic in the eighteenth century.

MILLS

The Domesday survey of 1086 listed mills in the following parishes:

Village	Value of the mill
BROUGHTON	0s.
CALDECOTE (Newport Pagnell)	5 ora and 4d.
CALDECOTTE (Bow Brickhill)	10s.
CALVERTON	13s. 4d.
LITTLE WOOLSTONE	10s.
MIDDLETONE (Milton Keynes)	6s. 8d.
NEWPORT PAGNELL	8s.
STANTONBURY	10s. 3d & 50 Eels.
WOLVERTON	32s. 8d (Mills).

TABLE 1: Domesday Mills in Milton Keynes.

The mill sites established in the late Saxon period and listed in the Domesday survey remained in use until very recent times. Watermills existed in most of the parishes in the city (Fig. 10) and the leats constructed to control the flow of water to them can still be seen at several sites.

It is assumed that all these mills were of undershot type, and were probably similar to the timber-framed example dating from the eighteenth century which was excavated at Caldecotte (Petchey and Giggins 1983). Most mills were rebuilt on the same site several times, and this process invariably seems to have destroyed the remains of any earlier buildings. It was hoped that the excavations at Caldecotte might reveal evidence of the Domesday mill in Bow Brickhill. However, no traces of it or any subsequent medieval mills were found.

The only parish in the Ouzel valley which did not have a watermill was Walton. The reasons for this are uncertain, but may be connected with its tenurial association with Milton Keynes and Caldecotte, discussed in detail in the parish essay. During the medieval period Walton was part of the De Greys' manor, and would most likely have used the demesne mill at Water Eaton.

Only two sites in the Ouzel valley have surviving mill buildings, namely Water Eaton in Bletchley and Caldecote in Newport Pagnell. The mills at Little Woolstone and Willen are known from nineteenth-century illustrations (Rec. Buckinghamshire 1982, pl. 1a: Fig. 64). However, both were demolished before the development of the city, and their sites were destroyed by the construction of Willen Lake in 1972.

The reasons for the failure of mills are tied in with the relative stability of the manor and village that they served. However, the reverse can also be true; for example, Caldecotte had become so small by the end of the sixteenth century that only one or two families remained, but because of its association with Bow Brickhill it retained its watermill well into the eighteenth century. Mills at Milton Keynes, Woughton on the Green and Great Woolstone all disappear from the historic record by the end of the medieval period.

The upper reaches of Bradwell Brook do not appear to have been suitable for watermills. There are references to a mill in Loughton, adjacent to Manor Farm, Little Loughton, of which no trace can be seen today, even though the medieval description of the site suggests a fairly extensive complex with ponds and banks to control the water flow (Jenkins 1952, No. 87).

There were also windmills in many of the local parishes, but the only survivor is at Bradwell. Windmills were introduced into this country in the middle of the twelfth century by returning Crusaders. The local topography influenced the need for a windmill, and usually those parishes without watermills had one. The most common indicator of a windmill site is the name 'Windmill Field'; particularly good examples occur on the 1769 map of Loughton (Figs 43 and L5) the 1641 map of Great Linford (Figs 36 and L3) and the 1698 map of Shenley (Fig. L7). In the sixteenth century Bradwell had a windmill to the south-east of the village, which probably survived into the seventeenth century (see parish essay). The present stone tower mill in the north of the parish next to the canal was not built until 1815 (Plate 7).

The only local mill mound examined by the Unit was at Great Linford where excavations in 1977 (Mynard and Zeepvat 1992, 104ff) revealed the cross-tree trenches of the mill set within the mound. Several large fragments of oak survived, and radiocarbon dating of this material suggests that the mill (Fig. 12) was constructed in the first half of the thirteenth century. This is the earliest dated mill so far (1992) excavated in this country.

Plate 7: Bradwell windmill. *(MKAU)*

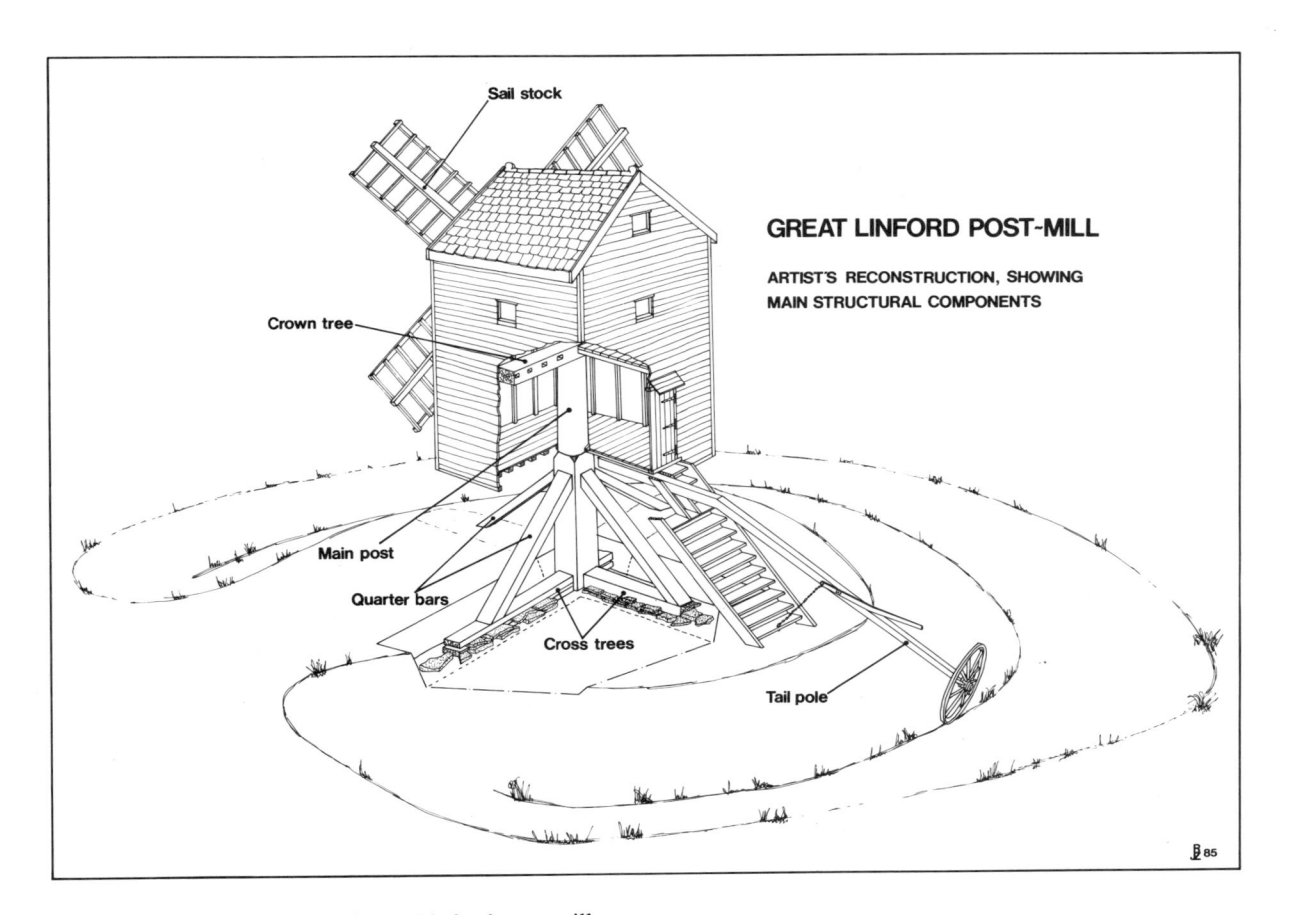

Figure 12: Reconstruction of Great Linford post-mill.

Windmills, like watermills, were always part of the demesne, and windmills at Shenley and Tattenhoe are recorded in the early thirteenth century (see parish essays). The windmill at Tattenhoe (RCHM 1913, 294) survived as an earthwork on the edge of Tattenhoe and Bletchley parishes until the construction of the Windmill Hill golf course in the late 1960s.

Post-mills survived as the main type of windmill well into the eighteenth century, and are occasionally depicted on early estate maps, for example the 1793 map of Bow Brickhill (Fig. 19). The site of this mill, like that at Tattenhoe, has also been incorporated into a golf course.

MOATS

Many of the local moated sites have been scheduled as Ancient Monuments by the Department of the Environment, and most are preserved within the city's Linear Parks. The majority are located in the Ouzel valley where most parishes, with the exception of Walton, contained an example (Fig. 10).

These moats were often constructed upstream of mill sites, being fed with water from the mill leat. Not all were homestead moats containing buildings; in fact, many were no more than fishponds made in the shape of a moat. They would also have served as safe places for ducks and geese, or even as gardens. The moat at Fenny Stratford was in an area called 'Saffron Gardens' (see parish essay).

Many moats were close to the river in locations so liable to flooding that they would have been unsuitable as house sites. However, the moats at Great Woolstone and Milton Keynes village are both adjacent to the church, and are likely to have been the sites of manor houses. The moated site at Woughton on the Green, which is some distance from both the river and the church, had a building within it which was the rectory in the sixteenth century.

Only two moated sites were excavated by the Unit, namely Caldecotte and Willen, both in the Ouzel valley. The Caldecotte moat (Plate 8) was a well-preserved example, in spite of the backfilling of two sides in the late 1960s. There is evidence that this moat was the site of a former manor house. A document of 1641 states that '. . . the site of the manor house is still known by the name of *Buriestead*, compassed with an ancient ditch but lieth continually common' (New College Ms. 1450). Excavation of this site produced no firm evidence of a building which could be interpreted as a manor

Plate 8: Caldecotte moat from the north-east, before backfilling. (© *British Crown Copyright 1993/MOD reproduced with the permission of the Controller of Her Britannic Majesty's Stationery Office*)

house, although quantities of medieval tile and fragmentary remains of stone walls did suggest the presence of buildings during the medieval period (Zeepvat *et al.*, forthcoming). The moat at Willen was excavated in 1972, in advance of its destruction during the construction of Willen Lake. No evidence was found to suggest that there had ever been any substantial medieval building within the moat.

A number of moats occur on the western side of the city, in the Loughton Brook valley. At Loughton, a small rectangular moat is associated with an extensive fishpond system, and the moated platform is thought to have been used for servicing the pond rather than as the site for a house. In Shenley and Tattenhoe parishes a number of moats survive. The geology and topography of this part of the city provided ideal conditions for moat construction, and the manorial organisation of this area suggests that individual estates had their own manorial buildings, often associated with a moat, as at Westbury.

FISHERIES

Those villages in the Ouse and Ouzel valleys which were sited relatively close to the flood plain had important fishing rights in the river, frequently mentioned in manorial documents throughout the medieval period. The use of nets in rivers, moats and ponds was a very common method of catching fish, but archaeological evidence for such techniques rarely survives. However, numerous stone weights used on fishing nets and basket traps have been dredged up from the local rivers, showing that fishing by these methods was a common practice in this part of the south Midlands (Mynard 1979).

Fishponds were often associated with moats, whilst many moats could easily serve as fishponds, and indeed may have been constructed for this purpose. The monastic fishponds can still be seen at Bradwell Abbey, and the name of the largest pond there (Plate 9) was recorded as *Western Hall* in the sixteenth-century survey of the site (Mynard 1974, 34).

An important fishpond was situated on Loughton Brook, to the south of Tattenhoe village. Here the valley had been dammed to create a large pond covering approximately 4.8 ha. The presence of this was first suspected in 1984 when the field names *Pond Tail* and *Water Spinney* were noted on the Tattenhoe estate map of 1801 (Fig. L9). The site was subsequently visited, and identified as the only fishpond of its type in Milton Keynes. The Unit advised the Development Corporation and its tenant farmer of the existence of the site in 1985, and recommended to English Heritage that it should be scheduled as an Ancient Monument.

Plate 9: Bradwell Abbey; the large fishpond after cleaning, 1975. *(MKAU)*

Unfortunately, the site was badly damaged early in 1986 by ploughing, levelling and drainage works. More recently the city grid road V1 was constructed across the pond. In 1991 the site was actually scheduled, somewhat belatedly, as an Ancient Monument.

FIELD SYSTEMS

The organisation of the lands of the manor for the benefit of both the lord and his tenants resulted in the development of the common- or open-field system of agriculture. This type of field system has its origins in the Saxon period, and Hall (Rowley 1981) has suggested that the fields and the villages or manors to which they belonged were organised and laid out at the same time.

The main feature of this type of field system was that the arable lands of the parish were sub-divided into two or three large fields, usually of at least fifty acres, which were used in rotation. Individual holdings were scattered among the fields in strips (Plate 10) and were of a more or less uniform size, each having a fixed rent or service due to the manor. The land of the lord was known as the demesne land, and was mostly intermixed in the fields. Blocks of strips within the fields were called furlongs, and the names of these furlongs are frequently found in medieval documents, sometimes surviving as later field names.

Many of the parishes, such as Wolverton and Bradwell, were partly enclosed by private agreement by the fifteenth century, but it was not until the Parliamentary enclosures of the eighteenth century that the land was extensively hedged to form the fields which survived up to the development of the city.

Occasionally, maps of the common fields recording the strips and the names of their holders survive, but this is not the case for any of the parishes within Milton Keynes. The pre-enclosure estate map of Great Linford, drawn up in 1641 (Figs 36, L3), shows the furlongs and gives their names, but this is the only map of its type in the city.

In the absence of contemporary maps, the layout of the medieval fields has been reconstructed by plotting the surviving ridge and furrow by ground survey and from aerial photographs. The plans for each parish are contained within the parish studies in this volume. The original drawings recording the numbers and direction of strips at a scale of 1:5000 are preserved within the Unit's archive. The maps published are semi-schematic, each strip on the published map representing two strips on the ground.

In addition to the sub-division of the arable lands, the meadow too was divided into allotments or

Plate 10: Ridge-and-furrow in Great Linford parish, *c.*1975. *(MKAU)*

'doles' which were distributed by lot to individual tenants annually.

WOODS AND PARKS

Woodland was one of the most important factors in the rural economy of the manor. It was used as a source of fuel and timber for building, fencing and manufacturing small tools and implements. It created employment for numerous rural craftsmen such as tanners and charcoal burners, provided food for browsing animals feeding off the autumn mast, and for hunting and the keeping of game.

It is thought that no areas of primary woodland survive in this part of the Midlands (Rackham 1980). In south Northamptonshire the forests of Salcey and Whittlewood are extensive areas of surviving medieval woodland. Whaddon Chase, on the west side of the city, is an ancient wood of very early origin. Parts of Shenley and of Tattenhoe were once within the Chase, which covered over 9000 ha (22,000 acres) at its greatest extent, containing common land, heathland and woodland. The existence of these large tracts of woodland is not due to passive neglect of the 'wildscape', but to careful management and re-planting through the medieval period (Pettit 1968).

The earliest references to woodland in this area occur in the Domesday survey, where it is recorded in relation to the number of pigs it could support rather than to the rent it was worth or its actual acreage. Woodland in the city area listed in the Domesday survey is at Shenley, where two of the four separate manorial holdings each had woodland sufficient to support fifty pigs, and at Great Woolstone, where there was woodland for a hundred pigs. The absence of any other references to woodland in Milton Keynes in 1086 does not imply that there were no other woods in the area, merely that they were probably not sufficiently large or valuable to be recorded.

The surviving woodland in the city should be thought of as being in the general category of parks, part of the demesne land of the lord of the manor, relatively small in area (41–82 ha; 100–200 acres) and securely enclosed (Cantor 1982, 56).

In the Shenley area, three areas of medieval woodland survive; Shenley Wood, Oakhill Wood and Howe Park Wood, all of which contain, or are bounded in whole or in part by, some form of earthwork defining the park from the surrounding fields. The best example of an earthwork bank was found in Shenley parish (SP 83053590) where the southern boundary of Shenley Wood coincided with the boundary between the townships of Church End and Brook End. This bank, although levelled by ploughing, was still visible as a soil mark (Plate 11) before the area was developed.

Plate 11: Shenley township boundary, visible as a soil-mark, 1980. *(MKAU)*

No traces of deer leaps or park pales have been noted locally, but woods such as Howe Park were probably bounded by a park pale on the outer boundary bank.

A medieval deerpark is recorded in Bow Brickhill parish in 1220 (Hughes 1940, 40) and the earthworks at SP 916344 are likely to have been associated with it. The extensive area of woodland which now exists in Bow Brickhill parish was planted in the late eighteenth century by the Bedford estates, largely on open heathland.

The best example of a medieval park which still retains the name 'park' occurs in Bletchley parish, where a park is first recorded as being part of the de Grey manor in the fourteenth century. Its position adjacent to the church and later manor house of Water Hall is confirmed by the 1718 map of the estate of Browne Willis (Fig. 15). The line of the park can be clearly seen as a curving boundary surrounding the area to the north of the church, and the survival of placenames such as *Great Park* and *Little Park* are further confirmation that the medieval park was in this area.

Post-medieval coverts such as Woughton Covert in Woughton and Milton Hill in Milton Keynes parish were planted to encourage game, and for the benefit of foxhunting.

Two woods known from early map evidence have been totally removed from the modern landscape. One, at Simpson, was a wood of 12.1 ha (30 acres) recorded in 1781. The other, in Bletchley parish, was known as Rickley Wood, and covered 24.3 ha (60 acres) in the northern part of the parish. Subsequently the area was called Denbigh Hall Farm, and is now part of the Denbigh industrial estate.

RELIGIOUS HOUSES

The north part of Buckinghamshire had several small monastic houses, most of which had been founded by *c*.1200. The only example within Milton Keynes was Bradwell Priory (later Bradwell Abbey) where Benedictine monks from Luffield Priory in Northants. were given land by Meinfelin, baron of Wolverton, to establish a religious house in about 1135. The reconstruction of the Bradwell Priory plan (Fig. 29) is based on a post-suppression survey undertaken in 1524, the layout of the existing buildings, and limited excavation evidence (Mynard 1974).

The monks at Bradwell acquired land in most of the surrounding parishes, often scattered amongst the holdings of the local lords and peasants, consisting of strips of land which were either farmed or leased out by the monks. They also held a

Plate 12: Snelshall Priory earthworks, 1975. *(MKAU)*

watermill in Wolverton parish, later known as 'Meademill' which was destroyed in about 1840 when the railway viaduct over the Ouse was constructed.

Other priories held land in Milton Keynes, notably the priory of Snelshall (Plate 12), situated to the west of Shenley Brook End, just outside the city boundary. More than two hundred deeds recording land held by the priory in Shenley, Loughton, Bradwell and Wolverton and the names of their tenants survive (Jenkins 1952). A similar collection of documents is extant for the Newton Longville area, including parts of Bletchley parish.

A priory at Clattercote, Oxon. had a small grange (farm) in Wolverton which was later held by the priory at Chicksands, Beds. The site, now Manor Farm, was sold to a London merchant in the fourteenth century, and later became part of the main Longville manor of Wolverton, but was still known by the field name of 'The Grange' in the middle of the nineteenth century (Sheahan 1863, 645).

It was common practice for the lord of a manor to give the advowson of a church to a monastic house, and there are several instances of this in Milton Keynes. Bradwell church was given to Tickford Priory in the middle of the twelfth century, and Bow Brickhill to Woburn Abbey in 1185.

POST-MEDIEVAL LANDSCAPE

R.J. Zeepvat

Much of the more recent history of the Milton Keynes area, from the sixteenth century onwards, has been more than adequately chronicled by a number of authors, in particular Sir Frank Markham (1973, 1975), so to repeat their efforts in this volume is unnecessary. Therefore, in keeping with the theme of this volume, this section will deal with those aspects of the history of the area that have contributed to change in the North Bucks. landscape prior to the building of Milton Keynes. The sites mentioned are shown in Fig. 13 by capital letters A–G.

AGRICULTURE

From the fourteenth century onwards, the greatest change to the agricultural landscape was the enclosure of the common fields. These early enclosures, undertaken by individual landowners, affected only a part of any parish. In the sixteenth century such enclosures had taken place in most of the parishes described in this book. However, in the seventeenth and eighteenth centuries a process of large-scale regulated enclosures was encouraged by Parliament, the intention being to organise land improvements better, and consequently increase profits from agriculture. In the Milton Keynes area, the first large-scale enclosure was at Great Linford in 1658, the last at Bow Brickhill in 1790. The process involved the owner or owners of the majority of the land, and with most rights of commoning, obtaining a Private Act of Parliament to enclose. A surveyor and commissioners were appointed, highways and rights of way were marked out, and land allotments were more or less amicably agreed and ratified, after which the new fields were fenced, and recorded on a map by the surveyor. Many of these maps survive for the area, and some are reproduced in this volume.

The most noticeable change made to the landscape by this procedure was the replacement of the large unenclosed medieval furlongs by smaller rectangular fields delineated by fences or hedges, a pattern which remained largely unaltered until the advent of the new city. Within the new pattern of fields, much of the medieval ridge-and-furrow was preserved by a change of land use from arable to open pasture, particularly in the areas of heavy clay soils in the Shenleys, in Great Linford and in some of the Ouzel valley villages.

SETTLEMENT

Along with the changes to the agricultural landscape described above, great changes have occurred to the pattern of settlement in the area over the last four centuries. The first of these was the total or partial desertion of villages in the area. Tattenhoe was the first settlement in the area to be wholly deserted, sometime in the fifteenth century. Partial desertion of Caldecotte, and total abandonment of Westbury-by-Shenley, had taken place by the early sixteenth century. Although commonly cited as a reason for abandonment, enclosure in the parishes containing these settlements did not take place until the seventeenth or eighteenth centuries. In the case of Tattenhoe and Caldecotte, the causes of abandonment may be found in their subordinate relationship to other manors; Tattenhoe to the Shenleys, and Caldecotte to Bow Brickhill.

However, this is not to say that enclosure did not result in changes to the plan of some villages in the area. Almost all of the crofts excavated in Great Linford (Mynard and Zeepvat 1992) were abandoned as a result of the 1658 enclosure, which swept away much of the south end of the village. Wolverton too became almost totally deserted as a direct result of the enclosures and emparking carried out by the Longville family in the mid sixteenth century. Because the process of enclosure resulted in individual holdings in a parish often becoming a tightly-knit block of land, farms began to move out of the villages to be nearer their fields. This led to a certain amount of village depopulation, and also to the creation of isolated farmsteads (Plate 13).

In contrast to the decline of older agricultural settlements in the area, the coming of the Industrial Revolution to North Bucks. brought about the creation of two new settlements, Wolverton and New Bradwell, and extensions to Stony Stratford, Bletchley, Fenny Stratford, and Great Linford, in the mid to late nineteenth century. In all these cases, expansion was a direct result of the coming

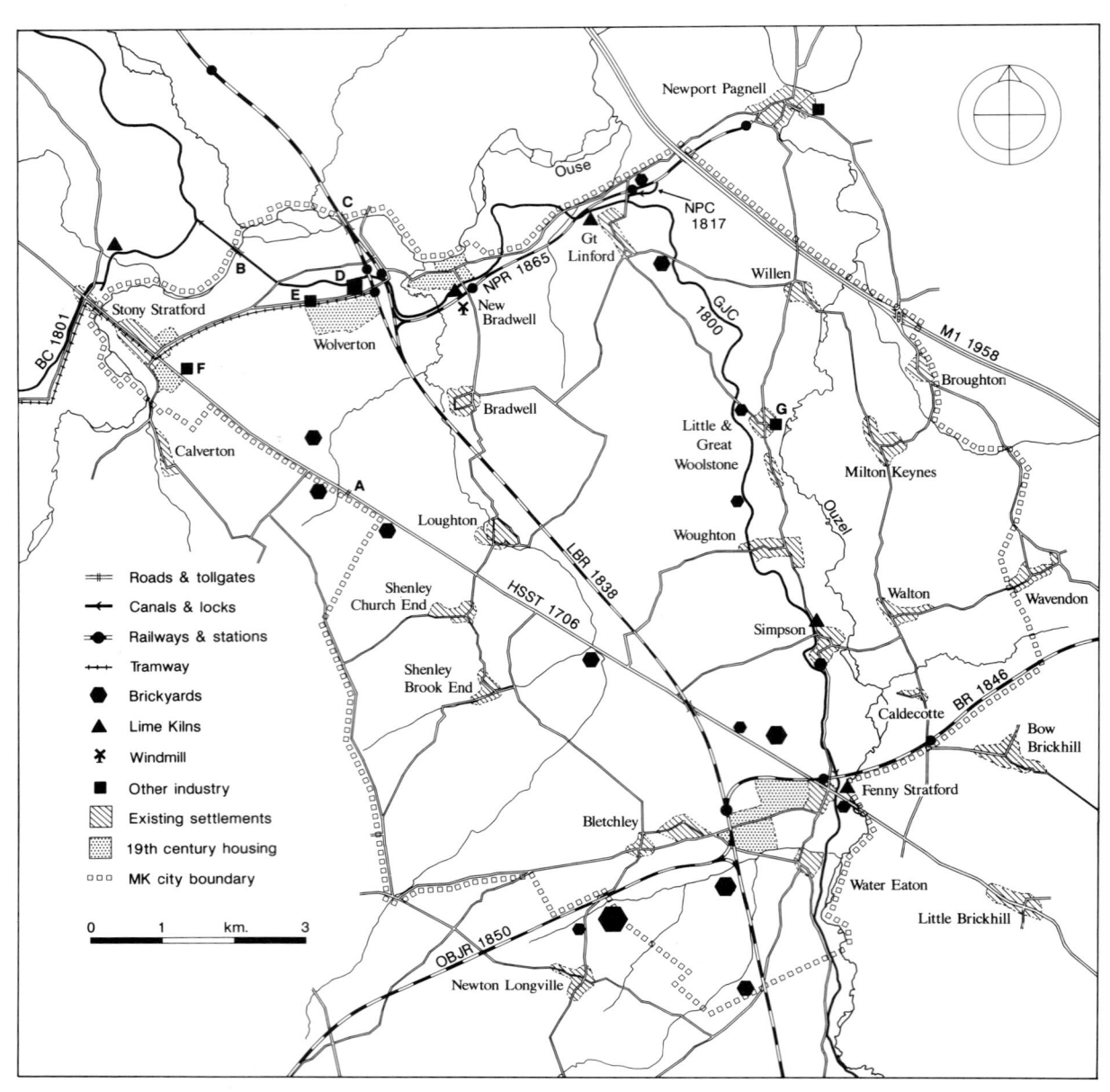

Figure 13: Distribution of post-medieval industrial sites.

Init.	Original name	Open	Present situation
BC	Buckingham Canal	1801	Closed 1921
BR	Bedford Railway	1846	now BR Bedford branch
GJC	Grand Junction Canal	1800	now Grand Union Canal
HSST	Hockliffe to Stony Stratford Turnpike	1706	now A5(T)/grid road V4
LBR	London & Birmingham Railway	1838	now BR West Coast Line
NPC	Newport Pagnell Canal	1817	closed 1864
NPR	Newport Pagnell Railway	1867	now the 'Railway Walk'
OBJR	Oxford & Bletchley Junction Railway	1850	now goods only line

KEY TO FIG. 13

of the railways to the area (see below). The establishment of the railway works at Wolverton, and the increasing importance of Bletchley as a junction between two major cross-country routes, necessitated the provision of housing for employees on a large scale, resulting in the appearance, in what had been a quiet rural area, of terraced housing more at home in towns of the industrial Midlands and North.

TRANSPORT

ROADS AND BRIDGES

Markham (1973, 301) records that by the late seventeenth century the roads in North Bucks. were all in a terrible state, and that despite the requirements of the Statute Labour Act of 1669, parishes in the area were persistently shirking their statutory obligation to repair roads. Ruts on Watling Street were two to three feet (0.6–0.9 m) deep, and there was mud everywhere. This situation was worsened by an increase in stagecoach and wagon traffic at this time. In 1706 Parliament authorised the creation of the Hockliffe – Stony Stratford Turnpike Trust to take charge of that 22 km stretch of Watling Street. Toll gates, at Stony Stratford and Two Mile Ash (A), remained on this road until 1868, by which time it had become a part of the London – Holyhead Trunk Road, engineered by Thomas Telford. Following this example, other turnpikes were set up on roads in the area. The Stony Stratford to Newport Pagnell road was split between two trusts, with Wolverton as the junction. Further road improvements in recent years have swept away the toll houses in the area. The last to go was that at Two Mile Ash, one of the oldest.

As has been mentioned above, the pattern of minor roads in the area was formalised as part of the land enclosures. Many of the routes shown in Fig. 13 have existed since the early medieval period, but were formerly less direct, following the headlands separating the medieval furlongs. Some 'short-cuts' appeared before the large-scale enclosures, where fields were turned over to pasture and traffic could cross formerly cultivated areas instead of skirting them. With the advent of the motor vehicle most minor roads were eventually surfaced, though a few remained fairly basic until the 1970s.

In 1959 the opening of the M1 motorway, which forms the north-east boundary of the city, introduced changes of a slightly different nature to the area. Its construction was partly responsible for increased gravel extraction in the Ouse valley, particularly at Great Linford and Tongwell, and its opening brought both London and Birmingham within easy reach by car as well as by rail,

Plate 13: Wood Farm, Great Linford, 1974. *(MKAU)*

Plate 14: Canal basin, Great Linford, *c*.1880. *(Mansell coll.)*

Plate 15: Arch of medieval Tickford Bridge, Newport Pagnell. *(MKAU)*

heralding the inclusion of North Bucks. in the commuter belt.

Improvements to the roads necessitated improvements to the crossings of the Ouse at Old Stratford and the Ouzel at Fenny Stratford. The former was rebuilt in its present form in 1835, replacing a three-arched, humpbacked medieval structure, while the latter, on the site of the Roman river crossing, was replaced by a bridge on the present alignment, some 200 m upstream, in 1800.

Following an Act of Parliament in 1809 to replace the Tickford (Ouzel) and North (Ouse) bridges at Newport Pagnell, the medieval stone Tickford bridge was replaced in 1810 with an iron bridge (Harris 1968). This structure, which was designed by Thomas Wilson and cast by Walkers of Rotheram, is the oldest iron bridge in the country still open for traffic, and is a scheduled Ancient Monument. An arch of the medieval North Bridge, replaced at the same time by a new stone bridge on a different alignment, can be seen in Ousebank Gardens (Plate 15).

CANALS

Canals came late to the Milton Keynes area, for it was not until 1797 that the Grand Junction, a broad canal linking the Thames at Brentford with the Oxford and Warwick and Birmingham Canals at Braunston, Northants., was opened to Fenny Stratford. The single 14 km pound running northwards to Cosgrove was not opened until 1800, and a narrow-gauge branch from Old Stratford to Buckingham followed in 1801. In 1817 a narrow canal was opened between Newport Pagnell and the Grand Junction at Great Linford (Plate 14). Wharves were opened at Water Eaton, Fenny Stratford, Simpson, Woughton, Great Linford, and Wolverton on the main line, while Stony Stratford was served by a wharf and basin at Old Stratford, on the Buckingham branch. With the growth of New Bradwell a wharf was opened there later.

The coming of the canal brought down the price of coal, which rapidly replaced wood as the principal domestic fuel in the villages, as well as that of many other commodities, including building materials, some food items and crockery. It also encouraged the export of agricultural produce, and the growth of local industries, particularly brickmaking (see below). However, it was also responsible for the death of the local pottery industry, centred on Potterspury, Northants., by making accessible the much finer products of the Staffordshire potteries.

The history of the Grand Junction and its branches is well-documented elsewhere (Faulkner 1972), and the problems relating to the aqueduct (B) over the Ouse at Wolverton are dealt with briefly in that parish essay. The Grand Junction main line (now the Grand Union) remains in use to this day, albeit for pleasure traffic, but the two branches have long since disappeared.

RAILWAYS

The coming of the railways to the Milton Keynes area was to an extent a chance occurrence. Richard Creed, secretary to the London and Birmingham Railway company, proposed that their line should be constructed through Whitchurch, Winslow, Buckingham and Brackley, the most direct route between London and Birmingham. However, fierce opposition from the Duke of Buckingham necessitated a revision, which led to the adoption of the present route through Leighton Buzzard, Fenny Stratford and Wolverton. In the city area the principal engineering problem, as with the canal, was the crossing of the Ouse. This was accomplished by building an embankment nearly 3 km long, in the middle of which was a six-arched viaduct (C), 200 m long and nearly 20 m high. The story of its construction, and the history of the railway, later the London and North-Western Railway, is well-documented elsewhere (Leleux 1976). The line was opened in 1838, with stations at Wolverton and Bletchley.

As happened with the canal, a number of branch lines were constructed in the area, linking Bletchley to Bedford in 1846 (Simpson 1983) and Oxford in 1850 (*ibid*., 1981), and Wolverton to Newport Pagnell in 1867. The latter was constructed partly along the line of the Newport Pagnell Canal, and is now part of the city's public footpath/cycleway system. Additionally, being midway between London and Birmingham, Wolverton was chosen as the site for the L&BR's locomotive, carriage and wagon works (D). These developments led to an increase in the importance of Wolverton and Bletchley, and thus to the large-scale housing developments (Plate 16) mentioned above. In addition, the coming of the railways further encouraged the growth of local industries, particularly brickmaking and engineering.

The growth of Wolverton Works in the latter half of the nineteenth century also brought about the construction of a 3'6" gauge steam tramway between Wolverton and Stony Stratford. This carried the large numbers of workmen who commuted from Stony Stratford and its outlying villages to Wolverton Works. The line was opened in 1887 and extended to Deanshanger in 1888. It was transferred to the L&NWR in 1919 and closed in 1926,

Plate 16: Wolverton; industrial housing and railway works, c.1960. *(Aerofilms)*

largely as a result of competition from motor buses.

INDUSTRY

With the expansion of the canal and railway system, various industries were encouraged in what had been an essentially rural area. Some, like brickmaking and lime burning, used locally available raw materials, and represented expansion of existing small-scale industry. The appearance of new industries such as engineering was related to increasing mechanisation in agriculture, and the demands of other local industries.

BRICKMAKING AND LIME BURNING

Considering the fact that much of the Milton Keynes area is underlain by Oxford clay, it is surprising that large-scale brickmaking did not come to the Bletchley area until the construction of the railway. Before that time, small-scale production had been carried out around Buckingham and Newport Pagnell, though the arrival of the canal had encouraged brickmaking at Simpson and Great Linford. The subsequent growth of brickmaking around Bletchley, encouraged by the development of Wolverton and promoted by Gregory Odell Clarke and others, resulted in the creation of the Bletchley Brick Company in 1919, and the vast brickworks near Newton Longville, which were only recently closed.

The ready availability of brick led to its use even in stone villages like Great Linford, and to the ending of the quarrying of limestone for building in the area. However, stone was still quarried for the production of lime for building and agricultural use, and the 1881 OS map records lime kilns at Fenny Stratford, Simpson, Great Linford, New Bradwell and Old Stratford, the last three all in or near to stone quarries.

OTHER INDUSTRIES

These included cottage industries such as lace making and straw plaiting, long-standing local industries such as tanning and brewing, and new introductions to the area, such as engineering and printing. Most had little impact on the landscape of North Bucks., but some deserve a brief comment.

Lacemaking and straw plaiting had employed much of the area's rural female population until the nineteenth century, when the introduction of machine-made Nottingham lace in 1820, and the arrival of Chinese and Japanese plait in the latter years of the century caused both industries to go into terminal decline.

However, female employment in the area was to a small extent rescued by the establishment of a printing works (E) in 1878 next to the railway works at Wolverton by George McCorquodale, a printer from Newton-le-Willows. McCorquodale's intention was to provide work for the daughters of railway employees, and in this he was successful. Although the firm remains in Wolverton, the distinctive brick frontage of the former main works, built in 1884, was sadly pulled down in 1986 in advance of re-development.

With the increased use of the steam engine as the motive power in an increasing variety of agricultural machinery, it is not surprising that a number of engineering firms sprang up in the area in the mid nineteenth century. One of these was Hayes of Stony Stratford (F), established by Edward Hayes in 1840 to develop and build agricultural machinery. However, as a result of their success with steam engines, the firm found itself changing direction towards the construction of marine engines, and later complete boats, normally tugs or launches. These were either towed by traction engine to Old Stratford and launched sideways into the canal, or shipped in kit form. Hayes closed in 1925, and the site of the works is now (1992) occupied by North City Motors.

Not unconnected with Hayes was another local innovator in the field of agricultural machinery, whose work had a much greater effect on the landscape. This was William Smith of Church Farm, Little Woolstone (G). Smith was a farmer, whose interest in agricultural improvements led him to design and patent a 'combined double-breasted trench plough and subsoiler', a type of cable-hauled steam plough, in 1855. By 1862 he had sold nearly 200, and the previous year had staged an exhibition of steam-powered agricultural machinery at Hayes' works. Smith ceased production in 1877, after problems with the newly-formed National Labourers' Agricultural Union.

CONCLUSION

Since the early years of the twentieth century, the North Bucks. landscape has seen many more changes than those detailed above. Following the Second World War, the balance of agriculture shifted to some extent from husbandry to cultivation, and the development of much more powerful machinery led to the removal of some field boundaries, particularly in Woughton, and the flattening of many areas of ridge-and-furrow. Increases in road traffic led to a number of road improvements, such as the Loughton and Stony Stratford bypasses, as well as the construction of the M1. New industries have entered the area, particularly around Wolverton and Bletchley. From the 1920s, many villages were added to in a small way by the construction of council housing, while the towns saw large estates of the same spring up. In the 1960s, Bletchley was designated as a London overspill area, and was further expanded by the construction of the 'Lakes' and other estates. Finally came the designation of Milton Keynes new town in 1964 – but that is another story.

PLACE NAMES
OF THE MILTON KEYNES AREA

Margaret Gelling

Place-names are multi-faceted, and can be used to throw light on a variety of historical and geographical concerns. Perhaps the most important facet for the local historian is the information they provide about topographical aspects of settlement in the Anglo-Saxon period. In the Milton Keynes area this information can be classified under the several headings of woodland, water supply, river-crossings, hills and valleys. 'Topographical' names will be discussed first under these headings, and a concluding section will offer some notes on the group of 'habitative' names, of which *Milton* is, of course, a member.

WOODLAND

Names in the Milton Keynes area which refer to woodland are *Bletchley* and *Shenley*, *Weald* and probably *Walton*. Among the surrounding parishes are *Cosgrove*, *Gayhurst*, *Horwood*, *Nash* and *Deanshanger*.

Weald is likely to be the most ancient of these names. A study of the use of Old English *w(e)ald* in place-names (Gelling 1984, 222–27) suggests that it is an early Old English term for a large area of wood, and that it was used primarily in district-names. *Walton*, some eight kilometres east of Weald, is probably *wald-tun*, and may be named from the other edge of the same wood. If so, the district-name may have persisted until c.700, since *tun* was not commonly used in the earliest period of English place-name formation. Bletchley and Shenley both have as their main element Old English *leah*, the commonest topographical term in place-names. This can mean either 'wood' or 'clearing'. These two places could reasonably be seen as settlements situated in clearings in a hypothetical forest called *Weald*. They would not necessarily be new settlements of the Anglo-Saxon period; it has been argued (Gelling 1974) that the term *leah* was sometimes used by English speakers to denote settlements in a woodland environment which were established long before the English people came. The two meanings 'wood' and 'clearing' co-existed, and in place-names the crucial consideration for a choice between translations is whether the *-ley* name is isolated or a member of a cluster. Isolated *leah* names (such as Fawsley, Northants.) can often be plausibly interpreted as referring to a relatively limited stretch of ancient woodland. But the presence of other *leah* names around Milton Keynes (Chicheley and North Crawley to the north east, Yardley Gobion to the north-west, Apsley to the east) suggests that 'clearing' is the appropriate translation here.

Round the perimeter of the area under study there are several names which refer to less extensive areas of woodland. Horwood is 'dirt wood', perhaps referring to the soil. Cosgrove contains Old English *graf(a)*, the word which developed into modern *grove*, but which perhaps denoted a more valuable stand of timber than is suggested by the modern word. It has been argued in Rackham (1976, 56) and Gelling (1984, 192–4) that *grove* in ancient settlement-names denotes a carefully managed wood in an area where timber was becoming scarce. Gayhurst, on the northern fringe of the region, means 'wooded hill of the goats'. Old English *hyrst* probably described a hill with a rather thin covering of trees. Association of such a wood with goats is mentioned also in Gathurst, Lancs., and Goathurst, Somerset; Ticehurst, Sussex, and Tickenhurst, Kent refer to kids. Deanshanger refers to a sloping wood (Old English *hangra*); but as with most settlement-names containing this term the place is low-lying, and the slope a gentle one.

Names which refer to particular trees, like Nash ('at the ash-tree'), Willen ('at the willow-trees') and Potterspury ('pear-tree') may conveniently be mentioned in this section, though they are likely to indicate a stretch of landscape which was predominantly free from trees. *Shrob*, between Pottersbury and Deanshanger, derives from a word related to 'shrub' and 'scrub', and this also suggests absence of heavy tree-cover.

WATER SUPPLY

There is one name referring to a spring, and one to a brook: these are *Bradwell* and *Broughton*. The scarcity of names of this type indicates that the area is one in which an adequate water supply could be taken for granted. Bradwell must have had an exceptionally good spring. Broughton (Old English *broc-tun*) is the only settlement on

Broughton Brook, a tributary of the Ouzel, a good example of the type of stream to which the word *broc* was applied.

RIVER CROSSINGS

These are referred to in *Fenny Stratford*, *Great* and *Little Linford*, and *Old* and *Stony Stratford*. The Stratfords refer to river-crossings made by Watling Street, which runs from south-east to north-west across the area. Fenny Stratford is beside its crossing of the Ouzel; Stony and Old Stratford are on either side of its crossing of the Ouse. Great and Little Linford are higher up the Ouse, also on either side of the river, but so far apart as to suggest that the name referred not just to a crossing-place but also to a causeway across a belt of wet ground. The meaning is probably 'limetree causeway'. This ford, like the great majority of those referred to in settlement names, was probably of considerable local importance, though not situated on a major cross-country route. *Furtho* in Potterspury and *Tickford* in Newport Pagnell also refer to minor fords.

HILLS

Three Old English words for hills are contained in the names *Brickhill*, *Furtho*, *Moulsoe*, *Tattenhoe*, *Wavendon* and *Whaddon*. Wavendon and Whaddon contain *dun*, the hill-term most frequently used in settlement names. This word is characteristically used in the names of settlements which stand on low, whale-back-shaped hills. Whaddon and Wavendon are outliers from a large concentration of *dun* names which lies south of Buckingham. This is the predominant type of parish-name in the area between *Hillesden* and *Long Crendon*, indicating that the low hills of this area offered the most desirable settlement sites.

Brickhill contains Old English *hyll*, modern *hill*, characteristically used in place-names for a spikier and less comfortable eminence. In this name the word has been added, tautologically, to a British name meaning 'hill'.

Moulsoe, Tattenhoe and Furtho contain *hoh*, literally 'heel', in place-names 'sharp projection of land'. These are outliers from a concentration of 'hoh' names on the western scarp of the Chilterns, *Ivinghoe*, *Totternhoe* and *Sharpenhoe* being the major settlement-names in the group. *Houghton Regis* is *hoh-tun*.

VALLEYS

By contrast with the 'hill' names, settlement names referring to valleys have to be searched for in this area. *Salden*, on the southern fringe of the region, means 'shallow-valley'. *Beachampton*, on the western edge, contains *baece*, 'stream-valley', used in place-names of a well-marked but not dramatic feature, of a type rare in the east Midlands. The word is characteristic of Shropshire, Herefordshire and Cheshire, where the topography produces many examples of this type of stream valley. There is an unusual absence of the common element *halh*, which is used of depressions not sufficiently well-shaped to be classified as *baece*, *cumb* or *denu*.

The main points to be deduced from the topographical names of the area are that shelter was not a requirement, that water supply could be taken for granted although there was very little marsh, and that a belt of woodland extended from Weald to Bletchley.

SETTLEMENT

The 'habitative' settlement-names of the Milton Keynes area contain the Old English elements *tun*, *cot(e)* and *byrig*. Parishes and townships with names ending in *tun* are Broughton, Calverton, Loughton, Milton Keynes, Newton Longville, Simpson, Stantonbury, Walton, Water Eaton, Wolverton, Woolstone and Woughton. Some of these have affixes, mostly derived from the names of medieval lords, but all of them are dithematic compounds with *tun* in their earliest-recorded forms.

The presence of *tun* names on all sides of the belt of land running from Weald to Bletchley accords well with the suggestion that there was a block of woodland surrounded by open land in which the 'grove' of Cosgrove and the 'wood' of Horwood were discrete items. *Tun* is the commonest habitative term in place names. There is no semantic reason why it should not have been employed for the naming of settlements in a forest environment, but it is clear that it was, in fact, reserved for settlements in open country.

Tun, like *leah*, did not become fashionable as a place-name element until c.750, and it is likely that most names that contain it have replaced earlier names for the settlements concerned. Some of the replaced names might have been British, but in this area most were probably English names of the topographical kind. It is possible that names of the Broughton, Stanton and Walton type, in which the *tun* is defined by a topographical feature or a geological characteristic, stand at the beginning of the series, and that those in which the qualifying element is a personal name, as it is in Loughton, Simpson, Wolverton, Woolstone and Woughton, came into use later. The *Luhha*, *Sigewine*, *Wulfhere*, *Wulfsige* and *Weoca* of these names are likely to have been thegns who were given the overlordship of the places by a royal or ecclesiastical donor, and 'estate' may be a better translation than 'settlement' for *tun* in these compounds. In Calverton ('*tun* of the calves') the translation 'farm' seems appropriate.

An intriguing problem is presented by the names *Milton* and *Newton*, which are defined by their relationship – spatial in one case, chronological in the other – to surrounding settlements. Milton was earlier *Middeltone*, perhaps because it lies between Broughton and Walton. It might be an infill settlement of later date than those two, but until the whole category of 'middle *tun*' names has been carefully studied, the precise implications should remain an open question. Newton (with its variants Newington and Naunton) is the commonest English place-name, and here again a study of the whole corpus might lead to some conclusions about the date at which these settlements were 'new'.

Water Eaton, 'river settlement' with 'water' prefixed is the only instance in the region of a possible 'functional' -*tun* name. Some recurrent names, like Wootton, Moreton, Stratton, are now suspected of referring not just to the geographical situation of the *tun* – near a wood, marsh or Roman road – but also to a specialised role which this situation enabled them to fulfil in the economy of a large estate. Eaton is one of a number of settlements beside the Ouzel, so the name is not distinctive as a geographical statement. It is possible that this place had some specialised function in relation to the river.

Caldecote is a recurrent name which has alternative modern forms such as Calcot(t), Calcutt, Caldicot, Caucot. There are more than twenty examples in England. The literal meaning is 'cold cottages', and the name has been considered to refer to a shelter for travellers, but the status of the Buckinghamshire place is not consistent with this interpretation. The Caldecote near Newport Pagnell contained three Domesday estates whose collective tax assessment was for ten hides; and the borough of Newport Pagnell, which had been established in its territory, was rated at another five hides. It is possible that Caldecote was a new settlement of the middle Saxon period, and acquired this derogatory name at an early stage of its history, but it must have ceased to deserve the description quite quickly. There is reason to think that *cot(e)* is predominantly a middle, rather than late, Saxon place-name element.

Caldecotte in Bow Brickhill is a humbler example, not noted in records until 1247, but the archaeological evidence suggests that middle Saxon settlement occurred in the area of the medieval moated site (Zeepvat *et al.*, forthcoming).

Old English *byrig*, dative of *burh* 'fortified place' is poorly represented in this area. The affix to Stantonbury is *Barri*, a thirteenth-century owner's surname. In Westbury Farm near Shenley the meaning is probably 'manor-house', and this seems the likeliest sense also for Lathbury, across the Ouse from Newport Pagnell. Another habitative term occurs in Castlethorpe, which was probably originally a simplex name from Old English *throp*, thought to denote a settlement initially dependent on a more important place.

There is probably no instance in this area of a name containing Old English *ham* 'village'. Passenham, which adjoins the north-west perimeter of Milton Keynes, is *Passanhamm* in 921, which proves that (like Buckingham) it contains the topographical term *hamm* in its earliest sense 'land in a river-bend'. Haversham, on the north perimeter, has no diagnostic -*hamm* spellings, but it is enclosed by a bend of the Ouse in a similar fashion, and this is the case also with Tyringham, further down the river.

CHRONOLOGY

Current thinking about place-name chronology considers the 'topographical' names as likely to be earlier than the 'habitative' ones, but this does not apply to Shenley and Bletchley, as there is evidence that *leah* (like the commonest habitative term *tun*) only became fashionable in place-name formation in the mid eighth century. Shenley and Bletchley, if they do not refer to middle Saxon assarts, might be seen as English replacements for British names which survived until the eighth century. Little trace remains in place-names here of the British-speaking precursors of the Anglo-Saxons. We have only the first part of the name Brickhill, apart from some river-names which do not belong specifically to this restricted area.

PARISH ESSAYS

● Prehistoric

▲ Roman

⬢ Saxon

■ Medieval

◆ Post-medieval

Key to archaeological sites
                  on parish maps

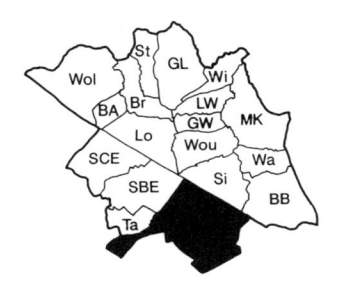

BLETCHLEY, FENNY STRATFORD AND WATER EATON

INTRODUCTION

Situated at the southern end of Milton Keynes, the parish of Bletchley (Fig. 14) covered an area of 1361 hectares. Within the parish were three townships: Bletchley, 529 ha; Water Eaton (formerly Etone), 40 ha; and Fenny Stratford, 420 ha. The parish was rectangular, but with a long finger of land extending from the south-west corner in the direction of the neighbouring parish of Whaddon. It was drained by three small streams flowing eastward to the River Ouzel from the higher clayland in the west.

The underlying geology is largely Boulder and Oxford clays, with a central band of gravel between Bletchley and Fenny Stratford. The Ouzel valley contains first and second terrace gravels and some alluvium. The soils are mainly a clay loam, and the western side of the parish is covered with the wetter and heavier clay soils. The local building stone comes from outcrops of ironstone which occur in the Greensand escarpment at Brickhill, about 3 km to the south of the parish. This can be seen in a number of older buildings, such as St Mary's Church, Bletchley and the Chantry House, Fenny Stratford.

The parish boundary on the east was the River Ouzel, beyond which lay Little Brickhill and Great Brickhill, whilst to the north Watling Street formed the boundary with Simpson. To the north-west the boundary with Shenley and Tattenhoe was unusual, being very straight and almost at right angles to Watling Street, which suggests that it was of considerable antiquity, perhaps of Saxon or even Roman origin. This north-western boundary continued westwards following the Buckingham to Bletchley road for 1.4 km before turning south and returning along Weasel Lane. The south-western boundary with Newton Longville was also fairly straight, but contained two dog-leg sections which followed medieval furlong boundaries. The southern boundary with Stoke Hammond ran relatively straight for 2 km before joining the River Ouzel.

The Roman Watling Street was an important route during the medieval period, as was another Roman road which ran west through the centre of the parish from the Roman town of *Magiovinium*, near Fenny Stratford, to the Roman temple complex at Thornborough, eventually joining the Roman road from Towcester (*Lactodorum*) to Alchester in Oxfordshire. A medieval road through the eastern side of the parish followed the Ouzel valley, linking the market town of Newport Pagnell in the north with Fenny Stratford and Leighton Buzzard to the south. The intersection of this road with Watling Street influenced the siting of Fenny Stratford, with its wide market area on the south side of the crossroads.

The two ends of Bletchley, West or Far Bletchley and Bletchley Church, were linked to Shenley and the parishes to the north-west by trackways. One of these ran through the parish and crossed the Ouzel at Etone (Water Eaton) mill, continuing to meet Watling Street south-east of Fenny Stratford. This route provided a short-cut for drovers who wished to avoid passing through Fenny Stratford (Tull 1980). The poor state of the roads, particularly Watling Street, is recorded in the fourteenth century, when it was impassable at certain times of the year (Bradbrook 1924, 291–292). This situation was not properly remedied before the early nineteenth century, when Watling Street was rebuilt as part of Telford's London to Holyhead turnpike.

Although the location of the Roman crossing of the Ouzel at Fenny Stratford, some 200 m downstream of the present bridge, is marked by a 'kink' in the parish boundary, it is not known whether a bridge or a ford existed at this point. However, from the Saxon name *Stratford* meaning 'street ford', given to the settlement that developed nearby, it is evident that at that time only a ford existed. The earliest references to a bridge occur in the fourteenth and fifteenth centuries (VCH 1927, 276) as grants for bridge building or repair, while in 1573 Thomas Searles left £40 towards the making or mending of the bridge at Fenny Stratford. The 1718 map of Eaton and Fenny Stratford (Fig. 15) shows a multi-arched bridge across the Ouzel, which presumably survived until the existing bridge was built in the early twentieth century.

Figure 14: Bletchley parish in 1967, showing major archaeological sites.

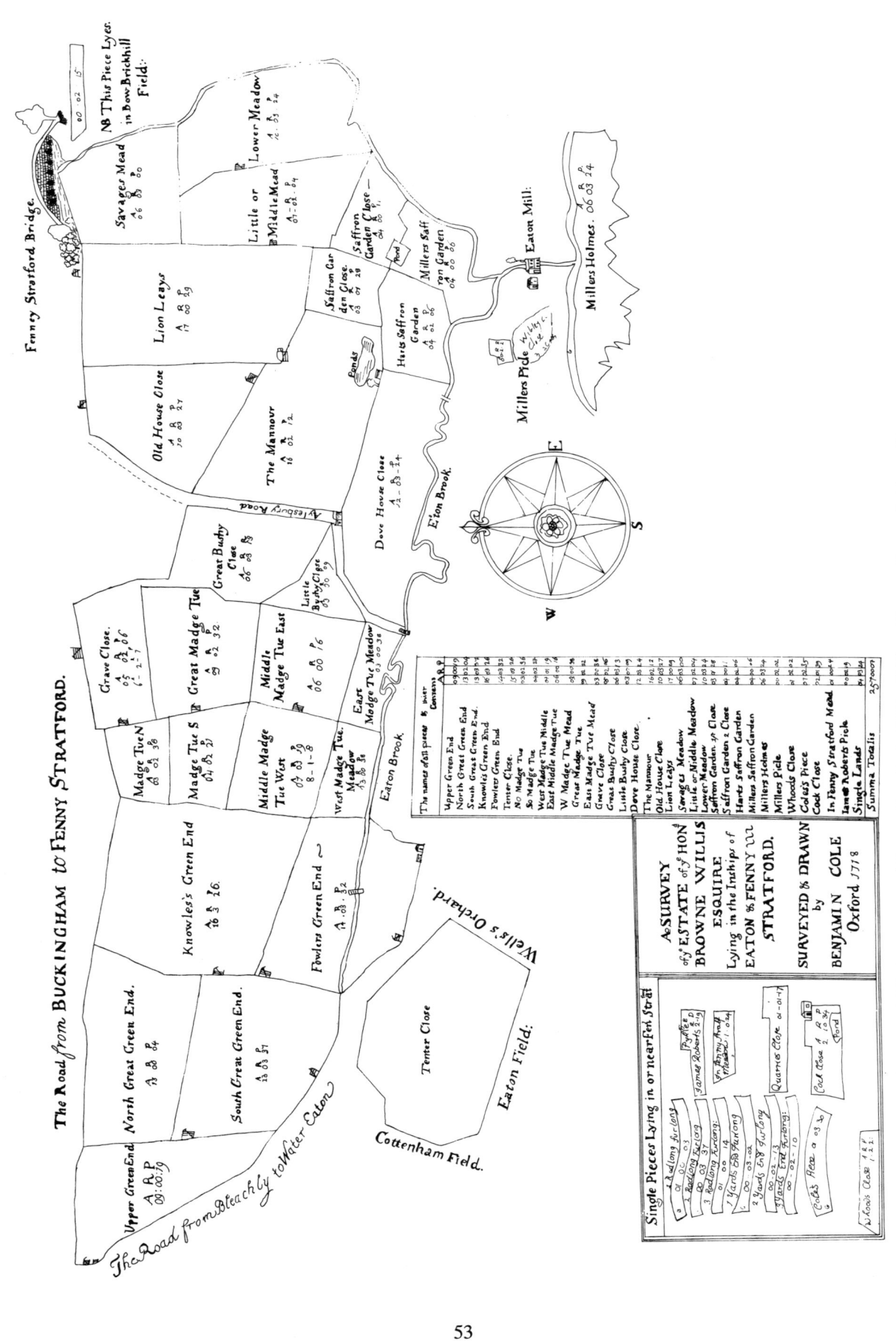

Figure 15: The estate of Browne Willis in Eaton and Fenny Stratford, 1718. *(Milton Keynes Borough Council)*

ARCHAEOLOGY

A few isolated flints of Bronze Age date have been found, but no evidence of any prehistoric settlement is known in Bletchley parish. In view of the proximity of Bletchley to *Magiovinium*, it is not surprising that a number of Romanised occupation sites have been discovered (Mynard 1987, 30ff). These represent small farmsteads at least 0.5 km south of the Watling Street. Two of these were partly recorded by rescue excavation; one in Sherwood Drive (MK100) and one at Holne Chase (MK45), on the south side of the Roman road to Thornborough. Three other sites are known in this area; Shenley Road (MK46), Whaddon Way (MK58) and Windmill Hill (MK96). Many of these small farmsteads are associated with grain-drying kilns, suggesting that this was a reasonably productive arable area in the second to fourth century.

THE MEDIEVAL AND LATER VILLAGE.

The Domesday survey only refers to *Etone*, which Geoffrey Bishop of Coutances held himself. The entry continues:

. . . "It answers for 10 hides. Land for 18 ploughs; in lordship 4 ploughs. 35 villagers with 6 small holders have 14 ploughs. 12 slaves. 1 mill at 20s; meadow for 12 ploughs. Total value £12; when acquired £8; before 1066 £10. Edeva held this manor; she could sell to whom she would."

The relatively high figure for the number of villagers, small-holders and slaves suggests a population of more than 170, which is high for this part of the county and may indicate that in Etone there were already several dispersed settlements, which later became the three main settlements of West or Far Bletchley, Bletchley Church and Water Eaton.

Earthworks on the west side of the Ouzel, north of Water Eaton mill and east of the canal, represent the medieval village of *Etone*. Limited fieldwork in this area suggested that the village of *Etone* extended across a substantial area towards the allotment fields to the north. A plan of the earthworks has not been produced.

A square banked enclosure, 60 m sq. internally, beside the Ouzel about 400 m north of Water Eaton mill was described as a fishpond or reservoir in 1913 (RCHM 1913, 114). This pond, shown on the 1881 OS map as an area of wet scrub or poor grass, was a silted-up fishpond, and the plan (Fig. 16) is drawn from that map. In 1964 this pond was backfilled with domestic refuse by Bletchley Urban District Council, and the banks were bulldozed over it. The destruction of the site was watched by Richard Griffiths, who found evidence of Late Iron Age, Roman and early medieval occupation sealed beneath the banks (Waugh *et al.* 1974, 373; Millard 1967, 109).

This earthwork was within a field called *Millers Saffron Garden*, and three adjacent closes were called *Saffron Gardens*. It is likely that saffron was grown in this part of the parish, since it was commonly used during the medieval period as a colouring and flavouring for cooking, as a source of yellow dye for cloth and as a medicinal herb (Gerard 1985, 35–39).

There are several fourteenth-century references to a fishery in Water Eaton manor, and it is generally assumed that they refer to the fishery rights in the Ouzel, which continued as late as 1681 and 1735 (VCH 1927, 279).

The medieval manor house of Water Eaton, called Waterhall, was situated to the north of the village of Eaton and south of Fenny Stratford. The 1718 map gives the field names of *Old House Close* and *The Mannour*, indicating the site of this house which survived until *c.*1560, when Arthur, Lord Grey de Wilton, lord of Bletchley and Whaddon, pulled it down and removed all re-usable building materials in order to build his new manor house at Whaddon. Willis records that an old man who was an eye-witness to the proceedings described how Lord Grey had summoned an enormous number of horse teams from all over the county to remove the materials, and that they were so numerous they reached from Fenny Stratford Town's End to Bletchley Leas Gate (BL Add. Mss 5840, 366). During the seventeenth century the Lords Grey de Wilton were living at Whaddon rather than Bletchley, and therefore there was no need for a manor house in Bletchley.

By the end of the seventeenth century the Willis family had acquired both Bletchley and Whaddon manors, and Browne Willis brought about a number of changes to the local landscape, financing repairs to St Mary's Church, Bletchley and the re-building of Fenny Stratford church. Browne Willis was also responsible for the construction of a new manor house about 100 m to the north of St Mary's Church, and Jenkins (1953) suggests that Willis undertook this venture because he had doubts about the success of his other major building scheme, the rebuilding and repair of Whaddon Hall, which was going on at the same time. Willis's new manor house, which he called *Water Hall*, was finished in 1710. Willis gave the name *Water Hall* to the new house through sentimental attachment or antiquarian interest, and his friend the Rev. William Cole described this action as 'very absurd'.

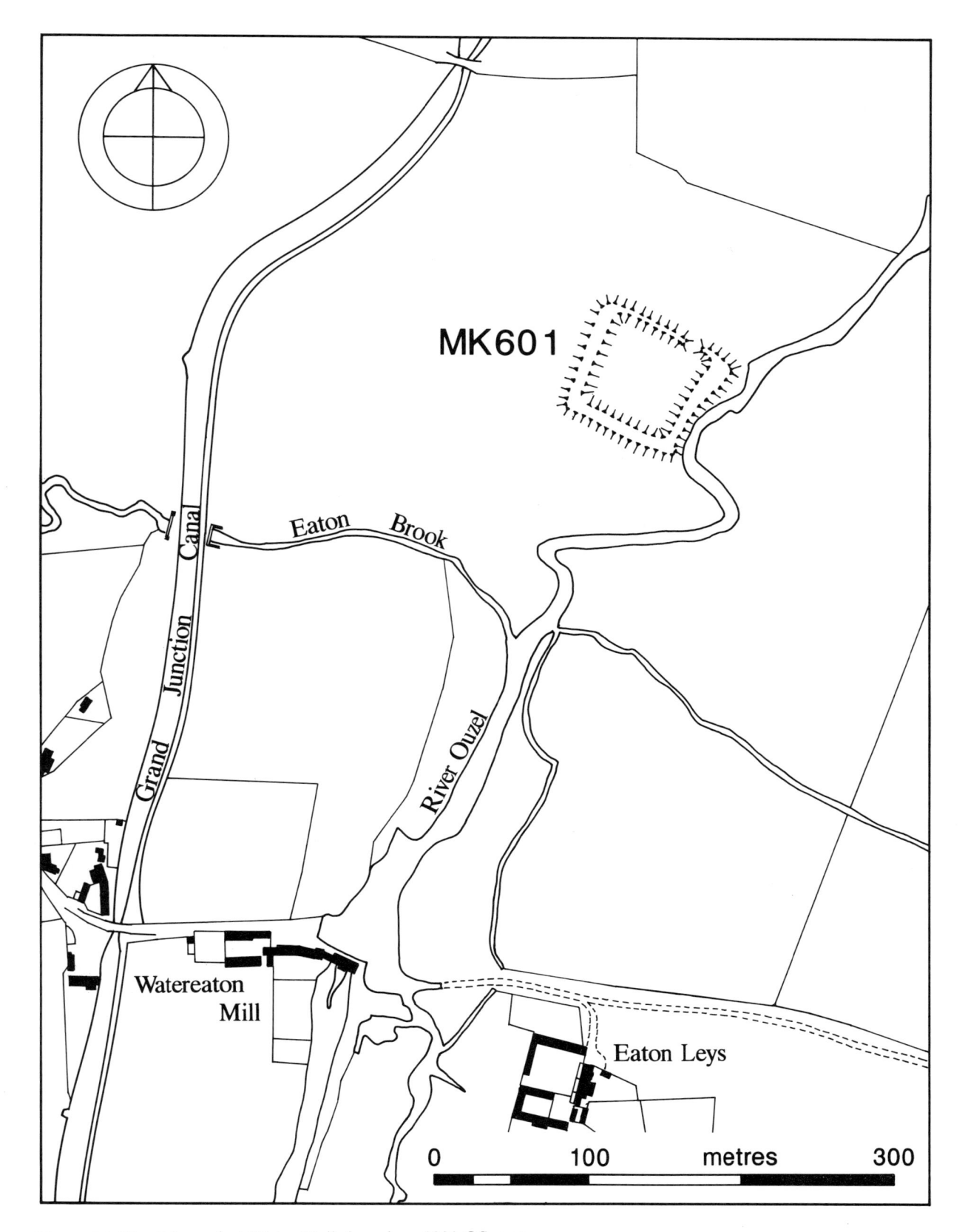

Figure 16: The fishpond at Water Hall, based on 1881 OS map.

Plate 17: Watercolour of Water Hall, Bletchley, 1710–60. *(Sir Philip Duncombe)*

The plan of this house and the layout of its grounds are shown on the 1718 map of Bletchley (Fig. L1), and a contemporary watercolour (Plate 17) shows that it was a substantial building. In the vicinity of the new manor house the 1718 map shows two ponds, which were either constructed as landscape features or may have been survivals from the medieval period. These ponds can still be seen today, but little else survives of any formal landscape laid out by Willis. The name *Bletchley Park* is still used for this part of Bletchley, and will long be remembered for the role the buildings played in housing military intelligence operations during the second World War.

To the south of Water Eaton on the road to Stoke Hammond the 1881 OS map shows a farm called 'Waterhall', but apart from the re-use of the name this site had no connection with the medieval manor house.

FENNY STRATFORD

The earliest documentary reference to a market is in 1204, when Roger de Cauz was granted the right to hold a market at Eaton by the king (VCH 1927, 276). The early market place was in what became the centre of Fenny Stratford at the north end of Aylesbury Street at its junction with Watling Street. When Browne Willis sketched Fenny Stratford in *c*.1730 (Bodleian, Willis Ms. 52b) he drew part of Aylesbury Street, showing that the central part of the road had been used as an animal market or shambles, suggesting that the early market square had been partly infilled by that time.

The development of the market town is directly linked to the manorial history of Water Eaton and Simpson. By the thirteenth century the de Cauz family had acquired both Simpson and Eaton, which made it relatively easy for Roger de Cauz to establish a market adjacent to Watling Street with a view to increasing the income of his manors. A number of tenements or burgage plots were laid out on the Simpson side of the road, but the main development was southwards along Aylesbury Street. In 1324, four months' tolls and stallage fees from the market were worth 7s 6d (37½p) for water Eaton manor (VCH 1927, 276).

In 1252 the lord of Fenny Stratford, John de Grey, who also held West Bletchley and Water Eaton, was granted permission to hold an annual fair in the town on the vigil and feast of the Nativity of the Virgin (8th September) and the six following days (VCH 1927, 276). This is the first reference to the town by the name of Fenny Stratford. This market was regularly held in Fenny Stratford until the first World War, although it had essentially become a livestock market by the turn of the century.

TOWN AND GUILD

Fenny Stratford had acheived borough status by 1370, when the burgesses paid forty shillings rent to the lord for half the vill of Fenny Stratford (VCH 1927, 276). Burgage tenements are noted in documents of fifteenth and sixteenth-century date, but no archaeological evidence for any of the medieval tenements has been found during redevelopment in the past twenty years.

In 1493 Roger and John Hobbs of Fenny Stratford founded the Guild of St Margaret and St Katherine, and the building which was erected (Fig. 17), known as the Brotherhood House, survives on the south side of the Watling Street. A chapel was established in the guild, and two priests were appointed to provide services and other deeds of charity. In 1495 the brotherhood held an estate of 251 acres in various parishes in the Milton Keynes area (Cal. Pat. Rolls 2 Hen. VII, part 1). The chantry estate with the Brotherhood House was leased from the manor, and in 1547 it was worth £14 16s 9d per year, and 15s rent was paid to Lord Grey (VCH 1927, 282).

In 1985–86 the Brotherhood House was restored and converted into offices, providing an opportunity for a detailed architectural investigation and some very limited rescue recording of archaeological deposits. A report on the architectural significance (Giggins 1983) confirms that the house was a good example of fifteenth-century timber-framed construction.

THE FIELD SYSTEM

The large amount of development in the parish, which had already taken place before the designation of Milton Keynes and the establishment of the Unit, destroyed much of the evidence of the medieval field system, and it has not been possible to reconstruct the layout of the medieval furlongs. It is likely that the townships within the parish each had their own field systems, and that Fenny Stratford's lands were carved out of the fields of Bletchley and Etone.

The fields beside the River Ouzel were liable to extensive flooding both in Water Eaton and in Fenny Stratford. The field names shown on the 1718 map (Fig. 15) confirm that this area was chiefly used as meadow land, with names like *Great Madge* and *The Madge*.

Parts of the parish had been enclosed by the early years of the fifteenth century, and Bletchley was included in Wolsey's Commission of 1517 (Leadam 1897), which identified parishes already partly enclosed. The enclosure of the parish did not take place until 1810 (Tate 1946, 36) which is relatively late for this area, and probably was occasioned by the dispersed ownership of the land in the parish. Fig. L2 shows the parish at the time of the enclosure.

OTHER LANDSCAPE FEATURES

MILLS

The references to a watermill in Bletchley parish refer to Water Eaton mill, which at the time of the Domesday survey was valued at twenty shillings (Table 1). Repairs to the mill, water wheel and mill spindle are mentioned in 1390 (VCH 1927, 279). The mill site, like most other mills on the Ouzel, is on a purpose-built straight mill leat rather than on the main stream itself. This provides a number of advantages in the control of the water flow, particularly during periods of high water and flooding. The mill was also used as a bridging point linking Bletchley and Little Brickhill parishes.

There are no references to a windmill in the parish, and the windmill mound on the western edge of Bletchley remembered in the local name 'Windmill Hill' was in fact in Tattenhoe parish.

PARKS

Two parks in Eaton are mentioned in a description of the manor in 1308 (Chan. Inq. P.M. Edw.II, 54) which refers to a 'deer park', and a 'great wood' which was also a park. The location of these parks can be established from the 1718 map of the Browne Willis estate. This (Fig. L1) records the field names of *Great Park*, *Little Park*, and several *Lawne* names which are all indicative of former parkland.

In describing part of the Bletchley estate, William Cole mentions that a park existed here in 1563 complete with

. . . "a keeper's lodge in the middle and was moated about, the park came down to the great road at Watling Street Way and was deparked before 1735." (BL Add. Mss. 5831, 148d).

The reference to the keeper's lodge and moated site in the park provides few clues as to its

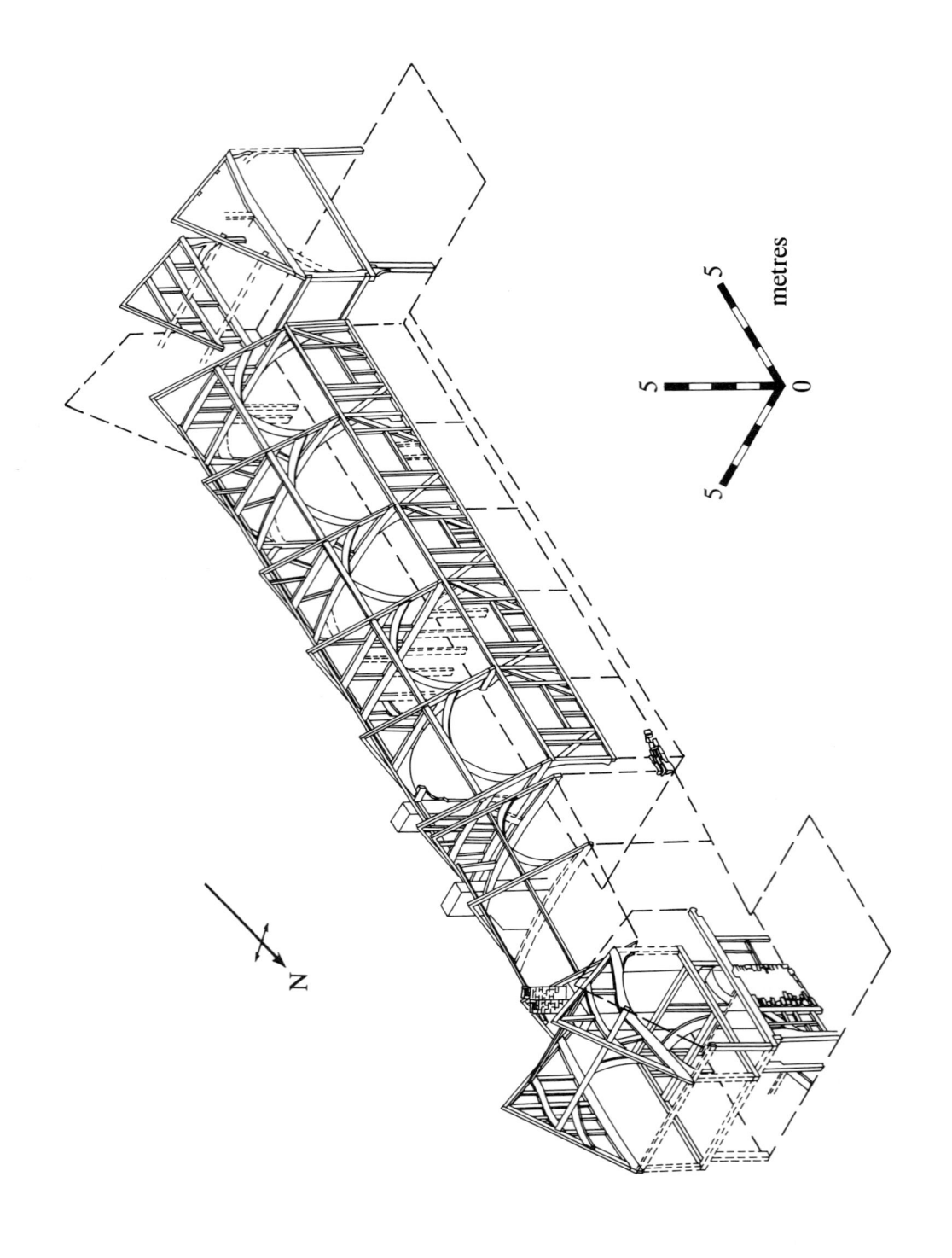

Figure 17: The Guild of St Margaret and St Katherine the Virgin, Fenny Stratford; reconstruction of medieval framework. *(P. Woodfield)*

location. On the 1718 map the name *Lodge Coppice* occurs at SP 863346, just to the west of a small group of buildings, one of which might be moated and could be the keeper's lodge. The 1881 OS map shows a small building and several ponds in the area, and the site was occupied by Home Farm until it was redeveloped in the 1970s.

The park which was also the 'great wood' was in the area of Rickley Wood at the north-west corner of the parish, adjacent to Shenley parish and Watling Street. The wood covered just over sixty-six acres in 1718, but the trees had been cleared by the time of the 1813 tithe map (Fig. L2). The boundary of the park survived as a field boundary well into the present century until obliterated by modern development.

OTHER FEATURES

Archery butts in the area of the manor house (Bodleian, Willis Ms. 98, 31a) were levelled by Browne Willis during the landscaping of the park around the manor house which he had built by 1710. The name survives on the 1718 map as *Archers Wells*, which covers several fields in the east side of the parish adjacent to Watling Street and north of Fenny Stratford.

INDUSTRIAL ARCHAEOLOGY

The Grand Union Canal follows the Ouzel Valley northwards through the parish in the direction of Fenny Stratford and Simpson. When opened in May 1800, the Grand Junction Canal, as it was then known, terminated at Fenny Stratford. The canal from Braunston was not completed until October 1800, when the shallow connecting lock was completed on the Simpson side of Fenny Stratford.

The parish is crossed by the London to Birmingham Railway, now part of the West Coast main line, constructed in 1838. From April to September 1838 the line from London ended at Denbigh Hall Bridge on Watling Street. In 1846 a small station was opened to the east of the parish church, and became important because Bletchley lay at the junction of the lines to Oxford in the west, and Cambridge in the east.

Bletchley was nationally famous for its brick industry, which began in the seventeenth century and developed with the construction of the canal. The brickworks supplied local towns, while later the bricks were sent further afield via the railway. The main area of brick production was at the southern end of the parish on the boundary with Water Eaton and Newton Longville (BCM 1980).

BOW BRICKHILL

R.J. Zeepvat

INTRODUCTION

Bow Brickhill parish (Fig. 18) is the northernmost of the three Brickhills, and covers an area of some 750 hectares, straddling the south-eastern city boundary of Milton Keynes. About one third of the parish falls within the new city, the boundary being marked by the BR Bletchley-Bedford branch line. The parish contains two settlements; Bow Brickhill itself, located some 0.5 km outside Milton Keynes, and the hamlet of Caldecotte, inside the city boundary in the north-west corner of the parish. The latter settlement and its surrounding area are the subject of a detailed study based on the results of archaeological fieldwork and excavation carried out by the Milton Keynes Archaeology Unit (Zeepvat *et al*., forthcoming).

Bow Brickhill parish is roughly rectangular in shape. Its west side is bounded by the river Ouzel, and its north side by Caldecotte Brook, with the exception of an area of some sixteen hectares, which extends northwards along the east bank of the Ouzel into Walton parish. On its south side the parish is bounded partly by Watling Street, but much of its southern and eastern boundaries with the parishes of Great Brickhill and Wavendon respectively run across the former heathland of the Woburn Sands Heights, now Brickhill Woods, and are not related to any landscape features.

The western part of the parish falls within the flood plain of the River Ouzel, a low-lying area prone until recent times to flooding, and referred to in a thirteenth-century document as *Magna mersa de bollebrichill*, or "the great marsh of Bow Brickhill" (BAS Mss 103/36). Moving east from the river the ground rises slowly, so that the medieval village of Caldecotte, 0.5 km from the river, is only two metres (67 m OD) above the level of the flood plain. Much of this low-lying part of the parish consists geologically of shallow deposits of river terrace gravels overlying Oxford Clay, which is exposed on the edge of the terrace toward the river, and also to the east of the second terrace gravels. The soils produced by the terrace gravels are loamy and well-drained, and were considered useful for both arable and pastoral agriculture.

Beyond the immediate environs of the hamlet of Caldecotte, the land continues a gradual rise south and east from the river to the foot of the escarpment of the Woburn Sands Heights, about 1.7 km from the river. A steep slope then rises to the highest area of ground for some miles around, with especially high spots being the site of Bow Brickhill parish church and the hill fort of Danesborough, both at about 170 m OD. The Woburn Sands Heights are, as their name suggests, formed by sands of the Lower Greensand, and produce a hungry podzolic soil which supported a dry-heath vegetation until the late eighteenth century, when extensive conifer plantations were established which survive to the present day. There are deposits of Fuller's Earth which have been exploited since the medieval period, and some of the sand is cemented by iron oxides to form rusty-brown-coloured ironstone, the only locally available building stone. There are former quarries near Bow Brickhill church.

Between the Woburn Sands Heights and the river the land is underlain by Oxford clay, which produces a tenacious and heavy soil, often difficult to plough in wet winters. However, across about half the area the clay is masked by head deposits which are often sandy, as they are derived from the Woburn Sands, and these lighten the soil considerably.

The Greensand escarpment is a slight natural barrier to north-south movement, not as severe as the Chilterns, further to the south. The Ouzel valley provides a easy route through it, followed by the Grand Junction Canal of 1800 and the London and Birmingham Railway of 1838. It is reasonable to suppose that this is a long-standing natural route, especially as it leads to the Tring Gap in the Chilterns. By analogy with the Icknield Way on the scarp of that latter ridge, Simco (1984, 67) postulates a pre-Roman east-west route along the Greensand ridge, but this is very speculative.

Apart from Watling Street, Bow Brickhill parish is traversed by three communication routes. The first of these (Walton Road/Galley Lane) runs northwards from Watling Street along the east side of

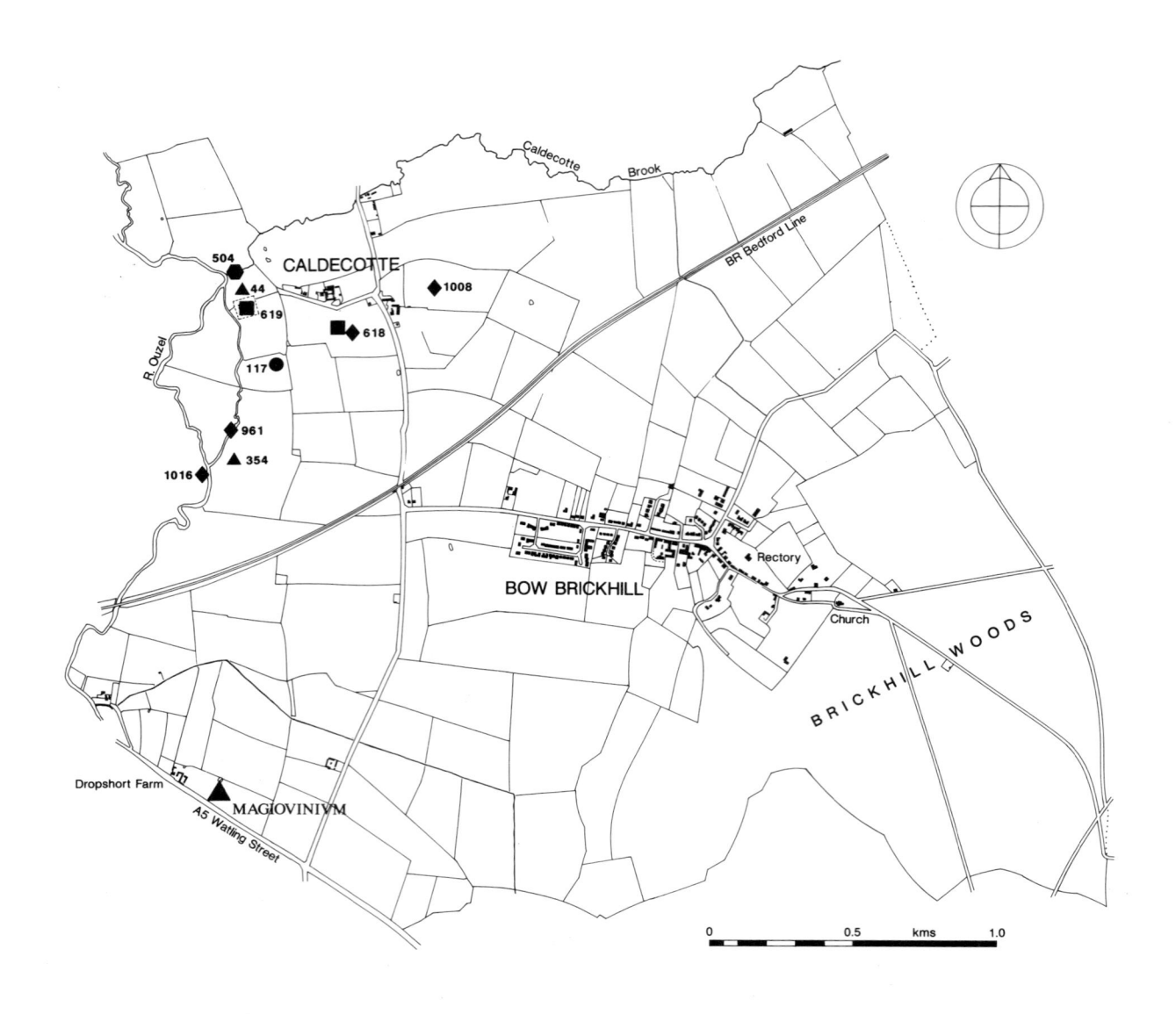

Figure 18: Bow Brickhill parish in 1967, showing major archaeological sites.

the Ouzel valley to Newport Pagnell, linking the settlements of Caldecotte, Walton, Milton Keynes and Broughton. It is evident from the archaeological and historical record that this route is of long standing, though its course has varied. The Roman road from *Magiovinium* to Irchester must have followed the east side of the Ouzel valley, though its exact course is not known, apart from a length of road discovered during excavations at *Magiovinium* itself (Neal 1987). A possible alignment for at least part of the Roman route can be seen on the 1791 enclosure map (Fig. 19) of the parish (BuCRO Occ. pub. 3/10/1961), where in addition to the modern road a parallel route is shown midway between the river and the present road, running southwards from the northernmost extremity of the parish, passing to the west of Caldecotte and joining Watling Street about 180 m west of Galley Lane. Part of this route survives as a hollow-way forming the west boundary of the scheduled area encompassing the medieval village earthworks at Caldecotte (MK618). From this road about 600 m north of Watling Street a branch led south-west to the Ouzel river crossing, while close to its northern end it was linked to the later route by the lane running through Caldecotte, marked on the 1791 map as Simpson Road. Beyond the parish, it appears to have joined the route crossing the Ouzel between Walton and Simpson.

The second of these routes, branching off the first half-way across the parish, runs through Bow Brickhill to Woburn Sands and Aspley Guise. Currently designated the B557, it is named 'Green Way Road' on the 1791 map.

The third route is the Bletchley to Bedford railway branch line, which was opened in 1846, and now marks the south-eastern city boundary of Milton Keynes. It crosses Walton Road on the level immediately north of its junction with the Bow Brickhill road, at which point is located the halt serving Bow Brickhill.

The village of Bow Brickhill developed around the junction between the Galley Lane to Wavendon road and a route which climbs the Greensand escarpment, leading south-eastwards to Woburn and Little Brickhill. The parish church is interestingly located along the latter road, on the south-eastern edge of the village, which it overlooks. In the early eighteenth century Willis recorded that the village consisted of fifty-six houses, with five more in 'London End' (possibly on Watling Street, close to the river crossing), and ten at Caldecotte (Bodleian, Willis Mss 98, 756).

The hamlet of Caldecotte lies to the west of Walton Road, in the north-west corner of the parish. It consisted (1990) of two farmhouses, a row of three nineteenth-century farm labourer's cottages, and two modern houses. Of the farmhouses, the older was Old Caldecotte Farmhouse, a seventeenth-century timber-framed house which stood at the east end of the village (Woodfield 1986, 155) until destroyed by fire in 1987. In contrast Caldecotte Farmhouse, to the north of Caldecotte Lane, is a nineteenth-century brick house with a slate roof, currently in a state of disrepair. From the 1791 enclosure map it is evident that this replaced an earlier house in a similar location.

To the south of Caldecotte Lane are the earthworks marking the original extent of Caldecotte, while to the west of the hamlet, close to the river, is a moated site which was noted in 1641 as having been the site of the former manor house (New College Ms. 1450). The moat and part of the village earthworks were excavated by the Unit in 1978 and 1990/91, and will be reported on in detail elsewhere (Zeepvat *et al.*, forthcoming). The earthworks are described below.

ARCHAEOLOGY

Most of the archaeological evidence relating to Bow Brickhill parish (Fig. 18) comes from two areas. The first of these is Caldecotte and the northern part of the parish, where intensive fieldwork and excavation in advance of the development of Milton Keynes was undertaken by the Unit. The second is around the site of *Magiovinium*, where excavations have been carried out in advance of road improvements on several occasions since 1978 (Neal 1987; other reports forthcoming).

Flints have been recovered from several locations in the parish, and a larger concentration (MK353/2) found during the construction of Caldecotte Lake in association with bone and burnt stones beneath alluvial deposits close to the Ouzel suggests a possible occupation site.

Much of the evidence for activity in the Iron Age comes from excavations in advance of Caldecotte Lake, with the discovery of a complex late Iron Age ditched enclosure (MK117), and contemporary cultivation evidence in the form of ard or plough marks sealed beneath a Roman yard surface (MK44).

Excavations at MK44 also produced evidence of extensive early Roman field systems and settlement, including industrial activity in the form of two pottery kilns and features related to bronze working. Much of this latter activity was probably encouraged by the establishment of the town of *Magiovinium*, two kilometres to the south, pro-

No.	Name	Owner	Acres	Roods	Poles
1	Nortons north meadow	APr	10	0	22
2	Nortons middle meadow	APr	11	1	17
3	Nortons south meadow	APr	15	2	28
4	Nortons close	APt	1	3	7
5	Caldecot close	APr	7	1	11
6	Back leys	APr	11	3	9
7	Outfield	APr	2	2	22
8	Long hades ground	APr	16	1	35
9	Crab-tree west ground	APr	13	3	49
10	Crab-tree east ground	APr	13	1	27
11	Garden bridge ground	APr	7	2	19
12	Far meadow	APr	9	1	37
13	Long hedge ground	APr	10	3	2
14	Mougher north field	Rec	11	3	15
15	Mougher west field	Rec	15	0	35
16	Mougher east field	Rec	10	3	15
17	Home ground	NH	44	2	39
18	Kiln furlong ground	CP	9	0	21
19	KIln pits ground	CP	13	2	31
20	Home close	SO	2	0	1
21	Well close	APr	13	3	28
22	An orchard	APr	2	0	34
23	Little Berrystead close	CP	4	1	24
24	Great Berrystead close	CP	8	1	31
25	The great holmes	Rec	12	0	6
26	The great holmes	Rec	9	0	30
27	Mill close	CP	4	2	22
28	Mill close	Rec	9	0	3
29	Broad gate piece	CP	10	1	4
30	Ditch furlong ground	CP	9	2	31
31	Ditch furlong ground	CP	8	3	38
32	Mill corner north ground	Rec	8	2	27
33	Mill corner south ground	Rec	17	1	14
34	Maedow ground	Rec	15	0	23
35	Fullbuddy meadow	NH	15	0	16
36	Rowland north field	WP	10	1	39
37	Rowland south field	WP	12	3	3
38	Milking yard	Rec	0	2	1
39	Gravel pit	CP	0	2	0
40	Gravel pit	NH	1	2	0

Key to landowners

APr	Anne Parker	APt	Anne Parrott
CP	Charlotte Primatt	NH	Nathaniel Hilliard
Rec	the Rector	SO	Samuel Odel
WP	William Page		

KEY TO FIG. 19:
Field names, acreages and landowners in the Caldecotte area in 1791.

ADDENDA:

THe key given opposite Fig. 19 refers to another map of the same date. The following key is the correct one for Fig. 19.

Landowners	Field no.	Allotment	Description/comments	Acres	Roods	Poles

Major landowners (in order of size of holding):

Landowners	Field no.	Allotment	Description/comments	Acres	Roods	Poles
Joseph Ager	8	-	'Berrystead Close'	4	1	24
	20	2nd	-	122	1	38
	30	-	'Caldecot Close'	not shown		
	61	-	'Sheveralls Closes'	9	2	18
	81	1st	-	279	0	35
The Rector	17	-	'for tithes of the fields'	44	3	22
	18	-	'for tithes of old enclosures'	24	0	0
	33	3rd	'for tithes of the fields'	35	3	25
	57	2nd	'for tithes of the fields'	90	3	28
	60	2nd	'for glebe'	22	2	30
	70	1st	'for tithes of the fields'	9	1	4
	79	5th	-	11	0	36
	82	4th	'for glebe'	19	2	12
Anne Parker	1, 10	1st	-	38	2	1
	2, 11, 37	2nd	-	18	0	3
	12	3rd	-	4	1	36
	14	5th	-	0	3	0
	29	4th	-	85	2	6
	46	7th	-	0	1	32
	73	-	'Chapel Close'	1	2	30
Thomas Ager	22	2nd	-	31	3	34
	45	-	'Farmhouse'	1	3	16
	72	-	'The Wicks'	7	0	32
	83	1st	-	69	1	37
Francis Moore	3	6th	-	0	3	17
	39, 53	1st	-	37	1	16
	55	2nd	-	9	0	1
	56	3rd	-	35	0	23
	59	4th	-	35	2	17
	65	5th	-	2	2	2
	67	-	'The Parks'	not shown		
	69	-	'Allotment for Manor'	10	3	25
	88-90	-	'Kiln Ground'	not shown		
	91	-	'Bell Coppice'	7	2	37
Charlotte Primatt	16	2nd	-	37	0	23
	31	1st	-	23	0	35
	78	3rd	-	9	1	21
John Chapman	4	2nd	-	1	0	28
	9	-	'Caldecot Close'	7	1	11
	38	1st	-	56	3	1
	44	-	'farm and homestead'	2	2	25
Thomas Cook	23	-	-	39	2	13

Minor landowners (in alphabetical order):

Name	Plot		Description	A	R	P
Gregory Austin	58	-	-	10	0	35
Thomas Bennett	63	-	-	2	1	21
Thomas Carpenter	25	-	-	1	0	24
Rev'd D. Chelsum	52	-	-	9	2	2
Joseph Clark	48	-	-	1	2	10
Thomas Clark	41	-	-	1	0	37
William Clark	40	-	-	1	2	10
H.W. Cowley	75	-	-	0	3	13
Mrs Duncombe	87	-	'Cut Mill Close'	not shown		
Thomas Edwin	76	-	-	1	0	13
William Elkin	35	-	-	18	0	12
Rev'd William Ellis	28	-	-	1	0	36
Rev'd Charles Este	19	2nd	-	3	1	32
Ann Hack	5	-	-	0	3	17
John Hammond	74	-	-	0	3	4
John Hart	42	-	-	0	3	39
William Henman	77	1st	-	3	0	35
Francis Hobbs	47	-	-	2	0	25
E. Masters	26	-	-	1	3	3
W. Merryman	7	2nd	-	0	0	21
Walter Mills	84	-	-	1	3	26
George Norris	36	-	-	16	3	17
Samuel Odell	27	-	'Orchard'	not shown		
	32	-	-	2	0	1
William Page	34	-	-	18	1	3
Page, (?) & Norris	13	-	'Caldecot Close'	1	2	8
Richard Parrott	50	-	-	1	0	31
Thomas Parrott	6	-	-	0	3	14
Joseph Pettit	49	-	-	1	0	30
Edward Shouller	62	-	-	2	0	36
S. Smith	80	1st	-	0	0	21
	86	2nd	-	0	1	9
John Stevens	24	-	-	16	2	10
Thomas Wootten	51	-	-	1	1	11
Others	15	4th	'for gravel'	0	2	0
	21	-	'for gravel'	1	2	0
	64	2nd	'stone pit'	1	3	8
	66, 68	-	'part of the Poor's allotment'	4	3	4
	71	3rd	'stone pit'	0	3	33
	85	-	'Town land'	6	0	19
	92	-	'The Poor's allotment'	198	0	5
Unknown	43	-	-	0	2	38

KEY TO FIG. 19: Landowners and acreages allotted in the 1791 enclosure of Bow Brickhill parish.

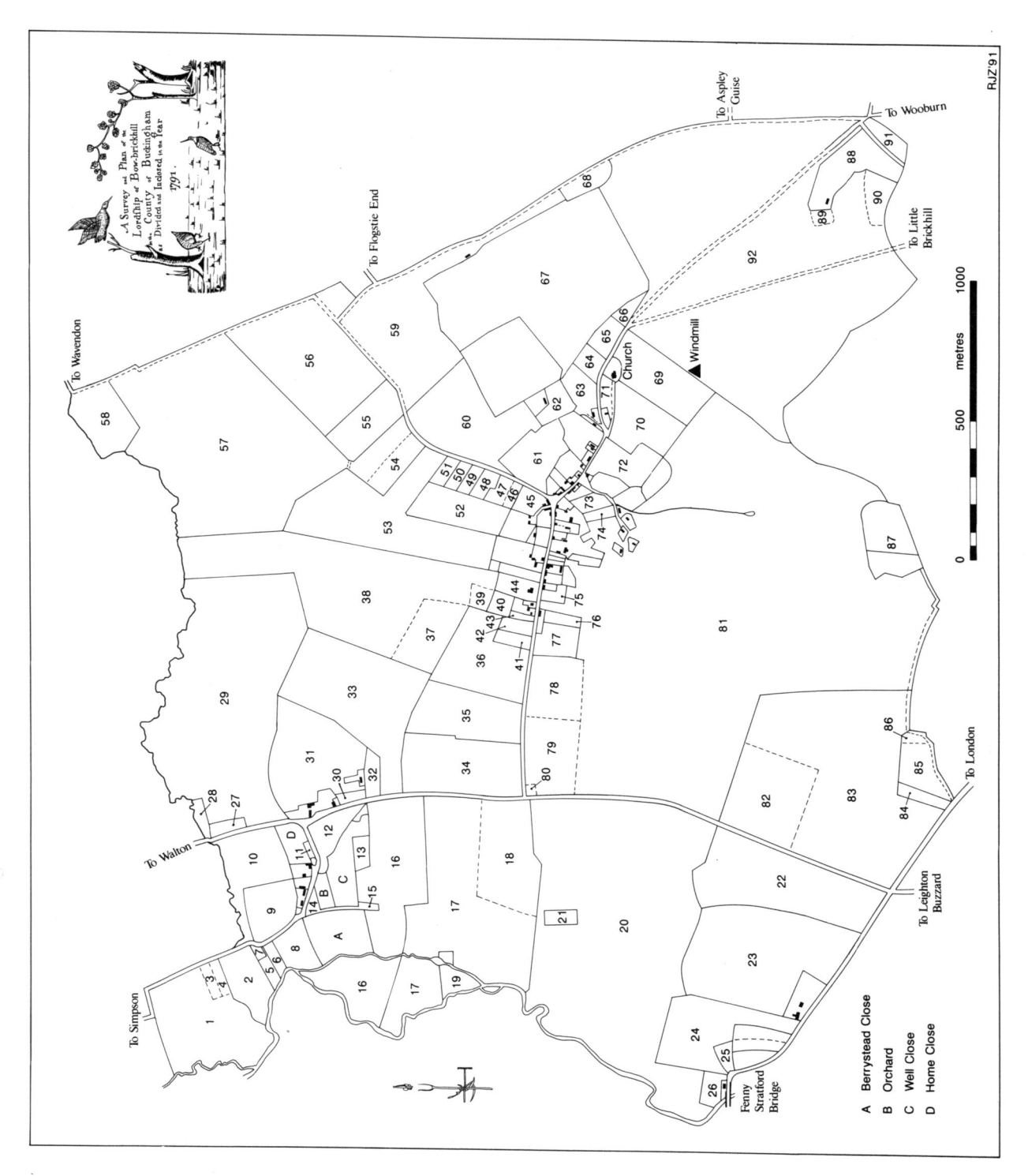

Figure 19: Bow Brickhill; reconstruction of the 1791 enclosure map.

viding a ready market for the goods produced. Occupation appears to have ceased in the area west of Caldecotte by the end of the second century, although the land continued to be farmed.

During the late Saxon period, settlement in the Caldecotte area was located (MK504) to the north-west of the village, slightly to the north of the former Roman settlement, close to the junction of Caldecotte Brook and the Ouzel. By the early medieval period, the focus of settlement had shifted to the area now occupied by the village earthworks (MK618).

Bow Brickhill appears in the Domesday survey, apparently as an amalgamation of two manors (VCH 1927, 289), while Caldecotte is not mentioned, presumably because it was included in the lordship of Bow Brickhill. By the early thirteenth century the Chauncey family, lords of Bow Brickhill, were also lords of Caldecotte manor, and the holdings descended from that time as one knight's fee but two manors, the principal holding being Bow Brickhill. The subsequent history of the two manors is detailed elsewhere (VCH 1927, 289–92), and little new information has been added as a result of the Unit's historical researches.

The only surviving archaeological earthworks in the parish are the village (MK618) and moat (MK619) at Caldecotte (Fig. 20), of which the former, now reduced from its original extent by encroaching housing development, is a scheduled ancient monument (Bucks. No. 100).

Well Close, the field containing the village earthworks, originally covered some 6.25 hectares. A number of long rectangular ditched enclosures were visible along its north and east sides, while the south-west part of the field was given over to larger enclosures containing ridge-and-furrow. The north-east corner appeared devoid of earthworks. Apart from the enclosures, the most prominent feature in the field was a hollow-way, running south-eastwards from Caldecotte Farm and cutting across several of the enclosures. Excavations have shown that this led to a complex of post-medieval buildings close to the south-east corner of the field. The date of the hollow-way is not certain; its line appears on the 1791 enclosure map as a field boundary, and the area containing the buildings to which it led as a small irregular plot of land. As no buildings are shown, the site must have been deserted by that time.

The moat (Plate 8) lies one hundred metres west of the village in *Berrystead Close*, adjacent to the same side channel of the Ouzel which supplied Caldecotte Mill. Only the west and north sides of the moat are now open, the other two sides having been filled in during the 1960's. The moat ditch is about 12 m wide. The enclosed area measures 37×40 m, and there appears on aerial photographs to have been an entrance near the north-east corner (Cambridge Univ. Coll. no. AEF36; Aerofilms A/54099/54), consisting of a narrow causeway. The only internal features were a series of pits in the north-west corner, associated with gravel extraction.

FIELD SYSTEM

As is shown in Fig. 21, most of Bow Brickhill parish was cultivated, apart from low-lying meadowlands in the Ouzel valley, and the high heathlands on the Greensand escarpment, which were common land. By the seventeenth century the parish was farmed on the three-field system, the fields being named in a terrier of 1639 as *South Field*, *Middlefield* and *Northfield* (Bodleian, Willis Mss, 81a). Exactly how these divisions related to the medieval field system is not certain. Only a small number of pre-enclosure field and place names survive for Bow Brickhill (BAS Record Ser. 4, 1940, 16 & 40), and few can be located with any certainty. The post-enclosure field names appear on the 1791 enclosure map (BuCRO Occ. pub. 3/10/1961).

OTHER LANDSCAPE FEATURES

Bow Brickhill is unique among the parishes of Milton Keynes in possessing both a watermill and a windmill, which appear to have been operational simultaneously. The watermill, to the south-west of Caldecotte on a side-channel of the Ouzel, was excavated by the Unit in 1980/81 (Petchey and Giggins 1983), while the windmill, located on high ground to the south of Bow Brickhill village, is known from documentary sources only.

Caldecotte Mill is first mentioned in Domesday Book (VCH 1927, 291) as a part of the manor of Caldecotte. In 1208 it was separated from the manorial estate, and in 1293 passed to that branch of the Grey family who became Earls of Kent. Following the collapse of their fortunes in the first half of the sixteenth century it passed to the Crown, who conveyed it in fee farm to Edward Ferrers and Francis Phillips in 1610. At that time the miller, Humphrey Blackshaw, paid a rent of £4 13s. 4d (£13.69). By 1652, both the watermill and the windmill belonged to Robert Morgan, who sold them in that year to William White. There is no record of more recent owners or tenants of the watermill.

There are two eighteenth-century references to the mill. On 25th May 1754 an Aylesbury newspaper recorded that a man washing some sheep at Caldecotte Mill was dragged by one of them into

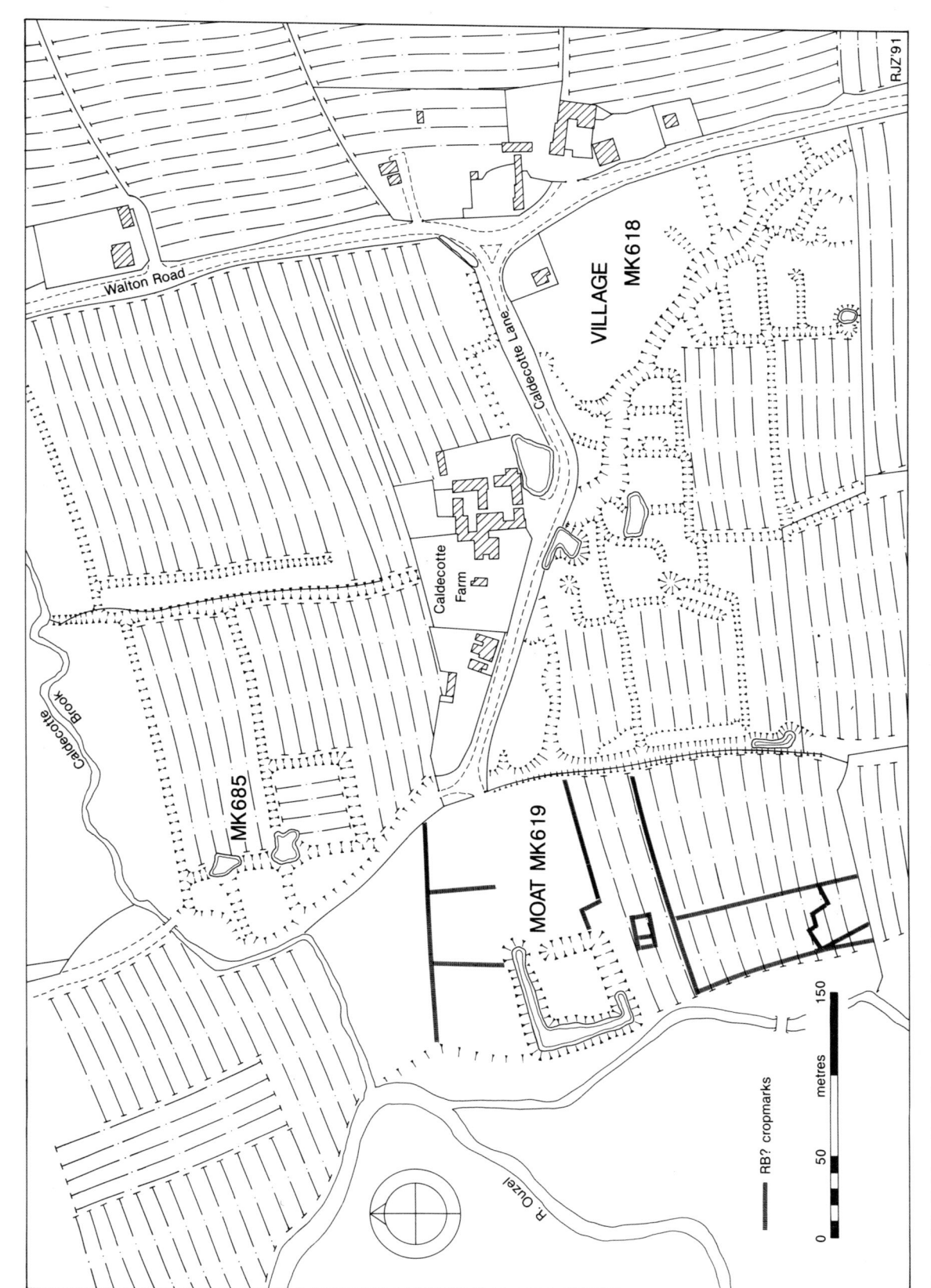

Figure 20: Caldecotte village earthworks and moated site.

Figure 21: Bow Brickhill medieval field system.

the mill-pond and drowned (Gibbs 1879, 106). On 12th June 1766 the vicar of Bletchley, the Rev'd William Cole, noted in his diary that his manservant, Tom Wood, had gone fishing at Caldecotte Mill, and had actually caught some fish (Stokes 1931, 58).

On the 1791 enclosure map the mill-pond is shown, and two neighbouring fields are named as *Mill Close*, but no mill building is shown. As other buildings are shown, including a milking parlour in the corner of Mill Close, this can be taken as evidence that the mill had been demolished by that date. Evidence from the excavation (Fig. 22) confirmed the presence of a mill in the seventeenth and eighteenth centuries only, with no trace of the earlier mill suggested by the documentary evidence.

The location of the windmill at Bow Brickhill is clearly shown on high ground to the south of the church (approx. NGR SP 913 341) on the 1791 map. It is depicted as a post-mill, with a conventional pitched roof and four-armed sails, similar to the reconstruction proposed for the post-mill excavated at Great Linford (Fig. 12). As has been mentioned above, the mill is known to have been in existence in 1653, and apparently remained standing into the nineteenth century, when it was shown on a map of the parishes of Bow Brickhill, Wavendon and Aspley Guise (BedsCRO R1/221).

RECENT HISTORY

In 1968 the northern part of the parish, including Caldecotte, was included in the designated area of the new city of Milton Keynes, from which point development became inevitable. The first major construction project in the area was the construction of Caldecotte Lake, the function of which is to prevent flooding, followed by associated lakeside development and a major road. Construction of the lake started in 1981 (Plate 18) and was finished two years later, but lake-side development is only now (1992) well under way. To the east of the lake, much of the northern part of the parish has been covered by the Tilbrook industrial development, and the Brownswood and Old Farm Park housing areas. Beyond the city boundary there has been little change to the parish, except for major road improvements to the A5.

Plate 18: Construction of Caldecotte Lake, 1981. *(MKAU)*

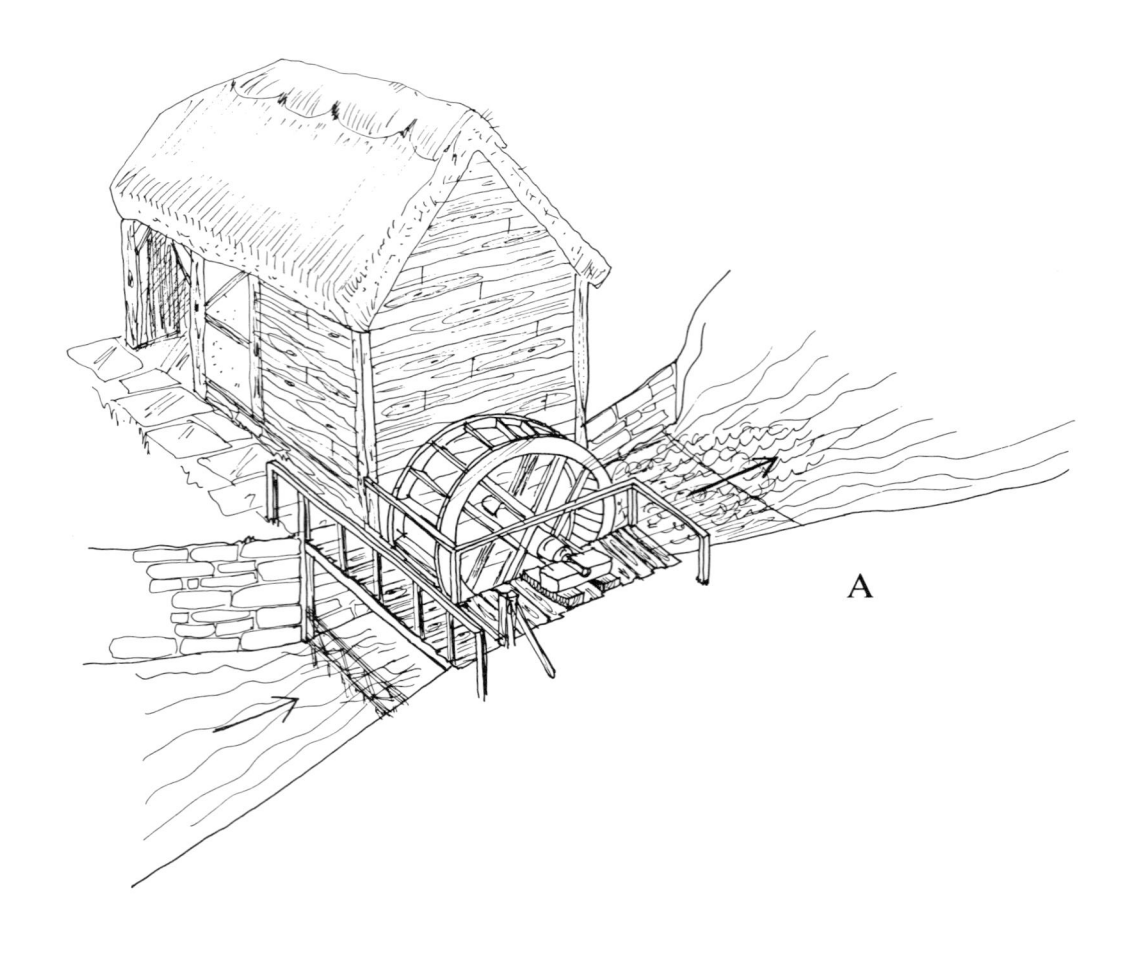

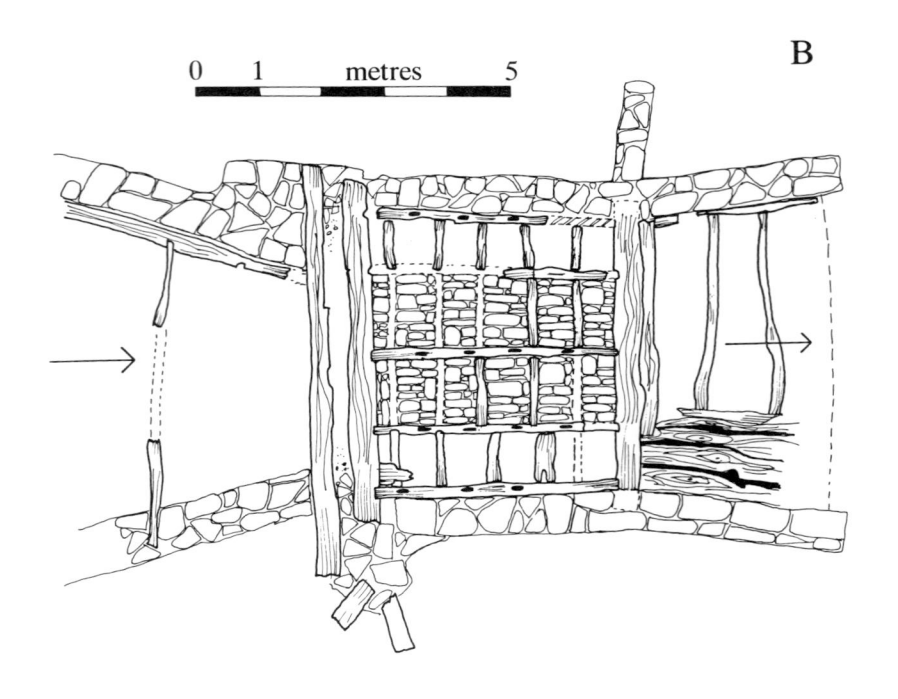

Figure 22: Reconstruction of Caldecotte watermill. *(John Crooks)*

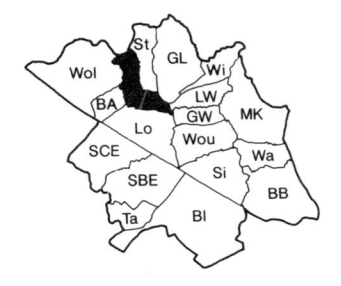

BRADWELL

INTRODUCTION

The parish of Bradwell (Fig. 23) ran southwards from its northern boundary at the Ouse to the southern boundary with Loughton parish. The parish then extended eastward, climbing to the higher ground of Bradwell Common, now central Milton Keynes. The northern and western boundaries were marked by the Ouse and Bradwell Brook. The southern boundary followed medieval furlong boundaries, except for one section where it dog-legged along the ends of individual strips. The eastern border with Stantonbury followed furlong boundaries to the point where it turned eastward and followed the medieval or earlier road leading to Secklow mound, the meeting place of Secklow Hundred.

The parish covered some 392 ha, and the geology is similar to that of the adjoining parishes, with lighter well-drained soils in the valley at the north end and heavy clayland in the south of the parish.

The medieval village developed in the south-west corner of the parish, at the intersection of two roads. One, an east-west route, ran from Wolverton down to Bradwell Abbey, then to Bradwell village. This road continued through the village as a deeply sunken way (Primrose Lane, formerly Bury Lane) and continued eastwards across Bradwell Common to the Woolstones, passing the Secklow meeting mound *en route*. East of the village this road was known as 'Common Lane' and was the parish boundary with Stantonbury until it reached Great Linford parish at Wood Corner, so-called because of the proximity of Linford Wood. Here it forked, one road leading to the Woolstones and the other to Linford Wood and eventually Great Linford village. The latter route was not made up in modern times, remaining as a grassy track.

The other road, the north-south route, ran from a junction with the Stony Stratford to Newport Pagnell road at the northern end of the parish, southwards through the parish to Loughton and the Shenleys. The Stony Stratford to Newport Pagnell road crossed the northern end of the parish. This was a principal route between Oxford and Cambridge, passing through Buckingham, Newport Pagnell and Bedford, and is presumably of late Saxon origin. A stone bridge which carried this road over Bradwell Brook was referred to as the *Stanbruge* in the early thirteenth century (VCH 1927, 506).

A possible Roman road (Viatores 1974, 336 and map 443) ran through the eastern end of the parish. In the late Saxon and medieval periods this road linked the Loughton valley villages with the market town of Newport Pagnell, and was called *Portweie* in the thirteenth century (Jenkins 1952, No. 8).

ARCHAEOLOGY

Apart from a scatter of flints along the east side of Bradwell Brook, the most significant evidence of prehistoric occupation in the parish comes from Heelands, where a group of Neolithic pits (MK342) was discovered during topsoil stripping prior to housing construction in 1979. About 500 m to the east, during the construction of Dansteed Way, evidence of an Iron Age settlement site was recorded (MK294).

Activity during the Roman period in the parish was represented by a single native occupation site at Wood Corner (MK64), on which limited excavation was carried out in 1976/77, in all too frequently atrocious conditions. That occupation and farming activity in the vicinity was rather more widespread than the excavated area was demonstrated by the discovery of a Roman corn-drying oven (MK137) some 200 m north-east of Wood Corner. About 1 km to the west, evidence of Roman smithing activities was uncovered during the construction of Bradwell Middle School (MK127).

Pottery of middle to late Saxon date was found during the excavation of the later manor site, Bradwell Bury (MK506/623). However, it was considered that this originated from nearby occupation and not from the site itself.

Figure 23: Bradwell parish in 1967, showing major archaeological sites.

THE MEDIEVAL AND LATER VILLAGE

The village (Plate 3) has an interesting plan, the roads almost forming a square, suggesting that there may originally have been a central green with the older buildings and earthwork sites disposed around it.

There are two medieval earthwork sites (Fig. 24) in the village: a small motte-and-bailey castle (MK621) near the church, and the moated site of the early manor house (MK623) on the west side of Abbey Road. Both are Scheduled Ancient Monuments.

The remains of the castle are in the field to the north-east of the church and south of the village hall. The mound is approximately 20 m in diameter and 3 m high. Traces of the ditch around the mound now survive on the west side only, but were visible on the north side until the construction of the village hall in 1921.

A shallow pond to the south of the mound must represent quarrying. Traces of a partly backfilled trench on the north side of the mound are all that remains of an abortive attempt to construct an air raid shelter at the beginning of the second world war by the Rev'd Conway Davies and villagers.

Fifty-five metres to the south of the mound a section of ditch 6 m wide, aligned east to west, may represent the southern boundary of the bailey. At its western end this ditch dog-legs to the south and then continues to the west, forming the southern boundary of the churchyard. The eastern side of the earthwork has been destroyed by the car park and garden of the 'Prince Albert', a nineteenth-century public house. It is likely that the bailey continued eastwards for approximately 120 m to the Loughton road; the deviation in the line of this road as it enters the village could be explained by its running around the earthworks of the outer bailey.

The castle is thought (VCH 1927, 283) to have been erected by a member of the Bayeux family, who held a manor in Bradwell during the reign of King Stephen. William de Bayeux held the manor of the honour of Wallingford, which was in the hands of Brian Fitz Count, a friend of the Empress Matilda, and presumably he built the castle at her request (Chibnall 1965, 23, note 6).

The second site (MK 623) is that of the medieval moated manor house which was partly excavated prior to the construction of the village sportsfield in 1975 (Mynard forthcoming). The remains of the medieval moat around the Moat House are all that survive of Bradwell Bury, a once substantial homestead moat, one of the largest in the city area. The site was first occupied in the sixth to seventh centuries, but the manorial complex has its origins in the tenth to eleventh centuries.

The moat was originally rectangular in shape enclosing an area of 115 m by 55 m and was 5 m wide. The manor house was centrally located, with a stone barn and two stone dovecotes to the north. At some time after the sixteenth century, perhaps as late as the late eighteenth century when Moat House was built, the moated area was reduced in size to 45×55 m by the excavation of a new north arm, cutting off the barn and a new square dovecote (which replaced the circular one) from Moat House, which now stood in a central position within the smaller moated enclosure. Access to these buildings was by way of a narrow causeway across the north ditch. The former north end of the moat was later destroyed by quarrying, and only slight traces of it remained on the east side.

The field in which the barn and dovecote stood was *Dovecote Close* in 1839 but was called *Bradwell Bury* in 1792 (Fig. 25), a name which is indicative of an early manorial site. Primrose Lane, which runs across the northern side of the village, and Abbey Road both led to this site, and were called Bury Lane until the later years of the nineteenth century.

The remaining moat around Moat House has gradually been destroyed. The east side was filled in in 1963 by the Newport Pagnell Rural District Council in order to widen Abbey Road. The southern side has been changed by the removal of the inner face to create a terraced garden in front of the house.

Moat House has a datestone set above the main door which bears the initials 'TM' and the date 1784. 'TM' are the initials of Thomas Mercer, a descendant of an earlier Thomas who in 1707 had married Elizabeth Fuller, heiress of Roger Fuller, lord of the manor of Bradwell. Thomas presumably built Moat House on the site of the old manor house, and may have demolished the remains of the earlier buildings and reduced the area of the moat at that time. The Mercers held the manor until 1787, when it was sold by Thomas to William Bailey.

From the surviving documents it is clear that during the sixteenth and seventeenth centuries several yeoman farmers became prominent landowners in the parish, and the names Cooke and Newman frequently occur.

The Newman family is first mentioned in 1402 when Thomas Newman and Isabell his wife granted property in the village to John Padbury of Deanshanger (Jenkins 1952, 39). The property,

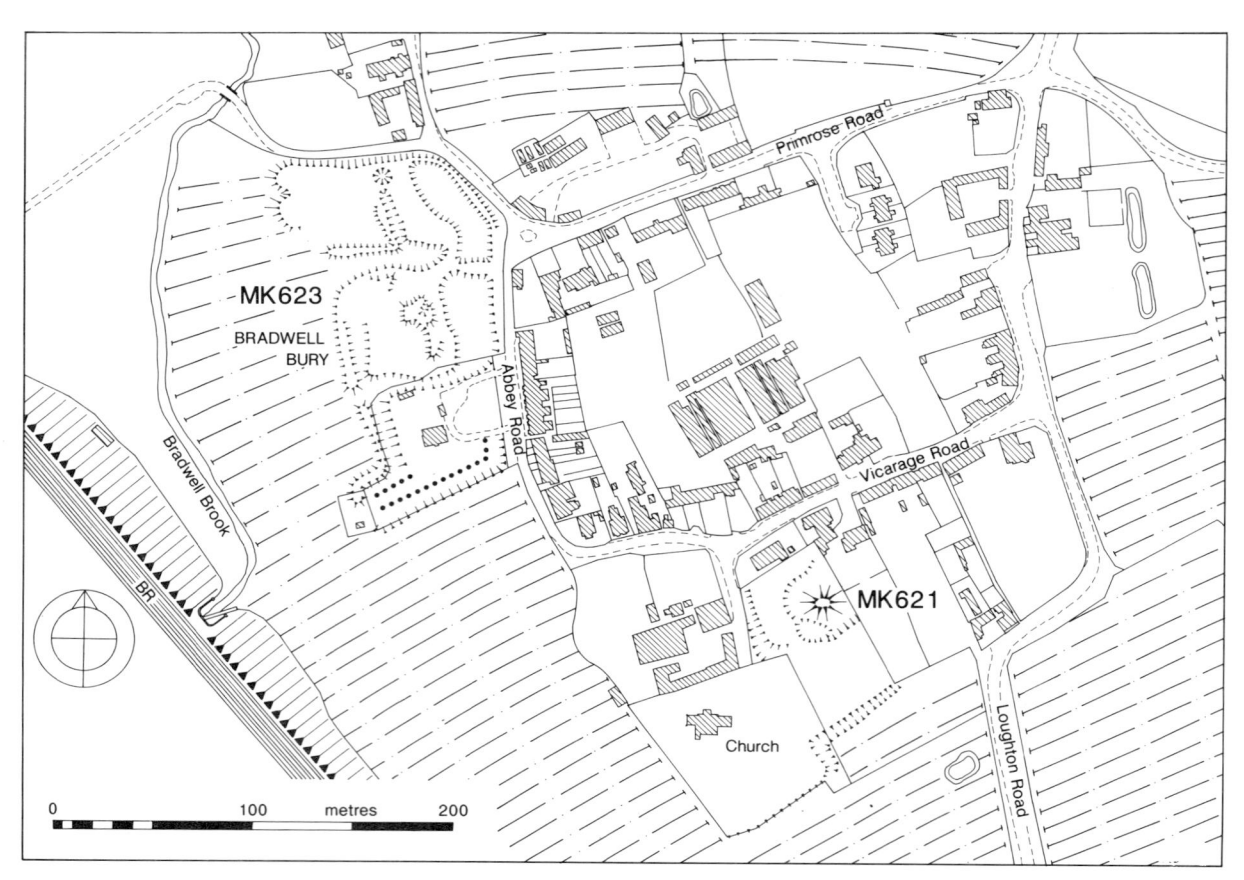

Figure 24: Bradwell; earthworks of the medieval manor and the motte-and-bailey castle.

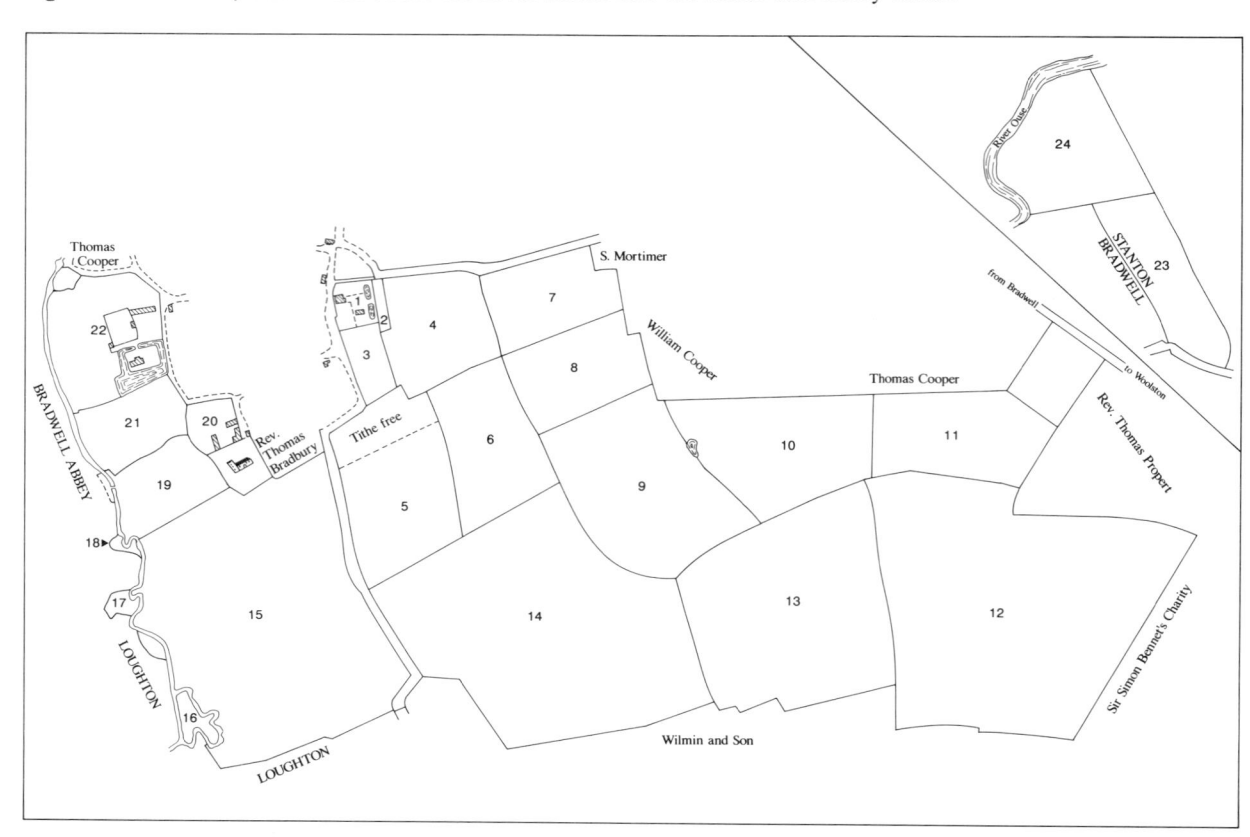

Figure 25: Bradwell: reconstruction of the estate map of William Bailey, 1792. *(Mrs Fossey, Bradwell)*

which they rented from Snelshall Priory, was described as '...Messuage and adjacent croft, hedges, ways and ditches belonging to the inclosure in Bradwell, next to the tenement of Roger Rabat on one side and the inclosure of lord Thomas de Aylesbury on the other'.

Nicholas Newman was the tenant of a farm belonging to Bradwell Abbey in the early sixteenth century. The property is described in the post-suppression survey of 1530 (Lipscomb 1847, 43) which gives details of the adjacent properties, but without further information it is not possible to locate its site within the village. John Newman too held a messuage, a close and various land in the parish at this time. The survey also mentions John's *Mansion Place* in Bradwell, suggesting that he lived in a substantial farmhouse or even one of the manor houses. However, the manorial accounts do not survive and there is no further proof of this.

John Newman's will of 1558 listed substantial bequests to his wife Elisabeth including 'the occupation of my mylne (mill)' (BuCRO D/A/Wf/4/237). This must be the windmill situated to the south-east of the village. The following year John died and his wife remarried, her second husband being Thomas Cooke, who in his will of 1559 promised that Elisabeth's children by her first marriage would be provided for according to the will of their father (BuCRO D/A/We/12/357). At the end of the century a subsidy assessment lists John's son as the second wealthiest person in the village (PRO D/X 398, E 179.220).

In 1530 John and William Cook were also tenants of the land formerly held by Bradwell Abbey (Lipscomb 1847, 43). When William died in 1552 he left to his son Thomas 'the lease of my farme at the church stile in Bradwell' (BuCRO D/A/We/7/110). The Cookes became wealthier in the early seventeenth century, and in 1649 John Cooke purchased his farm of fifty-five acres from Sir John Longville for £400 (NRO Litchborough Grant, Box A [6] x5255). The farm is referred to as 'Cook's Farm' until the end of the century in surviving documents (*op.cit.*). The Cook family are not mentioned in the parish registers after the death of Richard in 1695 (transcript in MKAU archive).

The oldest buildings are those related to the village farms and the manor. Home Farmhouse on Primrose Lane is probably the oldest secular building in the village. It was originally a late medieval or sixteenth-century house with a hall and solar, and was enlarged in the seventeenth century. Brookfield Cottages, formerly Brookfield Farmhouse, named after the *Brookfield* at the time of the enclosure, also has its origins in the sixteenth century. Moat House, described above, is dated 1784, but probably contains some earlier work (Woodfield 1986, 13) and was rebuilt shortly after the enclosure of the parish at a time of reorganisation of the manorial farms. Reconstruction and enlargement of Manor Farm, on the north side of the church, also took place at this time. Manor Farm, now a youth hostel, stands on the site of one of the village's medieval manor

No.	Field name	Acres	Roods	Poles
1	Homestead and gardens	1	–	39
2	Pightle	–	1	20
3	The Highlands	1	1	27
4	Goodys Leys	6	2	15
5	Butler's Piece (inc. Tithe free)	10	–	20
6	Lower Greenway	7	2	8
7	Crass Furlong	5	2	26
8	Upper Greenway	6	1	19
9	Spurfoot	12	3	14
10	Watering Pond Hill	10	1	32
11	Honey Plot	11	2	–
12	Long Summer Hill	32	2	23
13	Rooksley	20	2	2
14	Broad Slade (inc. manorial allot.)	30	2	6
15	Church Piece	29	3	14
16	Lower Hook	–	3	17
17	Middle Hook	–	1	20
18	Upper Hook	–	1	2
19	Church Leys	4	–	8
20	Homestead and Orchard	1	1	19
21	Rookery	3	3	3
22	Bradwell Bury	7	–	4
	Total	207	1	18
	in Stanton parish (inset):			
23	Lowney Moor	5	3	24
24	Stevens Meadow	7	2	30
	Total	13	2	14
	COMBINED TOTAL	220	3	32

KEY TO FIG. 25:
Field names shown on the William Bailey estate map, Bradwell, 1792.

Plate 19: Bradwell village; Vicarage Road in the mid nineteenth century. Painting by Col. Duncan. *(Northamptonshire Record Office)*

houses, and is a seventeenth-century house onto which an imposing east front with a datestone of 1790 has been added.

The 'Victoria' inn was the farmhouse occupied by John Newman in the seventeenth century (Bodleian, Willis Mss 12, 138). The stone building at the rear of the 'Victoria' inn and the row of houses immediately to the west of it was formerly a barn of Newman's farm. Some idea of the character of the village until the middle of the nineteenth century is conveyed in a painting of that part of Vicarage Road opposite Manor Farm, now in Northamptonshire Record office (Plate 19).

THE FIELD SYSTEM

The ridge-and-furrow map of the medieval field system (Fig. 26) shows that the whole parish was cultivated, apart from the flood meadows of the Ouse. The village and the road running eastwards from it neatly divided the parish into two blocks, which became the 'North' and 'South' fields.

These fields are referred to in several medieval documents (NRO, misc. ledger 383). The South Field also had the alternative name of *Wood Field*, owing to the proximity of Linford Wood.

From at least the later sixteenth century the parish was farmed on a three-field system (LRO Ter. 15/11). There are further references to these three fields in seventeenth-century documents (NRO Litchborough Grant) which give the names of the fields as *Brook Field*, *Seckley Field* and *Stanton Field*. The names were not consistently used, and *Seckley Field* later became *Windmill Field*, while *Stanton Field* is referred to as the *Pasture* or *Middle Field*. *Brook Field* contained all of the land north of the village lying between Bradwell Brook and the road to Stantonbury, *Stanton Field* was all of the land to the east of the Stantonbury road, and *Seckley* or *Windmill Field* contained all of the land south of the village and Common Lane.

Some land in the parish was enclosed in the medieval period. A document dated 1402 refers to the 'Hedges, Ways and Ditches belonging to the Inclosure of Bradwell' (Jenkins 1952, No. 107). However, this may only indicate small closes around the village. Three hundred acres of land enclosed in 1506–7 by the Prior of Bradwell were said to be in Bradwell (Leadam 1897, 181) but this is more likely to refer to land in Bradwell Abbey, since the Prior did not hold that much land in Bradwell parish.

The parish was enclosed in 1788, and although no

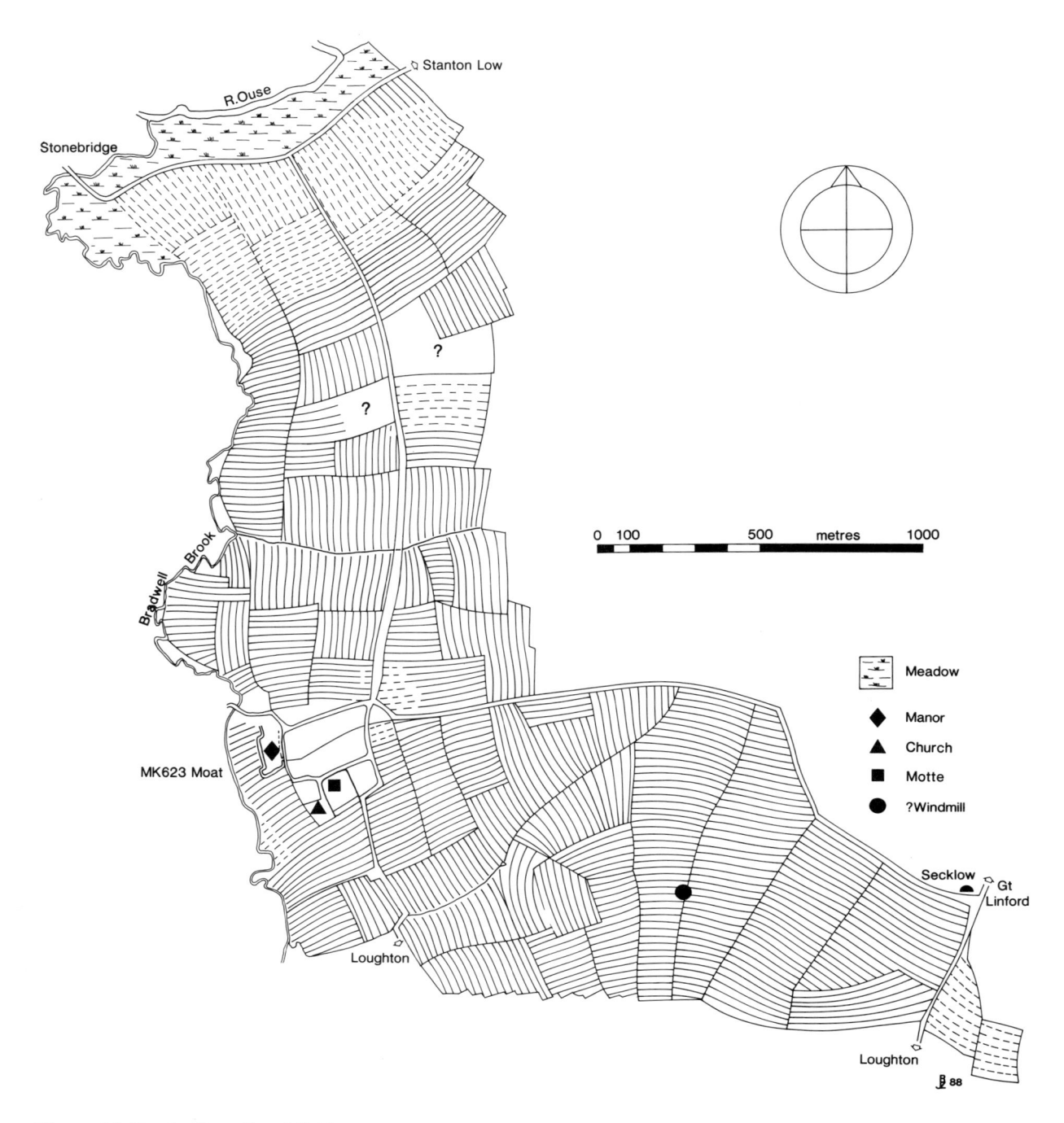

Figure 26: Bradwell medieval field system.

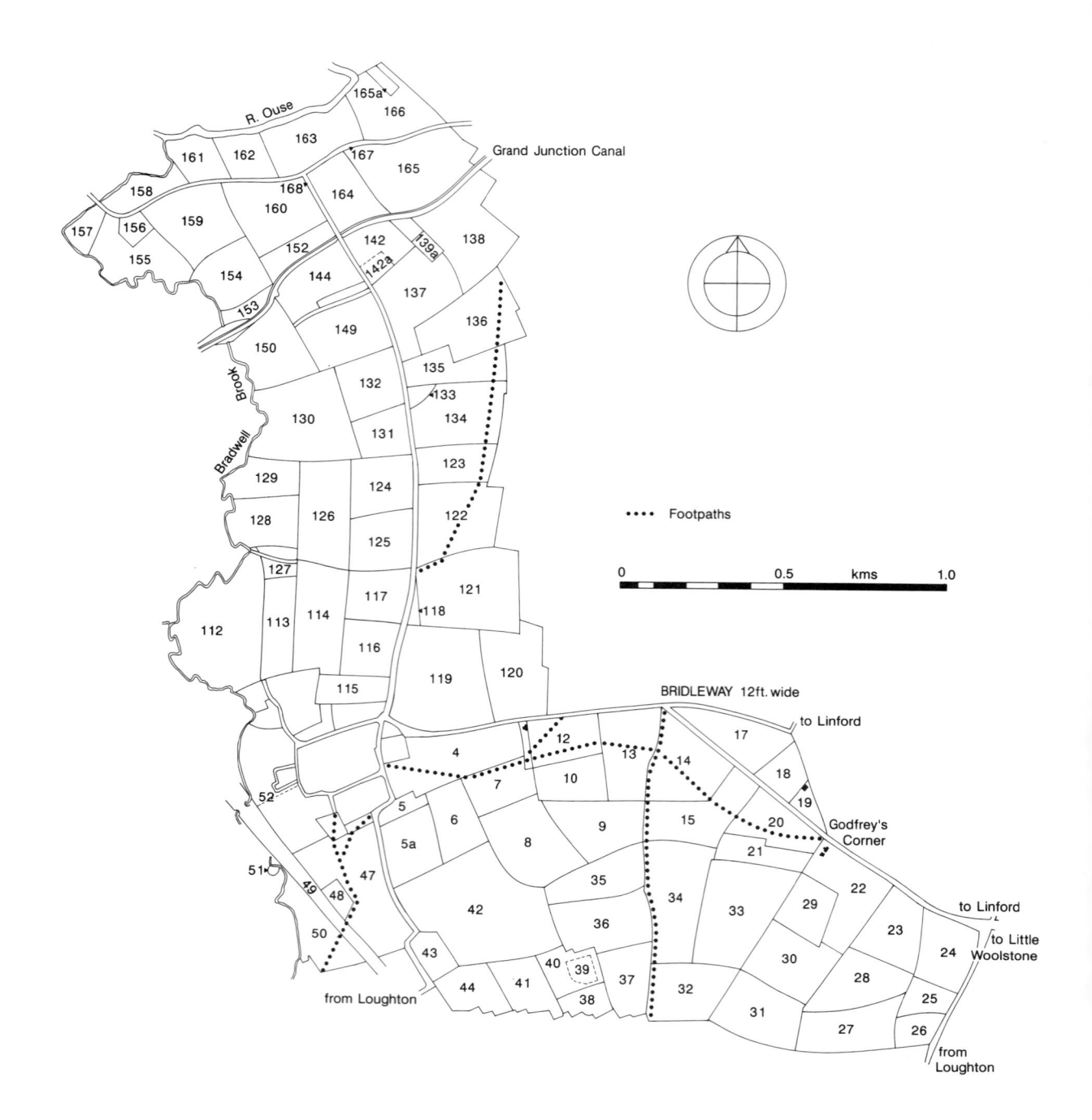

Figure 27: Bradwell; reconstruction of the tithe award map, 1839.

4	The Leys	37	Rooks Ley	131	First Double Hedge
5	Butler's Leys	38	Little Rooks Ley	132	Far Double Hedge
5a	part of Butler's Leys	39	part of Rooks Leys	133	Spinney
6	Lower Greenway	40	Rooks Leys	134	Long Deadland
7	Breast Ploughed Field	41	Furzen Field	135	–
8	Spurfoot	42	Broad Slade	136	Clare's Corner
9	Watering Pond Hill	43	Lower Earl's Willow	137	Pepper Hill
10	Higgin's Piece	44	Upper Earl's Willow	138	Earl's Willow
12	Short Dukes	47	–	139a	Pightle
13	First Common	48	Stone Pits	142	Stone Pit Close
14	Long Dukes	49	Railway	142a	–
15	Honey Pot	50	part of Church Piece	144	–
17	Wood Corner	51	A Hook	149	Long Furlong
18	Blacksmith's Close	52	Dovehouse Close	150	Gravel Pit
19	Blacksmith's Close	112	Bradwell	152	Close
20	First Common	113	Town Piece	153	Waste
21	The Five Acres	114	Benty Field	154	Gold Slipper Pits
22	Barn Close	115	Spinney Close	155	Furzen Leys
23	First Common	116	Lower Bancroft	156	–
24	Pond Piece	117	Upper Bancroft	157	Stonebridge Leys
25	Furnace Corner	118	–	158	The Meadow
26	Furnace Corner	119	Home Ground	159	Stonebridge Furlong
27	Wood Hill	120	Smith Hill	160	Furzen Leys
28	Wood Hill	121	Mortar Pit Field	161	Lower Meadow
29	Hasty Ridgeway	122	Newport Two-Stiles	162	Furzen Leys
30	Hasty Ridgeway	123	Short Deadland	163	Sidelands
31	Hasty Ridgeway	124	Upper Stonehill	164	Seven Acres Field
32	Rooks Leys	125	Lower Stonehill	165	Money Land
33	Over Field	126	Fox Holes	165a	March Meadow
34	–	127	Town Piece	166	March Meadow
35	Stonestead	128	Spring Fields	167	–
36	Rookesley	129	Far Fields	168	Toll House
		130	The Plain		

KEY TO FIG. 27: The field-names of Bradwell parish, from the Tithe Award of 1839.

enclosure award map appears to survive, the 1792 map (Fig. 25) of the estate of William Bailey, the lord of the manor (In private ownership) and the 1839 tithe award (BuCRO 57 AR 130/81) record the fields shortly after enclosure (Fig. 27). Many of the names of the new fields on these maps are those of the earlier furlongs. Typical examples are:

A	B	C
Stanbruge	–	Stonebridge Leys
Sliperfurlong Pits	–	Gold Slipper Pits
Bancroft	Bancroft	Bancroft
Church Furlong	–	Church Piece
Rokesle	–	Rooks Leys
Newport Slade	–	Newport Two Stiles
Le Dedeland	Long Deadlands	Long Deadlands
Tun Furlong	Bradwell Furlong	Bradwell
Sumerwellslade	Somerwellslade	Broad Slade
–	Stonne Rood	Stonehill
–	Butlers Furlong	Butlers Leys
–	Ley Furlong	The Leys
–	Short Willow Beds	Upper Earls Willow
–	Long Stunstead	Stonestead

A: From late thirteenth- to mid fourteenth-century documents.
B: From seventeenth-century documents.
C: From maps of 1792 and 1839.

TABLE 2: Continuity of field names in Bradwell parish.

OTHER LANDSCAPE FEATURES

Although no surviving earthwork was ever located, the village had a windmill in the medieval period. The mill is mentioned in the will of John Newman, who died in 1558 (BuCRO D/A/Wf/4/237). The site of the mill is suggested by the name *Windmill Furlong* in 1648 (NRO Litchborough Grant Box A [6] x5255). This furlong was within the field called *Windmill Ridgeway* in 1839 (Fig. 27). The windmill was in fact such a prominent feature that the common field, *Seckley Field*, in which it was situated was called *Windmill Field* in the mid seventeenth century (NRO Litchborough Grant box A [2] x5251).

The enclosure of 1788 took place shortly after William Bailey bought the manor, and it is likely that he was the prime mover behind it. The enclosure award map for the parish has not survived, but a map of the estate belonging to William Bailey in 1792 and the tithe award map of 1839 are probably based on it. These maps show that between these two dates Bailey had sold the manor and his land to William Hooton, and had acquired a large farm on the north side of the village.

The principal landowners at the time of the Tithe Award in 1839 were Bailey and Hooton, and the land was divided into the two main farms, Home Farm and Manor Farm, which both survived until the development of Milton Keynes.

Only one of the smaller landowners in 1839 was a descendant of a local family. This was John Wilmin whose family, like the Cookes and Newmans, held land in the parish from the sixteenth century.

The parish saw little change until the construction of the Grand Junction Canal in the late eighteenth century. The route of the canal passed through the north of the parish, and shortly after the canal was opened the 'New Inn' was erected at the point where the road running north from the village crossed it. A wharf was also established at this point so that goods including gravel, limestone and lime from the nearby quarries and kilns could be despatched by narrowboat.

The canal crossed the Bradwell Brook valley on a large embankment, through which ran two brick culverts carrying the brook. Part of this earthwork has now (1992) been replaced by a concrete aqueduct carrying the canal over Grafton Street, the first canal aqueduct to be constructed in Britain during this century.

The potential of the 'New Inn' area was also exploited by Samuel Holman, who purchased an acre of land to the south of the canal and built the large stone tower mill. This ground local corn, which was then despatched to its destination by boat until declining business forced the mill to close in the 1890s. Fortunately the Wolverton Urban District Council acquired the mill in 1949 and partially restored it, ensuring its preservation until the coming of Milton Keynes, when it was purchased by the Development Corporation and totally restored.

The opening of the London and Birmingham Railway in 1838 with a station at Wolverton led to the development of the northern end of the parish. Wolverton, midway between London and Birmingham, was chosen as the location for the railway company's works for building and repairing both locomotives and carriages. This inevitably led to a demand for local housing for the railway workers, the works employing nearly eight hundred men by 1851. Initially, workers were accommodated in local villages and some houses were built at Wolverton but, to satisfy the demand, land at Bradwell situated between the canal and the Newport Pagnell to Stony Stratford road was purchased by the railway company and the village of New Bradwell was established. It is said that the Radcliffe Trustees who owned most of the land in Wolverton parish were reluctant to sell more land to the railway company, and for this reason the company had to purchase suitable land at Bradwell.

New Bradwell was called Stantonbury for many years, because its church took over the nearby parish of Stantonbury, formerly assigned to the old parish church which stood alone in the fields amidst the earthworks of its deserted village (see parish essay). New Bradwell had its own railway station on the branch line from Wolverton to Newport Pagnell, and rapidly became a thriving community in its own right, eventually expanding to the south towards the old village, which became called Old Bradwell.

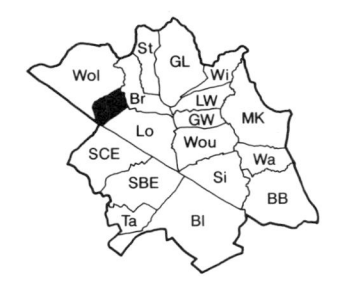

BRADWELL ABBEY

INTRODUCTION

The parish of Bradwell Abbey (Fig. 28) consisted of a rectangular area of some 181 ha of land running from Bradwell parish south-west to Watling Street. The northern boundary with Wolverton followed Stacey Brook, and the southern boundary with Loughton formed an almost straight line from Watling Street to Bradwell Brook.

The parish consisted of the land granted in about 1154 to the monks of Luffield Abbey, near Silverstone, Northants., by Meinfelin, lord of Wolverton, for the establishment of a Benedictine monastery (Mynard 1973, 31). Whether this land was part of Wolverton or of Meinfelin's holding at Little Loughton is unknown.

The monastic buildings were established at the western end of the parish, beside Bradwell Brook. The choice of this location was determined by the proximity of the Wolverton to Bradwell road and Bradwell village. On the south side of the priory complex a minor road ran to Loughton and the Shenleys.

ARCHAEOLOGY

Apart from the priory, only one notable archaeological site has been found in the parish. At Bradwell Abbey Barn (MK63), on high ground towards the south-west end of the parish, a palisaded enclosure of Roman date, possibly a livestock enclosure, was excavated in 1971 (Niblett 1974). Whilst fragments of Roman tile have been found at Bradwell Abbey, these probably were brought to the site with building materials salvaged from Bancroft villa, 1 km to the north.

THE PRIORY

The history of the Priory and an interpretation of the surviving buildings has been published in recent years (Mynard 1973) and an updated popular account is forthcoming (Baines *et al.* forthcoming). The following summary is based on these works.

The priory was at first dependant on Luffield, but obtained its independence by the late twelfth century (Westminster Abbey Muniments, Index B2, Deed 2813). Little is known of the priory during the thirteenth century, but it was probably a period of prosperity, with much building taking place (Mynard 1973, 31). By the middle of the fourteenth century times were harder, and the priory was badly affected by the plague (VCH 1905, 291), many of its buildings falling into disrepair (*ibid.*, 350). Despite all this, the Chapel of St Mary was constructed as a healing shrine in about 1350 (Mynard 1973, 65). The building of the chapel may have been an act of piety after the priory had suffered the ravages of the plague, and was probably also a useful source of income from trade generated by the growth of pilgrimages at this time.

The priory was suppressed in 1524 when Sir John Longville, its patron, granted it to Cardinal Wolsey for the endowment of his new college at Oxford (Letters and State Papers, Henry VIII, VI, [1] 536; PRO E.40, 683). The priory and its lands soon reverted to the crown, and in 1531 were granted to Sheen Priory, Surrey, in exchange for other lands (Letters and State Papers, Henry VIII, V, 403 and 627). A rental of Sheen Priory's property in 1532 lists the tenants of the former Priory at Bradwell (BL Add. Mss, Cotton Julius, C11, fol. 282.)

THE PRIORY BUILDINGS

After the suppression of the priory a survey was carried out which recorded all the buildings. This survey, undertaken in 1526 by William Brabazon (L. and P. Henry VIII, IV, II, 2217) was largely concerned with the condition of the buildings, and the value of any reclaimable materials within them. The reconstruction of the priory plan (Fig. 29) is based on the information in the survey, limited excavation at the site, and a study of the surviving buildings (Mynard 1973, 35–37). The buildings and associated earthworks are also shown on Plate 20.

Several buildings survive from the medieval

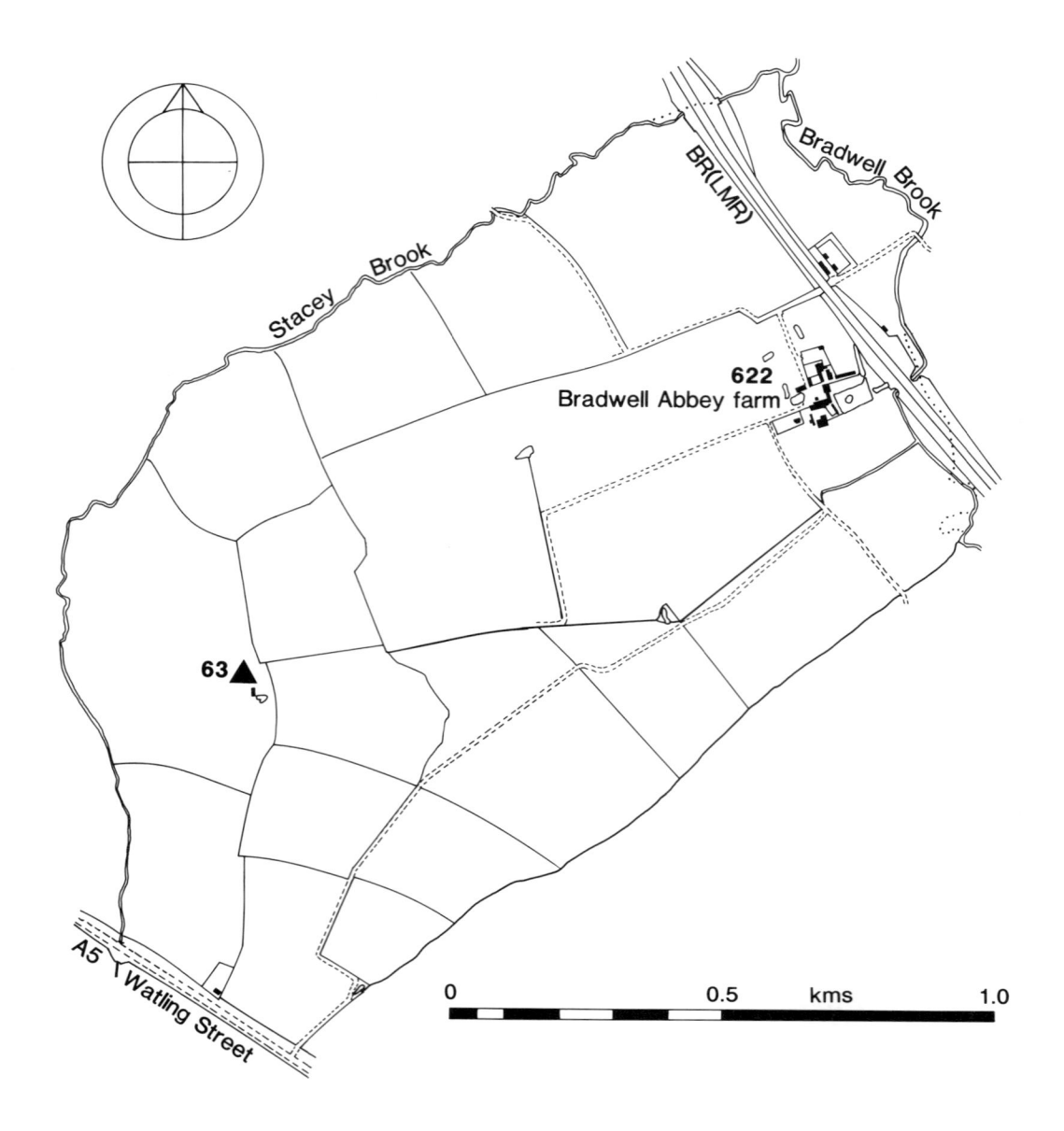

Figure 28: Bradwell Abbey parish in 1967, showing major archaeological sites.

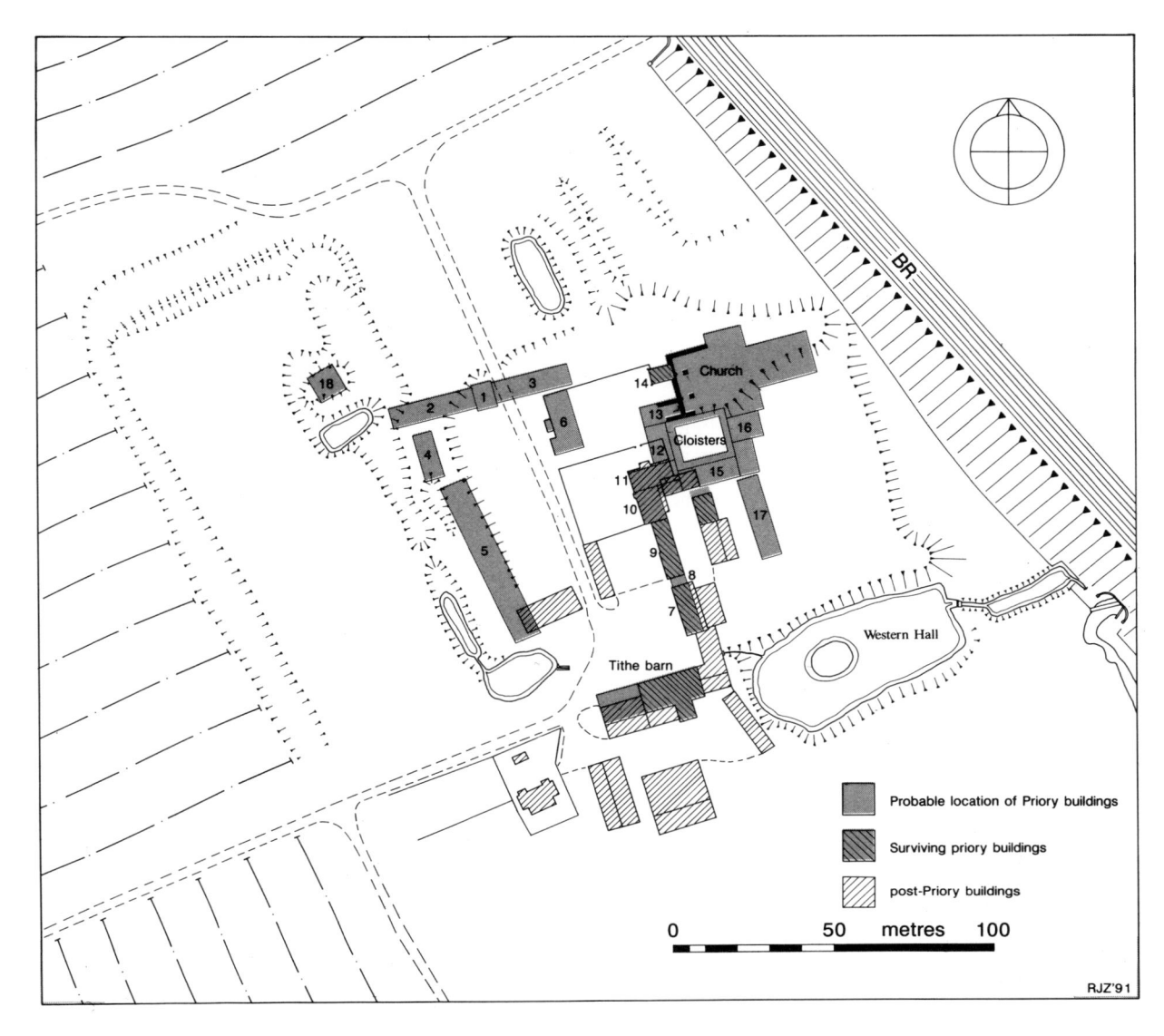

Figure 29: Bradwell Abbey; the earthworks and a reconstruction of the plan of the priory buildings.

1	Gatehouse	10	Low parlour
2	Several houses	11	Prior's chambers
3	Two houses	12	King's chamber
4	Barn	13	Low parlour
5	Several old houses	14	Chapel
6	Barn	15	Hall (frater)
7	Malt and kiln house	16	Chapter house
8	Chamber over gate	17	Row of houses
9	Four houses under a roof		

KEY TO FIG. 29: The buildings of Bradwell Priory.

priory; of these only the chapel, which was built against the west wall of the priory church, remains intact. The large barn that flanks the southern side of the main yard, known as the 'Cruck Barn', which has been dated dendrochronologically to the early fourteenth century (unpublished report in MKAU archive), has been reduced in length, having originally extended further to the west. The farmhouse, the range of lesser buildings running south from it and the barn beyond, which all contain traces of medieval walling, were retained after the Dissolution, being partly demolished and rebuilt to form the nucleus of the sixteenth-century farm complex.

The priory church lay to the east of the chapel, its west wall forming the east end of the chapel. The cloister and related buildings were to the south of the church, east of the present house. On the west side of the farmhouse was the outer courtyard of the priory. Traces of the earthworks marking the site of the northern and western ranges of buildings flanking this courtyard can be seen in the grass field in front of the house, whilst the Cruck Barn marks its southern limit.

The large pond (Plate 9) between the barns and the railway line was the priory's main fishpond, while the pond to the south-west of the house served the farmyard until recent times, and may be of medieval origin. The other ponds around the grounds are probably post-medieval garden features.

LATER HISTORY

After the suppression, the tenant of the Abbey farm was William Wogan, who leased it from Cardinal's College in Oxford for an annual rent of two pounds, also agreeing to collect the college's other rents from former monastic properties in the area (BAS Muniments 85/50). Wogan retained the chapel as a place of worship for his household, obtaining a license from the Bishop of Lincoln to do so (BL Add. Mss 5839, 438) and carried out the demolition and conversion of the other priory buildings mentioned above.

On the dissolution of Sheen priory in 1539 the Bradwell lands reverted to the Crown, and were granted to Arthur Longville in 1543 (L. and P. Henry VIII, XVIII, [1], g.346 [38]). The Longville family moved into the Abbey after Wogan's death in 1558 and remained there until 1650. The next owner was Sir John Lawrence, who sold it in 1666 to Joseph Alston, who was created Baron of Chelsea and Bradwell Abbey in 1688 (VCH 1927, 287). The Longvilles were responsible for some rebuilding and enlargment of the house, but much work was carried out by Sir Joseph Alston, including a restoration of the chapel and the creation of a park with a fine elm avenue on the west side of the house (Fig. 30).

Abbey Farm (Plate 20), as it became known, passed through several owners and was eventually purchased by a Mr G. Field in 1950, who owned it until it was purchased in 1971 by the Development Corporation. During Mr Field's ownership many interesting features were destroyed, including a barn on the west side of the chapel, the elm avenue, the old orchard and several stone walls. However, Mr Field did carry out temporary repairs to the chapel, ensuring its survival.

During their period of ownership, the Development Corporation meticulously restored the chapel, and re-roofed the farmhouse and other buildings. The Corporation based its archaeological and ecological staff at the farmhouse and attempted to establish it as a local Field Centre, but without any support from the County or National authorities this was not successful.

THE FIELD SYSTEM

The ridge-and-furrow map of the priory fields (Fig. 30) shows that at one time or another all of the land was ploughed. There appear to be no surviving documents recording the names of the furlongs in the parish, which may suggest that the monks farmed all of the land themselves, and that none of it was leased out to tenants.

In 1507 three hundred acres of land were enclosed by the Prior and laid down to pasture (Leadam 1897, 181). This represented a considerable area of the parish, and probably created the seven great closes referred to in a rental of 1532 (BL Add. Mss, Cotton Julius, CII, fol.282). These were; *Dove Close, Stubbernhill at Fursen Close, Busshe Close, Fursen* or *Loughton Meadow Close* and *The Grove*. Several of these names were still in use in 1797, and can be seen on the map of the Earl of Dartmouth's estate at Bradwell Abbey (Fig. 31), which was based on an earlier map of 1744.

Figure 30: Bradwell Abbey medieval field system.

No	Name	State (1796)	Acreage Acres	Roods	Poles	Ann. value £ s d		
1	House, barn, stables, yard, orchard, etc.	–	3	?	10	5	0	0
2	Dovehouse Close	p	5	3	16	33	10	3
3	Warren	m	9	3	15			
4	Lime Close	m	6	0	10	15	19	3
5	Lower Corn Close	m	5	1	3			
6	Lingards Pightle	m	1	1	10			
7	Corn Close	?	11	–	–	47	17	11
8	Great Bare Pasture	m	12	1	11			
9	Little Bare Pasture	a	20	0	6	21	0	9
10	Bare Close or Stone Pit Close	a?	18	2	6	33	10	9
11	Hill Ground	a	15	0	0			
12	Great Meadow	p	76	3	19	92	4	10
13	Barn Close	m	7	3	20	15	15	0
14	Bridge Close	p	12	1	4	18	8	3
15	Green Close	p	18	2	12	23	4	4
16	Slanch	m	4	2	16	6	4	2
17	Cow Close Meadow	p	10	0	0	8	0	0
18	Park Meadow	p	21	3	11	19	12	8
19	Cow Close	a	21	0	10	13	17	10
20	Spinney	w	–	1	10			
21	Great Monks in two closes	a	18	1	4	13	14	1
22	Two Mile Ash	m	9	0	16	12	14	7
23	House, Barn. Road Close	p	18	0	16	13	11	6
24	Crabtree Close	m	6	1	14	8	17	5
25	Little Monks	a	12	2	30	10	3	0
26	Park	a	15	0	4	13	11	6
27	Great Brickfield	a	31	1	20	25	12	2
28	Little Brickfield	a	8	0	3			
29	Square Close	p	18	2	20	13	19	9
	Total		430	1	6	466	15	0

Notes:
a   arable
m   meadow
p   pasture
w   woodland

Acreages are taken from a plan drawn up in 1744.

KEY TO FIG. 31: Bradwell Abbey estate, 1797.

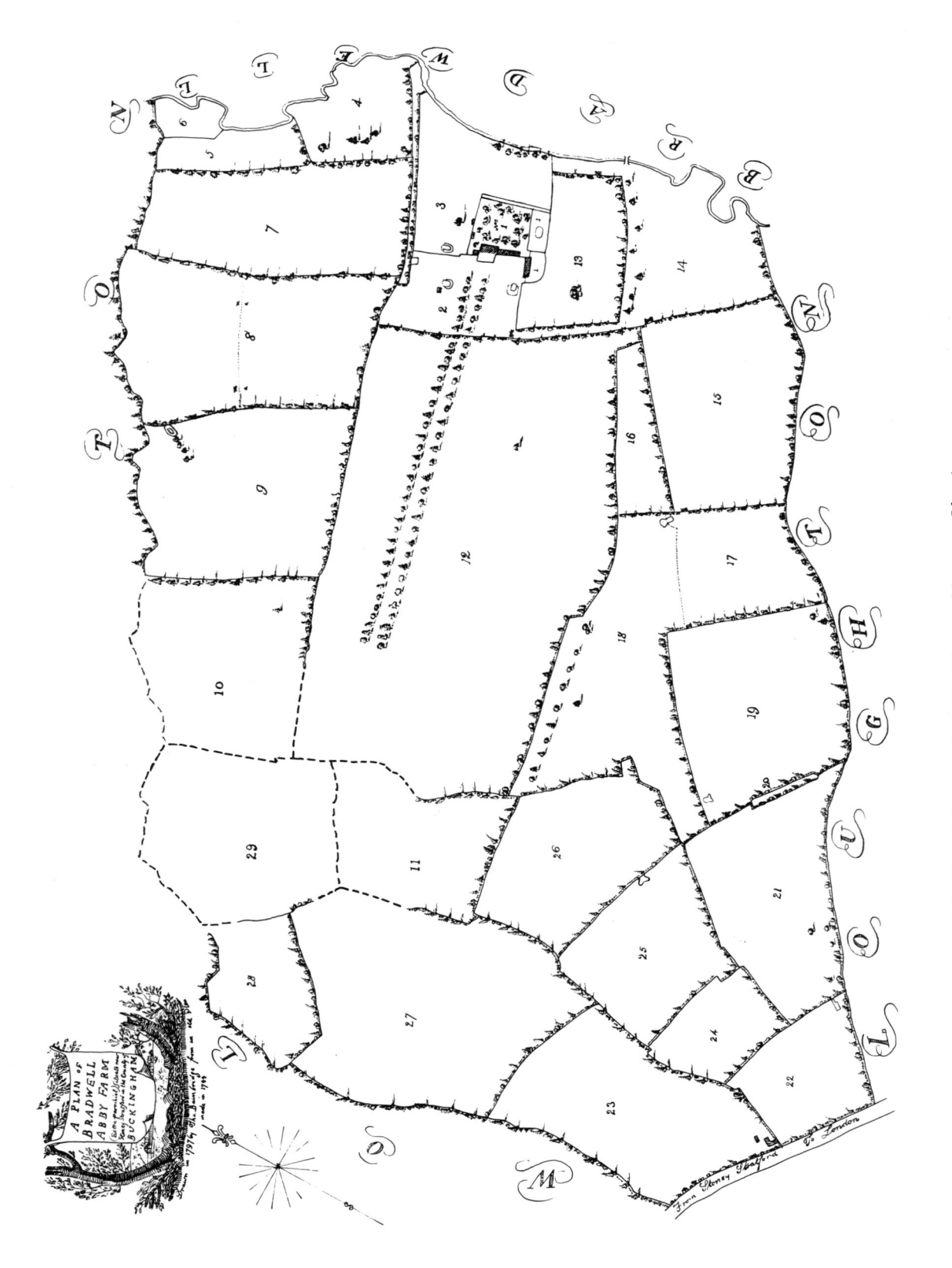

Figure 31: Bradwell Abbey; the estate of the Earl of Dartmouth, 1797. *(Cowper Museum, Olney).*

Plate 20: Bradwell Abbey from the south, c.1969. *(Cambridge University Collection of Air Photographs copyright reserved)*

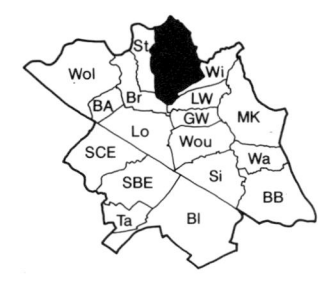

GREAT LINFORD

INTRODUCTION

The parish of Great Linford (Fig. 32) covered an area of some 743 hectares on the south side of the River Ouse, between the parishes of Stantonbury and Newport Pagnell.

Both the geology and topography of the parish are greatly influenced by its situation in the 'angle' between the converging valleys of the rivers Ouzel and Great Ouse. Much of the south-west part of the parish is formed of Boulder clay uplands, rising to a height of about 110 m OD, drained by streams running north or north-east down steeply-cut valleys to the major rivers. One of these streams, Stanton Brook, forms the western boundary of the parish. On the east side of the parish, the slopes leading down to the floodplain of the Ouzel are composed largely of Oxford clay overlying outcrops of Kellaways sands and clay, all covered in the valley bottoms by extensive head deposits.

To the north, on the slopes overlooking the flood plain of the Ouse, the picture is very different. Moving northwards from the extensive deposits of glacial lake material to the west of the village one finds in quick succession outcrops of Kellaways beds, Cornbrash limestone, and Blisworth clay and limestone. This latter outcrop, which was quarried extensively in the area north of the church, provided abundant supplies of building stone for the village (Horton, Shepherd-Thorn and Thurrell, 1974). Gravel has recently been extracted in the flood plain of the Ouse, and clay for brickmaking from the Oxford Clay beds to the south-east of the village.

Prior to the development of Milton Keynes most of the parish was pasture, but almost all of it had been ploughed in the medieval period.

The parish was roughly rectangular, its northern end bounded by the River Ouse. The western boundary with Stantonbury followed Stanton Brook, which ran northwards towards the Ouse. The southern boundary bordered with Willen and Little Woolstone, and followed the line of a ridge running from the Secklow mound, the Hundred meeting place at the southern end of the parish, north-eastward towards Willen village for a distance of 3 km. The eastern border followed medieval furlong boundaries to the Ouse.

Two early east-west routes traversed the parish. The first, crossing the northern end of the parish, partly the modern A422, was a principal route between Cambridge and Oxford, passing through Bedford, Newport Pagnell and Buckingham, and is presumably of late Saxon origin. The second road crossed the southern end of the parish, and was considered by Charles Green (Viatores 1974, 336 and map 443), to be a Roman road, no. 175a, running from Little Horwood to Willen, where it joined another road running northwards to the Roman town at Irchester, Northants. This road is referred to in medieval documents for the adjoining parish of Loughton, where it was called *Portweie* before 1225 (Jenkins 1952, No. 68), and *Portweye* in about 1250 (*ibid.*, No. 92). The names of many of the medieval furlongs are recorded in early documents, and one on the slope below this road was called '*Belowe the Street*' in the early thirteenth century (BuCRO D/U/1/65). This is considered to be evidence of the Roman origin of this road. It survived as a substantial agger, respected by the medieval furlongs as a boundary on its route through the parish. The meeting mound of the Saxon Secklow Hundred (MK300) was situated on the edge of the parish adjacent to this road (Adkins and Petchey 1984).

In the medieval period, a route led eastwards from the north end of the village to Newport Pagnell. At the southern end of the village, minor roads running from the green to Linford Wood, Willen and Woolstone are shown on the 1641 map (Figs 35, 36 and L3), and these must have existed in some form during the medieval period.

At the north end of the parish a bridge over the River Ouse was in existence by the early fourteenth century, when an indulgence was granted for its construction and repair (VCH 1927, 392). The way to this bridge ran around the edges of the furlongs on the line of the stream, as shown on the 1641 map.

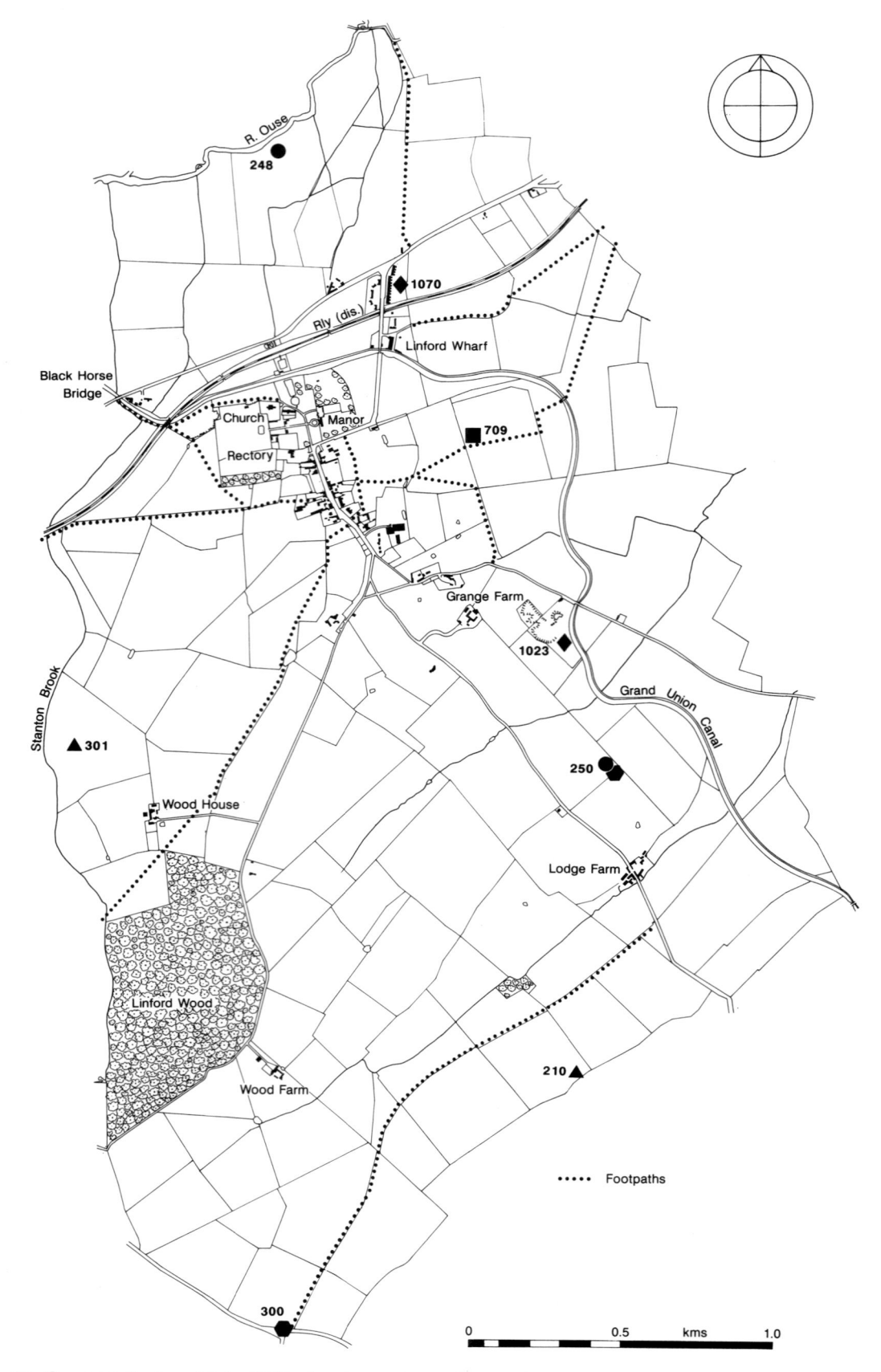

Figure 32: Great Linford parish in 1967, showing major archaeological sites.

ARCHAEOLOGY

Within the parish several archaeological sites have been located, confirming settlement from the Iron Age to the Saxon period (Fig. 32). In addition, a number of flint scatters of Mesolithic to Bronze Age date have been found but no definite evidence of occupation sites of those periods has been found.

Major excavations have taken place on the medieval village and on two other sites in the parish; Stantonbury Roman villa (Mynard 1987, 97–104), and the Iron Age and Saxon settlements at Pennyland (Williams 1993).

At Pennyland (MK 250), excavations revealed a mid to late Iron Age settlement consisting of four ditched enclosures and eleven penannular house drainage gullies. The site was on a gravel spur overlooking the Ouzel valley, and the environmental evidence recovered there demonstrated that its inhabitants were cultivating the surrounding heavy clay soils.

In 1975, a possible Roman villa site (MK 301) was located at Stantonbury Campus, and excavations were subsequently undertaken. A number of outbuildings were found, including a tower granary and a small bath suite. A geophysical survey located the villa farmhouse beneath the adjoining football pitch, preventing further examination. Occupation of the site was dated to the early second to mid fourth centuries.

Excavations in Great Linford village revealed small quantities of Roman pottery and at least one coin, suggesting the existence of a Roman site nearby. However, neither fieldwork nor construction work have located it.

Returning to Pennyland, excavations revealed a Saxon settlement of sixth to early eighth-century date, overlying the Iron Age settlement. It contained eleven 'sunken featured buildings', two timber halls, three unusual 'four-post' structures and a timber-lined well, along with associated boundary ditches. The presence of a settlement in this area was suspected in view of the field names '*Long Dunsted*', '*Short Dunsted*' and '*Dunstead buts*' on the 1641 estate map. *Dunstead* is derived from *Tunstude*, meaning the site of a deserted settlement.

During re-ordering of St Andrew's Church in 1980, a quantity of pottery sherds of seventh to eighth-century date were found in an old ploughsoil layer sealed beneath the church, suggesting the existence of a nearby settlement.

THE MEDIEVAL AND LATER VILLAGE

The earliest archaeological date for the establishment of the village comes from around the southern green, where occupation commenced in the late tenth to early eleventh century and expanded rapidly during the twelfth century.

The medieval village contained houses and crofts around an almost rectangular green, aligned north-east to south-west. From the north of the green a wide hollow-way, the main village street, ran north to Pipard's manor, the church and rectory. The street was some 600 m in length and further houses, crofts and closes lay on either side of it. To the south of the present manor house the road turned to the east, serving as an access to the fields in the north-east of the parish before eventually leading to Newport Pagnell. A sunken back lane which joined the main street at the north end of the green ran northwards leading to Croft L, creating a roughly triangular area of crofts and closes between itself and the main street.

South of this back lane and on the north-east side of the green was Walshes manor, later called *Walshes Place*, beyond which several crofts lay on the north side of Fullwell Lane. The windmill, located on a high spot within the fields approximately 400 m east of the village, was approached by *Mylleway*, which ran along headlands linking Fullwell Lane with the road to Newport Pagnell.

The principal water supply for the village came from two springs. One, at the north end of the village near the church, was called the *Hine Well* in 1641 (Figs 35, 36 and L3), but no earlier references to this spring have been found. The other, *Fullwell*, east of the green on the north side of the lane leading to Willen, became a village landmark, giving its name to land nearby as early as the thirteenth century (BuCRO D/U/1/66/1), when an adjacent furlong was called *Follewellshul*, becoming *Fullwellehyll* by 1477 (BuCRO D/U/1/46/1). In 1505–6 a rental of Walshes Manor (BuCRO D/U/2/11) refers to "the common street called *Fullwellend*", which became *Fullwell Lane* by 1524 (BuCRO D/U/1/46/3). In more modern times this was known as Willen Lane, and is now (1992) Harper's Lane.

The village earthworks (Fig. 33) were best preserved to the south and east of the green in Hern's Close and Newman's Close, fields which became and remained pasture after the abandonment of the houses within them. To the south-west of the green the earthworks had been the subject of considerable ploughing, and were much reduced. On the east and west sides of the main street they

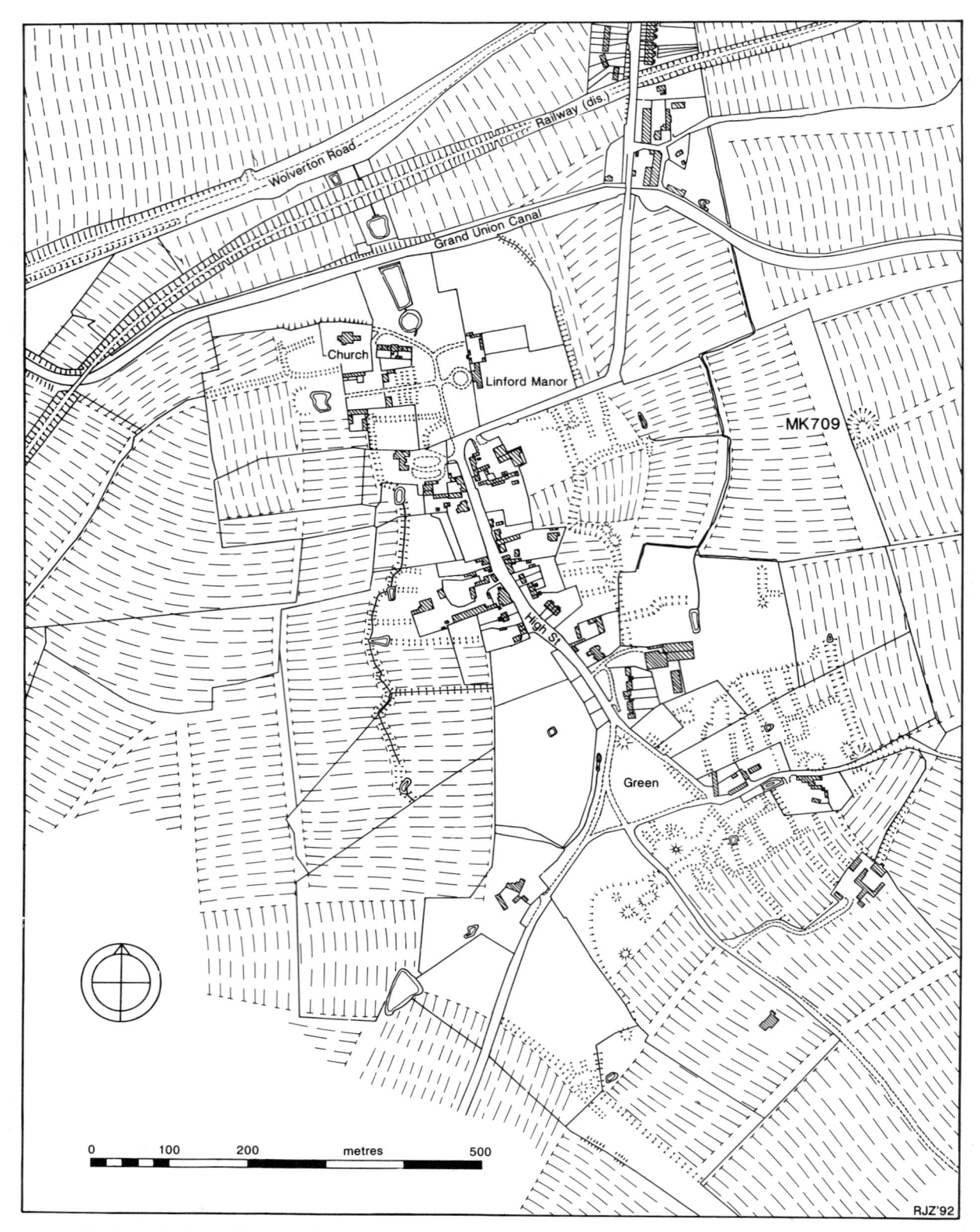

Figure 33: Great Linford village earthworks.

were more fragmentary, only traces of croft boundaries surviving.

The following description of the earthworks commences in the south-west corner of the village green. At this point a route defined by a ditch on either side, called 'Drove' in 1641, may have led across the fields to Woolstone. To the north-east along the southern edge of the green, were a series of house sites and crofts. The first croft (A), of which only traces of the ditches survived, was shown on the 1641 map as a small croft in the corner of a close called *Great Picknuts*, which is referred to as early as 1321 (BAS Mss 347/44). Beyond Croft A, the 1641 map showed eight larger crofts fronting onto the southern side of the green. The boundaries of these crofts were fairly well preserved, apart from those of Crofts N, O and P, between Croft A and Croft B, which had been levelled by ploughing.

The development of the crofts on the southern side of the green is interesting. The house sites were inserted along the southern edge of the early sub-rectangular green and the small closes behind them were taken from the field, enclosing strips that were formerly part of *Greens End Furlong*. The houses on Crofts B, C and D date from the late twelfth century; whether the closes attached to them were taken from the open field at that time or later is uncertain. Excavation of the boundaries of the closes produced no dating evidence to confirm their origin. This encroachment on the green in the late twelfth century suggests that it was a period of expansion for the village. On the green itself a number of fragmentary irregular hollows and mounds represented random clay pits or other post-medieval disturbance.

To the east of the green on the north side of Fullwell Lane, five medieval crofts were identified, only one of which, Croft F, was totally available for excavation. Croft T contained an occupied cottage, 'The Mead', and the remains of Croft G were largely within the garden of that cottage. Excavation revealed that Croft F was occupied from the late tenth century, Croft G from the late twelfth century and Croft H/J from the mid thirteenth. On the east side of Croft F, a close identified as Croft M, which may be the *King's Close* referred to in a rental of Walshes Manor (BuCRO D/U/2/11), contained one possible house platform, but trial excavation there revealed no evidence of occupation or structures.

The pattern on the east side of the main street is less clear since few earthworks survived. The rental of Walshes Manor in 1505–6 (BuCRO D/U/2/11) lists five properties, two crofts and a capital messuage running north from the "comon street called *Fullwellend*", and these must have been on the east side of the main street. The 1641 map shows cottages on this side of the street but no croft boundaries, presumably because they had become redundant by that time.

The layout of the northern end of the medieval village is unclear owing to the building of the Rectory in the mid sixteenth century, the building and enlargement of the manor house in the mid seventeenth century by Sir Richard Napier, and finally the demolition of that house and the building of the new manor house in about 1679 by Sir William Pritchard. Excavation has shown that the medieval manor house lay on the south side of the church, to the west of and partly under the two pavilions of the eighteenth-century manor house. This house, with its pavilions, almshouses and school house is within a landscaped setting (Plate 21) that removed virtually all traces of this end of the medieval village. It is likely that the green extended to the north end of the village. A document of 1460 (BuCRO D/U/1/77/1) relates to two messuages, and mentions the highway leading to the church, which abuts against the church on one side and *lee comyn greene* on the other.

On the west side of the main street, particularly at the north end, fragments of croft boundaries survived in the gardens behind the village houses. These, coupled with evidence from the 1641 map, suggest that medieval crofts fronted much of the village street.

The earliest evidence of occupation comes from pottery of sixth to seventh-century date recovered from beneath the church. Whether or not this material is from a Saxon settlement which went on to become the principal manor of Great Linford is uncertain. Excavation within the church in 1980 suggested that it was built in the tenth or eleventh century, and that the surviving twelfth-century tower was an addition.

Excavation of house sites confirmed that the village was established by the ninth to tenth century, and that by the late twelfth century it was expanding, with houses built along the southern edge of the green. By the late thirteenth to fourteenth century the village plan, with regularly laid out crofts, must have been fully developed (Fig. 34). During the fourteenth and fifteenth centuries the changes that resulted in the plan recorded by the 1641 map began. Many of the properties referred to in fifteenth-century documents can actually be located on the 1641 map. Most of the excavated crofts appear to have been continuously occupied until the mid to late seventeenth century, although Crofts C, E, F and possibly X2 were abandoned in the early to mid fifteenth century.

The 1641 map drawn up for Sir Richard Napier

Plate 21: Great Linford manor, almshouses and church, 1980. *(MKAU)*

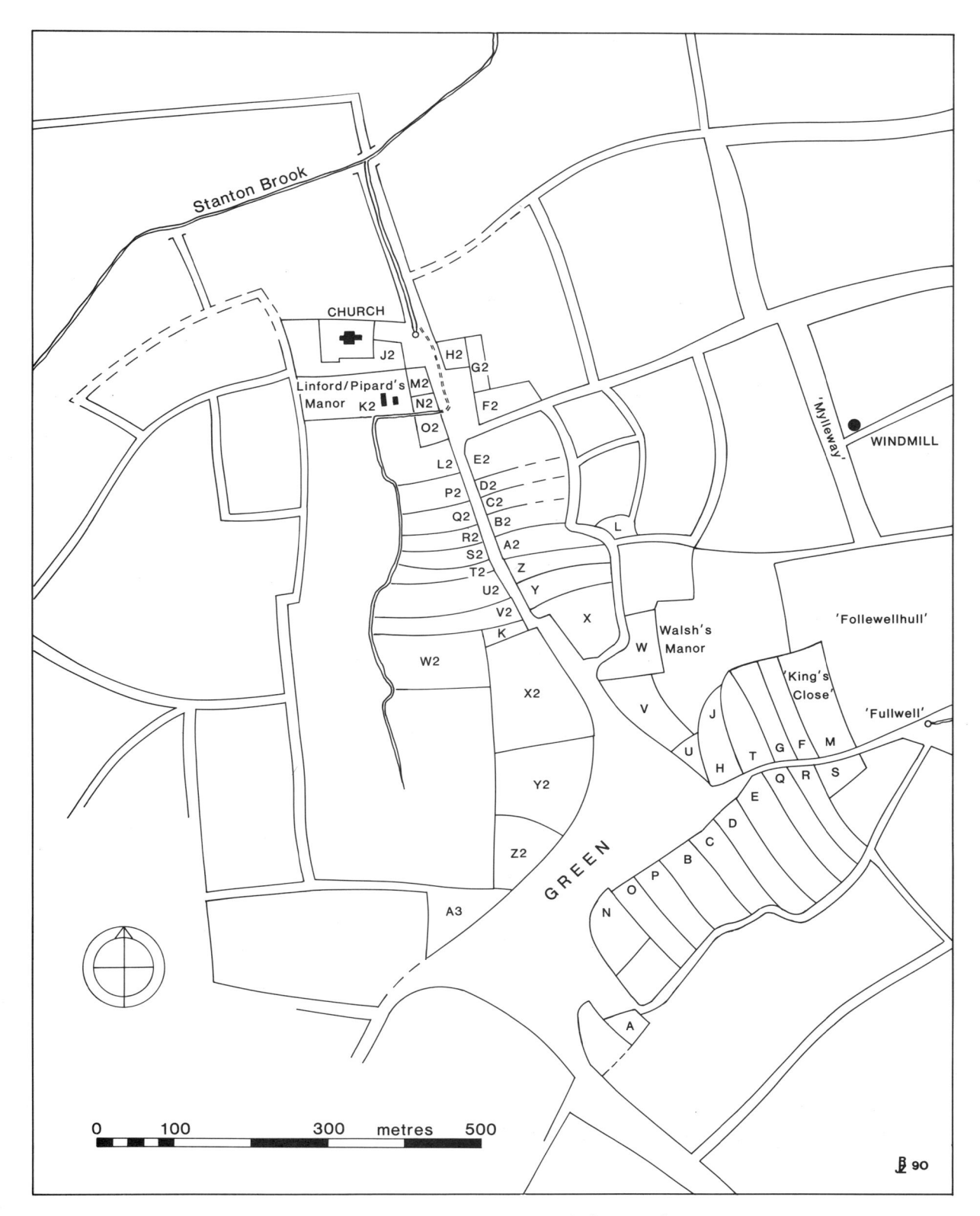

Figure 34: Great Linford; probable extent of the village by the early fourteenth century.

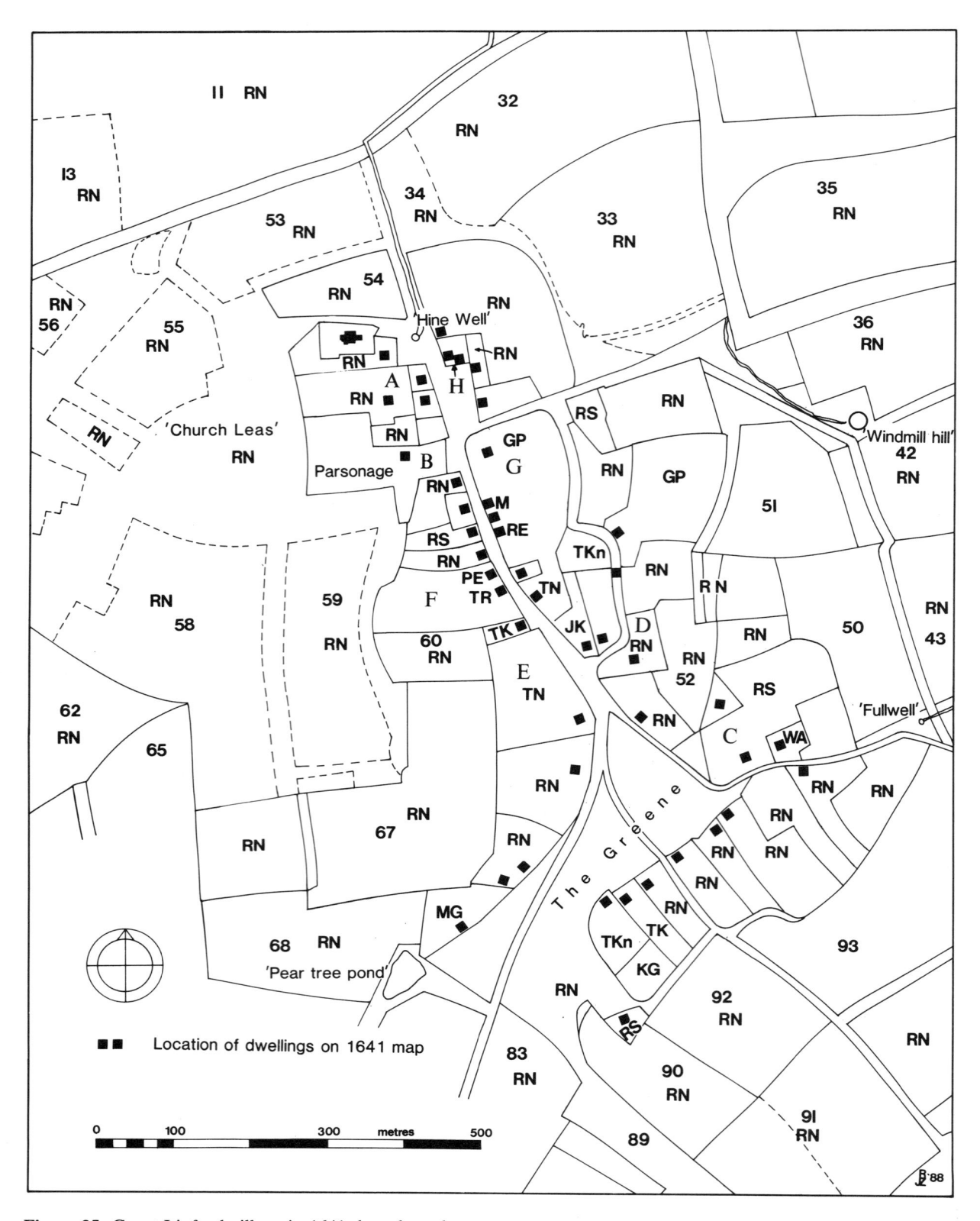

Figure 35: Great Linford village in 1641, based on the estate map.

FIELD NAMES
0. Midsomer Homes
1. Furlong next Linford Bridge
2. Furlong with Great Doles
3. Furlong between the Ditch and the River
4. Furlong shooting on Lo Hill
5. Furlong on east side the Meadow
6. Tithe Meadow
7. Roody Doles
8. Furlong shooting on Twenty Lands
9. First furlong shooting on Morro Leas
10. Second furlong shooting on Morro Leas
11. Morro Leas
12. Salt Marsh Gogg
13. Salt Marsh Pees
14. First Dirty Doles
15. Second Dirty Doles
16. Short ends
17. Pits
18. Long ends furlong
19. Furlong shooting to ould Pits
20. Mare furlong
21. Furlong above Whetstone hades
22. Furlong beneath Whetstone hades
23. Whetstone Hades
24. Doggeds Furlong
25. Furlong to Newport Headland
26. Furlong shooting to Newport Willows
27. Furlong on the other side Marsh
28. Mortar Pits
29. Butts from Marsh to Mortar Pits
30. Butts at Newport Bush
31. The Common Sward of Marsh
32. Stratford peas
33. Farland peas
34. Dove house Leas
35. Over Path Furlong
36. Furlong between Windmill Hades
37. Long Marsh
38. Green Grove furlong
39. Willow stub furlong
40. Blakeland
41. Bean Hill furlong
42. Furlong on Upper Side Windmill hades
43. Butts to Fulwell hades
44. Seven acres
45. Tongwell
46. Wet side caldecud Brook severall Swarde
47. Sevrall sward drie side the Brook
48. Furlong shooting on the brooke
49. Fulwell hill furlong
50. France furlong
51. Furlong against the grove
52. Farm close
53. Ash Leas pees
54. Ash Leas
55. Stoney Pees
56. Butts
57. Pees against Stanton hedge
58. Long and part of short woollan
59. Linford pees
60. Linford close
61. Stone pits furlong
62. Head ditch furlong
63. Furlong under West Hill
64. West Hill hades
65. West Hill furlong
66. Garland furlong
67. Furlong at Mallens Gate
68. Pear Tree Furlong
69. Furlong under Whitsons path
70. Furlong above Whitsons path
71. Furlong under Netherley Way
72. Nether Way hades
73. Rowlo Furlong
74. Furlong between the Ley wayes
75. North Hill Furlong
76. Gutter slade
77. Wood close
78. Linford Wood
79. Furlong between Ridge Way and Ley way
80. Overley Way
81. Furlong above greene end
82. Greens end furlong fallow field
83. Greens end furlong pease field
84. Higher worse way furlong
85/86. The furlong under ridge way
87. Lower worse way furlong
88. Brook sward
89. Drove
90. Great Picknuts
91. Under Picknuts
92. Granes end furlong
93. Furlong at Weatherheads backside
94. The belowe hill
95. Furlongs stone hades
96. Ducks headland
97. Springe hill
98. Furlongs
99. Hither Penniland
100. Penniland Field
101. Penniland furlong barley field
102. Further field
103. Langage furlong
104. Long Dunstead
105. Short Dunsted
106. Dunstead buts
107. Elder stub furlong
108. Radge Croft
109. Moor
110. Furlong pease
111. Buts on the other side the Brooke
112. Furlong shooting to Under street hades
113. Under street furlong
114. Under street butts
115. Malzmead
116. Malzmead furlong
117. Short well
118. Long Neath hill
119. Long Lewell
120. Long layes
121. Brier hedge
122. Balland Furlongs
123. Neath hill fallow field
124. Garebroad butts
125. Balland Furlongs
126. Wood furlong
127. Connie Burrough Hill
128. Pigs Hill
129. Cow Pen
130. Down head furlong

LANDOWNERS
SRN Sir Richard Napier
GP   George Person
TK   Thomas Kent
M   Malyns
RS   Richard Smith
MC   Matthew Cardwell
RE   Richard Evens?
TN   Thomas Nicholls
WA   William Adkins
KG   Kent's Grove
PG   Parratt & Gaddesden
TKn. Thomas Knight
TR   Thomas Roughead
JoK. John Kent

KEY TO FIGS 35 and 36: Great Linford; field names and landowners in 1641.

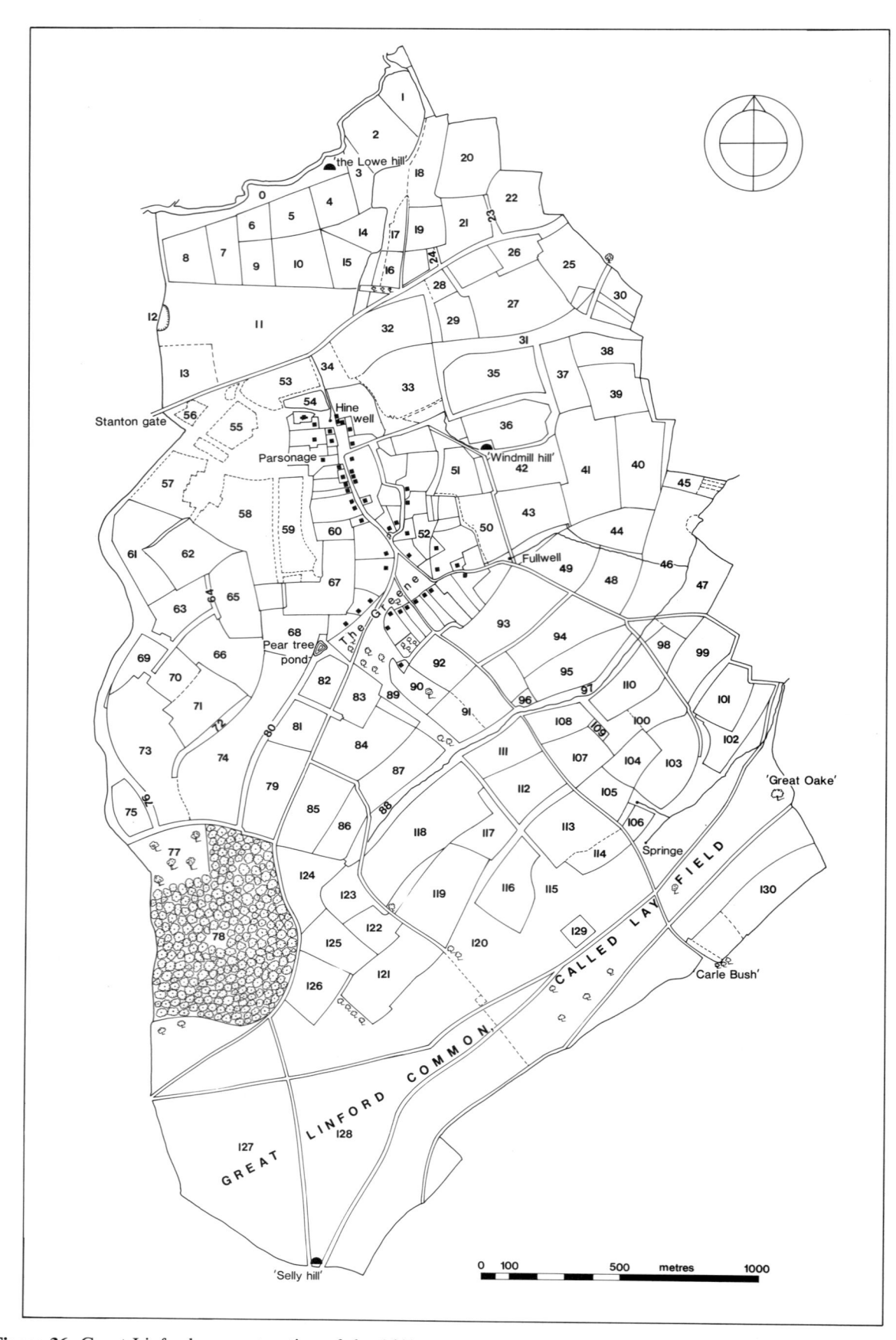

Figure 36: Great Linford; reconstruction of the 1641 estate map.

predates the enclosure of the parish by seventeen years, presenting a picture of the village and its fields much as they were during the late medieval period. A second estate map (Figs 37 and L4) drawn up in 1678 for Sir William Pritchard on his purchase of the Great Linford estate, records the parish after enclosure.

By comparing the 1641 map with the earthwork survey, the changes that took place over the years can be identified. In particular, several croft boundaries had been removed, creating larger plots of land around houses. On the north side of Fullwell Lane a small cottage occupied a plot at the south end of Croft G, while the other crofts had been combined to form the close associated with Moulsoe's farm house, which occupied the south end of the former Croft H. Many of the new closes around the village enclosed areas of ridge and furrow which were formerly part of the arable lands of the village.

On the east side of the village the windmill had gone, but its site was marked 'Windmill Hill', and the road leading to it and Newport Field was still open. The main street ran northwards to the church, the manor house, a farm, several cottages and the Hine Well, at which point it ended and did not continue down into the meadows beyond. Before entering the church and manor house area, the road turned to the right, opposite the Rectory, and led to Newport Field, Newport Pagnell and Little Linford.

The 1641 map illustrates forty-six properties in the village, consisting of the church, the parsonage, seven large houses and thirty-seven smaller village houses and cottages. Neither of the manor houses nor any of the principal farms were identified by name. However, several properties have been identified by linking the initials of the owners, shown on the map, with the names of contemporary village people obtained from local property deeds and other documents. These properties, identified by the letters A to H (Fig. 35), have been identified by various means as explained below:

A. GREAT LINFORD MANOR HOUSE (Croft K2)

This house, between the church and the Rectory, belonged to Sir Richard Napier in 1641. The site is that of the principal manor house built when the two Domesday manors held by Hugh de Bolebec were combined. This manor, held by the Pipard family from the late twelfth until the early fourteenth century, passed to the Butlers, Earls of Ormonde, who retained it until the early sixteenth century. The Butlers were probably never resident in the village, and the occupants of the manor house were the de Linford family.

In 1460 two messuages in Croft J2, called *Isabella Mason* and *Potens*, immediately to the south of the churchyard, were said to be on the north side of a tenement "late of Thomas Lynford" (BuCRO D/U/1/77/1), which in 1485 was described as "a tenement of the Lord of Linford" (BuCRO D/U/1/77/2). A glebe terrier of 1607 (BuCRO D/A/GT, box 6), describes the parsonage as "lying betweene the strete on the east side, the wood field on the west, the close of Henry Cowley on the south and a farmhouse belonging to the lord of Great Linford on the north". This farmhouse must be the building excavated in 1980, which was considerably enlarged in the early seventeenth century, at which time it was occupied by Sir Richard Napier.

B. THE PARSONAGE (Croft L2)

This building is clearly identified on the 1641 map. The present Rectory which occupies the same site dates from the seventeenth century, and incorporates parts of an earlier building.

C. MOULSOE'S FARMHOUSE

The location of this property is confirmed by the fact that it is the largest of the three properties owned by Richard Smith, and is marked with his initials on the 1641 map. Richard Smith obtained these properties from his father on his marriage in 1626 (BuCRO D/U/1/44). Moulsoe's Farm took its name from the Mulso (Mulsho) family who held land in Great Linford from at least 1449 (BuCRO D/U/1/76). William Mulso was a tenant of Walshes Manor in 1491, and earlier in 1480 (BuCRO D/U/1/33/6) he and a William Bruse had been given power of attorney to deliver seisin of the manor when it was acquired by Robert Gillibrond. On the death of William Mulso in 1557, the farm was purchased by Christopher Troughton and later passed to his son of the same name, who retained it until 1595. It was then purchased by John Blundell, and subsequently sold by him to John Smith of Little Linford in 1610, who settled it on his son Richard in 1626 (BuCRO D/U/1/44).

D. WALSHES MANOR HOUSE (Croft W)

The capital messuage of Walshes Manor is probably referred to as early as the late thirteenth century (BuCRO D/U/1/70). At that time the estate which became Walshes Manor was held by William le Waleys, and his house was described as "a messuage with curtilege, hedges, buildings and

Figure 37: Great Linford; reconstruction of the 1678 estate map.

ditches". In 1505/6 the tenant of the capital messuage was John Malyns (BuCRO D/U/2/11), and in 1510 (BuCRO D/U/1/33/8) the property was referred to as "Walshes' Place". Whilst no documents survive to give the precise location of Walshes Manor House, others confirm that it, and most of the property belonging to this manor, was situated on the east side of the main village street.

In 1638 (BuCRO D/U/1/33) Sir Richard Napier purchased "the Manor of Great Linford *alias* Lindford Manor and the capital messuage called Walshes Place *alias* the Manor of Walshes". In the more detailed description of the property the manor is called "The Manor of Great Linford alias Lyndford Manor alias Walshes Manor or Walshes Land or Tyringham Manor." The principal residence of the manor is described as the "capital messuage, farm and demesne of which Sir Thomas Tyringham was in his lifetime seized."

The main manor of Great Linford was purchased by Sir Richard Napier in 1640 from Sir John Thompson (BuCRO D/U/1/34), and no capital messuage or manor house is mentioned in that transaction. This leads one to suspect that at that time Walshes Manor House was the principal residence in the village, and that the original manor house was no longer in use as such.

Documentary and excavation evidence have shown that the house of the main Great Linford Manor (A) was nothing more than a substantial farm house. The excavation confirmed that the house was extensively rebuilt and enlarged in the mid seventeenth century. This work must have been carried out by Sir Richard Napier soon after his purchase of that manor in 1640. Having acquired both manors he combined them as one and planned a new manor house on the prime site adjacent to the church. Whilst this all took place he must have had a residence for his use when in the village, and this would have been Walshes Place, since it was the principal house there at that time. Turning to the 1641 map, there is only one other large house owned by Sir Richard and this is the only property which is likely to have been Walshes Place. This house occupied Croft W and was not in an area available for excavation. Later in the seventeenth century Walshes Place became a farm house, and was the subject of a lease in 1666 and various mortgages (BuCRO D/U/1/11).

FIELD NAMES					
1	Sickley Hill	21	Nicholas Meade	42	Hulls Close
2	Kents Ground	22	Drieside Brooke	43	Upper Green
3	Lynford Wood	23	Cockel Brooke Meade	44	Pegnuts
4	Wood Close	24	Fullwell Ground	45	The Grove into 2 parcils
5	Horse Ground	25	Tongwell Meade	46	Lower Greene
6	Neath Hill Close	26	Marsh Ground	47	Herns Close
7	Neath Hill	27	Mare Furlong	48	The Close adjoyning
8	Upper Meadow	28	Shorte End	49	Newmans Close
9	Lower Meadow	29	Soames Feild	50	Taylors Close
10	Greate Ground	30	Morral Lees	51	Hicks Shepherd
11	Stanton Slade	31	Ashe Lees	52	Turners Meade totherside River
12	Little Stanton Slade	32	Church Lees	53	The Island
13	Long Lees	33	Church Lees		
14	Charles Bush Ground	34	Turnees Meadow	LANDOWNERS	
15	Greater Cowpen Meade	35	Townes End Meadow	A	Glebe Land
16	Little Cowpen Meade	36	Lower Meadow	B	Hospital Land
17	Long Ground	37	Kents Ground	C	W. Kent
18	Hetther Long Ground	38	Kents Ground	D	Manor
19	Oake Ground	39	Newground Pastor	E	Parsonage
20	Pennylond Field	40	Upper Green Close	F	J. Ruffhead's Land
		41	Upper Green Close adjoyning		

KEY TO FIG. 37: Great Linford; field names and landowners in 1678.

From this time on, Walshes Place became less important. By 1881 the site was occupied by an imposing eighteenth-century property, called "Great Linford House" (6" O.S. Map, 1st edition), which was demolished without record in about 1961.

The ownership of virtually all of the parish by Sir Richard Napier and its enclosure in 1658 resulted in considerable changes in the village. Many of these are recorded on the estate map drawn up in 1678, which shows that many of the village houses, particularly at the south end, had been demolished, and that the back lane to the east of the main street had gone out of use. At the north end of the village, the cottages (Crofts N2 and O2) had been replaced by barns and their site added to the manor complex. By 1678 when the second estate map was drawn up the manor house, rebuilt and enlarged by Sir Richard Napier, sat within much larger grounds, which included an area formerly part of the Rectory garden. The Rectory had also acquired a much larger curtilege, the garden being extended to the south and taking in land formerly the rear of Crofts P2, Q2 and R2. The 1678 map records the village and parish as it was when the estate was purchased by Sir William Pritchard. Whilst Sir William never spent much time at Linford, he developed it as his principal country seat and totally remodelled the manor complex, creating a beautiful country house in landscaped grounds, which included pavilions, a school house and almshouses.

THE FIELD SYSTEM

The plan (Fig. 38) shows the full extent of the field system, which may not all be contemporaneous. The date of establishment of the field system within the parish is uncertain, but it is most likely that its origins are contemporary with those of the village. When the furlongs were first laid out, they respected only two roads. Both were east-west routes, the southern one probably of Roman origin, while the northern route running along the Ouse Valley may be earlier. The village was not sited on either of these routes, but in a more favourable location, overlooking the Ouse Valley and adjacent to a source of limestone for building.

An indication of the date of the establishment of the furlongs, or at least those in that area of the parish, comes from Pennyland, where the Saxon settlement of sixth to early eighth-century date lay totally sealed beneath ridge-and-furrow.

The village had its origins in the ninth or tenth century, and it is most likely that the field system was established at that time. The Domesday evidence suggests that in the late eleventh century a proportion of the parish was not cultivated, this waste land gradually coming into use as the expanding population of the village required it. Possibly most of the available land in the parish was under the plough by the mid to late twelfth century.

The 1641 map shows the field system and all of the furlongs with their names, as they existed at that time. A number of early documents dating from the middle of the thirteenth century onwards survive giving the names of local landowners and of the individual furlongs in which their land was situated. The thirteenth-century furlong names are fairly descriptive and their likely interpretations are:

Le Smeye: possibly misread for Smeþe (OE þ= th), and this is 'smooth place' or perhaps more likely 'smithy.'
Rowelowe: possibly the site of a burial mound, 'rough tumulus'.
Below the Streete: the Street referred to here was a Roman road.
Eldefeld: Old field or elder field.
Westhul: West hill.
Le He Ditch: *He* might be 'high' or 'enclosure'; 'the head of the ditch' is a later rationalisation.
Le Forde: 'the ford'.
Follewellehull: Fullwell Hill.
Foxhole:
 Land occupied by foxes.
Tun Stude : Site of a deserted settlement, OE *tunstede* means 'settlement-site.'
Banland: Beanland.
Heldhul: Most likely 'sloping hill' from OE *held*.
Upon Kingstret: On King Street, possibly the same street referred to in 'Below the Streete'.
Corndich: Might be Heron Ditch, OE *cran* = 'heron'.
Stantonbroc: Stanton Brook.
Goseland: Gooseland.
Springewelle: The name of a spring.
Nerhombroc: *hom* in field-names is OE *hamm* 'river meadow'. There was probably a meadow called 'Near Ham'.
Segeloweslade: Secklow Slade.

Many of these names survived with only minor changes until they were again recorded on the 1641 estate map, suggesting that the layout of the furlongs remained much the same for over three hundred years.

The parish was originally farmed on the two-field system, for in 1449 the earliest located documentary reference to the names of the great fields (BuCRO D/U/1/76) mentions only two, *Segelowfeld* and *Le Dounefeld*. *Segelowfeld* is Secklow Field, which took its name from the Secklow Mound, the meeting place of the Saxon Secklow Hundred, situated at the southern end of the parish (Adkins and Petchey 1984). *Dounefeld* probably means the lower field.

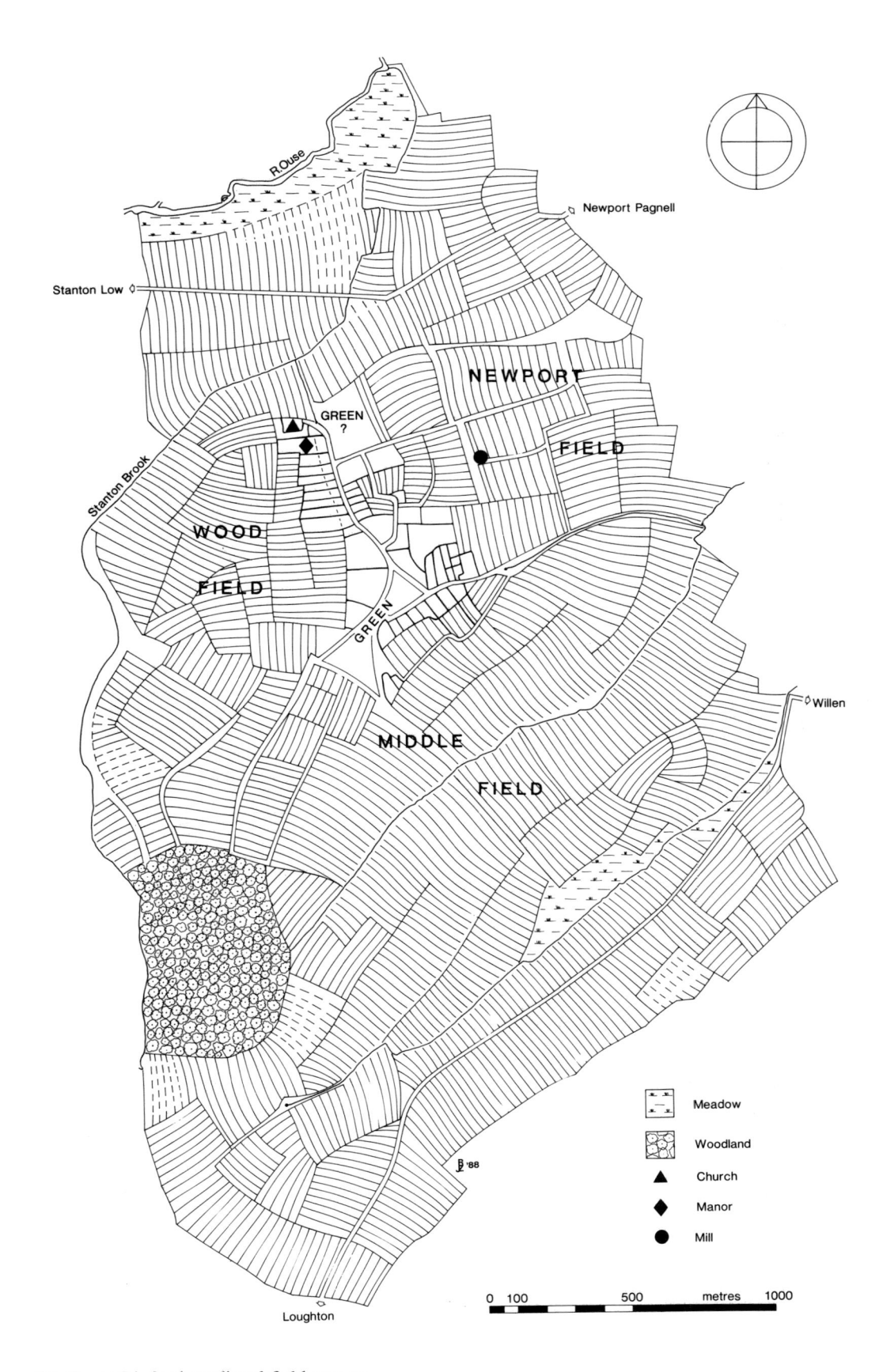

Figure 38: Great Linford medieval field system.

Later in the medieval period the parish operated a three-field system, but it is not until the early seventeenth century that documents have been found which refer to furlongs within these fields. The names of the three great fields were *Wood Field*, *Middle Field* and *Newport Field*, although the latter is sometimes called *Newport Side Field*, and was referred to as the *North Field* in 1608 (BuCRO D/U/1/103/1) and 1626 (BuCRO D/U/1/104/3).

Some of the fields which had previously been ploughed must have become permanent pasture at quite an early date. For example, at the south end of the parish, the large area shown on the 1641 map as *Great Linford Common called Layfield* which was approached from the village by the lanes called *Ley Way* and *Rygeway*, was found during the survey to be completely covered by ridge-and-furrow.

The Leyfield was already established in 1477 (BuCRO D/U/1/46/1) when Richard Prentys purchased lands within it from Robert Malyns. It may still have been arable land at that time but by 1525 (BuCRO D/U/1/46/3), when Richard Prentys sold these lands to Harry Logge, a grazier from Stantonbury, it was probably pasture. On the 1641 map the western end of the Leyfield was divided into two fields called *Connie Burrough Hill* and *Pigs Hill*. These names suggest an area of grazing for pigs which also supported a large rabbit population.

In 1649, the prenuptial settlement of Sir Richard Napier and Mary Kynaston (BuCRO D/U/1/2) gives an extent of the manors of Great Linford and Walshes. This document lists the rights of common held by each manor, the total of which came to grazing for 460 sheep, 38 cows, 14 dry beasts and 8 horses. In addition, the manors were entitled to 1900 furze faggots yearly "to be taken off the common called Layfield", which suggests that the common must have been extensively covered in scrub in order to supply such a large number of faggots. The 1641 map shows several trees on the Leyfield. One in particular is identified as *Great Oak*, which may suggest that the area had been partly overgrown and not ploughed for some considerable time.

Much of the low-lying land adjacent to the River Ouse in the north of the parish was originally ploughed, but was pasture when a large part of it called *Morrowe Leaze* was subject to grazing regulations in 1567 (BuCRO D/U/2/2).

The actual management of the meadow land can be hinted at from documents which show that it was divided up into lots called *doles* and *swathes* (BuCRO D/U/1/46/1), and that grazing was strictly controlled (BuCRO D/U/2/2,5 and 6). A post-enclosure document of 1663 (BuCRO D/U/1/11) refers to a forecrop or share of meadow land, which might suggest that two crops of hay were obtained from some of the meadows.

The enclosure of the parish in 1658 changed not only the system of farming, but also the structure of the community. The large estate that was created in the seventeenth century remained until the present day, with eight to nine tenant farmers and a larger group of labourers, dependent upon wage labour. Unlike the open-field villages which escaped the earlier depopulating enclosures, Great Linford had a declining population, probably controlled at the level of potential employment by the main estate owner. The decline in the number of houses prevented extra people coming to live in the village, and indeed there is evidence that part of the labour requirements were met by day labourers from outside. By 1700, Great Linford must have appeared a very modern estate by the prevailing standards of the area; totally enclosed, with a varied and up-to-date pattern of farming.

OTHER LANDSCAPE FEATURES

ROADS AND WAYS

Several medieval documents refer to the paths and ways into the fields. The earliest, dating from the first half of the thirteenth century (BuCRO D/U/1/66/1), refers to the street mentioned above. A document of similar date (BuCRO D/U/1/66/2), lists *Kingstret*, which may be the same road. A document of 1449 (BuCRO D/U/1/76), refers to the main street of the village as the *Highway*, and to the *Lanezend*, which is believed to have been the end of the back lane on the east of the main street. This document also lists *Hacketweye* and *Whystone Path*, the latter being situated to the north of Linford Wood. *Hacketweye* was a furlong name in 1449, but by 1477 (BuCRO D/U/1/46/1) there was a way called *Hachetwaye* beside land called *Lynffordes* and land called *Welsch*, both of which were names of manors in the parish. A document of 1649 (BuCRO D/U/1/2), refers to *Hatchett Pitts* but gives no location, and the name does not occur on the 1641 map.

A terrier of lands acquired by Richard Prentys in 1477 (BuCRO D/U/1/46/1), lists *Highway*, *Mylleway*, *Beyond the Way*, *Beyond Waye End*, *Hacketlane*, *Hacketway*, *Worseway*, *Lywaye* and *Nether Ruggewaye*. Several of these have been dealt with above. The location of the others is not absolutely certain but may be as follows:

Mylleway: a route leading to the mill on the east side of the village.

Beyond the Way and *Beyond Way End*: may refer to land in the west of the parish approached by the *Lywaye*, which is presumably the *Ley Way* shown on the 1641 map.

Worseway: may be an early name for the *Drove*, a way shown on the 1641 map and located to the north-east of two furlongs called *Higher Worse Way* and *Lower Worse Way* respectively.

LyWaye: see above.

Nether Ryggeway: this is the main way from the village running parallel to *Ley Way*, leading to Linford Wood and eventually to Bradwell. This route on the 1641 map is shown adjacent to the furlong called *Under Ridge Way*. Further evidence comes from a terrier of 1515 (BuCRO D/U/1/82/5), which refers to land between the ways called *Le Whay* and *Ryg' Whay*.

A rental of Walshes Manor, dated 1505–06 (BuCRO D/U/2/11), refers to the *Lane Close*, the *Common Street* (presumably the High Street) and the "Common Street called *Fullwellend*" which was more recently known as the Willen Lane.

The 1641 map shows that the main road from Newport Pagnell to Stony Stratford, which runs across the north end of the parish, had been partly rerouted so that instead of running along the north side of the *Morro Leas* it ran along the southern side cutting across ridge and furrow. A lane leading from the green, at the south end of the village, to Little Woolstone is also shown, marked as *Woolson Way*. The route shown also cuts ridge and furrow, as does the lane leading from the village green to Willen.

The early ways to the nearby villages must have run along headlands and around the ploughed furlongs, their routes probably being varied according to the crops. Later, when more land was turned over to pasture, more direct routes running across the ridge and furrow came into use and continued until the coming of Milton Keynes.

WOODLAND

Although woodland in the parish is not mentioned in the Domesday survey, it is most likely that the present Linford Wood is of considerable antiquity. There are references to a Deer Park in the parish in the late thirteenth century (Cal. Pat. 1281–92, 103) and it is likely that this was on the site of the present Linford Wood. The absence of ridge-and-furrow within Linford Wood, apart from a late extension at the south end planted after 1678, confirms that the area it occupies was not cultivated during the medieval period.

WINDMILL

The windmill is first mentioned in 1302–3 (Feet of Fines Bucks., Hil. 31 Edw.I), when it was held by William le Waleys and Cecilia his wife. However, the radiocarbon dates for the cross-timbers of the mill suggest that it could have been constructed as early as the late twelfth century, a date which would accord with the expansion of the village at this time.

MANOR HOUSE

The original house built for Sir William Pritchard was much altered during the first half of the eighteenth century, most probably after the death of Sir William in 1705. By his will, Sir William left most of his estate in trust for his wife during her lifetime. When she died in 1718, the estate passed to Sir William's nephews and executors, Richard Uthwatt and Daniel King. Daniel apparently sold his interest in Great Linford to his cousin Richard, and the estate remained in the ownership of the Uthwatt family until it was purchased by Milton Keynes Development Corporation.

The present manor house, which incorporates parts of Pritchard's building, may be largely attributed to Thomas Uthwatt, who inherited from his father Richard in 1719, and died at Great Linford in 1757.

The accounts for the Great Linford estate survive for the period 1678 to 1888 (BuCRO D/U/4/1–20). These accounts are fairly extensive for the early part of this period, recording the building of the manor house, school and almshouses, repairs to the church, and landscaping of the grounds.

THE NINETEENTH-CENTURY VILLAGE

Whilst the village itself changed very little, many of the houses were rebuilt in the eighteenth and nineteenth centuries, and some infilling took place. Most of the existing farmhouses are said to date from the late seventeenth or eighteenth century (Woodfield 1986, 45–57), but may occasionally include fragments of earlier buildings. The last surviving cottages on the south side of the green (Plate 22) were demolished *c*.1930.

During the nineteenth century, Great Linford parish was not immune to the effects of the Industrial Revolution. The Grand Junction Canal, opened in 1800, passed through the parish from its easternmost point, skirting the village to the north and cutting through the manor grounds. As much of its route followed the contours, little major engineering was required, except for an embankment

Plate 22: Cottages at Granes End, Great Linford, *c*.1900, from postcard by Bartholomew, Great Linford. *(MKAU)*

Plate 23: 'Ye Olde Wharf Inn' and entrance to Newport Pagnell Canal, Great Linford. *(Mrs E. Tompkins)*

crossing Stanton Brook by the 'Black Horse' inn, which was built at about the same time. A wharf serving the village was opened where the canal crossed the road leading north from the village, and a second public house, the 'Old Wharf Inn', was established there (Plate 23).

In 1817 a branch was opened from the wharf to Newport Pagnell, falling by seven locks over 2.4 km to a wharf on the west side of the town. Both the Grand Junction (now the 'Grand Union') and Newport Pagnell canals are comprehensively detailed elsewhere (Faulkner 1972).

In 1814, the northern east-west route through the parish became part of the Stony Stratford to Newport Pagnell Turnpike, which operated until 1878. In 1865 a branch railway to Newport Pagnell from Wolverton was opened, using for its route part of the Newport Pagnell Canal, which had been sold to the Newport Pagnell Railway Company in 1864. The village was served by a station close to the canal wharf, and the branch line, which had been taken over by the London and North Western Railway in 1875, remained in operation to 1964. Much of its route is now a pedestrian/cycle way, the 'Railway Walk'.

The development of Wolverton and New Bradwell, and the consequent demand for building materials, led to the establishment of two brickworks in Great Linford during the nineteenth century. The first of these, Sheppard's, began operating in about 1840 to the north of Linford wharf, east of the road leading from the village. Traces of the clay pits can still be seen in Rowsham Dell, Giffard Park.

A second brickworks was established in about 1880 by George Price next to the Grand Junction Canal, south of the Willen road. The kilns here survive as listed structures, the only remaining examples of bottle kilns in Buckinghamshire, while the brickyard wharf is now the moorings belonging to the Lionhearts Cruising Club. Probably also connected with this demand for building materials were the lime kilns and quarry adjacent to the canal, west of the church.

In addition to building materials, the development of the railway works at Wolverton and Salmon's coachworks at Newport Pagnell created a demand for workmen and for houses for them in the surrounding villages. The effects of this, and the other developments described above, can be seen in the census returns for Great Linford. In 1801 the population of the parish was 313, which rapidly rose to 479 in 1851, reaching a peak of 577 in 1911 before dropping to 422 in 1931. The housing demand brought about by these Victorian 'commuters' was in part met by the construction of 'Station Terrace', adjacent to the site of Sheppard's brickworks and the railway station. However, throughout this period Great Linford remained very much an agricultural village, with the majority of its inhabitants working on the land.

The passing of Squire Uthwatt, and the subsequent sale of the contents of the manor house in 1963, marked the end of an era. Now the parish is totally developed, and the village has been engulfed by modern housing.

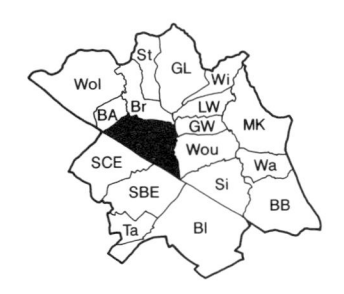

LOUGHTON

INTRODUCTION

This parish (Fig. 39), which covered some 621 ha, was on the north side of Watling Street, which formed its south-western boundary with the Shenleys. The north-west border with Bradwell Abbey ran at right angles to Watling Street in an almost straight line eastwards to Bradwell Brook. The north-east boundary with Bradwell ran from the brook to the higher ground of Bradwell Common, following the ends of medieval strips for part of the way. It then turned southwards following a gentle curve as it bordered Great Woolstone, and then ran around medieval furlongs in dog-leg fashion, bordering Woughton on the Green until it reached the Watling Street at *No Mans Land*, where it bordered Simpson.

The highest part of the parish is in the north-east, in the area of Bradwell Common (now the city centre), where the land rises to over 120 m OD. Drainage is by Bradwell (or Loughton) Brook which flows northwards to the Ouse. This stream neatly divides the parish into two parts, which until 1409 formed the parishes of Great and Little Loughton (VCH 1927, 400).

The underlying geology is chiefly Oxford and Boulder clay, with some alluvial deposits in the valley, and a small area of Cornbrash limestone in the northern end of the parish. Heavy clay soils cover most of the parish, with some lighter soils on the head deposits in the valley.

Several medieval routes ran from the village. One followed the brook to Bradwell Abbey and Wolverton in the north while another, which remained in use until recent times, ran through the medieval fields following the furlong boundaries to Bradwell. The third, a possible Roman road, was the medieval *Portweie* which led to the market town of Newport Pagnell. Of these, only the *Portweie* is older than the village, as the other two routes both respect the boundaries of medieval furlongs, suggesting that they are contemporary with the field system or of more recent date.

At the crossroads formed by the Bradwell to Shenley road and Watling Street several inns were established on the Loughton side of the road, the largest and most famous being the 'Talbot', which dates from the seventeenth century. This part of Watling Street became one of the first turnpike roads in England, the section from Two Mile Ash in Bradwell Abbey parish to Hockliffe, Beds., being opened in 1706 (Tull 1972, 50).

The parish was crossed by the London to Birmingham Railway, constructed in 1838, and four bridges were required to link the eastern fields with the main farms in the village.

ARCHAEOLOGY

Flint flakes recovered in the valley area are part of a larger spread evident to the north in Bradwell parish. One substantial Roman site, Wymbush (MK211), is known in the parish, on the west side of the Loughton Brook, to the north of the village. Excavations were carried out by the Unit in 1979, and the remains of a stone-built farmstead surrounded by a ditched enclosure were uncovered (Mynard 1987, 82–90; Zeepvat 1988). The evidence suggested that the site had its origins in the middle of the second century and became deserted by the end of the fourth.

THE MEDIEVAL AND LATER VILLAGE

Although the parish borders Watling Street the village was established some 600 m away from it. However, there are references to houses along the road in the early thirteenth century (Jenkins 1952, No. 73).

Before 1409 Loughton consisted of two settlements, Great Loughton and Little Loughton, each of which had parish status. Great Loughton developed on the north side of the brook, within a roughly triangular area bounded by Bradwell Road to the west, Church Lane and Pitcher Lane to the north and east and Leys Road, which followed the course of the brook, to the south. The triangle was subdivided by School Lane, running from the church to Leys road.

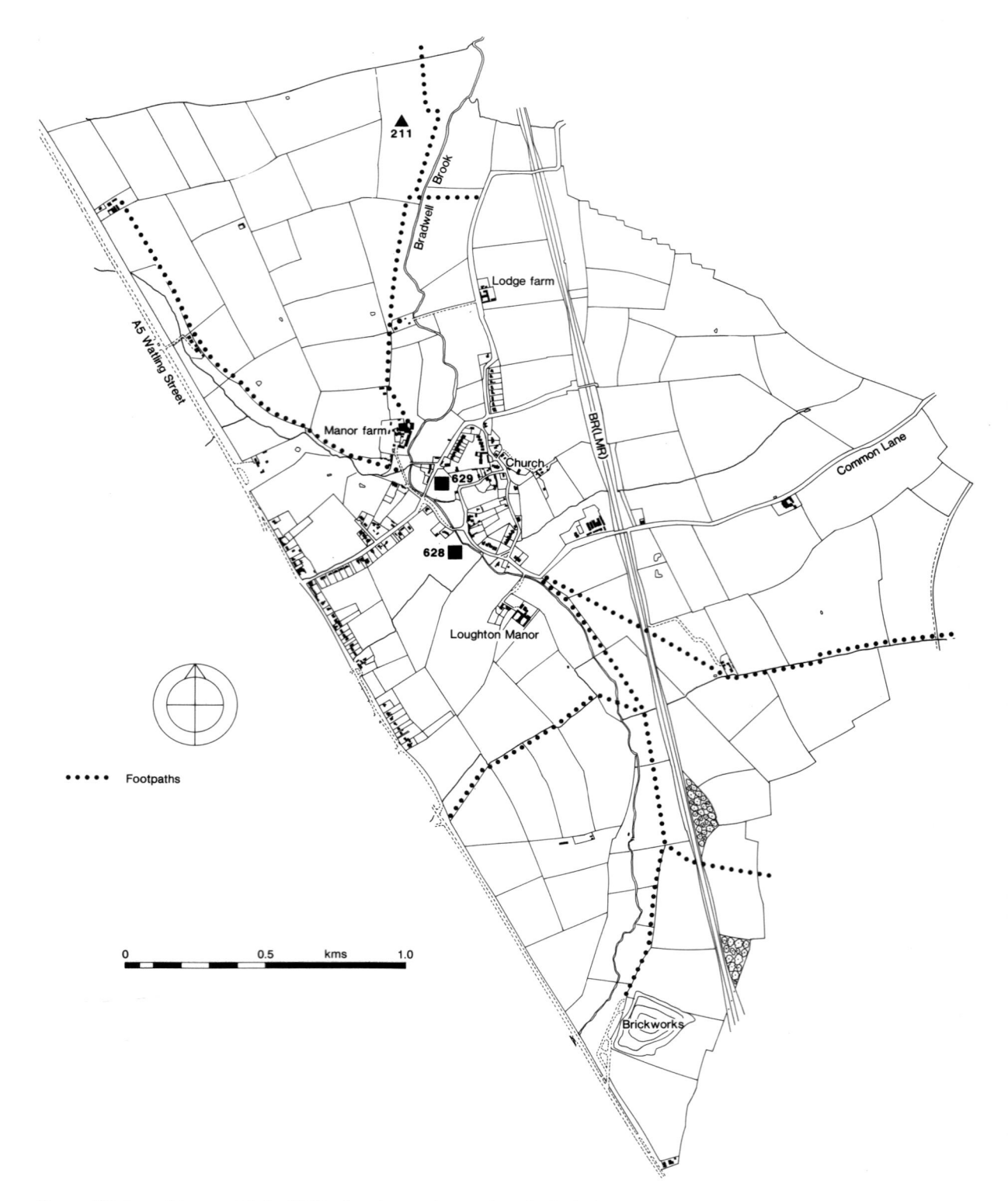

Figure 39: Loughton parish in 1967, showing major archaeological sites.

Little Loughton lay to the west and south of the brook. The western part was a rectangular green surrounded by Manor Farm and several old closes, which still contain the best group of late medieval buildings in the city. This green and the earthworks on the south side of the brook is all that remains of Little Loughton.

The earliest record of a church in Little Loughton is in 1219, when a rector was presented by William son of Hamon, confirming the early manorial connections with Wolverton. In the eighteenth century, when burials were found close to the manor house, it was suggested that the church stood nearby (BL Add. Mss 5839, 251). Local tradition placed the church in the close on the south west side of Manor Farm, but recent development there revealed no trace of it.

Manor Farm (Plate 5) is a particularly good example of a late fifteenth-century timber-framed house which was later encased in stone. The manor changed hands a number of times during the last quarter of the fifteenth century, eventually coming to the Piggot family, who were responsible for building and enlarging the house in the late sixteenth century.

With the amalgamation of Great and Little Loughton, the plan of the later village retains the basic elements of both settlements and is not of any particular type. The location of the original settlements was probably related to the proximity of the brook and Watling Street.

Medieval earthworks survived on the north and north-east sides of the village (Fig. 40). To the east of Pitcher Lane, in the field called *Dove House Close* on the 1769 tithe map (Figs 43 and L5), a 10 m wide ditch or sunken trackway aligned north to south ran for a distance of more than 100 m to a rectangular pond or pit, 29×23 m and 1 m deep. There were also two other small rectangular ponds with outfall ditches on the south side. Traces of

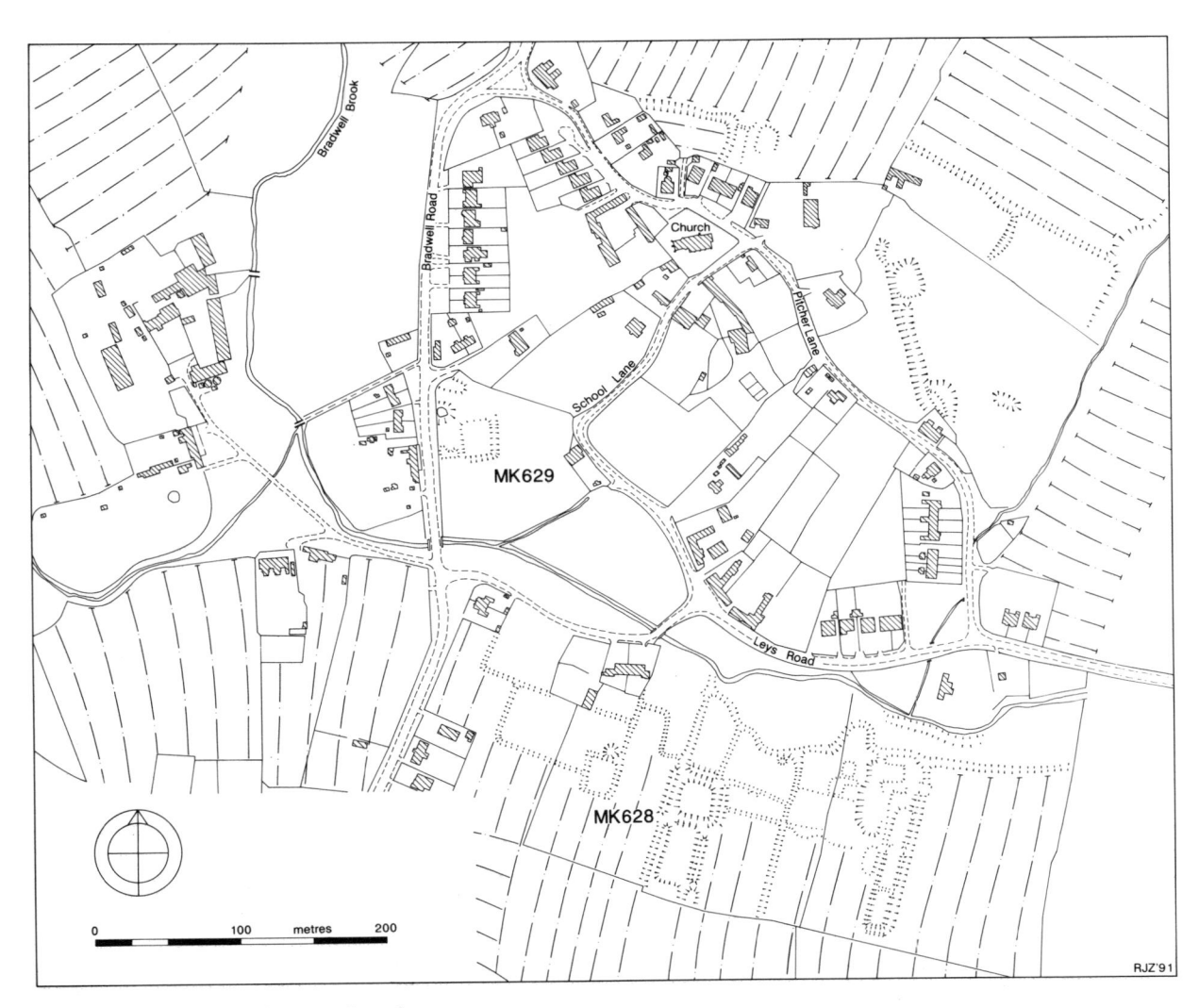

Figure 40: Loughton village earthworks.

Plate 24: Loughton moat and fishponds. Loughton Manor farm in top right corner. *(Cambridge University Collection of Air Photographs copyright reserved)*

the close boundary were visible to the north-east. Another close boundary and a house platform were recorded to the west, north of Church Lane.

Earthworks, possibly those of a banked and ditched stock enclosure, survived in School Field, which was called *Cross Close* in 1769. The name may be connected with *The Cross* in the Snelshall Cartulary (Jenkins 1952, No. 68), which could refer to a free-standing cross in the field. However, it is much more likely that it related to the crossroads location of this close, adjacent to the point where Bradwell Road crossed routes following the brook.

The earthworks on the south side of Loughton Brook and Leys road (Fig. 41; Plate 24) form an important complex containing house platforms, fishponds and a moat. They are situated along, and on the south side of, the old course of the brook and consist of three closes and five crofts, one of which contains a moat and associated fishpond, at least four other ponds, and seven house sites. The five crofts were defined by boundary ditches and leats. All of the earthworks appear to post-date ridge-and-furrow, and several were in use as late as 1769.

The crofts and closes have been identified by the letters A to G, commencing at the western end of the site. Close A is rectangular, 116×55 m, with its longest axis aligned with the brook. Close B, on the south side of A, is smaller, being only 82×44 m. Both closes share a common eastern boundary with Close D. The western half of this close survived as a square close in 1769. Close C, a small close measuring 20×15 m, is situated partly in the south-eastern corner of Close B, while on its north side within Close B is a small pond or pit, 10 m in diameter, linked to the eastern close boundary ditch. Close D is 'L' shaped, its frontage onto the brook measures 36 m; the western half of the close is only 34 m in length, whilst the eastern half measures 60 m. This close contained a house platform which was hollow internally, and was cut through by a sewer trench in 1975. Subsequent rescue excavation revealed the remains of a stone-founded house of fourteenth to fifteenth-century date (Mynard forthcoming). In 1769 this close was called *Well Close*, had no building on it and was larger, extending back some 140 m from the brook

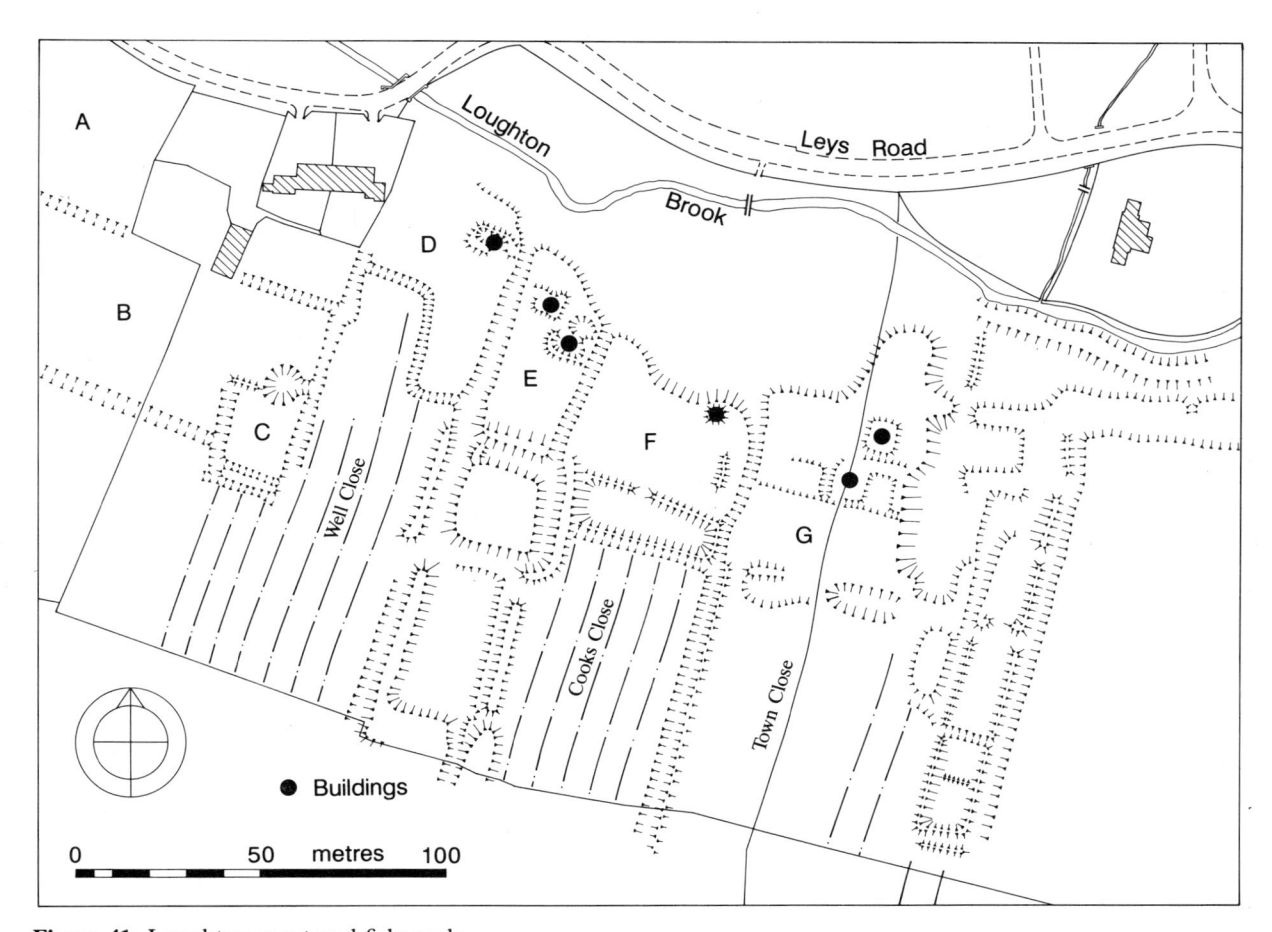

Figure 41: Loughton moat and fishponds.

to the medieval furlong boundary. The ditch between this close and Close E on the east was like a leat, being partly dammed at its northern end, nearest to the brook, as if to create a small head of water for some purpose.

Close E was a long narrow croft, 140×27 m, running from the brook to the former furlong boundary to the south. At its northern end were two possible house platforms, whilst the southern half was occupied by a moated platform and a fishpond. The following description of these features is based in part on notes from Mrs Charmian Woodfield, who surveyed the earthworks in 1975. The fishpond appears to have been fed in part by a small stream rising near the 'Fountain Inn' to the south, now culverted underground at the south-west corner of the fishpond. However, the original entrance for water into the pond appears to have been at the south-west corner, where the ditch entry was fed by drainage from the ridge-and-furrow uphill to the south. The pond was 20×40 m, and was probably at least 1 m in depth. There were banks on the east and west sides which continued for a short distance beyond the pond to the south. The moated platform was 24 m sq. and the arms were on average 5 m wide and 1 m deep. The platform was flat and was presumably for servicing the fishpond. The northern corners of the moat ditch were partly dammed to allow the moat to retain water to a certain depth, after which it would overflow into the croft boundary ditches. At the north-west corner of the moat is a footbridge onto which four footpaths converge, and it is likely that there was a bridge and a sluice here for many centuries. The moat and fishpond clearly postdate the ridge-and-furrow, which disappeared under the fishpond banks at an angle. It seems likely that this complex was connected with the rearing of fish, though there were no signs of complex fish breeding tanks, etc., as at Great Woolstone (see parish essay). The difference between the two sites is presumably either of date, or status, or both.

Close F, measuring 120×50 m, contained a house platform in its north-east corner and a large rectangular fishpond or enclosure, which extended across Close E. This pond was 35×10 m, and is currently 0.5 m deep. There is a bank on the south side with an outer ditch which carried surface water from the ridge-and-furrow to the croft boundary ditch on the east side. In 1769 Closes E and F were shown as one unit called *Cooks Close*. Although there were no buildings shown on this close in 1769, an apple tree still stands, and a house was said to occupy this croft late in the last century (*pers. comm.* Mrs Constance Kitchener, c.1960).

To the east, the area shown as Close G contains two house platforms, one large and two small ponds, a hollow area thought perhaps to be a pond, and a series of three enclosures. The house sites are at the north end of the area, and were occupied by buildings in 1769, at which time the western 25 m of this area were fenced off, forming a long narrow strip of land called *Town Close*, the boundary of which still survives.

South of the house sites are two small ponds both 7×10 m, lying side by side on an east-west alignment in the centre of the close. West of the house sites was a large rectangular pond, 27×12 m, on the south side of which a sunken area 30×20 m may be the yard associated with the 1769 buildings. The northern bank of the pond was bulldozed in advance of drainage works in 1975 and sherds of seventeenth-century pottery were found in it.

The westernmost earthworks are a series of three linked enclosures running north to south. They appear to have been laid out by surveyor's rule, the east bank and ditch of all three being exceptionally straight. The southern enclosure, 12×25 m, is the most dished of the three, and has two opposing entrances towards its northern end. Immediately uphill from these a small bank with a central gap divided this enclosure into two almost equal parts. The central enclosure, also 12×25 m, was separated from the southern one by a bank and ditch. This enclosure lacked the dished appearance of the first one, and differed also in being open to the north. The third enclosure, also 12×25 m, had an inturned entrance to the south and two gaps at its northern end.

The main water supply for this complex came from the higher ground to the south where a stream rising near the 'Fountain Inn' provided the water for the moat and the large fishpond, while drainage from the medieval furlongs delivered water to the other features.

These earthworks are of good quality, suggesting that they are either of late medieval or post-medieval date. It is known that the Piggott family were responsible for extensive works associated with the rebuilding of Little Loughton manor house, and it is possible that they were responsible for the construction of this fishpond complex. There is reference to a fishery in Loughton Brook which was held with Little Loughton manor in 1587 (VCH 1927, 399) and in 1603–4 James Farnell held fisheries in Loughton with lands and messuages (*op. cit.*).

THE FIELD SYSTEM

The ridge-and-furrow in the parish is shown in Fig. 42. Thirteenth-century documents refer to three fields; The *North Field, the South Field* (Jenkins 1952, no. 75, *c*.1225) and the *East Field* (*ibid.*, nos 104, 105, *c*.1250). However, the South and East fields were one and the same, since several furlong names occur in both. The boundary between these fields may have followed the road from Watling Street to the village, then east along Leys road and north along the Portway up to the boundary with Bradwell.

It is unlikely that the North field originally went with Little Loughton and that the South field belonged to Great Loughton, since the boundary between them is not the same as that between the Great and Little Loughton townships shown on the 1881 OS map, which was likely to have been the same as the medieval boundary. It seems therefore that although the two manors in Loughton each achieved parish status, they shared a common two-field system.

By the seventeenth century Loughton had a three-field system, the names *Moore Field, Prior's Marche Field*, and *Seckloe Field* being recorded on a Glebe Terrier of 1639 (BL Add. Mss 5839, 236). The location of these fields was not given, but can be suggested from the evidence of furlong names on the 1769 map. Moore Field was in the south of the parish between Watling Street and the brook, Prior's Marche would have been to the north of Moore Field, between the brook and Watling Street and bordering onto Bradwell Abbey parish, and Seckloe Field the land north of the brook on either side of Portway leading to Secklow mound.

A large number of field and furlong names are recorded in the Snelshall Cartulary (Jenkins 1952), many of which can be related to names on the 1769 enclosure map (Figs 43 and L5). The Snelshall Cartulary also refers to meadow which would have been adjacent to the brook. The main area of common or rough grazing is likely, in common with both Bradwell and Great Linford parishes, to have been in the east of the parish on the higher ground, in the area of Secklow. However, the 1769 map shows two areas of common, the first being *Furzen Hill Common*, at the north end of the parish, and the second *Wall Mead Common* and *Elfield Common* in the south.

The earliest record of enclosure in Loughton is in the mid thirteenth century, when the monks of Snelshall Priory were given permission to 'inclose' three acres of land (Jenkins 1952, No. 70). The document also records that the monks had a messuage nearby, already enclosed, presumably by a ditch or hedge. Permission was given with the proviso that the same method of enclosure should be used for the arable land. It would appear that the monks were attempting to consolidate their holding in Loughton and form it into a small close adjacent to their messuage. This is one of the earliest references to enclosure of arable lands in the Milton Keynes area, and shows that small-scale enclosure around the village was occurring well before the end of the thirteenth century. It was not until 1769 that the parish was enclosed (Tate 1946); the exact acreage is not recorded.

OTHER LANDSCAPE FEATURES

A watermill at Loughton was granted by William de Luftone to Simon, son of Walter the miller of Newport in about 1205 (Jenkins 1952, No. 87). The mill is described as "a fixed mill with pond and ways and with all its appurtenances below his messuage in Lufton; also two places for the repair of the pond, one at the head of and the other below the pond". Shortly after this Simon granted the mill, which was said to be next to his courtyard, to Snelshall Priory in Whaddon (Jenkins 1952, 88).

A windmill was recorded in 1361 in Little Loughton manor (VCH 1927, 399). The location of *Windmill Field* was confirmed by the 1769 enclosure map and the area examined, but no trace of a windmill mound was found. A slight mound was found nearby, but it was not possible to investigate this by excavation.

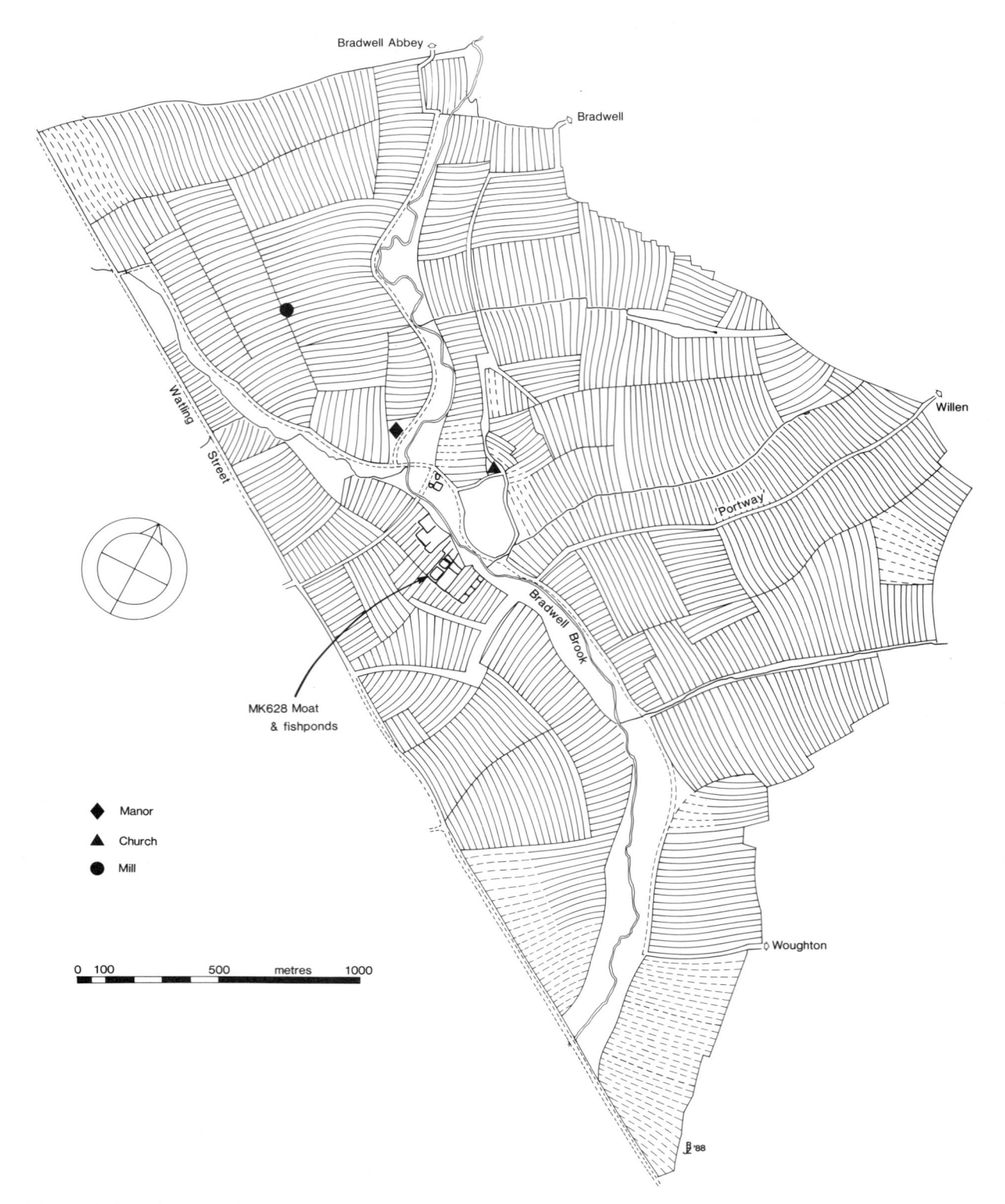

Figure 42: Loughton medieval field system.

Figure 43: Loughton; reconstruction of the 1769 tithe map.

#	Name	#	Name	#	Name
1	Furzen Hill Common	24	Rooksley Leys	48b	South Joint Oakhill
2	The Furlong under the Furzens	25	Rooksley Close	49	Ash Pole Furlong
3	The Furlong at Abbey Gate	26	Summer Well Common	50	Redland Furlong
4	Long Crown Hill Furlong	27	Bridge Foot Close	51	Wall Head Common
5	Short Crown Hill Furlong	28	Limeslade Furlong	52	Upper Brook Common
6	Green Hill Furlong	29	Long Land Furlong	53	Bow Back Furlong
7	Linceslade Common	30	Hoaridge Furlong	54	Butts shooting to the Brook
8	The Furlong shooting into Linceslade	31	Limeslade Close	55	Portway Knowls
		32	Clover Close	56	The Furlong over the Hole
9	The Furlong shooting into Upper Down Way	33	Hatchings Furlong	57	Childway Furlong
		34	Middle Furlong	58	Homeward Combs
10	Down Way Furlong	35	Long Ditch Furlong	59	The Furlong between Port Way and Potters Way
11	Butt Furlong	36	Short Ditch Furlong		
12	Specklane Corner Furlong	37	Shirtimoor Furlong	60	Knowlhill Furlong
13	Great Close	38	Dove House Close	61	Childway Furlong
14	Great Holm	39	Spinney Close	62	Pretage Furlong
15	England Close	40	Ricks Hedge Furlong	63	Combs Furlong
16	O'er Thwart Close	41	Whiteland Furlong	64	Goblings Ditch Leys
17	Barkers Close	42	Bay Well Furlong	65	Furlong above Goblings Ditch Leys
18	Fox Hill Furlong	43	The Furlong above the Moors		
19	New Hedge Furlong	44	The Furlong under the Moors	66	Burnt Bushes Furlong
20	Short Willow Bed Furlong	45	Broad Arse Furlong	67	Breach Furlong
21	Long Willow Bed Furlong	46	Short Oakhill Furlong	68	Elfield Furlong (?)
22	Staunch Hill Furlong	47	Long Oakhill Furlong	69	Elfield Common
23	Badland Furlong	48a	North Joint Oakhill		

KEY TO FIG. 43: Loughton furlong names in 1769.

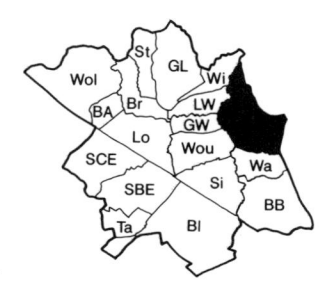

MILTON KEYNES

INTRODUCTION

The parish of Milton Keynes (Fig. 44) covered an area of some 772 hectares. The village, first recorded as *Mideltone* in the Domesday survey, became Milton Keynes in the thirteenth century with the addition of *Keynes*, the name of the family that held the manor at that time (VCH 1927, 402).

The River Ouzel formed the western boundary with Willen, Little Woolstone, Great Woolstone and Woughton on the Green. The northern and eastern parish boundary with Broughton and Moulsoe was Broughton Brook. The eastern boundary with Wavendon followed the line of the Woburn to Newport Pagnell road, before deviating slightly to the west along medieval furlong boundaries. The southern boundary with Walton also followed furlong boundaries on its route to the Ouzel.

The underlying geology is largely Oxford and Boulder clays, but extensive deposits of second terrace gravels occur in the western half of the parish. The highest land was in the south bordering Walton and Wavendon, where Milton Hill rises to more than 76 m OD. Two small streams which rose in the south of the parish ran to Broughton Brook, which joined the Ouzel at the northern tip of the parish. Extensive meadowland bordered the Ouzel throughout the parish. The only woodland was a small covert in the area known as *Kents Hill*.

The village (Plate 25) developed around a triangular green at the intersection of three roads. The main through road, which formed the western side of the green, was the north to south route which linked Willen and Newport Pagnell with Walton, Simpson and Fenny Stratford. The bridging point of this road over the Ouzel was at the north end of the parish, a short distance south of Willen Mill. An east-west route from Bradwell Common ran through Little Woolstone village, crossing the Ouzel at Little Woolstone mill to enter Milton Keynes village from the west, behind the church. This road continued eastwards from the green, joining the Newport Pagnell to Hockliffe road just outside Broughton Village. A road to Woughton left the Fenny Stratford road about 1 km south of the village and ran westwards to the Ouzel, which it crossed at the medieval mill site (Foxmilne). A fifth road, shown on the 1685 map (Fig. 45) was identified as "the way from Wavendon to Middeltone". This road followed furlong boundaries, but as it approached the village it ran over the ridge-and-furrow through fields that were enclosed in 1585 or slightly earlier (Bodleian, Willis Mss 99, 139.6).

ARCHAEOLOGY

Excavation on the edge of the terrace gravels in the western part of the parish, in the former Hartigans gravel pit, has confirmed extensive occupation dating from the Bronze and Iron Ages (MK19, MK23). Occupation at Hartigans continued into the early Roman period, by which time the focus of occupation (MK330) had shifted northward along the gravel ridge (Williams 1993).

Roman pottery fragments and tile suggest that a small site existed near Milton Hill, on the south side of the parish (MK72), though development of the area has failed to reveal any traces of occupation. Recent works around the churchyard have produced both Roman and late Saxon pottery.

One of the most extensive Saxon sites found in the city was sited at Hartigans pit, on the same site as the Iron Age settlement mentioned above, probably because the topographical requirements for Iron Age and Saxon settlements were similar.

In 1967 during gravel extraction a small burial ground (MK501) located to the east of the Rectory and 220 m east of the present parish church was briefly examined. The graves were all aligned roughly east to west, confirming that they were Christian burials. One of the graves was cut by a ditch containing twelfth-century pottery, suggesting that it was earlier than this date. No evidence of coffins was found. These late Saxon/early medieval burials were situated at the southern end of *Lancaster Close*, right against the boundary with a small close called *Chapel Yard* in 1685.

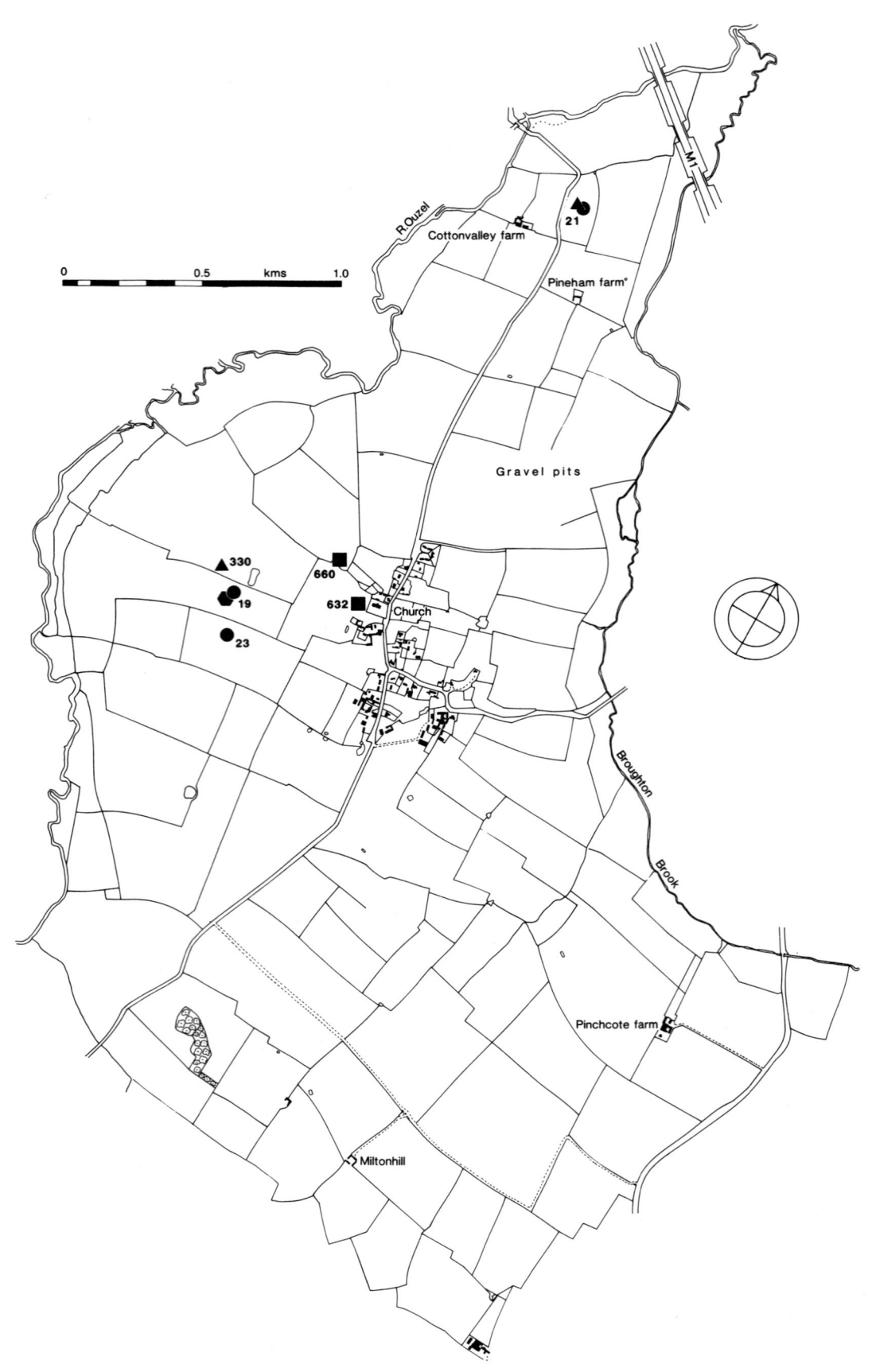

Figure 44: Milton Keynes parish in 1967, showing major archaeological sites.

Plate 25: Milton Keynes village, from the south-east, c.1960. *(Aerofilms)*

In May 1992, during the extension of the village community centre car park, further burials were discovered in Chapel Yard. The number of burials found and the fact that many graves had been cut through earlier ones indicated that the cemetery was extensive, and that burials had taken place over a considerable period. It is most likely that this cemetery was associated with an earlier village church. The present church dates entirely from the fourteenth century, and may have been built on a new site at that time.

There is a local tradition that a barn which stood in *Lancaster Close* about 100 m to the north of the burials was in fact an old church (*pers. comm.* Mr Peter Kent, whose family have lived in the village since the sixteenth century). The barn, which was destroyed in the 1960s, was described by Mr Kent, a local builder, as being of stone construction with walls about 1 m thick. Its west window had a rounded head, and the south door had a simple wooden lintel over it. Most houses and barns in the village were of timber-framed construction, perhaps with stone sills, so the building described was unusually substantial for a barn, not only in the parish but also in any of the Ouzel valley villages. The possibility that this barn might have been the surviving remains of an earlier church has been considered, but the distance from the burials makes this unlikely. In addition, it was not shown on either the 1685 or the 1782 maps of the village, and none of the local antiquaries, in particular Browne Willis who spent part of his youth in the village at the Rectory, had noted the existence of this building.

THE MEDIEVAL AND LATER VILLAGE

At the time of the Domesday survey the main manor in the parish was held by Godric Cratel, and at the time of the Conquest it had been held by Queen Edith. The village developed around the triangular green at the intersection of four roads. The church of All Saints, the medieval moat and the manor site are lie to the north of the green.

To the west of the churchyard a group of earthworks (Fig. 46) are the remains of an elaborate moat and fishponds complex, probably constructed in the early fourteenth century by Philip de Aylesbury, who held several manors in Buckinghamshire, namely Bradwell, Broughton, Milton Keynes and Drayton Beauchamp.

The moat, which abutted the western edge of the churchyard, was partly levelled and backfilled by a local farmer in 1947. The platform was approximately 38×33 m, and the northern and eastern arms of the moat are still clearly visible, each being on average 13 m wide at the upper edge and just over 1 m deep. The moat, which is usually dry, is drained at the north-east corner by a 5 m wide leat which runs to the fishponds.

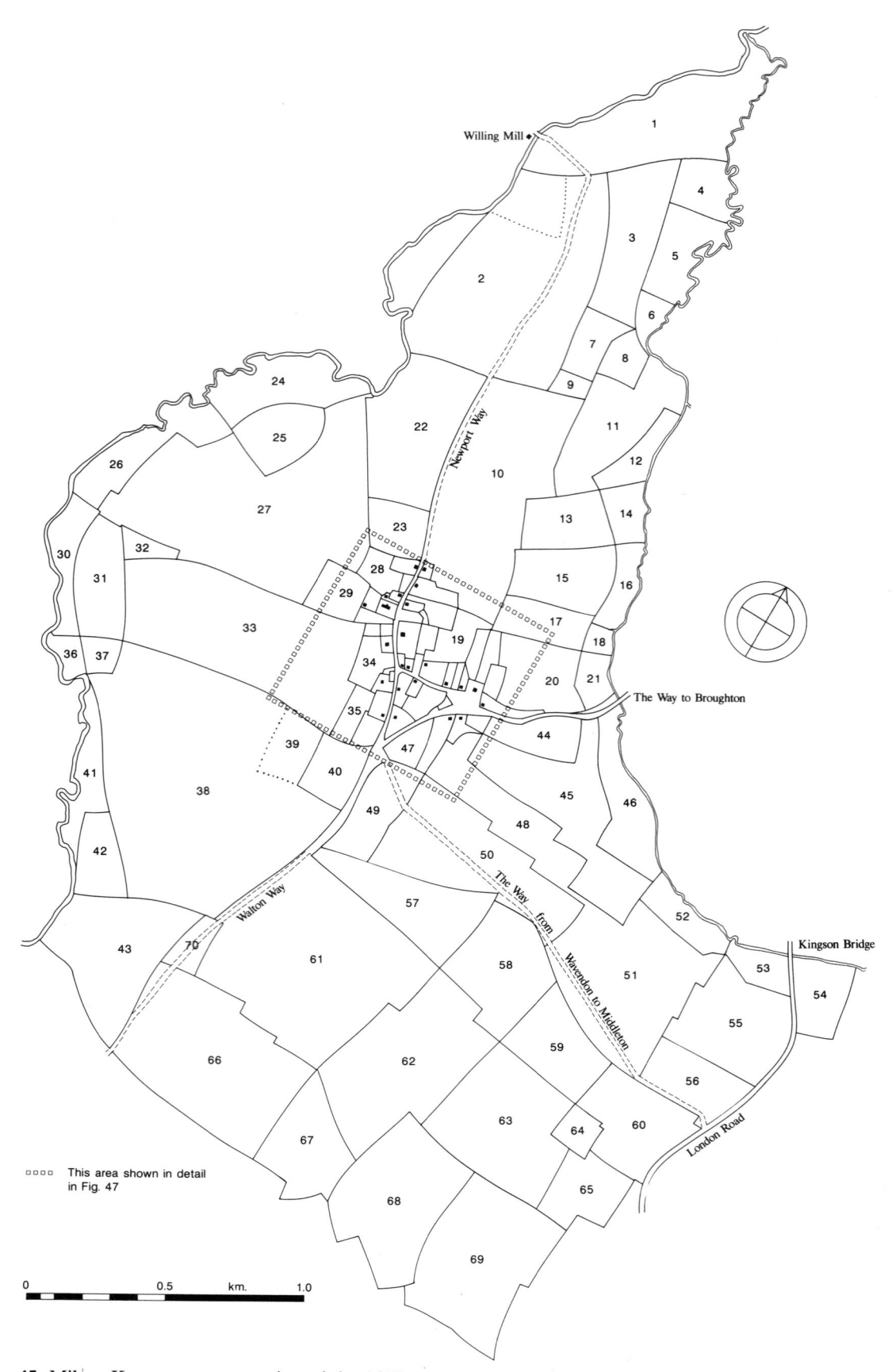

Figure 45: Milton Keynes; reconstruction of the 1685 estate map.

The main group of fishponds to the north-west of the moat are fed directly from the water table. They are all roughly rectangular in shape, and are linked to each other by leats. After the death of Sir Thomas Aylesbury in 1418 a post-mortem inquisition lists the manor house and its ponds called *Pondwykes* (Chan. Inq. PM. 6 Hen.V, no. 60).

In 1685 the field containing the moat was called *Dovehouse Hop yard* (Fig. 47), and the field to the south of the moat was the *Courtyard*. The dovehouse may have been in existence as late as 1585, when John Stafford, lord of the manor, granted the rector *Court Barn* and *Dovehouse* closes in exchange for land in the North Field (Bodleian Willis Mss 99, 140). It is worth noting that hops were still to be found in nearby garden hedges to the north of the church in 1983.

There were other earthworks in the field called the *Bowling Leys* to the south-east of the Rectory, which was enclosed before 1585 (Bodleian, *op. cit.*), and which now contains the village sports field. These earthworks were never very clear, and levelling of the sports field in the 1970s rendered them even more indistinct.

To the south of the Rectory the 1685 map shows a plot of land called the *Manor House and Close*. It has recently been discovered that No. 22 Milton Keynes village, which is situated within this close, is an important early fourteenth-century hall house of cruck construction, and is almost certainly a small medieval manor house (Giggins, unpublished report in MKAU archive). The discovery of this building is important, since it is the oldest known domestic building in the city (Fig. 48).

1	Mitch Meadow	27	Great Ground, or Compound Close	51	Fenn Field
2	Great North Field			52	Fenn Meadow
3	Corn Close	28	Smith's Close	53	Dole Meadow
4	Betts Holme	29	Fathering Yard	54	Noon Layers Hill
5	Kent's Holme	30	Ox Leys Meadow	55	Kingsoe Leyes
6	?	31	Great Oak Grove	56	Little Black Hedy Close
7	Lancaster Close	32	Renns Park Close	57a	Lesser Marsh, or Hopkin's Marsh
8	Hencemans Little Close	33	Oat Field		
9	Rickyard	34	New Close	57b	Great Marsh, or Saunder's Marsh
10	Little North Field	35	Glebe Close		
11	Hencemans Great New Close	36	Ellis, his holme	58	Hogs Hole Meadow
12	Ruff Holme	37	Little Oak Grove	59	Woodland Meadow
13	Bowlings Grounds	38	Great Ground, or Great Pasture	60	Great Black Hedy Pasture
14	Lowsy Holme			61	Thistle Field
15	Furs Close	39	'Part of Great Pasture ditched outside quick, 1685'.	62	Hogs Hole Field
16	Long Holme			63	Great Woodland Field
17	Long Close	40	Great Rycroft Close	64	'A little close belonging to Barn Close'
18	?	41	Lady Holme		
19	Bowling Leys	42	Bushey Close	65	Barn Close, or Little Woodland Close
20	Berd Leys	43	Walton Close		
21	Beards meadow	44	Smiths Close	66a	Great Hills
22	Great Linches Close	45	Cottagers' Pasture	66b	Dudley's Hills
23	Little Linches Close	46	Cottagers' Meadow Ground	67	Brinklow's Hills
24	Hames Stake	47	Robert Parrot's Close	68	Kent's Hill
25	New Close, lately taken out of Tenn Pound Close	48	Kent's Leech	69	'The Hill next to Wavendon that Kent's House stands in'
		49	Townsend Leys		
26	Woolston Meadow	50	Saunder's Leech	70	Common Close

KEY TO FIG. 45: Field names in Milton Keynes parish in 1685.

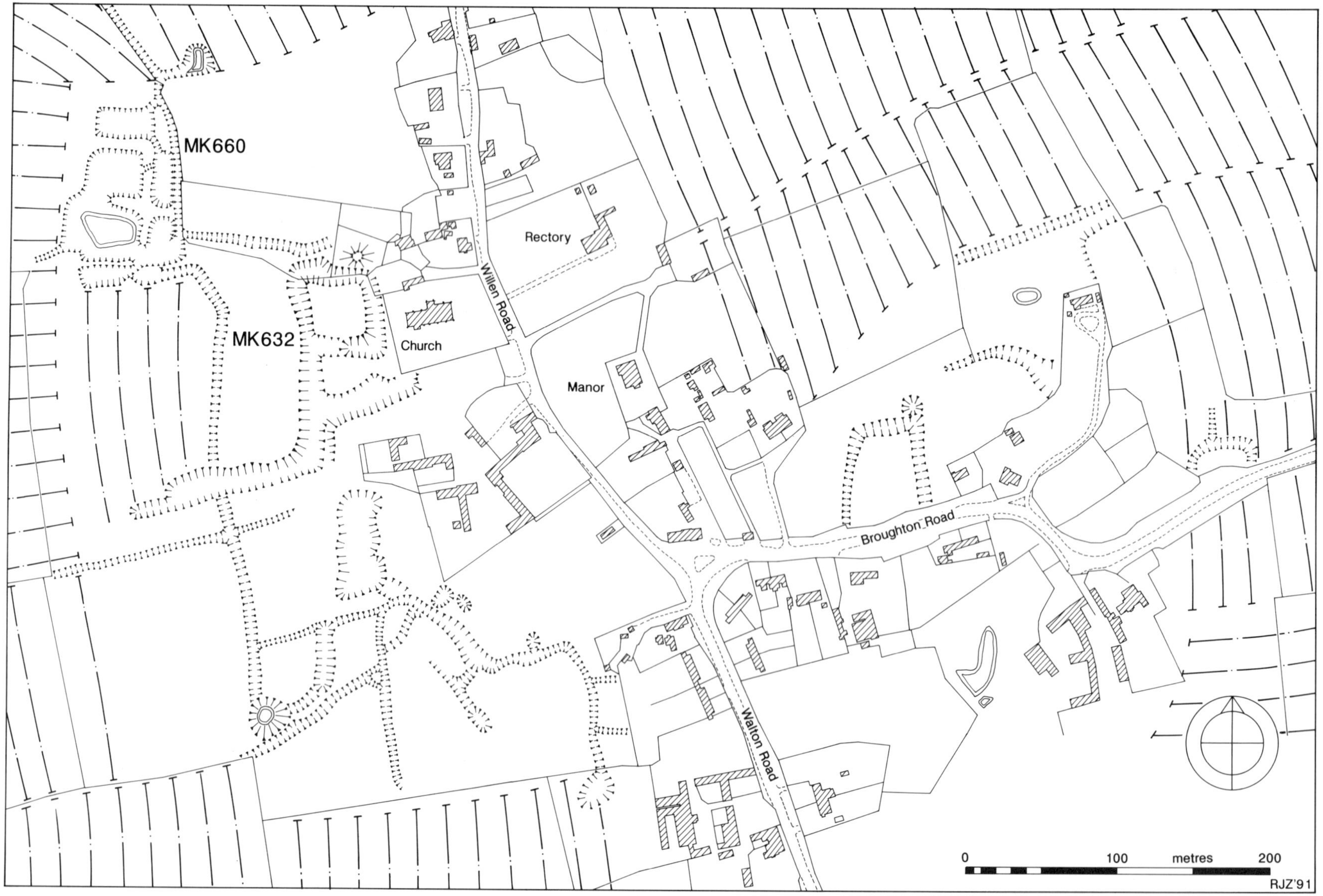

Figure 46: Milton Keynes village earthworks.

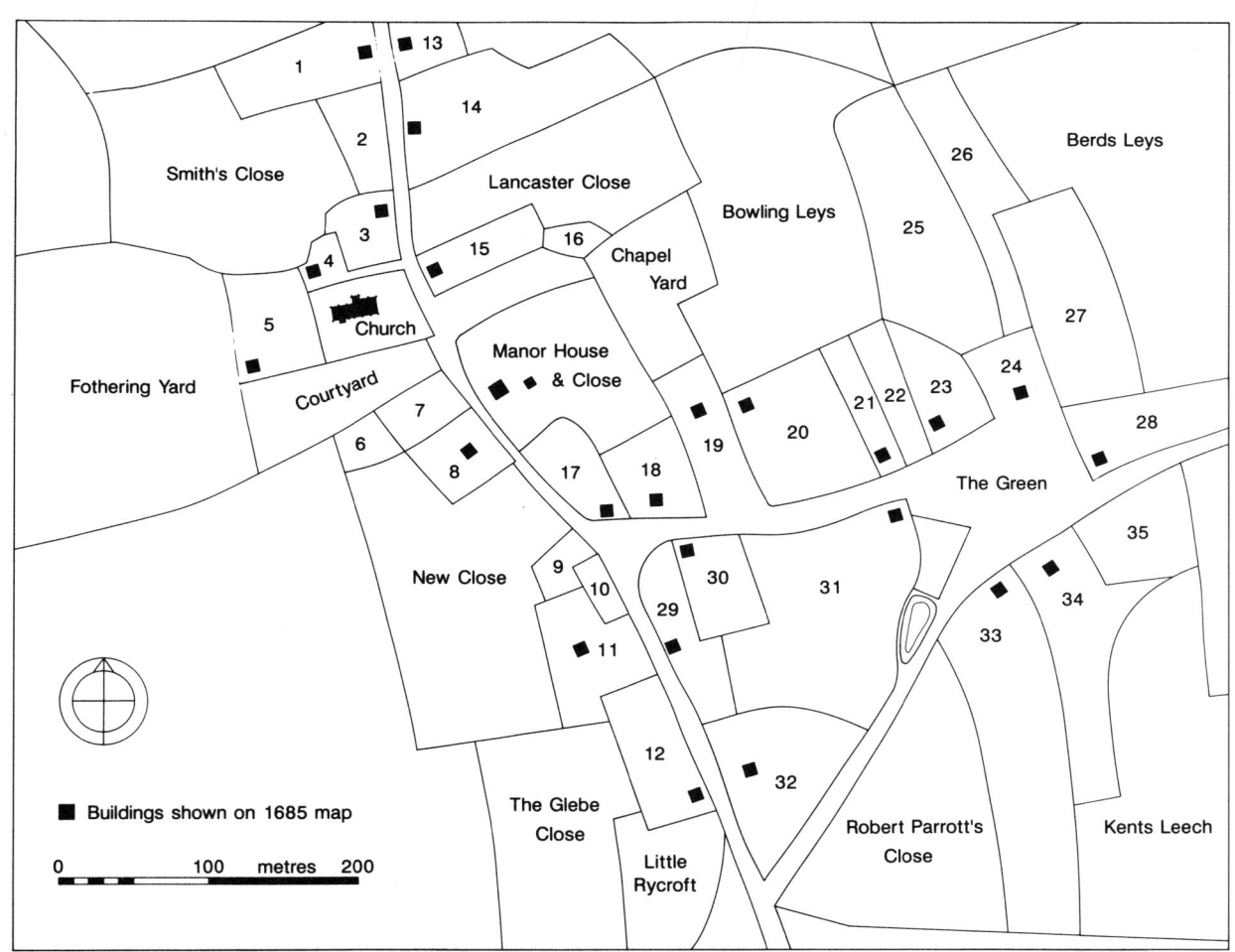

Figure 47: Milton Keynes village in 1685, reconstructed from the estate map.

1	Richard Pancoasts	19	Henry Smith's Close
2	Smith's Orchard	20	John Homes' House and Close
3	Smith's house and yard	21	Thomas Bell's Home and Pightle
4	John Ping's House	22	Francis Eldershaw's Pightle
5	Dove House Hop Yard	23	Hugh Smith Senior's House
6	A Great Barn	24	'A House upon the Waste'
7	Garwell's	25	'Hugh Smith Senior. One Close'
8	Widow Smith	26	Smiths' House Close
9	Francis Eldershaw's Pightle	27	'Hugh Smith Junior. One Close'
10	Widow Partridge's	28	Mr Ashby, his House and Close
11	John Hind's House and Close	29	John ? House and Close
12	Mr Sander's House and Homestead	30	Thomas Parneley's House and Pightle
13	Thomas Eaton's House and Pightle	31	Thomas Pickering's House and Close
14	Mary Smith's House and Close	32	Mr Purton's House and Pightle
15	Parsonage House, Yard and Close	33	Hopkins' House and Close
16	Widow French	34	Kent's House and Close
17	Francis Eldershaw's House	35	John King's Close
18	Henry Smith's House		

KEY TO FIG. 47: Landowners in Milton Keynes village, 1685.

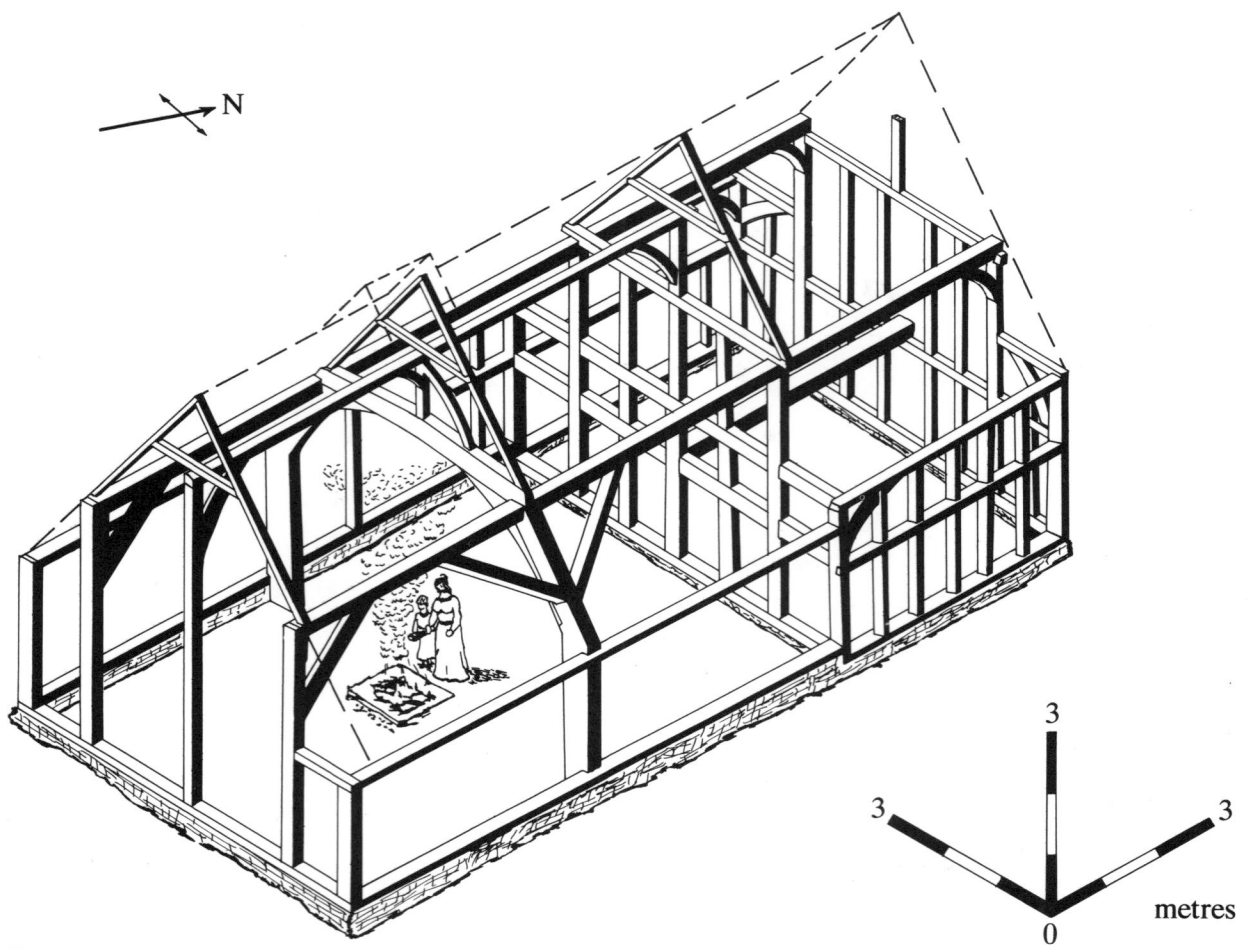

Figure 48: 22 Milton Keynes village; reconstruction of medieval framework. *(Brian Giggins)*

In a sale catalogue of the manor dated 1789 *Manor Close* was called *Lord's Close* (Fig. L7) and contained six small tenements (LRO DG/7/2/54). The manor passed through the ownership of many families including de Keynes, Bereville, de Aylesbury and Stafford, and was purchased in 1677 by Daniel Finch whose descendents held it until early this century, when the estate was purchased by the Society of Merchant Venturers, who remained the owners until it was purchased by the Development Corporation.

THE FIELD SYSTEM

The ridge-and-furrow map (Fig. 49) shows that most of the parish was ploughed during the medieval period. Very little documentary evidence relating to the fields has been found. The parish had three open fields, and apart from a reference to the *North Field* in 1583 (Bodleian, Willis Mss 99, 140) the earliest extant reference to their names is in a Glebe terrier of 1674 which lists *North Field*, *Kingsbridge Field* and *Town Field* (*ibid.*, 139). The possible location of these fields is shown.

Some enclosure took place in about 1566, when Richard Woodall, who leased the manor from Sir Humphrey Stafford, enclosed 240 acres of land and destroyed seven houses in the village (PRO E 178/424 1566). The 1685 map shows that most of the parish had been enclosed by that date. There is no enclosure award for the parish.

OTHER LANDSCAPE FEATURES

The Domesday survey refers to a mill in the parish held by Godric Cratel and worth 6s 8d. In 1313, Philip Aylesbury held one third of a mill in Milton Keynes, and at his death in 1349 a watermill was part of the manor (Cal. PM. Edw.III No. 249, 342.) In 1418 the mill was identified by the name *Foxmilne* (VCH 1927, 404) and was situated on the Ouzel at the point where the route from Woughton to Milton Keynes crossed the river. Traces of the mill leat survive on the Woughton side of the river. No later references to this mill have been discovered.

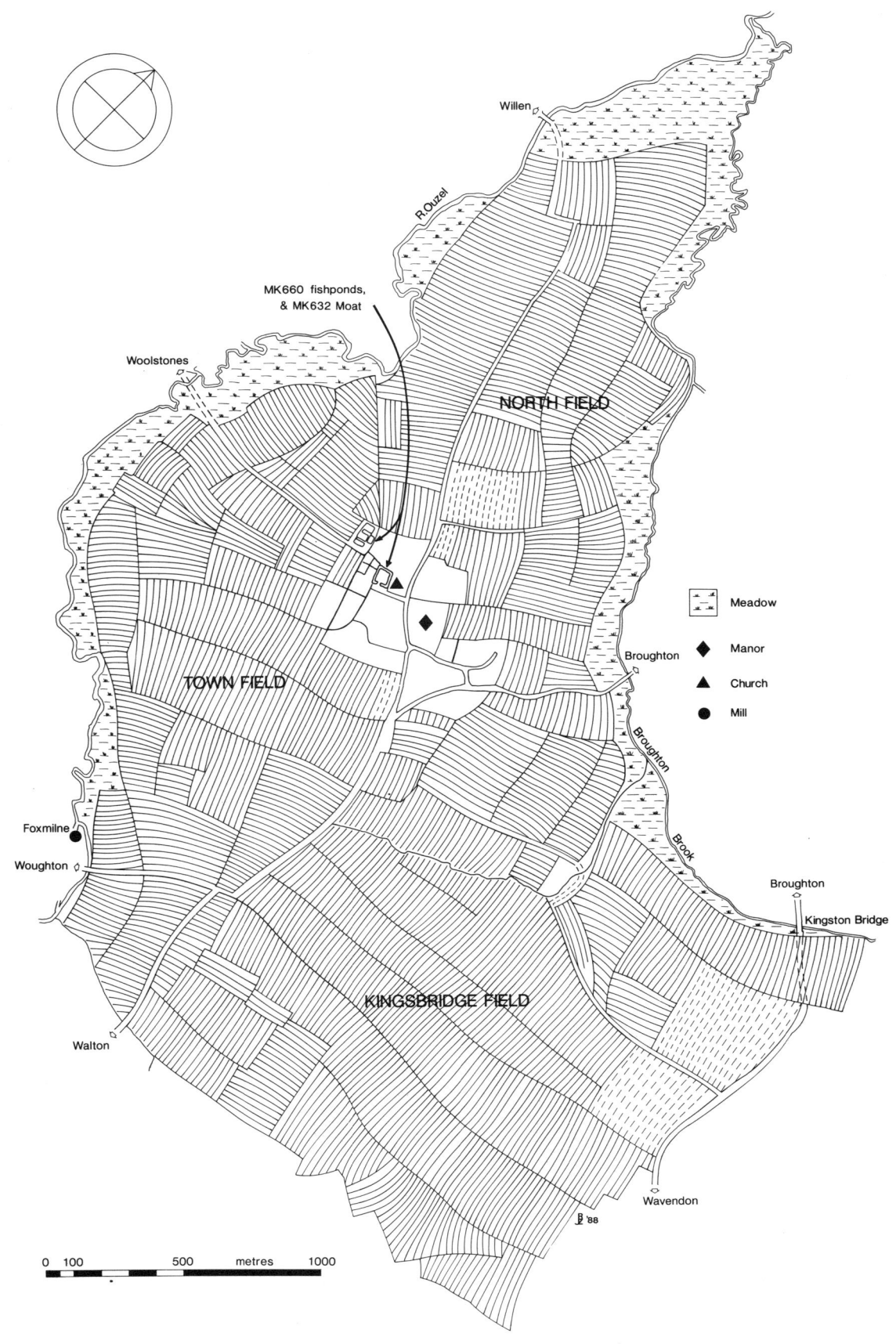

Figure 49: Milton Keynes parish medieval field system.

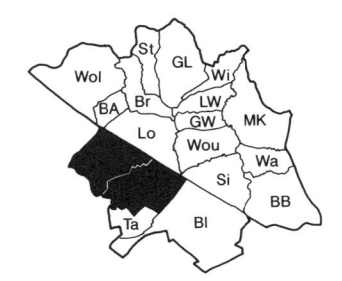

SHENLEYS

R.J. Ivens

INTRODUCTION

The parish of Shenley was situated to the south-west of Watling Street and covered an area of 1344 ha (3321 acres). It was split between the two townships or endships of Shenley Church End, 673 ha (1662 acres) and Shenley Brook End, 671 ha (1659 acres). The long and straight north-eastern boundary followed the line of Watling Street. The north-western border with Calverton parish ran almost at right-angles to Watling Street for some 2.5 km until it met Calverton Brook and then turned abruptly southwards. The boundary then followed the brook until it reached the site of Snelshall Priory where it kinked eastwards into Shenley Common for a short distance and finally continued southwards to Tattenhoe parish. The boundary with Tattenhoe was of 'dog-leg' pattern formed by following woodland and field boundaries. From the north-eastern corner of Tattenhoe the boundary returned to Watling Street following the straight line of Rickley Lane. The irregular east-west border between the two endships of Shenley followed field and woodland boundaries (Figs 50 and 51).

The area has rather ill-drained heavy clay soils derived from the underlying Boulder and Oxford Clays. Small pockets of sand and gravel outcrop in the centre of Shenley Church End village, and in Shenley Brook End between Howe Park Wood and the western edge of the village. The land is drained to the north-east by Loughton Brook and two small tributaries. The greater part of the parish slopes gently down from the north-west to the south-east although the extreme south-west of Brook End is a continuation of the low spur which gave Tattenhoe its name.

There were four main foci of settlement in the parish: Shenley Church End, Shenley Brook End, Westbury and East Green. Communications with the outside world would have been largely via Watling Street, the Drovers' Road, now known as the 'North Bucks Way', which runs along the western edge of the parish, and the *Riggewie*. This latter route ran in a south-easterly direction through the parish and so on to Bletchley, and can be traced from the thirteenth century onwards (Jenkins 1952, No. 33); in the eighteenth century it had become known as the *Bletchley Ridgeway* (OxonCRO, Peers 1/IV/6). Several small roads linked the settlements of the parish with each other, the fields and the outlying farms. These minor routes were far from constant and were created and abandoned as the needs of the local settlements dictated. Compare, for example, the Salden Estate Map of *c*.1599 with the 1698 Survey of Shenley Brook End (Figs L7 and L11). The Salden map records an abandoned road a little to the west of Two Mile Ash as 'Here was an highway before the enclosures'. The route which ran from Shenley Brook End to Whaddon until recent years is not marked at all on the Salden map, but is clearly evident on the 1698 survey. This new route effectively by-passes the deserted village of Westbury, and perhaps can be seen as the final recognition of its demise. Of course such changes in the road network do not necessarily mean that the old roads disappeared completely, for they often survived as footpaths and farm tracks, and sometimes their physical form remained carved into the landscape long after they ceased to have any real function. The old medieval street through Westbury survived as a sunken or hollow-way until the western extension of Childs Way finally destroyed both it and the remains of the settlement it once served.

ARCHAEOLOGY

There is little evidence of prehistoric occupation in Shenley parish, though a small number of possible Neolithic or even Mesolithic flints have been found during the excavation of later settlements; occasional Bronze Age artefacts have also been found. Such finds really indicate no more than transient use of the area and cannot be taken to suggest any permanent settlement. However, it should always be remembered that large parts of this area are still undeveloped, and have consequently received little archaeological attention. It is only from the late Iron Age that substantial archaeological remains are found in addition to such casual losses. For example at North Furzton (MK158), in the extreme south-east of the parish, a habitation site of a small group of stock farmers

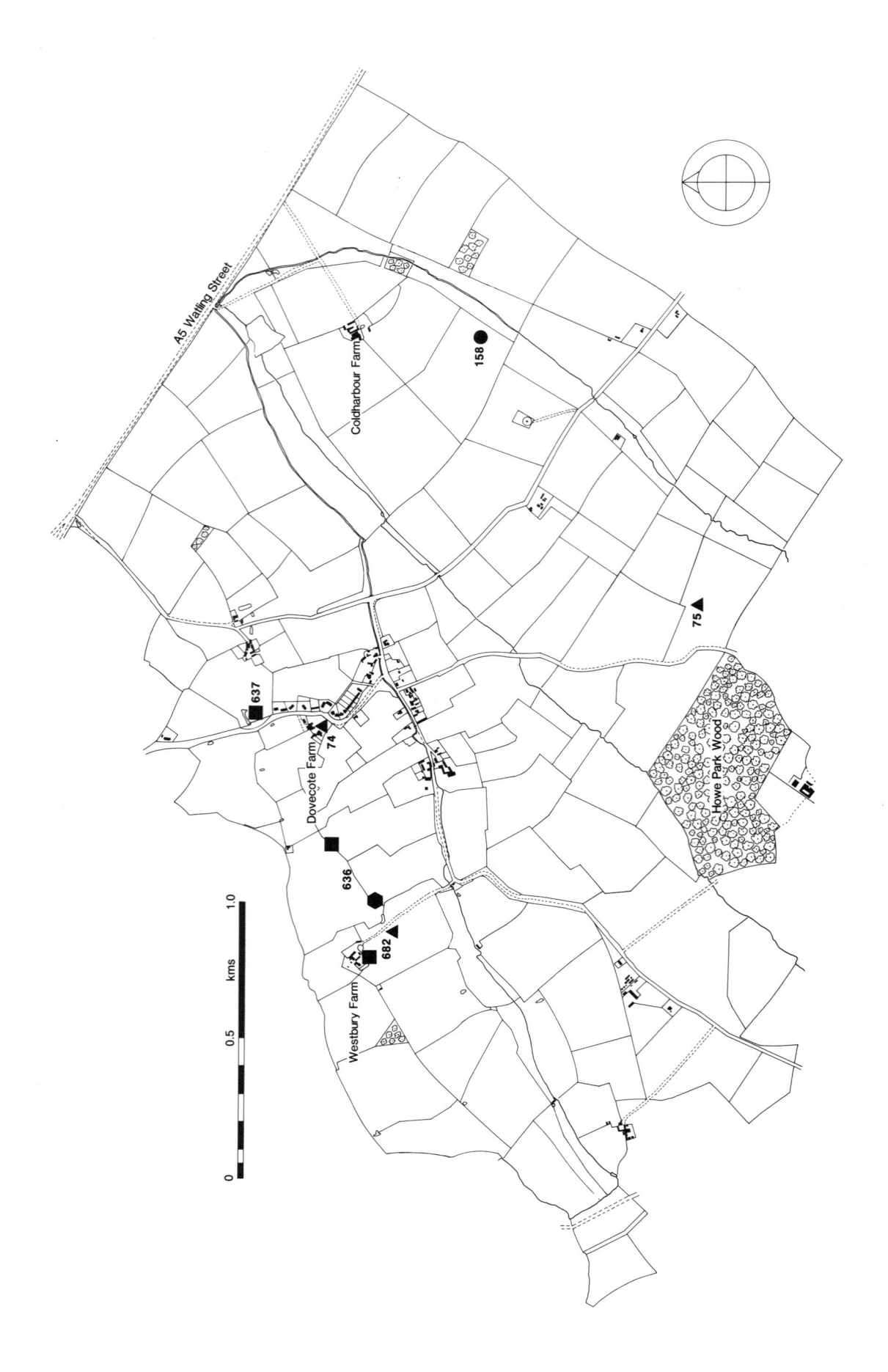

Figure 50: Shenley Brook End in 1967, showing major archaeological sites.

Figure 51: Shenley Church End in 1967, showing major archaeological sites.

dating to the first century BC was excavated (Williams and Hart, forthcoming).

Numerous finds of Roman coins and other artefacts have been made in almost all parts of the parish. A concentration of finds around the prison site (MK160) suggests that there may have been a settlement in that area. Below the western end of the deserted medieval village of Westbury an extensive and long-lived field system spanning most of the Roman period was discovered during the course of the excavations, and again this may indicate a settlement in the vicinity (Ivens *et al.*, forthcoming). A tessellated pavement was recorded at Dovecote Farm (MK74) in 1901 (RCHM 1914, 254). Despite trial excavations in the gardens of Dovecote Farm and extensive investigation of the adjacent fields, the site of this reputed Roman building has never been established. However, a small Roman building was discovered during the course of road building in nearby Baker's Close, but the remains do not tally with the earlier reports. (Ivens, *op. cit.*). Other concentrations of finds within the parish, which indicate probable habitation sites, are marked on the parish maps (Figs. 50 and 51).

Very little is known about the Shenleys during the centuries between the end of the Roman period and the Norman Conquest. A scatter of Saxon artefacts has been found, and they seem to cluster about three distinct centres: Shenley Church End, the deserted village of Westbury, and a third site on the southern margins of Shenley Brook End. The very name Shenley (*scienan-leage*, i.e. bright clearing) could indicate a new Saxon settlement in the forest (Mawer and Stenton 1925, 23; Gelling, above, for a discussion of *-ley* names in Milton Keynes). If this is the case then there may well have been a regeneration of the forest since the Roman period. Definite evidence of settlement at this period is provided by the discovery of a group of seventh-century burials below the medieval settlement at Westbury. Two wells complete with wooden ladders were found only a few metres from these burials, and these date to a similar period. One of these wells was subsequently used for the retting of flax, and a study of the pollen remains found in the silts indicates that the surrounding area was largely open grass and arable land with a very small amount of tree cover.

THE MEDIEVAL AND LATER VILLAGES

The Domesday survey records four separate holdings in Shenley. Two of these were in Church End and were held by one Hugh, of Hugh Earl of Chester. The remaining two were in Shenley Brook End and were held by Richard Ingania (Artificer) and Urso de Bercheres (Morris 1978, 13–14, 41–43 and 44–45). There are also several entries describing Westbury, but the descent of these lands demonstrate that these all refer to Westbury-by-Brackley, Northants; in fact there is no certain reference to Westbury-by-Shenley until the reign of Henry III (VCH 1927, 448–9). East Green is not mentioned in Domesday.

SHENLEY CHURCH END

Church End has also been known as 'Over Shenley' and 'Magna Shenley', and parts are sometimes referred to as the 'Manor of Shenley Maunsell'. Church End is and probably always was the main settlement in the parish. The church is the main focus for the village and occupies a slightly raised position on the west side of the road. Shenley Toot, the earthwork remains of the Earl of Chester's motte and bailey castle, is preserved about 0.4 km south-west of the church, towards Shenley Wood. The village has no distinctive plan, and could be described as a linear street village with a church and green at a road junction.

Manor Farm is the only major surviving farm in the village. The buildings date from c.1750, but the farm itself may be the main manor farm of the Maunsell family, who held lands in Shenley during the later twelfth and thirteenth centuries (VCH 1927, 445–6). It is also possible that the farm was associated with the site of the main manor at Shenley Toot. Shenley Park House and Shenley Old Rectory are two examples of very fine brick buildings of the early nineteenth century. A number of Victorian and Edwardian brick-built farm workers' cottages have also been erected in the village. The only other buildings of particular merit are the almshouses built by Thomas Stafford in 1615 (VCH 1927, 451).

Since it lies in an area of largely pastoral farming the township of Shenley Church End contains some of the best-preserved earthworks in the whole city. These are largely medieval in date, although some may be later. Examples of most earthwork types are evident, and range from irregular quarry holes to the remains of a substantial motte-and-bailey castle.

SHENLEY TOOT MK639

The castle (Plate 6) occupies a reasonably flat area, with what would have been a broad open view to the north in the direction of Watling Street and Loughton village. The embanked enclosure which forms the bailey is roughly rectangular in plan, although the southern side curves gently outwards (Fig. 52). The main enclosure measures some 200 m north to south, and approximately 150

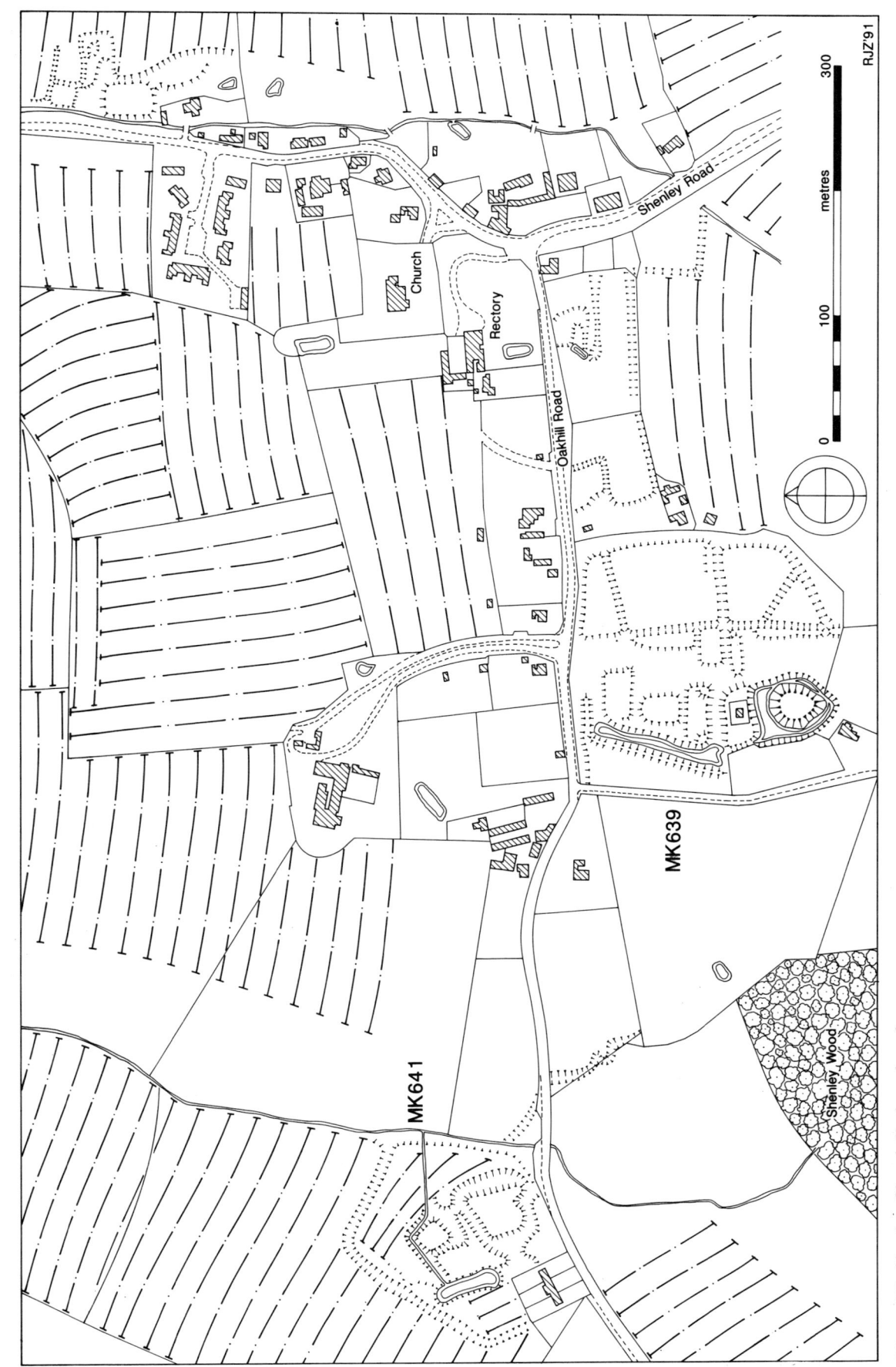

Figure 52: Shenley Church End earthworks.

m east to west. The motte is located in the south-western corner of the bailey, and is surrounded by a wet moat which runs 60 m north to south and 45 m east to west. The mound itself measures 40 m north to south and 35 m east to west, and stands some 3.95 m in height. The north-western side of the bailey is defined by a substantial and intermittently wet ditch. This pond measures 95 m north to south and has an average width of 10 m. The southern end of the pond has been damaged by a water storage reservoir built during the 1930s, and the exact relationship between the pond and the moat is unclear. The eastern side of the bailey does not have such a clearly defined boundary. The bailey is divided into two by a ditch some 5 m wide and 1 m deep running north to south. The eastern bailey contains what appear to be four closes. In the western bailey are five or possibly six platforms of differing sizes.

It is probable that some of these internal earthworks are post-medieval; certainly an old manor house stood in the grounds of the Toot until it was demolished by Matthew Knapp in 1774. A few years later the Rev'd Primatt Knapp, brother and heir of Matthew, built a 'rural cottage' on the motte, and constructed a drawbridge across the moat (Sheahan 1862, 598).

SHENLEY GRANGE FARM MOAT MK641

The earthworks of Grange Farm moat (Plate 26) lie about 700 m west of the parish church, on the north side of Oakhill Road. The moat is pentagonal in shape and covers an area of 1.86 ha, with maximum dimensions of 130 m, and is deliniated by a 6 m wide ditch (Fig. 52). Within this main enclosure are four platforms and a pond. The central platform is 18 m square and is surrounded by an 8 m wide ditch. To the south is a larger irregular platform some 30 m wide, surrounded by a 10 m wide ditch. The western side of the enclosure is occupied by a large pond 43 m in length, which appears to be cut into the two rather irregular western platforms. The pond would therefore seem to be a later addition. The moat was fed from a small stream which ran along its eastern side.

Documentary and field-name evidence suggests that this moated enclosure is the site of a monastic grange originally attached to Woburn Abbey and later to nearby Snelshall Priory. The name Grange has long been associated with this site; for example in 1599 it was known as *The Graunge* (Fig. L11). The earliest known reference to a monastic holding in Shenley dates to *c*.1190, when William Maunsell lord of the manor of Shenley Church

Plate 26: Moated grange, Shenley Church End. *(MKAU)*

End granted Woburn Abbey a "messuage in Shenley above which their barn (grangia) is situated forty acres on one side and forty on the other, and pasturage for two hundred sheep, five cows and five sows and their offspring" (Jenkins 1952, No. 44). Clearly this grant represents an extension to the Shenley holdings of Woburn Abbey. Woburn appears to have granted its Shenley estates to Snelshall priory between 1235 and 1241 (Jenkins 1952, No. 49)

There were a number of other minor earthworks strung along the Shenley and Oakhill roads (MK640). These were poorly preserved, and seem to be the remains of terracing and garden landscaping of the post-medieval period.

SHENLEY BROOK END

There is no real focus for this hamlet, other than the green area where the road from Shenley Church End meets the Whaddon and Bletchley roads. The hamlet is linked together today by a terrace of 1930s council houses which stretch from Dovecote Farm corner southwards towards the green. In its simplest form the village is a loosely linked collection of four farms: Shenley Lodge (formerly East Green), Dovecote Farm, Valley Farm and Emerson's Farm. Westbury Farm and Westbury deserted medieval village also lie within this township.

Valley Farm dates from c.1600, and contains several timber-framed buildings as well as a mid eighteenth-century granary. The field to the east of the main farmhouse contains traces of fragmentary earthworks which may indicate that settlement was more extensive along this northern side of the stream in the medieval or post-medieval period.

East Green Farm, now known as Shenley Lodge, dates from c.1600. There are no surviving earthworks in the area, but a number of possible house sites have been noted in the area to the south of the farmhouse. The 1698 map of Shenley Brook End shows the main green as East Green, an area of apparent open space with trackways leading off from all of its five corners (Fig. L7). A substantial farmhouse and outbuildings are also shown in the corner of the close marked *Mileses*. Two other closes in the area of the green contain buildings. A close on the south eastern side of the green is called *Dovehouse Close*, and perhaps formed part of Dovecote Farm. Settlement in this area of East Green was never very extensive, and in the absence of any substantial earthworks and finds of medieval pottery it seems likely that it was only occupied during the late medieval and early post-medieval periods. This would tie in with the date for some of the earlier enclosures in this part of the parish, for it is recorded that in c.1750 several houses, *i.e.* small cottages, were demolished at East Green by Mr Knapp (Oxon CRO, Peers 11/iii/2).

The present Dovecote Farmhouse only dates back to the early years of the present century. However, it was rebuilt on the site of an earlier and probably medieval farmhouse. Excavations have shown that the gardens have been substantially landscaped, and no traces survive of any earlier buildings (Ivens *et al.*, forthcoming). Despite the lack of archaeological information a considerable amount of detail is known about Dovecote Farm. It is marked on the Salden map of 1599 and on the 1698 survey. The latter also illustrates a small building which must surely be the dovecote itself. Even more informative is the 1656 Parliamentary Survey into the lands of the Guild of St Margaret and St Katherine at Fenny Stratford, founded in c.1485. This survey describes the Guild's lands in Shenley as "All ye Farme House with a Dovehouse two barns Stable and Garden together with a parcell of Pasture Ground . . . .". In all some sixty acres of pasture and arable land are listed (Parliamentary Survey Bucks. 18, PRO E.317/18).

SHENLEY BROOK END MOAT MK637

A little to the north-east of Dovecote Farm is the earthwork complex generally described as Shenley Brook End Moat (Fig. 53). The site has been partly filled in, giving it a somewhat irregular appearance. The main components are a curving wet ditch which forms its southern and eastern sides, and a straight pond-like feature which forms the northern side, thus giving the site its moated character. The ditch has an average width of 7 m, and the entire complex measures 150 m north to south and 140 m east to west. Within the moat is an enclosed area measuring 20 m north to south and 25 m east to west and this contains the slight remains of a ploughed-out platform area. On the western side the old Shenley Road curves as though avoiding the site, which suggests that it may have been more nearly circular than its present remains indicate. To the east side of the moat are a number of slight banks and ditches which have been heavily ploughed in recent years, and these may be the remains of former closes and gardens.

The 1698 survey of Shenley Book End clearly shows a large house on this site. The map indicates that this was a two-storey building set in an orchard or wooded garden. The name of the occupant is not recorded, and no other cartographic or documentary evidence has so far been discovered

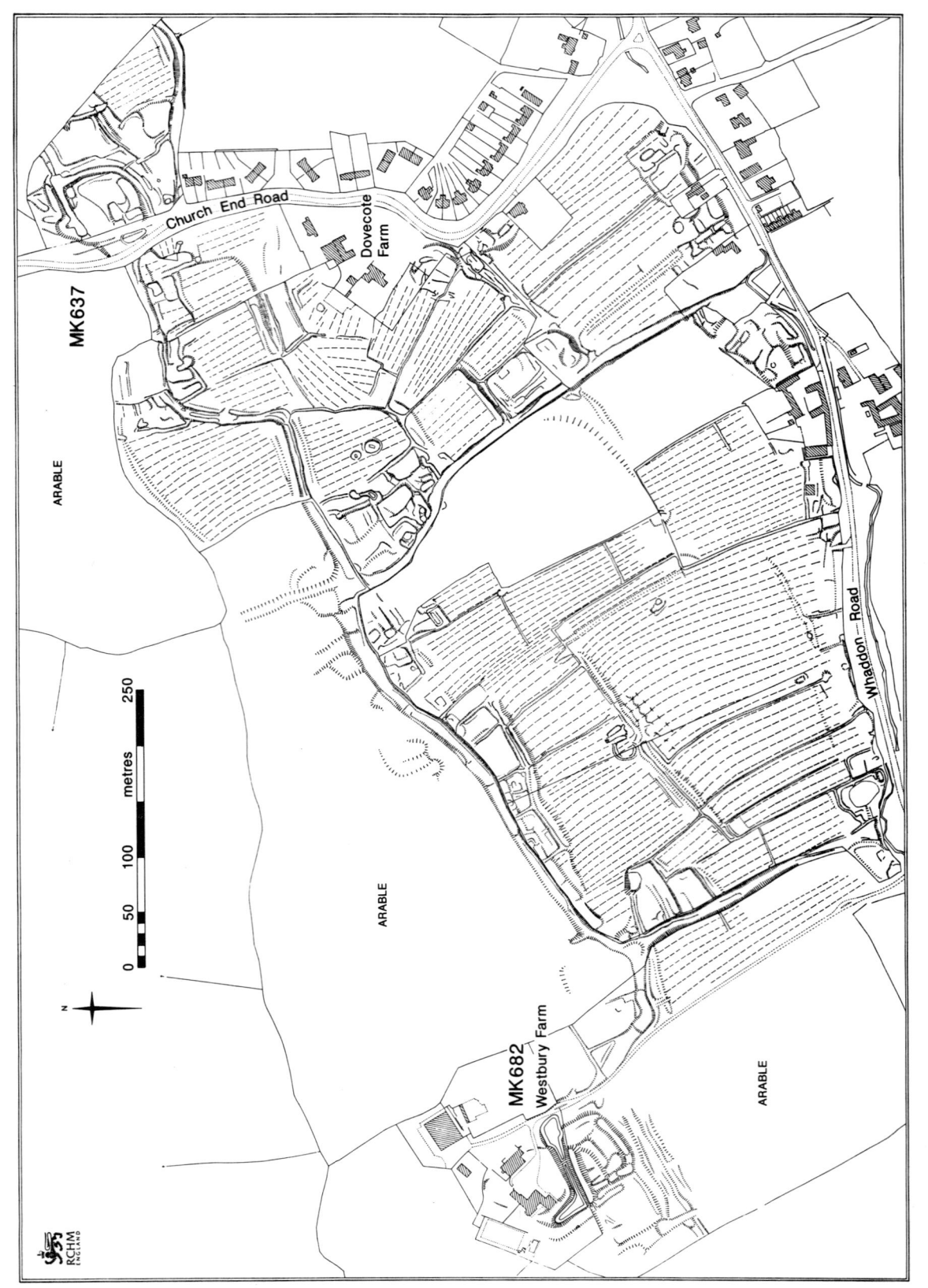

Figure 53: Shenley Brook End earthworks.

relating to this building or to its evidently wealthy owners.

The surviving earthworks reflect the use of the site for a post-medieval house and garden, but this may only be a re-use of a medieval moated or perhaps even earlier site. To the west are the moated site and village earthworks known by the name *Westbury*. This could imply that there was a more easterly site or manor after which it was named. The 'Bury' name element is often associated with manor sites and is known in several Milton Keynes parishes, for example Bury Street in Caldecotte and Bradwell Bury in Bradwell (Gelling, above). It is therefore possible that this site was once the focus for one of the Saxon manors noted in Domesday, which were subsequently taken over by Richard Ingania and Urso de Bercheres.

WESTBURY FARM MOAT MK682

The moat at Westbury Farm only survives on two sides, forming an L-shaped pond. The east-west arm of the moat has been partly filled in on its southern edge and now has a length of 38 m and a maximum width of 8 m. The smaller north-south arm is 15 m long and 7 m wide. A 2 m wide bank runs parallel to and south of the long arm of the moat for about 25 m of its length. The date and function of this are unknown, but its effect is to narrow the moat to approximately 5 m for most of its length. South of this bank are several irregular and plough-damaged platforms, again of uncertain date. The moat is fed from ground water, and in times of flood would overflow at its eastern end. What would have been the internal platform of the moat is now occupied by the modern farmhouse, farm buildings and gardens, and it is unlikely that any archaeological deposits survive. The present farmhouse was largely built of brick about 1670, although the east wall of the south wing is timber-framed with brick filling, and the lower parts of the west wall of the same wing are built of stone. The house contains a number of fine seventeenth and eighteenth-century details, particularly the timberwork (RCHM 1913, 254). The ornately carved Iberian baroque front door is perhaps the most striking element, though it is certainly a relatively modern addition (Woodfield 1986, 98).

It is generally assumed that this moated site was at one time the main focus for the manor known as Westbury, and that the manor was an amalgamation of the Domesday estates of Richard Ingania and Urso de Bercheres (VCH 1927, 448). The origins and descent of Westbury manor are complex issues, and there is no clear evidence as to who first constructed the moated site. In all probability it was a member of the Fitz Eustace family, who held the manor at the end of the thirteenth and throughout the fourteenth centuries, and may also have had an earlier interest in it. The most likely candidate for the construction of the moat at Westbury is Thomas Fitz Eustace who acquired the manor in 1327, and had already obtained permission in 1320 to have an oratory built at his house in Shenley (VCH 1927, 449).

WESTBURY DESERTED VILLAGE MK636

A vast complex of earthworks (Plate 27) occupied the fields between Westbury Farm and Dovecote Farm until the construction of Childs Way and its associated developments. The most obvious feature was a meandering hollow-way which ran for over a kilometre from Shenley Brook End Moat almost to Westbury Farm, at which point it turned sharply southwards to join the Whaddon Road. A second hollow-way ran northwards from Shenley Brook End, meeting the east-west route about halfway between the two moated sites. The fields to the north of the east-west route had been extensively cultivated in recent years, and only the slightest traces of earthworks survived. However, to the south a very fine series of house platforms were preserved, together with the boundaries of a number of enclosures and fields. The overall impression is of a straggling ribbon development along the two roads.

Extensive excavations on the site in advance of the development have to a large extent confirmed this initial impression (Ivens *et al.*, forthcoming). The major period of the village's occupation has been shown to be the thirteenth and fourteenth centuries; it continued to be occupied in a reduced form through the fifteenth century, and was virtually deserted by the sixteenth. Some evidence of earlier medieval settlement was also recovered in addition to the Saxon and Roman use of the area described above. Throughout its life the settlement was continually evolving, sometimes expanding and sometimes contracting, and can really best be described as a loosely connected series of farmsteads rather than an organised village community.

The 1599 Salden Estate map includes the area of Westbury village, and shows a landscape which is beginning to be enclosed but is still largely open fields (Fig. L11). The village of Westbury is not marked at all, although there is a building that appears to be Westbury Farm and sizeable settlements are indicated at both Shenley Church End and Shenley Brook End. A hundred years later the picture had changed somewhat (Fig. L7). The settlement pattern is very similar, although interestingly the medieval roads through the now deserted Westbury are clearly marked, but there is

Plate 27: Westbury-by-Shenley village earthworks, from the east. *(Cambridge University Collection of Air Photographs copyright reserved)*

now a considerable degree of enclosure. A number of close and furlong boundaries are also marked, presumably survivors of the medieval landscape. Many of these boundaries can be traced on the modern earthwork plan (Fig. 53), illustrating just how little this corner of Milton Keynes changed over the three hundred years before the coming of the new town.

WOODLAND AND THE MEDIEVAL FIELD SYSTEM

Shenley is one of the most heavily wooded parts of Milton Keynes with three substantial surviving woods: Oakhill, Shenley and Howe Park. It has already been suggested that woodland had regenerated in the area during the Dark Ages, and that Saxon settlers had started new clearances. The Domesday survey records that there was wood for 150 pigs in the Shenleys. Although the precise meaning of this form of measurement has never been established it does indicate that Shenley was fairly heavily wooded in the eleventh century (Morris 1978, 13–14 and 41–43). The map evidence suggests that the three surviving woods have changed relatively little, at least in size, since the sixteenth century. The nature of the woodland almost certainly has changed, for medieval and early post-medieval woods were not nature reserves, but were managed for the production of a wide variety of raw materials. Not the least of these was for fuel and this probably explains the construction of a small late medieval tile kiln within Shenley Wood (Edmondson and Thorne 1989, 78–87). Even today the remaining coppice stools bespeak an earlier and more rigorous system of management.

The southern side of Shenley Wood follows a gently curving boundary which was once also the boundary of the two Ends of Shenley and the Hundreds of Secklow and Mursley. An earthen bank survived along a part of this boundary (SP 8305 3595) until levelled by post-war agriculture, though its position could still be traced as a soil mark until the very recent past. It may be that this bank was the last remnant of an encircling boundary to the wood.

Traces of a similar bank and ditch can seen round considerable stretches of Howe Park Wood, which as the name suggests was a medieval park, and the embanking was a means of controlling the movements of deer. The earliest reference to Howe Park is made in an Inquisition following the death of John Fitz Eustace in 1369/70 (IPM. 43 Ed. III, No. 348).

The Shenleys occupy an area of relatively poor agricultural land, yet almost the entire parish has been cultivated in the past, and ridge-and-furrow can be widely traced on the ground and from aerial photographs. Only areas of woodland and the flood plains of several small streams seem to be exempt. Ironically it is the poor quality of the land which has allowed the ridge-and-furrow to survive, for much of the area has long been under permanent pasture. No plan of the open-field strips is known for Shenley, but the ridge-and-furrow maps included here reconstruct the field system as far as the physical remains allow (Figs 54 and 55). The long sweeping selions which cover most of Brook End contrast with the much more fragmented pattern in Church End. This is probably a reflection of relatively early enclosure of Church End, and the late (1762 and 1764) enclosure of most of Brook End. In fact, considerable parts of Shenley Common were not enclosed until the middle of the nineteenth century (Tate 1946, 33 and 38).

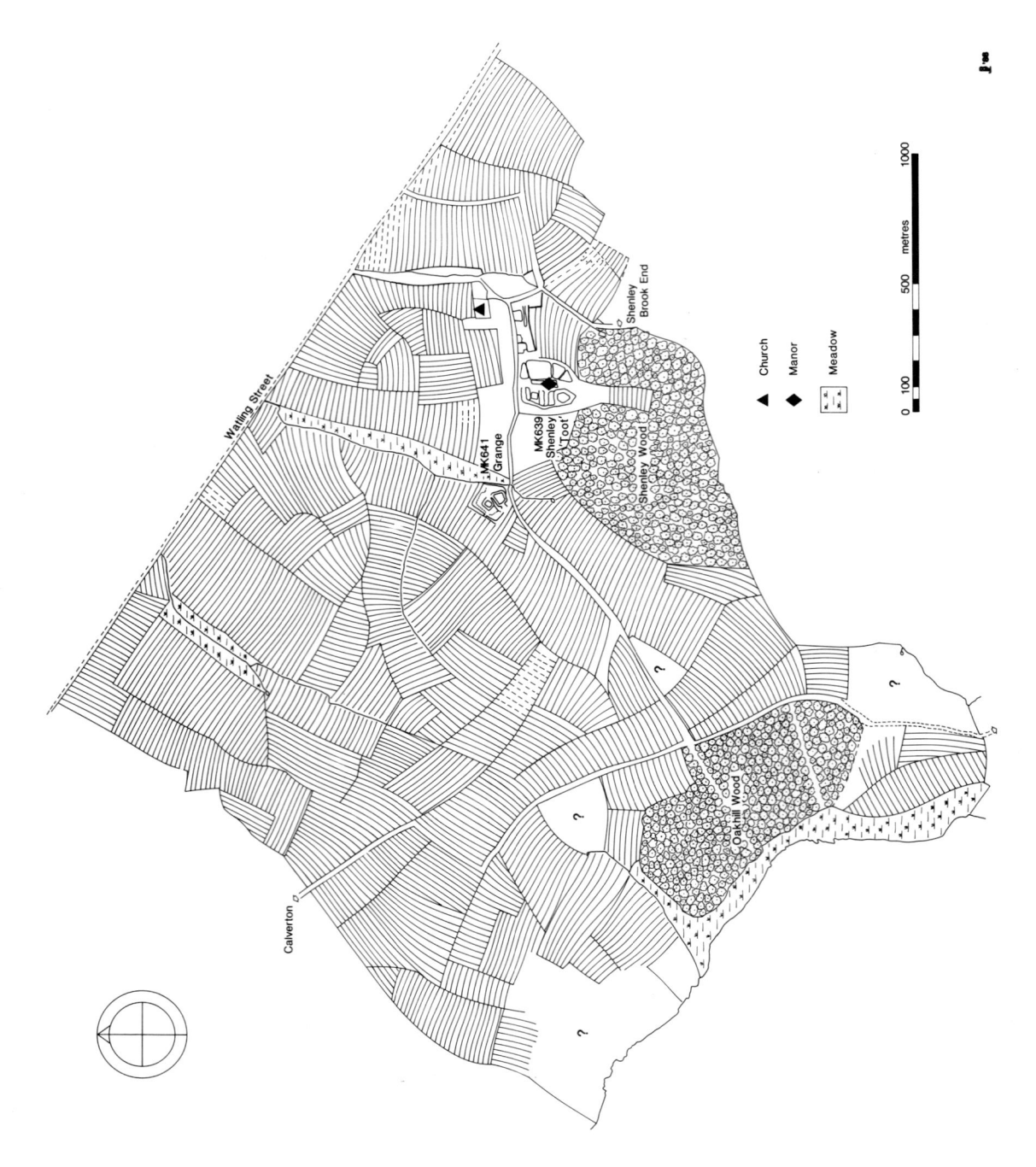

Figure 54: Shenley Church End medieval field system.

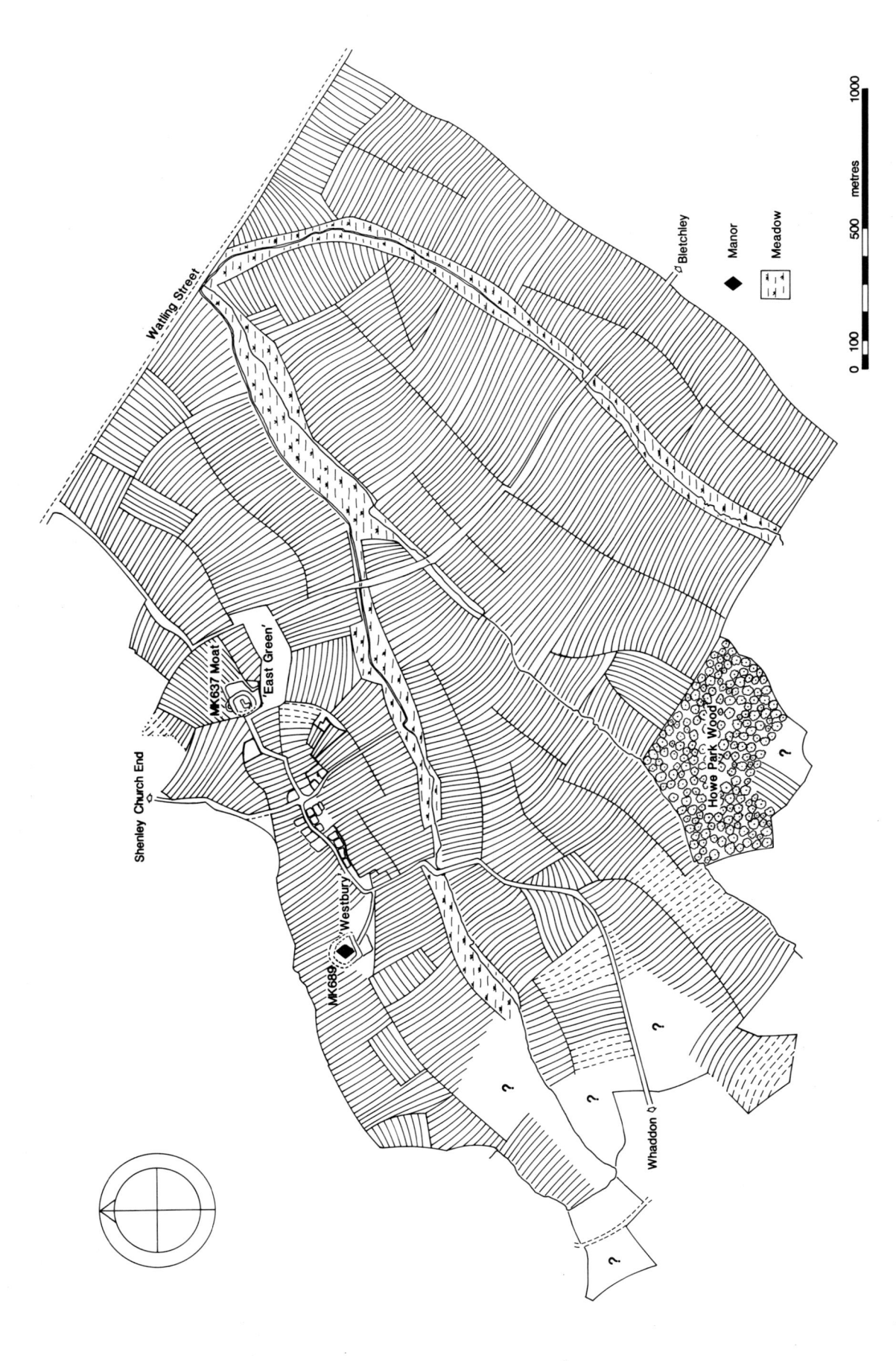

Figure 55: Shenley Brook End medieval field system.

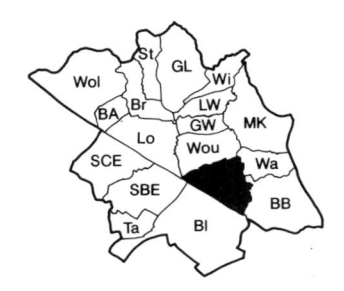

SIMPSON

INTRODUCTION

The parish of Simpson (Fig. 56) was triangular in shape, being bounded by Watling Street on the south-west, the River Ouzel on the east and Woughton on the Green on the north. The parish covered 552 ha and there were two main settlements, the village itself and a ribbon of houses, shops and inns along Watling Street which formed part of the medieval market town of Fenny Stratford. The name is first recorded in the Domesday Book as *Sevinestone* or *Suiuinestone*, meaning 'Sewines tun' or farm.

The parish rises gently from the low-lying meadows adjacent to the Ouzel to a height of 87 m OD in the west towards Denbigh Hall Bridge and Watling Street. Two small streams flow eastwards through the parish from the higher land to the Ouzel. The underlying geology is largely Boulder and Oxford clay, with first and second terrace gravels in the valley. In common with other Ouzel Valley parishes, the riverside fields are subject to extensive flooding throughout the year, providing some alluvial deposits and resulting in good meadowland.

The River Ouzel forms the eastern boundary with the parishes of Bow Brickhill and Walton. The north-west boundary with Woughton on the Green follows medieval furlong boundaries and meets Watling Street at a point known as *Nomansland*, a name often found at the edges of parishes, describing an area perhaps of unknown ownership.

The north to south route through the parish came from Fenny Stratford and ran northwards to the villages of Woughton and the Woolstones. Another medieval road ran through the western side of the parish, linking Bletchley with Woughton on the Green. This route respects the ridge-and-furrow, and a field adjacent to it is called *Portway Ground* in 1781, indicating that it was perhaps a way to the market at Newport Pagnell or Fenny Stratford.

An east to west road through the parish, linking the village with Walton and Wavendon to the east and Watling Street to the west was known as *Groveway* in 1781. This road is also of medieval origin, running along the straight boundary between the North Field and Middle Field of the open-field system (Fig. 59).

ARCHAEOLOGY

No major prehistoric settlement sites are known in the parish, although a number of chance finds of flints have been made in the Ouzel Valley. Two Roman occupation sites have been located, both in the Ouzel valley; to the south of Simpson village (MK351), and in the area formerly occupied by Simpson Sewage Works (MK309). Metal detecting on the latter has produced quantities of Roman coins, as well as Saxon metalwork.

THE MEDIEVAL AND LATER VILLAGE

The village developed in a low-lying position to the west of the Ouzel at the intersection of the roads mentioned above. It was roughly triangular in shape, with the parish church of St Thomas and its associated small green providing a focus for the through roads. The majority of the older timber-framed buildings are concentrated on the eastern side of the village fronting the Newport Pagnell road.

The site of the medieval manor, a scheduled ancient monument, contains extensive earthworks which consist of a moat, two fishponds, the site of the manor house and gardens, and some post-medieval landscaping (Fig. 57; Plate 28). In 1806 the Hanmer family sold the manor house to Charles Pinfold, who pulled it down in about 1810 (Hanmer 1877).

The moat and fishponds were to the south of the manor house on the west bank of the Ouzel. The moat was rectangular in shape, measuring 45×40 m internally, the southern and western ditches being the best preserved. It was about 20 m west of, and was fed by, an artificial cut which has been in recent years the main course of Ouzel, the original silted channel being just visible in the meadows to the east.

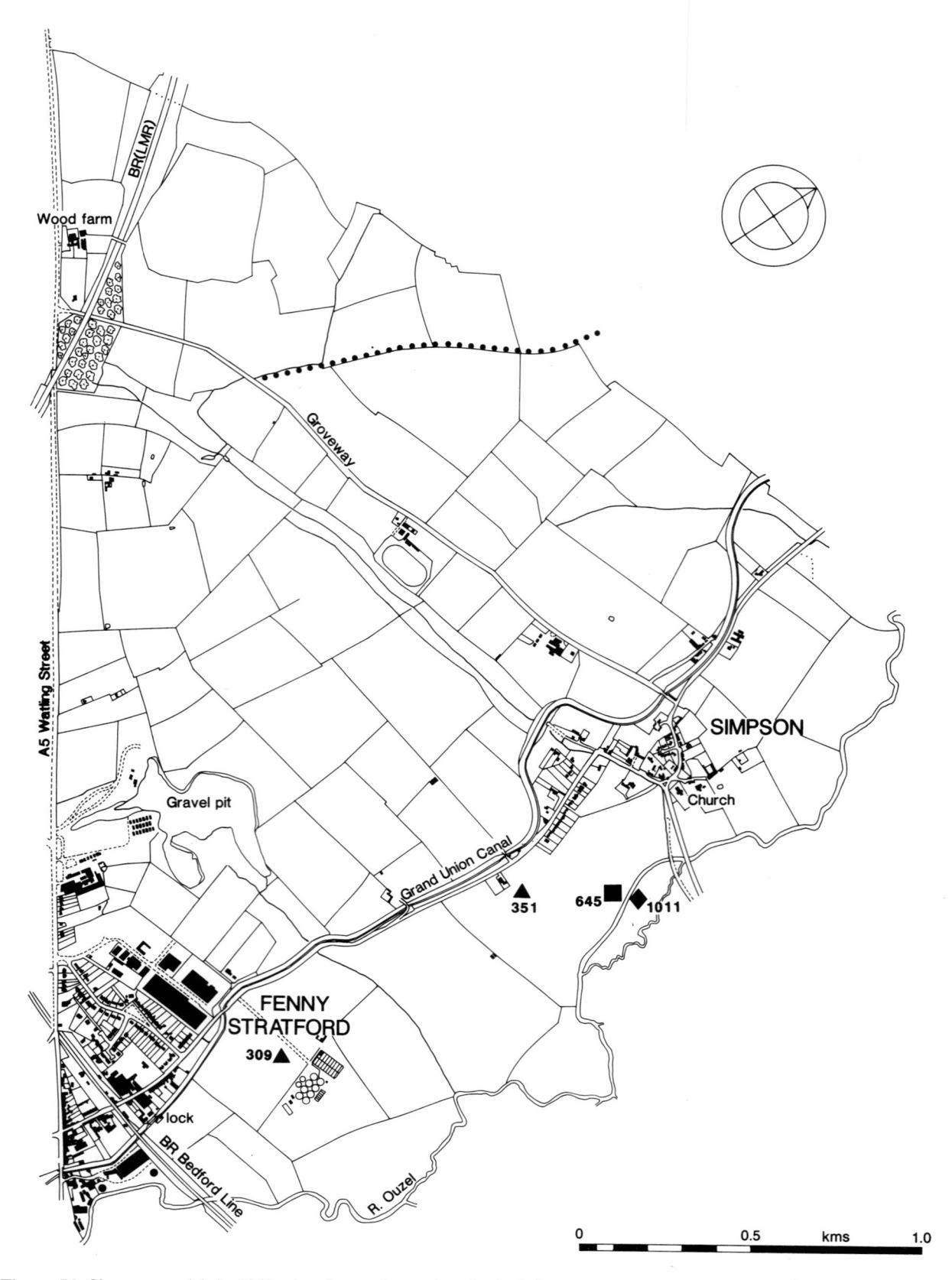

Figure 56: Simpson parish in 1967, showing major archaeological sites.

Figure 57: Simpson; earthworks of manor, moat and fishponds.

Plate 28: Simpson manor, moat and fishponds earthworks, from the south. *(MKAU)*

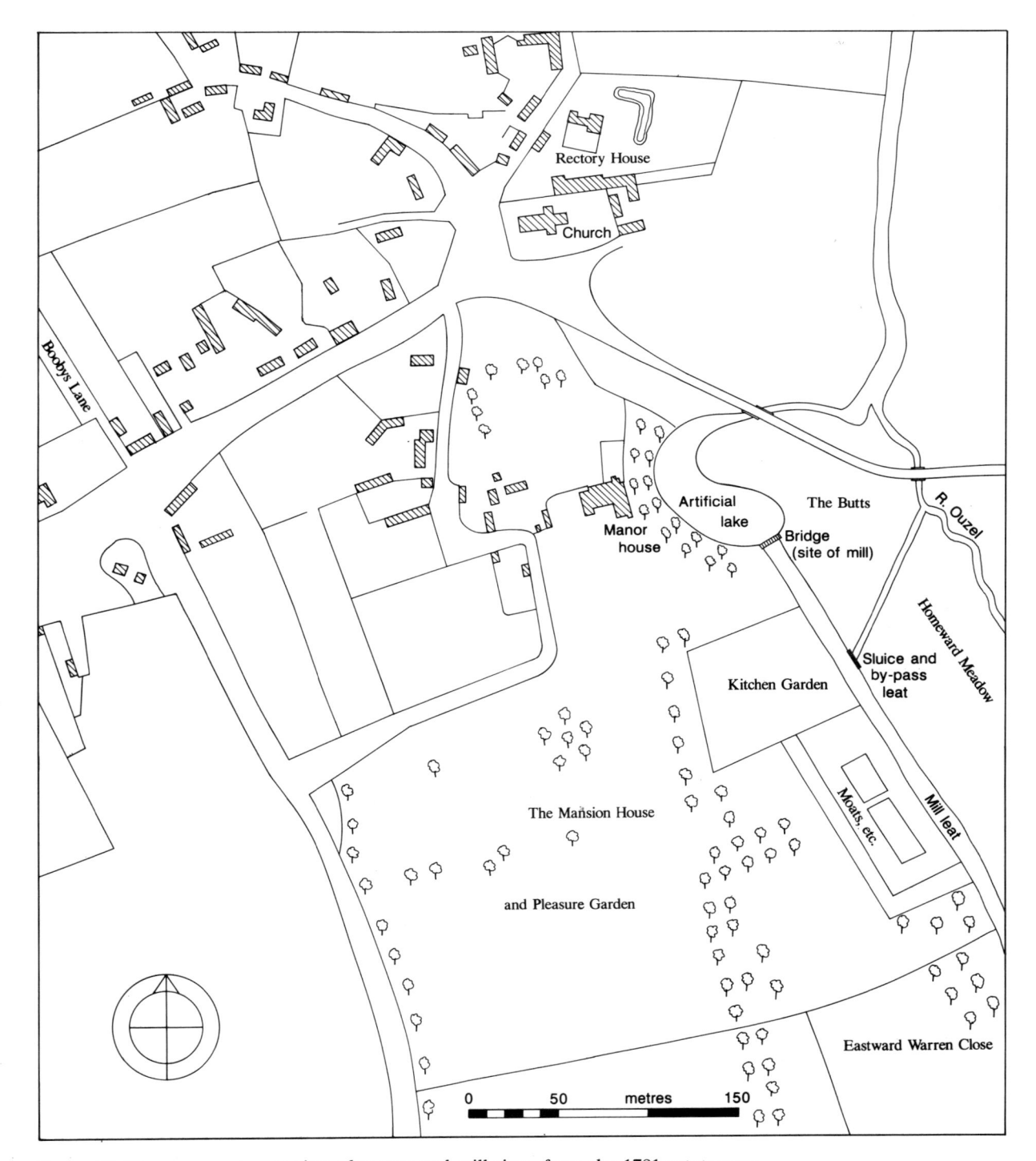

Figure 58: Simpson; reconstruction of manor and mill sites, from the 1781 estate map.

This cut followed the line of an earlier leat serving Simpson Mill, which stood a short distance downstream from the moat. Since the moat and fishponds were constructed against the leat they may post-date the mill. However, the possibility that the mill, moat and fishponds were contemporary cannot be excluded.

The moat was fed from the leat by a channel which ran to the south of the fishponds at right angles to the leat, and then turned north skirting the ponds, entering the south-east corner of the moat. There was a short overflow channel at this point back to to the leat so that the level of water could be effectively controlled.

The two rectangular fishponds lie between the river channel and the moat leat. There is no obvious feed to them, but slight breaks in the south-east and north-east corners may indicate entry and exit points for water. The ponds would also have been fed by seasonal rises in the water table. Although now silted up, the ponds were probably 1.5 m to 2 m deep when in use.

The interpretation of the site of the manor house and formal gardens is aided by comparison of the earthwork survey, the estate map of 1781 (Figs 58 and L8) and a watercolour of the manor house, reputedly by W.H. Hanmer and dated to about 1782, which shows the main house and a small timber bridge across the mill leat (Markham 1973, Plate 24).

The two fishponds, the line of the leat to the former water mill and the mill pool are shown on the 1781 map, although the mill pool had probably by then been landscaped into an attractive garden feature. The moat is shown as the *Kitchen Garden*, suggesting that the area within the platform was being cultivated to provide food for the main house.

The field name *Warren* occurs in 1611 in a survey of lands held by William Duncombe in Bletchley, Fenny Stratford and Simpson. In this survey there is mention of "a third of a close of pasture called the Warren also the Conygree lying in Sympson. . ." (Herts CRO. 12314). Both of these names suggest a place where rabbits were kept and allowed to breed, a common practise in the medieval period. The name *Warren Close* is recorded on the 1781 map, and the area had been divided up into three closes when the map was drawn. Three roughly circular mounds in this area were excavated in 1978. Their precise date was not established but they were clearly later than the ridge-and-furrow, and were perhaps constructed as small circular pillow mounds for rabbits in the grounds of the manor house.

THE FIELD SYSTEM

The ridge-and-furrow in the parish is shown in Fig. 59. A glebe terrier of 1674 gives the names of three fields; *North*, *Middle* and *South* (Bodleian Willis Mss 100, 126). The North Field probably consisted of all of the land to the north of the Groveway, the South Field all of the land to the south of the Fenny Stratford road, and the Middle Field the remaining land in between. The glebe terrier states that the North Field contained both arable and meadow land, and the 1781 map shows that the Rectory held two fields on the western side of the river, totalling more than eight acres. A number of meadow names are listed in 1674: *Little Mead*, *Land Mead*, *Great Mead*, *Calcotsham*, and *Watermead*, all of them presumably valuable meadowland adjacent to the Ouzel.

The parish was enclosed in about 1770, and the award was enrolled in 1771 (Tate 1946, 33). The enclosure map is missing, but oral tradition refers to a map surviving in the village into the 1970s. The 1781 estate map, drawn up only ten years after the enclosure, was almost certainly based on the enclosure map, and contains evidence of the ways in which lands were allotted amongst the various landholders in the parish. The demesne land held by Sir Walden Hanmer, baronet, amounted to just over 407 acres, and he was the largest single landholder at that date. A number of other individuals held large parcels; John Newman, Thomas Pancoust, Thomas Goodman and another branch of the Goodman family, John Goodman from Loughton. The Rectorial estate was centred in the North Field area and amounted to just over 227 acres. The majority of the hedgerows which survive in the parish date from this period.

OTHER LANDSCAPE FEATURES

THE MILL

A mill in the parish on the estate of the Bishop of Coutances valued at ten shillings is listed in the Domesday survey. There are a number of medieval references to the mill, but the most informative of these dates from the mid fifteenth century. This is the report of Gilbert Ippiswell, bailiff for the de Grey family estates in Woughton, Bletchley and Simpson, in which he states "Also in the decaye of the mille of Sewenestoun thys yere, overe 30s resseyuid there 33s 4d" (Grey of Ruthin Valor, Beds. Hist. Rec. Soc. XLVI, 1967, 118). In addition to this, Gilbert referred to John le Millere of Sewenestoun, who owed 13s 4d to the manor.

When the Hatch family held the manor in the middle of the seventeenth century there is refer-

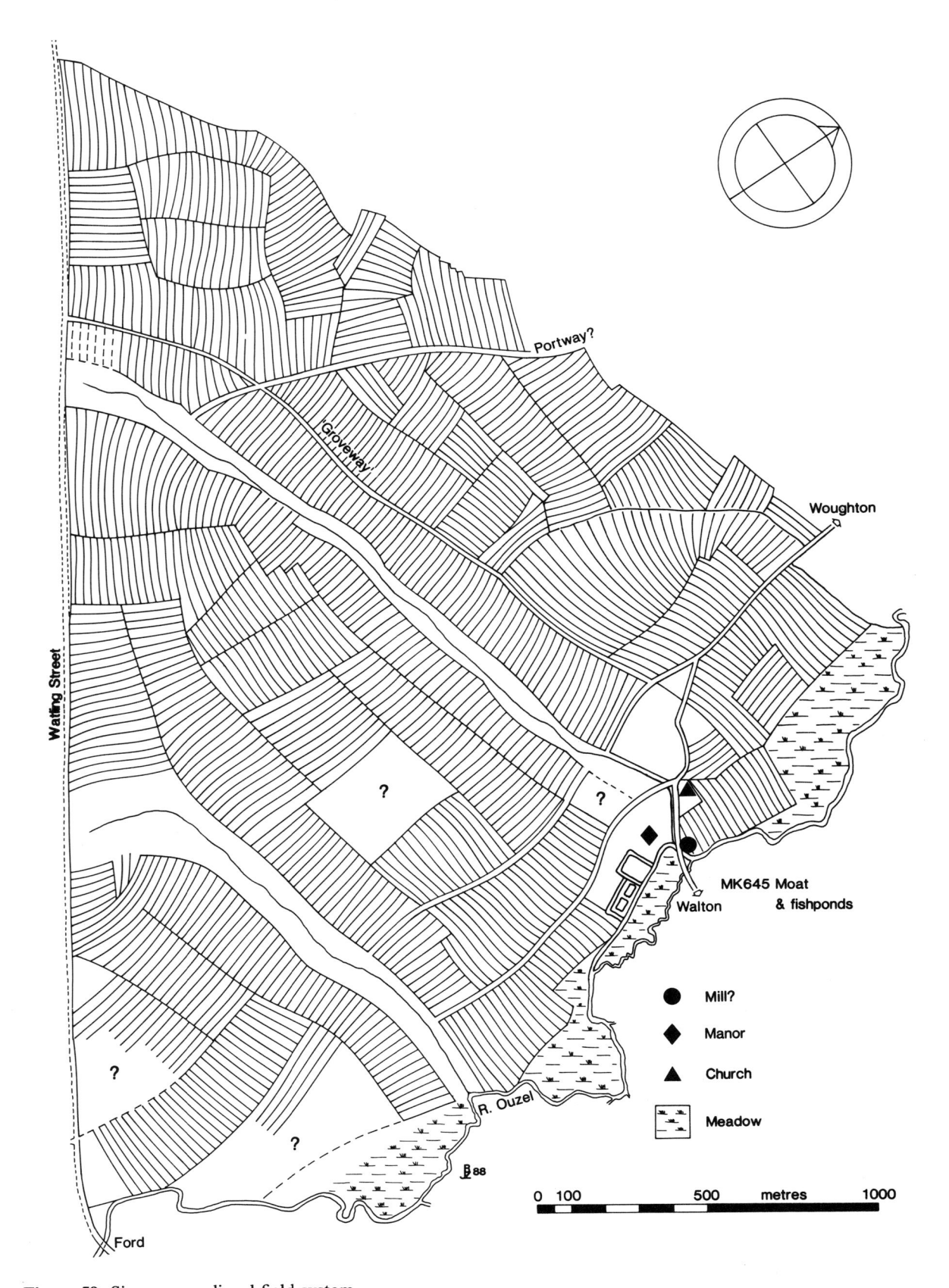

Figure 59: Simpson medieval field system.

ence to a mill in Simpson which contained "two mills under one roof". The same document also refers to a mill house and a field name *Mill Holmes* (VCH 1927, 460).

There are no mill-related names on the 1781 map, but the position of the rectangular structure at the end of the mill leat at the head of what appears to be the mill pond suggest that perhaps the base of the mill survived at that time. Until recently the surviving earthworks represented one of the best-preserved mill channels on the Ouzel. However, recent dredging works have seriously damaged them, and during this work traces of brickwork were found in the west bank.

The parish boundary follows the line of the old river channel, so the mill leat was cut through meadow land between the manor and the river. It is possible that an earlier meander was straightened and deepened to form the leat, as at Caldecotte, about 1 km upstream. In order to control the flow of water in this part of the valley it was necessary to construct a number of small sluice gates to prevent the mills from being flooded. During the construction of Caldecotte Lake in 1981 the remains of a sluice-like feature (MK1011) were found approximately 100 m south of the site of the mill. This feature consisted of a substantial brick and timber structure on the east bank of the leat, from which a silted channel led north-eastwards to the original course of the river (Fig. 57). It is suggested that this feature may have been an overflow sluice gate to take water away from the main channel to prevent flooding and to control water reaching the mill (Zeepvat *et al.*, forthcoming). The line of the overflow channel can be seen both on aerial photographs (Plate 28) and on the 1781 map. Whether this is the weir mentioned in 1574 (VCH 1927, 549) is uncertain.

WOODLAND

Although no woodland survives in the parish today, the place-name *Wood Farm* is an indicator of an area of former woodland which was shown on the 1781 estate map as *Simpson Wood*, covering just over thirty acres. There are several wood-related field names adjacent to the wood, indicating that it was previously larger. The road name *Groveway* may well have referred to the way to the wood or grove.

The wood was probably planted in the fifteenth or sixteenth century, since it overlay medieval ridge-and-furrow. The first documentary reference to the wood dates from 1635, when John Hatch, who held part of the manor, bequeathed *Pillgrove Wood* to his wife (VCH 1927, 459). The western side of the wood was destroyed by the construction of the London to Birmingham Railway in about 1839, while the remainder was cleared during the nineteenth century.

BRICKWORKS

A number of brickworks are known to have existed in the parish. The most extensive and long-lived was on the south side of the village, by the canal. This was operated by the Clarke family in the middle of the nineteenth century (BCM 1979, 32), and the associated wharf was used for the transfer of bricks to help build new houses in Bletchley, Wolverton and New Bradwell. A number of other brickyards and a limekiln existed in the parish.

CANAL

The parish is crossed north to south by the Grand Union Canal, which was constructed in about 1800. The route taken by the canal truncated the line of the old road along the east side of the green, resulting in the sharp right-angled bend in the village street and forcing all traffic to go past the church before rejoining the old route to Woughton. A shallow lock and a lock-keeper's cottage were built at Fenny Stratford, and a small wharf and swing bridge were built to the south of Manor Farm. The recent restoration of the keeper's cottage has preserved an interesting part of the industrial heritage in Milton Keynes.

RAILWAY

The south-east corner of the parish is crossed by the Bedford branch of the former London and North Western Railway line. A small station was erected at Fenny Stratford in 1846, when the line opened.

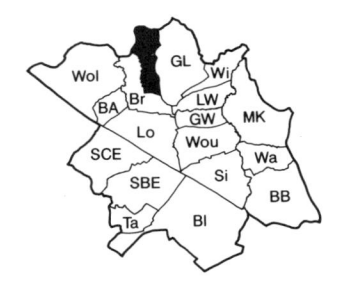

STANTONBURY

INTRODUCTION

The parish of Stantonbury (Fig. 60) was situated on the south side of the River Ouse, between the parishes of Bradwell and Great Linford. The parish, which contained some 326 ha, was a long thin rectangular area of land running southwards from the Ouse to the higher ground of Bradwell Common, near Linford Wood. Like its neighbouring parishes, its northern end was not included in the designated area of Milton Keynes. The geology is largely Boulder clay, with outcrops of Blisworth and Cornbrash limestone.

The northern parish boundary was the Ouse, into which Stanton Brook, the eastern boundary, ran northwards from Stanton Wood, which formed the western edge of Linford Wood. The boundary then turned westwards, running along the road to Bradwell village for a distance of 0.8 km before turning north to follow furlong boundaries back to the Ouse.

The village was established close to the river on the Ouse valley route from Buckingham to Bedford. A second road ran south from the village to the southern end of the parish, where it joined the road from Bradwell to Great Linford and Secklow.

ARCHAEOLOGY

A large part of the northern end of the parish was totally destroyed during gravel extraction in the thirty years before the development of Milton Keynes. The unhelpful attitude of the gravel company and the lack of adequate resources for archaeology resulted in the village site being destroyed with only a few days rescue work allowed (Mynard 1971) and extensive Iron Age and Roman settlements being only partly excavated (Woodfield 1989).

Before the Conquest, Stanton Low was the site of an Iron Age village, linked by a ford across the Ouse to a similar site at Haversham. With the arrival of the Romans, the settlement was abandoned and a series of ditches cut across it as part of an extensive land drainage project.

In the late first or early second century, a group of huge timber barns or storehouses and a timber wharf were built adjacent to the river, the whole being enclosed by a massive ditch, faced with stone on its inner side. The area thus enclosed covered some 3.75 ha. Some of the barns were later destroyed by fire.

In the mid second century a large bath-house was built, containing several mosaics and evidence of painted internal columns and other opulent decoration. Linked to this, and fronting the river, were more massive buildings. Further downstream were two more large and wealthy buildings, probably houses, one of which had a courtyard and tower granary added to it. Yet more buildings of a similar nature fronted the river. In the late third century there were signs of refurbishment in several of the buildings, including the insertion of heating systems into the two houses. In the later fourth century the site declined, and was used for iron and bronze working. Part of one house was turned into a lime kiln. By the end of the century occupation on the site seems to have ceased.

THE MEDIEVAL AND LATER VILLAGE

Whilst a few sherds of eighth to ninth-century pottery were found on the village site, there was no evidence of settlement of that date. The earliest pottery from the village was of the tenth to eleventh century, and as with most other local villages this was probably the date of its establishment.

The village was called *Stantone* at the time of the Domesday survey, and this name, meaning 'Stone Tun' (settlement), suggests that most of the buildings were constructed of local limestone. It was sited to the west of the Roman settlement mentioned above, which would probably have been visible as a series of ruined buildings, representing a useful source of building materials. It is therefore no coincidence that the rubble cores of the ruined walls of the village church contained Roman tile. The church dates from at least the twelfth century and was originally larger than the

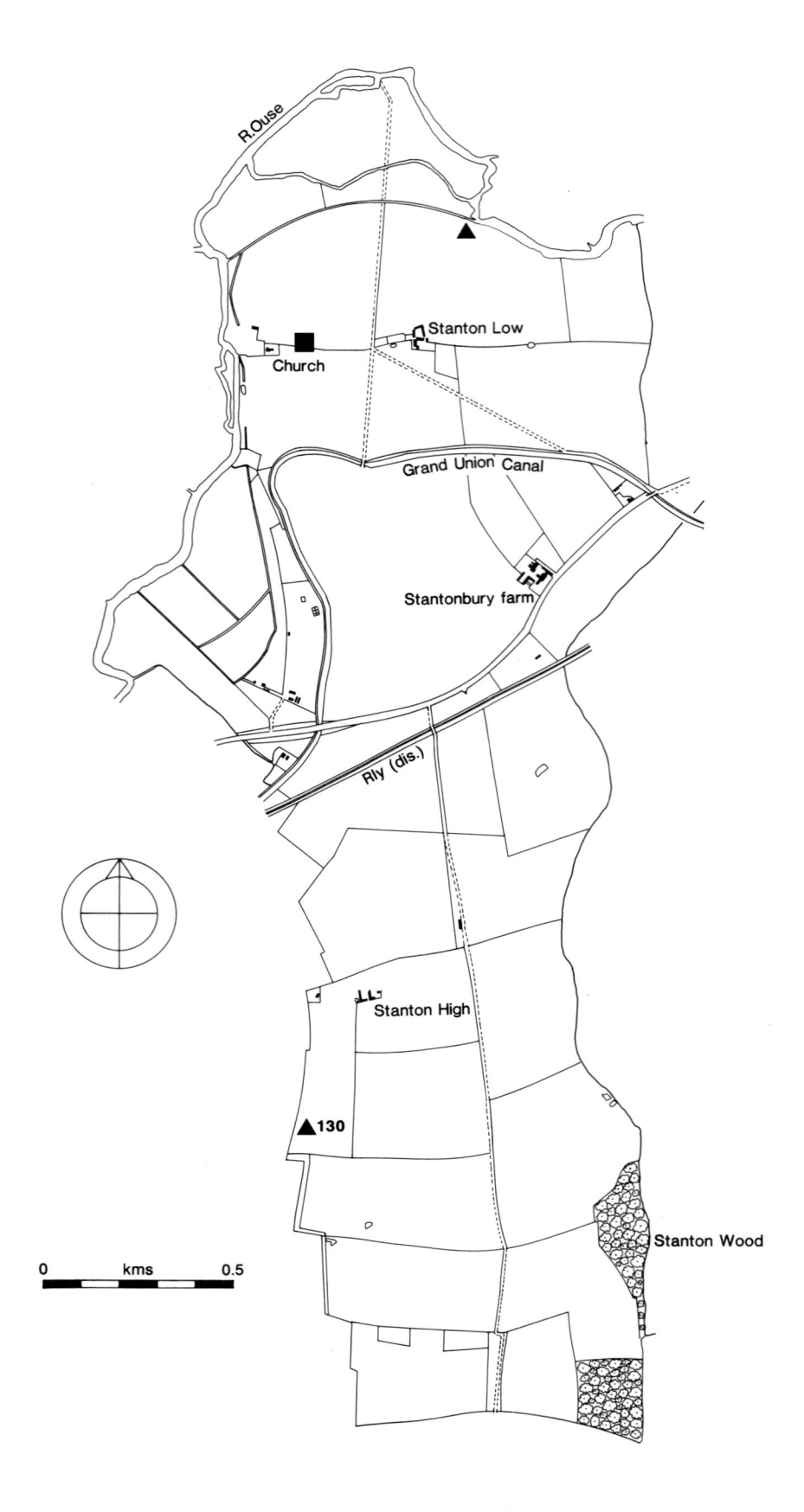

Figure 60: Stantonbury parish in 1967, showing major archaeological sites.

Plate 29: Stantonbury village earthworks and church, c.1950. *(MKAU)*

present two-cell ruin suggests (Mynard 1971, 21–22).

The village (Plate 29) was a linear development with the crofts and house sites laid out along the north side of the east-west road. The church and manor house were at the west end, and several of the crofts at the east contained ridge-and-furrow, suggesting that the village had extended eastwards from the church and manor into the ploughed furlongs of the open field.

The manor was held by the *Barre* family in the early thirteenth century, and their name was added to that of the village changing it to 'Stanton Barry' which eventually became Stantonbury (VCH 1927, 462). There are few references to the early manor, but an inquisition taken after the death of Thomas Barry in 1326 lists the manor house, a broken mill, a ruined dovecote, a fishery, 100 acres of arable land, 14 acres of meadow and 3 acres of wood. At that time there were only eight villagers paying rent to the lord for land and houses (PRO C/134/95/4). During the fifteenth century the manor came into the ownership of the Vaux family of Harrowden, Northants., who enclosed much of the parish and depopulated the village (Leadam 1897, 210).

In the mid seventeenth century the manor was owned by the Witterwonge family and Sir John Wittewonge, Baron of Stantonbury, rebuilt the manor house in the 1660s (Herts CRO, D/ELW). In 1721 the manor was purchased by Sarah, Duchess of Marlborough, and passed to her descendants the Spencers who demolished the house in 1791.

Lipscomb stated that there were only four houses left in the village in 1736 (Lipscomb 1847, 345). The 1881 OS map shows only the church and three farms, of which the only survivor is Stantonbury Farm, now called Stantonbury Park Farm, situated on the road from Bradwell to Newport Pagnell, which marks the city's northern boundary.

In 1857 the parish was extended to include the railway settlement in Bradwell parish, and the old church dedicated to St Peter served the new parish until the erection of the church of St James in New Bradwell in 1860. The old church was regularly used and was in good order until the 1920s, after which it was neglected and fell into disrepair. In the early 1950s the Norman chancel arch was removed from St Peter's and re-erected in St James' church. The old church suffered from vandalism in the next decade, and finally in 1956 the chancel

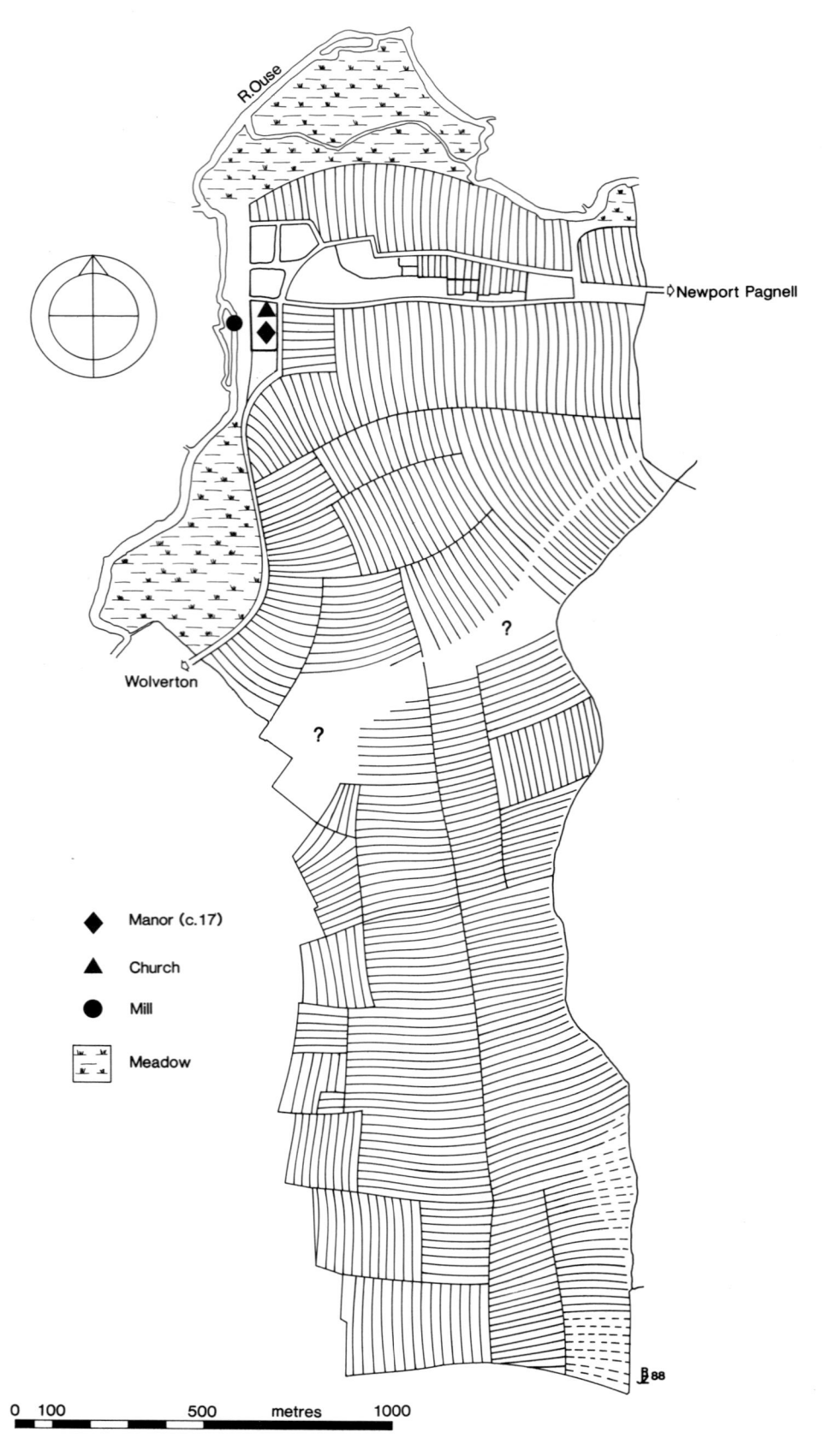

Figure 61: Stantonbury medieval field system.

roof collapsed and the church became the ruin that remains to this day. The farmhouse and buildings to the south-east of the church were demolished in advance of gravel quarrying, and the village site was destroyed in 1966–67.

THE FIELD SYSTEM

The ridge-and-furrow of the medieval field system is shown in Fig. 61, and all of the land apart from the low-lying meadows was ploughed. There are few extant documents that refer to the fields of Stantonbury. The Barre family held both Bradwell and Stantonbury manors in the thirteenth century, and whilst there are numerous documents relating to their land in Bradwell there is little for Stantonbury. It may be that the references to their fields in Bradwell actually include land in Stantonbury; for example is *Stanton Field* really in Bradwell (NRO Misc. Ledger 383)? Much of the parish was enclosed in the sixteenth century (Tate 1946, 18) and remained pasture until recent years.

OTHER LANDSCAPE FEATURES

MILL

The site of the mill was to the west of the village, where the mill leat and the island it created can be seen.

CANAL

The Grand Junction Canal passed through the parish, and had little effect apart from making access to the fields in the north of the parish difficult, in that they could only be approached by crossing the canal.

CLAY PITS AND BRICK KILNS

The earthworks to the south-east of the church and the manor contain clay pits, and presumably also the sites of the kilns that were used to make the bricks for the erection of the new manor house in the 1660s (Herts CRO, D/ELW, fol. 220).

TATTENHOE

R.J. Ivens

INTRODUCTION

The small and roughly rectangular parish of Tattenhoe was situated in the south-western corner of the city, and was bounded by the parishes of Shenley Brook End, Bletchley, Newton Longville and Whaddon. The parish's northern border with Shenley Brook End was of the classic 'dog-leg' pattern formed by following woodland and field boundaries. The eastern and southern boundaries were relatively straight, and appear to have followed the lines of early routeways (see also Bletchley and Shenley). Apart from a short border shared with Whaddon, the greater part of Tattenhoe's eastern end was occupied by a formerly detached portion of Newton Longville (Fig. 62).

The parish was one of the smallest within Milton Keynes, occupying only 262 ha. It was drained to the north-east by the Loughton Brook, which roughly bisected it. The highest part of the parish, over 120 m OD, was on the western edge where it borders Whaddon. On the northern side of the brook the land rises quite steeply before levelling off towards Howe Park Wood and Shenley Brook End. To the south of the brook the ground rises gently towards Windmill Hill in Bletchley where it levels off at around 120 m. The northern half of the parish was a low spur of land running from west to east. This topographical feature is mirrored in the name Tattenhoe, *i.e.* 'Tata's spur of land' (Gelling, above). The greater part of the parish contained heavy ill-drained clay soils derived from the underlying Boulder clay.

The deserted village of Tattenhoe was situated in the northern and central parts of the parish, well away from any of the modern through routes in Milton Keynes. The southern boundary of the parish ran along the Bletchley to Buckingham road, and the village earthworks and church were linked to this road by a footpath. This may represent the line of the original route through the parish which crossed Loughton Brook at a bridging point a little north of Water Spinney, and then snaked its way to Westbury and Shenley. On the southern side of the Buckingham Road, this path continued to Newton Longville. The North Bucks Way runs close to and parallel with the western boundary of the parish. During the post-medieval period this was an important drovers' road, used for taking livestock to London. There are no known links between Tattenhoe village and this drovers' road. A number of minor trackways link the three main farms with their surrounding fields.

ARCHAEOLOGY

A scatter of Bronze Age and other flints have been found in the parish, and Roman finds are relatively common. However, there is as yet no evidence of any prehistoric or Roman settlement. Similarly, there is very little evidence of Saxon occupation. Excavations on the deserted medieval village suggest a very late Saxon or more likely, a Saxo-Norman date for the first settlement on the site (Ivens *et al.*, forthcoming). The recent (1992) discovery and excavation of a small early Saxon cemetery near the southern boundary of the parish at least suggests there was a Saxon settlement in the vicinity, though not necessarily within the parish.

THE MEDIEVAL VILLAGE

Much of the village site will be developed and consequently destroyed. However, it was already badly damaged by modern ploughing and has been extensively excavated. The church, moat, fishponds and adjacent areas have been preserved as part of the City's parks system.

The site of the moat has been known for many years. It was noted by Lipscomb in 1842 and Sheahan in 1862. Sheahan described the site as "An ancient moat near the church, nearly full of water, encloses about a quarter of an acre of ground – the site of the ancient manor house. There are the remains of fishponds too in the vicinity of the moat". (Sheahan 1862, 759).

The village earthworks (Fig. 63) are aligned along a trackway which runs southwards for almost 700 m from the moat and church in the north to Loughton Brook in the south. Aerial photographs

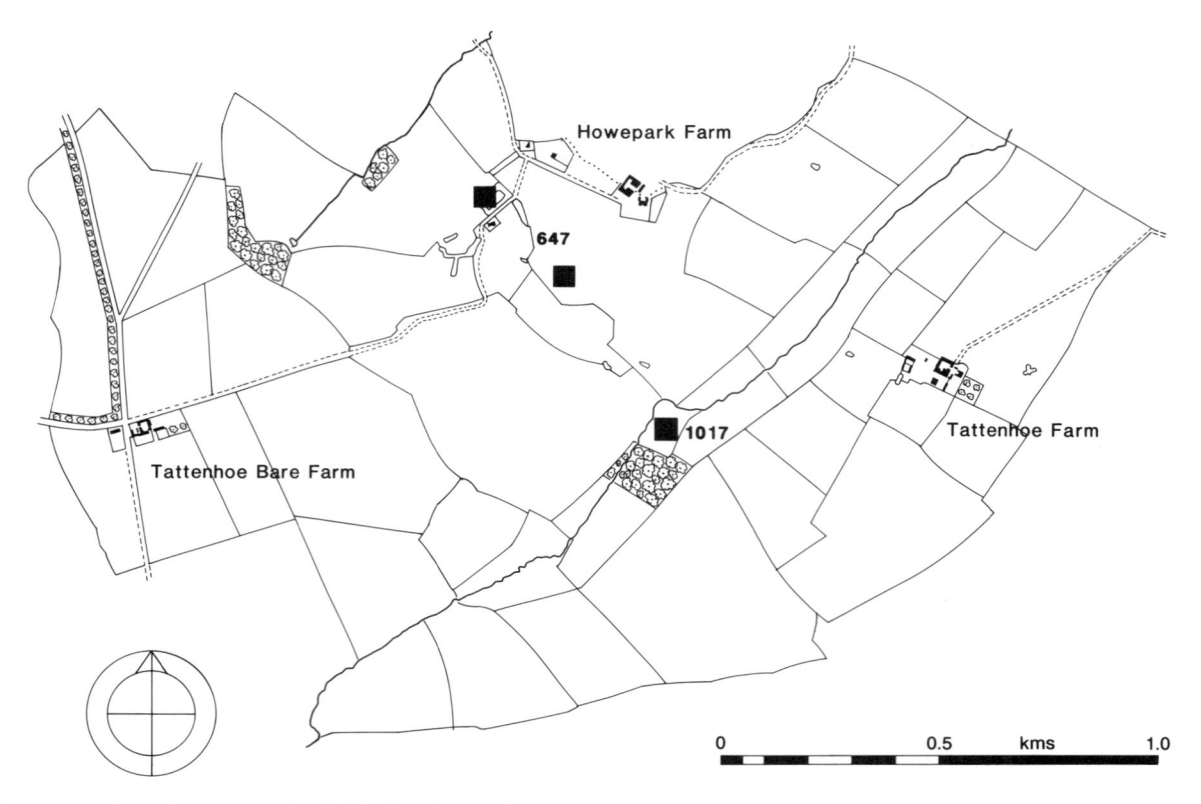

Figure 62: Tattenhoe parish in 1967, showing major archaeological sites.

taken in the mid 1960s show the extensive and relatively clear nature of the earthworks, and the effects of subsequent plough damage can be clearly seen by comparing these early photographs with those taken in 1979 by the RCHM(E) (Plates 30 and 31).

The most obvious feature of the earthworks is the moated site at the northern end of the village. It is rectangular in shape with a stone revetted causewayed entrance on its south-eastern side. The central platform is 40×20 m. The moat itself is very well-preserved, with straight and very steep sides. A pronounced external bank survives on three sides of the moat. At its northern corner a 5 m wide channel links the moat with a long rectangular fishpond measuring 70×15 m, which in turn drains away northwards into a roadside ditch. This pond has marked banks on its northern and southern sides, and its shape and regular nature suggests that it was in contemporary use with the main moat.

A short straight channel may also be seen at the east end of the churchyard, and a long narrow pond runs southwards from the south-east corner of the moat. Both of these appear to be fed from the moat, and are presumably part of the original design.

A little to the south-west of the church were a series of linked fishponds which have been partly filled in recent years; three survive in a reasonably intact form.

The area immediately south of the church has been ploughed almost flat, but excavation has shown that the remains of a number of substantial later medieval structures survive below ground level.

The church is the only surviving building on this part of the site. It is of sixteenth-century construction; tradition records that it was built in 1540 using materials from Snelshall Priory. The only medieval element that survives in the church is the fourteenth-century church bell which is inscribed " + PETRUS DEVESTON MEFACIT". Peter de Weston was a well known bell-founder who died in the summer of 1347 (Cocks 1897, I9 and 591). The present church is certainly a re-building of an earlier church that was probably on the same site, as in c.1215 Ralph Martel confirmed the grant of his grandmother Sibilla (Sibyl de Angerville) of the chapel of Tattenhoe to the monks of Snelshall (Jenkins 1952, No. 2). The record of Sibilla's land in Tattenhoe, which dates to before 1167, is the earliest known reference to the parish.

Tattenhoe is one of the few parishes in this area not mentioned in Domesday, and it was probably included with the Shenleys. Certainly at later periods the two manors are often described and held together. In the sixteenth century, the men of

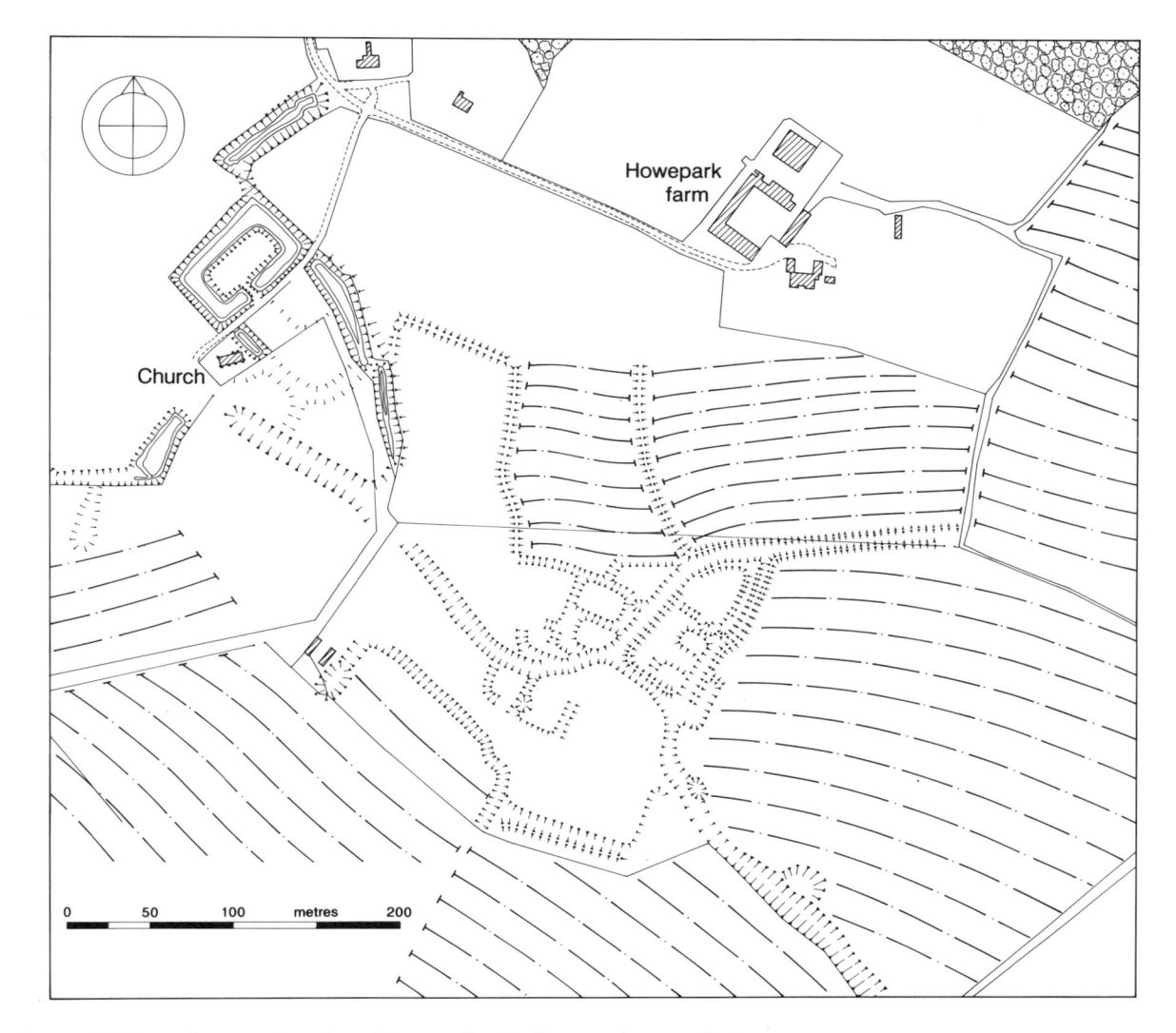

Figure 63: Tattenhoe; earthworks of the medieval village and moated site.

Shenley claimed that Tattenhoe was not a manor at all but merely a part of Shenley. This claim was disproved when Court Rolls and deeds were produced as evidence of Tattenhoe's manorial status (VCH 1927, 434).

The southern part of the village has been extensively excavated, and shown to consist of a number of small enclosures and house platforms set alongside a meandering hollow-way or sunken road.

In general terms it appears that the earliest settlement occupied the higher ground to the east of the present church and probably dates to the later eleventh and twelfth centuries. In the thirteenth and fourteenth centuries the village seems to have migrated southwards. It is likely that this was part of a reorganisation connected with the construction of the moated site and the fishponds. This southern part of the settlement does not seem to have survived the fifteenth century, and as a village the settlement was already deserted by the sixteenth century, though several individual farms survived until the present day.

If, as it appears, there was a major reorganisation of the village in the thirteenth century, then one may suppose that this was at the instigation of one of the families who held the manor during this period. Likely canditates are Paul Pever, or William de Jarpenville or his descendants, who held Tattenhoe for almost all of the thirteenth and fourteenth centuries (VCH 1927, 432–434). Coincidentally perhaps, Paul Pever also held Great Woolstone, where there is also a fine series of fishponds.

The only specific medieval reference to major earth-moving occurs in 1227 when Cecilia, abbess of St Mary de Pratis, Northants., later Delapre Abbey, brought a suit against Ralf de Totenhal and Nicholas Haversham for raising dykes in Totenhal. She later withdrew the action (Jenkins

Plate 30: Tattenhoe village earthworks, c.1965. (© *British Crown Copyright 1993/MOD reproduced with the permission of the Controller of Her Britannic Majesty's Stationery Office*)

1942, 17 and 21). While this may refer to the construction of the moat and fishponds or perhaps to the pond in Water Spinney, it could equally describe a feature such as the hedge-ditch which still survived in Tattenhoe Bare as recently as 1604 (VCH 1927, 434).

OTHER LANDSCAPE FEATURES

WATER SPINNEY

To the south of the village in the Loughton Brook valley is a small nineteenth-century covert known as *Water Spinney*. This is bounded on three sides by a substantial earthwork bank, up to 3 m high, and the site is probably best explained as a medieval fishpond and dam. The earthwork would have functioned as a dam, blocking the small stream which once ran through the site and so creating an extensive though shallow fishpond. No parallel for this earthwork exists within Milton Keynes, though several examples of this type of fishpond are known in South Northants., for example at Silverstone (RCHM 1982, 132–133). As well as acting as a fishpond this dam was probably also used to control the water level in this part of the valley; indeed, this may well have been its primary function.

WINDMILL

In 1910 a low mound situated about one kilometre to the south-east of Tattenhoe church was opened and sherds of medieval pottery recovered. This was interpreted as the mound of a windmill (RCHM 1913, 294). The site now forms part of Windmill Hill Golf Course. Its location is plotted by the Ordnance Survey and also on the Salden Estate map of 1599 (Fig. L11). There is good documentary evidence for the construction of this windmill, and it is firmly dated to the middle of the thirteenth century. In about 1250, William de Jarpenville (Jarpevile) granted Snelshall Priory a plot of land in the common pasture of *Tateho* within the parish of that vill, upon which the monks may construct a windmill. William also allowed free access to the Prior's men with their horses and baggage, presumably for the carrying of corn and flour (Jenkins 1952, No. 35). In return for this grant, the priory allowed William de Jarpenville and his heirs the right to grind his corn at their mill three times a year without payment (*ibid.*, No. 37).

THE FIELD SYSTEM

It is clear from Fig. 64 that virtually the entire parish was ploughed during the medieval period, and good examples of ridge-and-furrow lie under

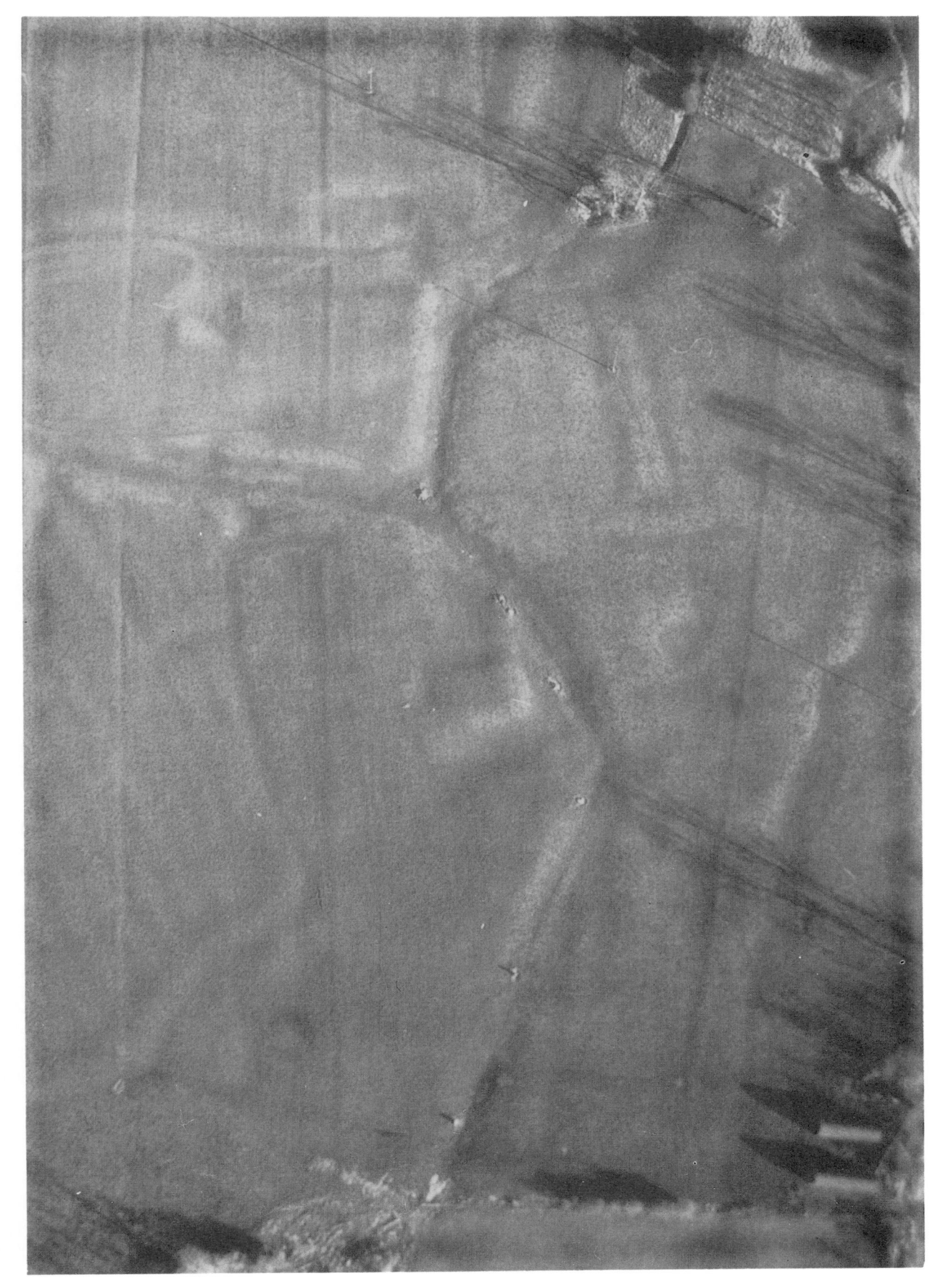

Plate 31: Tattenhoe village earthworks, 1979. *(Royal Commission on the Historical Monuments of England)*

Figure 64: Tattenhoe medieval field system.

pasture in several parts of the parish. Only the area of the village itself and the Water Spinney remain unploughed. The Salden Estate map shows that a limited amount of enclosure had taken place immediately around the village site by the end of the sixteenth century. The Selby Estate map of 1801 shows that the greater part of the parish was enclosed during the seventeenth and eighteenth centuries, with the exception of Tattenhoe Bare and Tattenhoe Common in the south of the parish, and Shenley Common on the western side (Fig. L9). The Selby family interest in the manor dates to the late seventeenth century, when they acquired extensive mortgages on property from Charles Stafford and eventually, in 1732, the estate itself. Thomas James Selby bequeathed the manor along with his Whaddon estates to William Lowndes, in whose family it remained until the twentieth century (VCH 1927, 433).

By the late nineteenth century, the agricultural land was mainly divided between three farms, Tattenhoe Bare Farm in the west, Howepark Farm in the north and Tattenhoe Hall Farm in the south-east. Tattenhoe Bare Farmhouse dates from the early part of the nineteenth century. Tattenhoe Hall Farmhouse is shown on the Selby Estate map, although the existing brick building dates to c.1840–50. The present Howepark Farmhouse was built c.1850, and is the successor to an earlier building located just over the parish boundary in Shenley.

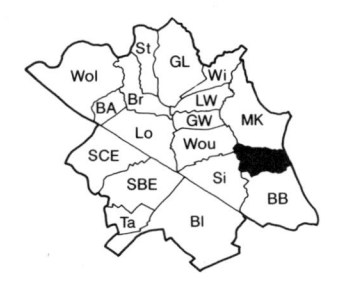

WALTON

INTRODUCTION

The parish of Walton (Fig. 65) was situated on the eastern side of the Ouzel between Bow Brickhill and Milton Keynes and covered some 312 ha. The soil is mainly a heavy clay loam with underlying Oxford and Boulder clays. An outcrop of sand and gravel occurs at the east end of the parish, towards Wavendon. Similar glacial head deposits occur along the northern boundary and in the south-east, towards Woburn Sands. The nearest source of building stone is an outcrop of ferruginous sandstone in the area of the Brickhills, to the south.

The parish rises gradually from the Ouzel to a height of some 89 m OD at its eastern end. Two streams, Caldecotte Brook in the south and a small stream in the north-west corner both drain westwards into the River Ouzel.

The parish was roughly rectangular in shape, with the Ouzel forming its western boundary and Caldecotte Brook its southern boundary, except in the south-west corner where part of Bow Brickhill projects into Walton, close to the river. The eastern boundary with Wavendon followed an almost straight line along medieval furlong boundaries. The northern boundary with Milton Keynes parish ran straight from the Ouzel for more than half of its length, and then followed furlong boundaries until it reached Wavendon parish.

The main road through the parish was the north to south route running along the Ouzel Valley linking Fenny Stratford with Newport Pagnell, passing through the villages of Caldecotte, Walton, Milton Keynes and Willen. The road to Wavendon left the village green at a T-junction and followed a fairly straight route, respecting the medieval furlongs. From Woughton a road crossed the Ouzel at *Monxton's Bridge* (VCH 1927, 515) and continued to the church, where it became the lane running eastwards to the main road, north of the village green. South of the green a road ran down through the meadows to a ford over the Ouzel and thence to Simpson.

ARCHAEOLOGY

Few prehistoric finds have been made in the parish, but it is likely that the terrace gravels may have been occupied, as in the adjacent parishes of Bow Brickhill and Milton Keynes. A few sherds of Belgic and Roman pottery were found during the construction of the Open University complex around Walton Hall.

A large late Iron Age and Roman site was located in 1989 in the north-east corner of the parish, at what is now Wavendon Gate (MK145). Excavation revealed extensive Iron Age occupation, as well as a large early Roman ditched enclosure containing pottery kilns, and both cremation and inhumation burials. The site also produced evidence of Saxon occupation (Williams *et al.* forthcoming). A second Roman site to the north-west of the village was partially examined in 1970 and 1972, when it was confirmed that the site dated from the early second to the mid fourth century (Mynard and Woodfield 1977; Mynard, 1987, 37). Recent evaluation of this site in advance of development has shown that it was similar in extent and character to that at Wavendon Gate, 1.5 km to the east (Zeepvat 1990).

THE MEDIEVAL AND LATER VILLAGE

Walton was not recorded in the Domesday survey, and the earliest evidence of occupation revealed by excavation dates from the twelfth century (Mynard forthcoming). The first known reference to the name dates from the late twelfth century, when the manor was divided into two holdings which became separate manors (VCH 1927, 286).

In 1190 the Bishop of Lincoln granted parochial status to the two manors, which had jointly founded a church and maintained two priests. (Bodleian Willis Mss 24, 125[7]). The right of each manor to present a rector to its half of the church persisted until 1458, when at the request of the two patrons the living was united and one rector represented both manors (VCH 1927, 488). From that time on the patrons presented the new rector

165

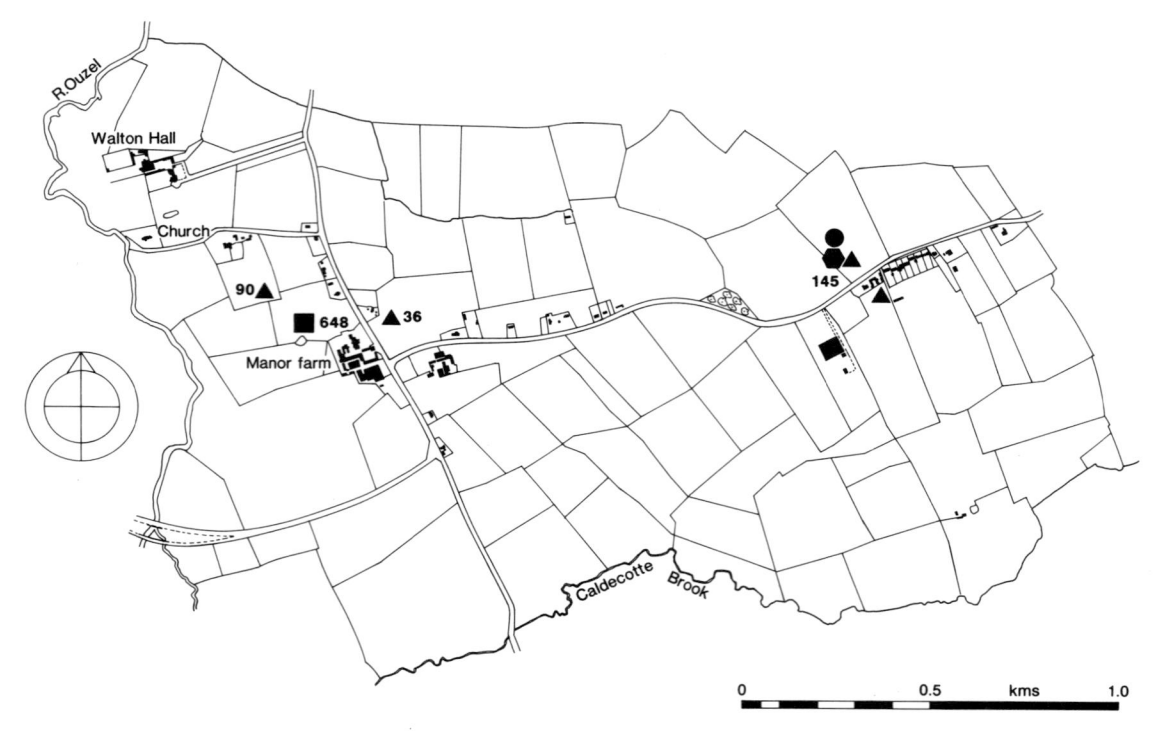

Figure 65: Walton parish in 1967, showing major archaeological sites.

alternately. A watching brief and partial excavation within the church during conversion work in 1975 revealed parts of a fine twelfth-century font buried beneath the Victorian font within the nave. This has been preserved in the Unit's collection.

The archaeological and historical evidence both from the church and the village suggests that the development of Walton occurred sometime during the early to mid twelfth century.

Early spelling of the name was 'Waleton' which may be derived from *Wald-tun* meaning the *Weald* (woodland) *tun* (village) (Gelling, above). There are other examples of *Weald* used in the area, notably in Calverton parish with *Upper*, *Middle* and *Lower Weald*. However, there is no evidence of any early woodland in the parish.

An interesting document of c.1200 records that William de Bray, son of Roger de Bray, lord of one of the manors of Walton, granted two acres of land in Walton to William de Astwith (Bodleian, Radcliffe Mss, deed 321). The description of the location of the land which was granted provides useful information about the parish at that time.

There were five roods in the *North field* next to the croft of Radulph Charge, three roods in the *Southfield* from *Hulwelle* to the croft held by Henry Godsouele; and one rood against *the Grena* next to the rood of Radulph Charge. The grant specifically mentions that on the first five roods William de Bray gave licence to build. This document confirms that the village and the green were already established, and that further building was proposed. It also confirms that a two-field system was in operation.

There are few other extant medieval documentary references to Walton. However, several thirteenth and fourteenth-century documents preserved amongst the Radcliffe Manuscripts in the Bodleian Library at Oxford record field names, tenant's names, and some topographical detail.

The earthworks of the medieval village (Fig. 66), surveyed in 1972 in advance of the construction of city road H9, showed that it consisted of two ends. The northern end, sited on the road to Woughton on the Green around the parish church, contained the site of an early manor house to the north of the church (VCH 1927, 485), and several house sites on the lane leading east from it.

The southern end of the village had a sub-rectangular plan, with a small triangular green at the eastern end, beyond which a road led to Wavendon. This road entered the narrow eastern end of the triangular green and formerly forked, forming two sides of the triangle. The northern fork became disused and remained only as a sunken grassy hollow way, whereas the southern fork survived, joining the Fenny Stratford to Newport Pagnell road at a T-junction. On the west side of the green was Walton Manor (Manor Farm), to the north-west of which another hollow

166

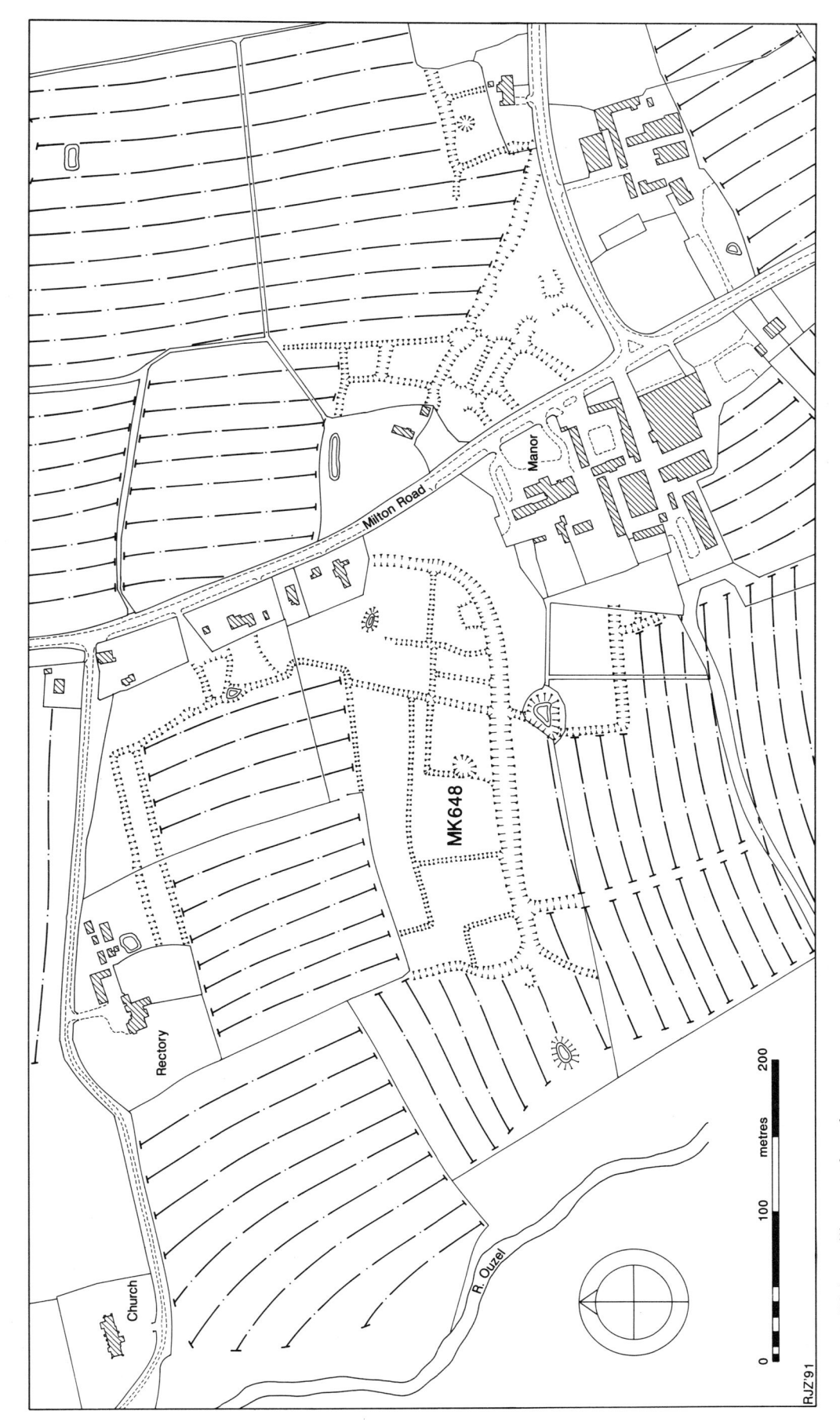

Figure 66: Walton village earthworks.

Plate 32: Walton Hall and Walton church, from south-west, 1968. *(MKAU)*

way led to a rectangular block of house sites and crofts which were partly excavated in 1972 (Mynard forthcoming).

The pre-city village consisted of a few cottages between the church and Walnut Tree Farm. Walton Hall, an early nineteenth-century house (Plate 32), stood within a small decayed park of sixty acres which included the church within its general boundaries and was one of the few surviving parks remaining in the city. This is now the campus of the Open University.

At the southern end of the village Manor Farm and Walnut Tree Farm stood on opposite sides of the Newport Pagnell to Fenny Stratford road. These farms lay adjacent to the green where the Wavendon road joined the north to south route. The 'Pine Tree' public house formerly stood at this junction. The earliest reference to an inn in the parish occurs in 1378, when Peter Bray had an inn next to the highway (Jenkins 1936, 182). We cannot say whether this early inn was on the same site as the 'Pine Tree', but this junction on an important market route was a prime site for such a building.

Walnut Tree Farm and Manor Farm are both timber-framed buildings dating from the sixteenth century (Woodfield 1986, 154–55).

THE FIELD SYSTEM

Apart from the meadowland, all of the parish was ploughed at some time during the medieval period (Fig. 67). As early as the twelfth century the parish had a North and a South Field (Bodleian, Radcliffe Mss, deed 321). The boundary between these fields is unknown, but it is likely that the road from Wavendon to Walton formed part of it, and that the road running west from the green was its western continuation.

An interesting document of 1345 records an agreement between Roger de Grey, lord of Walton, with his free tenants on one part and Philip de Aylesbury, lord of Milton Keynes, with his free tenants on the other part, concerning the rights of intercommoning in both Walton and Milton Keynes (BAS Mss 102/36). Disputes had arisen between the two manors and their tenants concerning the boundaries of the furlongs over which they had post-harvest grazing rights, which could not have been clearly defined. As a result of this, the boundaries would have been formalised, and the dog-leg section of the boundary between the two parishes may be a reflection of this re-arrangement, which obviously followed furlong boundaries.

Table 3 shows names which have been recorded

Figure 67: Walton medieval field system.

Name	Date and Deed No.	Possible Meaning
Le Gorhaluacre	c.1265/473	The Gore Half Acre
Hulwelle	c.1200/321	?
The Grena	c.1300/40	The Green
Le Marsh	" / "	The Marsh
Aladebruge	1296/323	Alade's Bridge
Dikedemede	c.1300/324	Ditch Meadow
Lutlemers	" / "	Little Marsh
Muchelm	" / "	?
Le Shortedole	" / "	The short Dole (area of meadow)
Le Brocfurlong	" / "	The Brook Furlong
Southfield	" / "	The South Field
Le inlande	" / "	The Inland
Genedit virgate	c.1300/325	?
Ashtonfurlong	1339/329	?
Bradeway	1341/331	Broadway
Zendore Smiethenhull	1347/332	?

TABLE 3: Medieval field-names in Walton.

from medieval documents which survive in the Radcliffe Collection of Deeds at the Bodleian Library, Oxford.

The marsh is also referred to as the *Magna Mers de Walton* (Bodleian, Radcliffe Mss 40). There are similar references to a large marsh area in the adjoining parish of Bow Brickhill, which was known as the *Magna Mersa de Bolle Brichull* (BAS Mss 103/36) and was in the area of the hamlet of Caldecotte. These documents show that this part of the Ouzel valley was very wet and presumably liable to extensive flooding, and was therefore used mainly for meadowland.

The reference in 1296 to "One rod of pasture in the meadows of Walton between the pasture of the parson of the town and that of John de Laycestre abutting on suth (south) on stream at *Alfladebruge*" (Bodleian, Radcliffe Mss 323) suggests that the bridge must have been on the stream on the southern parish boundary, later known as the Tillbrook.

There is no formal record of the enclosure of the parish which must have been enclosed by private agreement at an early date. The Lay Subsidy returns of 1524 record that there were twenty heads of households in Walton (Chibnall 1950, 87). Some forty years later the census of 1563 records only fourteen families (Cornwall 1959, 268), and it was perhaps during these years that enclosure and subsequent decline in the population took place.

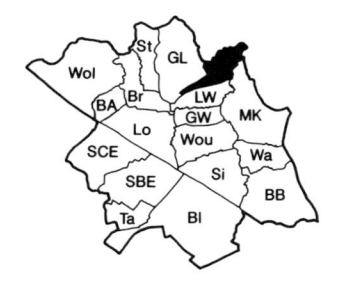

WILLEN

INTRODUCTION

Willen was one of the smallest parishes in the city, covering just over 274 ha (Fig. 68). The village was in the centre of the parish at the junction of the through roads. The church and manor occupied a slightly elevated position overlooking the Ouzel valley at a height of just over 60 m OD.

The underlying geology is mainly of Oxford and Boulder clay in the west of the parish, with an area of Kellaways sands and gravels south-west of the village. On the south and east sides of the parish the Ouzel valley contained areas of meadowland with underlying terrace gravels and head deposits, most of which have been removed with the development of the city. A small area of Cornbrash limestone occurs in the southern half of the parish, on the east side of the canal. The soils are essentially a brown clayey loam and are poorly drained, particularly in the south-west, towards Bradwell Common.

The Ouzel formed the eastern parish boundary with Milton Keynes and Moulsoe parishes. The southern boundary with Little Woolstone followed an almost straight line at right angles to the Ouzel. The northern boundary with Newport Pagnell was of dogleg type following medieval furlong boundaries, indicating that it was probably not a primary boundary. The parish was of an unusual shape, with a long finger of land extending south-westwards between Great Linford and Little Woolstone parishes towards Bradwell Common.

Willen is not mentioned by name in the Domesday survey, and is thought to have been included with Caldecote, a hamlet in the parish of Newport Pagnell, to the north. The manorial histories of Caldecote and Willen were connected in the early medieval period, and the two were described as one vill as late as the fourteenth century (VCH 1927, 503). This may explain the late boundary between these two parishes.

The earliest extant reference to the name of the parish dates from about 1151–54, when the advowson of the church at Willen was held by Tickford Abbey in Newport Pagnell (VCH 1927, 504). At that time the name was spelt *Wilinges*, and is thought to mean 'the place of the willows'.

The parish was crossed by two medieval roads. The north to south road was a route along the western side of the Ouzel Valley, linking Newport Pagnell and Fenny Stratford. The church and manor site were located just to the east of this road. The other road, from Great Linford to Milton Keynes village, crossed the parish from west to east. This route, which came via Willen to take advantage of the bridging point over the Ouzel at Willen Mill, respected the medieval furlong boundaries in Milton Keynes and Willen parishes, but not in Great Linford, and is thought to be of late medieval origin.

ARCHAEOLOGY

Very few prehistoric or Roman finds are recorded from Willen parish. The construction of Willen Lake in 1972 was expected to reveal evidence of prehistoric settlement, but none was found. Excavation of the moat (MK655) beside the Ouzel confirmed that minor Roman and Saxon activity had taken place on the terrace gravels.

THE MEDIEVAL AND LATER VILLAGE

The medieval village, one of the smallest in the city area, was located around the church, and on either side of Milton Road downhill from the church and the manor to the mill on the Ouzel. Medieval croft boundaries survived on the north side of Milton Road, and on the south side vague earthworks (Fig. 69), thought possibly to be the remains of house sites between the ridge-and-furrow and the lane, were watched when they were destroyed by the construction of Willen Lake, but only a few sherds of medieval pottery were found. At the bottom of the hill Milton Road forked, one branch leading to the mill and beyond to Milton Keynes village, the other, shown as a sunken way on Fig. 49, along the west side of the Ouzel to the small moated site and the meadows beyond.

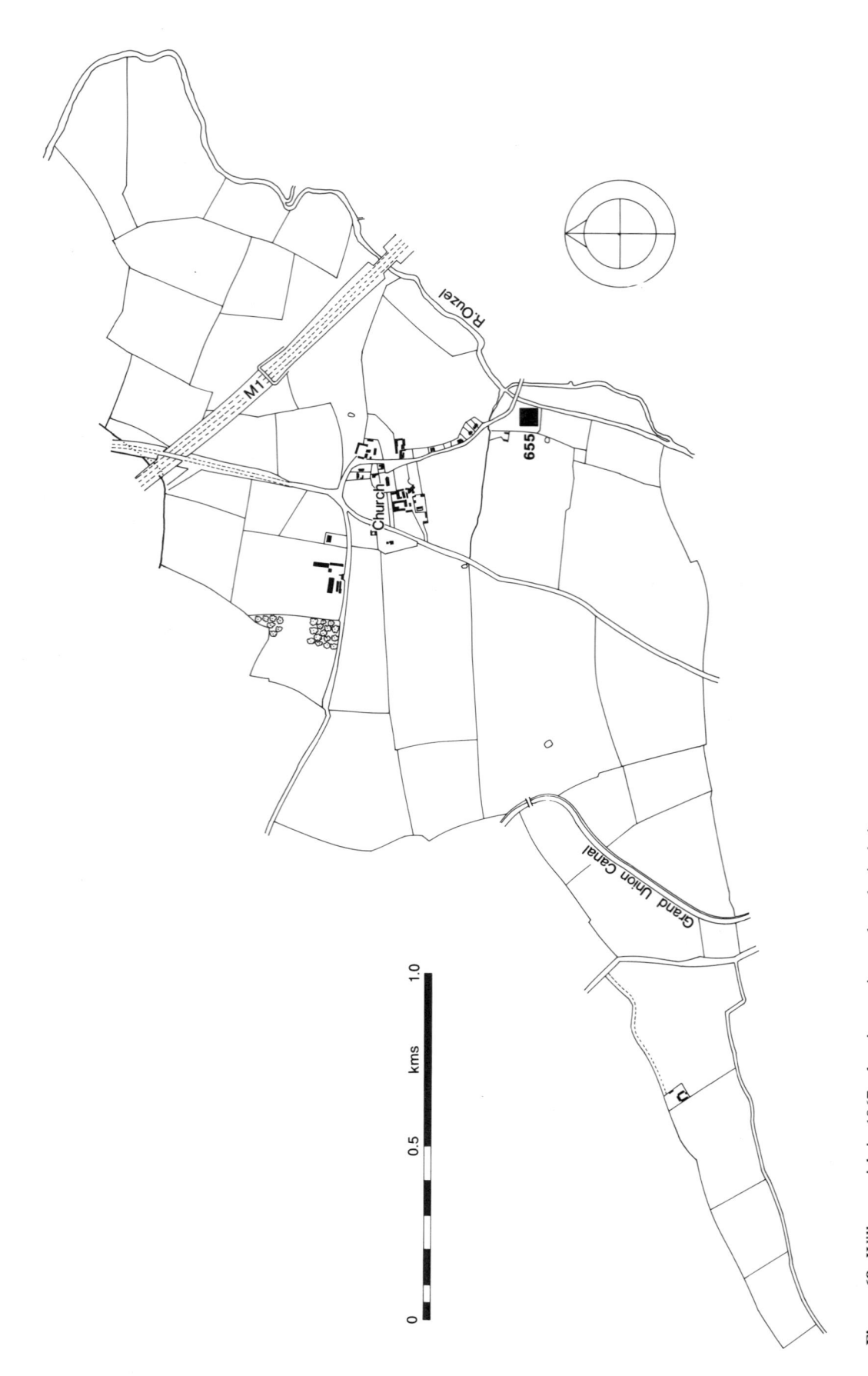

Figure 68: Willen parish in 1967, showing major archaeological sites.

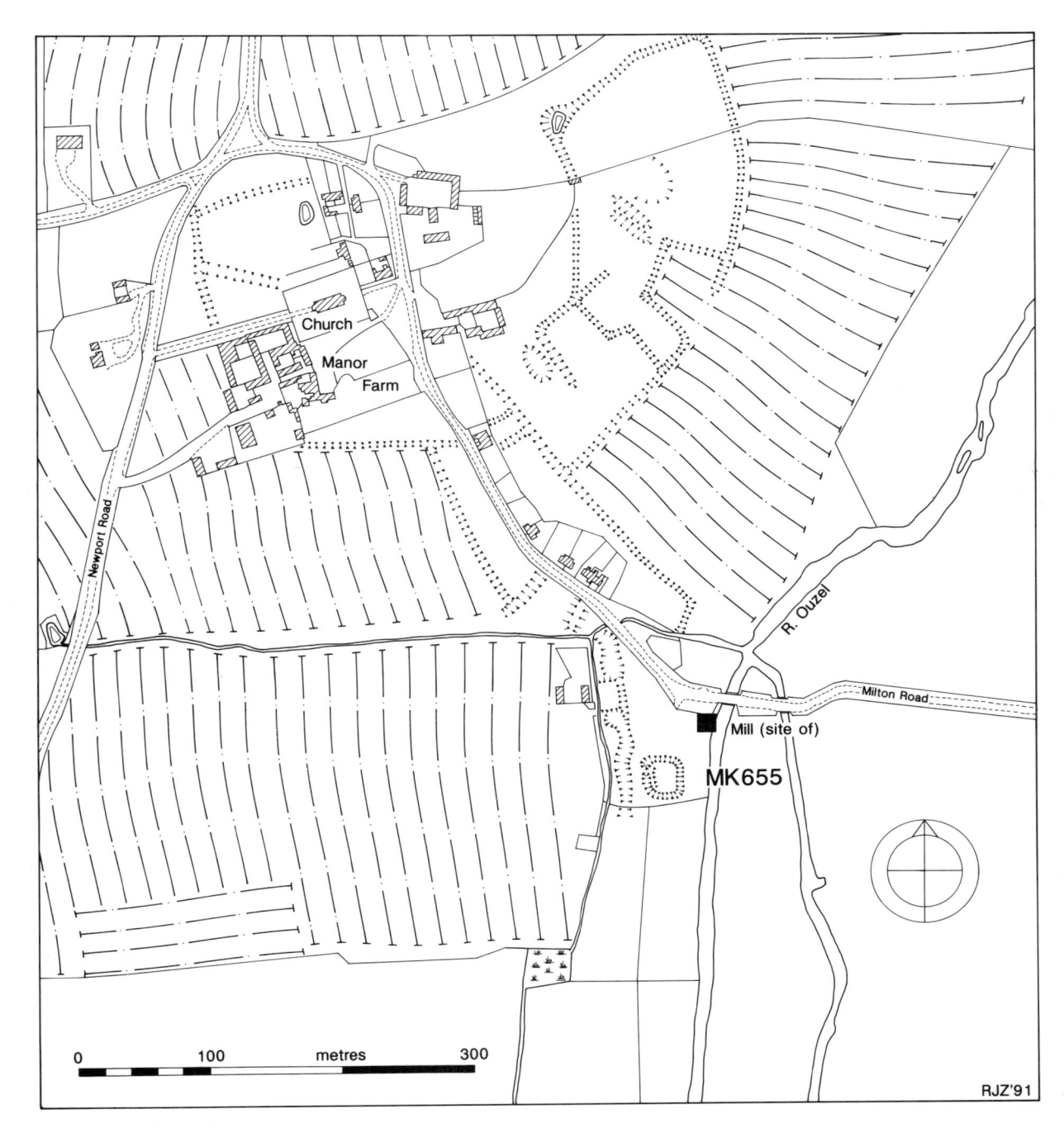

Figure 69: Willen village earthworks.

The mill (Fig. 70) straddled the mill race, and was a timber-framed and weatherboarded building. It was sketched in 1822 by a surveyor carrying out a survey of the estate for Dr Busby's trustees (Westminster Abbey Muniments, Busby Mss.). Three years later the mill equipment was advertised for sale owing to the impending demolition of the mill (Northampton Mercury, June 25th 1825) and in 1888 the vicar of Willen, describing the parish, stated "nor is there any trace of a ruin, except of one wretched little mill". The mill site survived until 1963, when the then Great Ouse River Board filled in the old course of the river, dredged and realigned the former mill race, and erected a new bridge. Subsequently all of these works were swept away with the construction of Willen Lake.

The moated site (MK655) and parts of two crofts between it and Mill Lane were excavated in 1973 prior to their destruction during the construction of Willen Lake, and revealed evidence of activity during the medieval period, ending in the fifteenth century.

north view of the Mill since fallen down

Figure 70: Willen Mill in 1822 (*Westminster Abbey Muniments*).

The moated site was first recorded in 1962 (Mynard, unpublished Ms.) and was surveyed prior to its destruction in 1973. In 1962 it consisted of an almost square island 26×10 m in area. The ditch around this was on average 8 m wide on the west, 6 m on the east, 5.5 m on the north and only 4.5 m wide on the south side. The average depth of the ditch was 1 m below ground level, and only the east and south sides contained water. The original access to the island was by a two-metre-wide causeway on the west side, towards the north-west corner. However, this causeway was blocked by both the outer and inner banks. The outer bank, breached at each corner, survived on the east, south and west sides. It was on average 2 m high and 5 m wide. The inner bank, some 2.5 m wide and 1 m high, remained on the east, north and south sides. The banks were constructed of clay, presumably upcast from the moat. At the north-west corner a small channel linked the moat to a channel 3×18 m aligned north to south, possibly part of an early mill leat. By 1971 the north ditch of the moat had been filled in, and the southern ditch was partly filled by the local farmer.

The rescue excavation of the moat took place over a period of only two weeks. The results confirmed that it was of medieval date and that there had been both Roman and Saxon activity in the area before its construction. It seemed most likely that the moat was constructed by or shortly after the early thirteenth century, and that it was probably contemporary with the mill (Mynard forthcoming). The location of the moat adjacent to the mill leat was similar to that of other Ouzel moats, at Caldecote downstream and Simpson and Woolstone upstream. It is suggested that the mills and moats were constructed at the same time, and that the moats were associated with some form of water or garden management and were not homestead moats.

To the north of the moat on the south-west side of Willen road was a slight house platform, the site of a rambling and decayed structure, possibly of medieval origin (Fig. 71), which like the mill was recorded for posterity by the Busby Trustees' surveyor in 1822 (Westminster Abbey Muniments, Busby Mss). A trial trench was cut through this platform, but no evidence of the cottages other than sherds of fourteenth to nineteenth-century pottery was found. A second house platform was situated to the south-west, on the east side of the sunken way leading to the moat and the meadows. This also was trial-trenched, and whilst no evidence of structures was revealed finds dating from the twelfth to the fifteenth century were recovered (Mynard, forthcoming).

The medieval manor house was on the site now occupied by Willen Hospice, formerly Manor Farm. The medieval church was a simple building consisting of a chancel and nave with a double-

Figure 71: Willen; cottages in Mill Lane, 1822 (*Westminster Abbey Muniments*).

arched bellcote (Bodleian, Willis Mss 186a). It was in poor condition in the early sixteenth century (VCH 1927, 503) and in the next century was replaced by the present church, which was designed by Robert Hooke and built between the years 1679–82 at the expense of Dr Richard Busby. This church is a remarkable building, and has been rightly described as one of the architectural treasures of Milton Keynes (Woodfield 1986, 165).

Dr Busby purchased the manor of Willen in 1671 and spent his retirement here. At his death in 1695 he bequeathed the manor to trustees, and they and their successors managed the estate until the coming of Milton Keynes. Dr Busby's action meant that for almost three hundred years Willen remained more or less unchanged, with little or no development apart from the necessary rebuilding of farmhouses and cottages and the erection of a new school for the village children in 1847.

The pre-city village consisted of Brook Farm and Manor Farm, with a few nineteenth-century cottages near the church and on the north side of Mill Lane. The only outlying farm building was Downs Barn, a nineteenth-century barn situated in the south-west of the parish (Fig. L10). This barn gave its name to the nearby area of Milton Keynes, also called Downs Barn.

THE FIELD SYSTEM

The ridge-and-furrow and the furlongs of the medieval field system of the parish are shown in Fig. 72. A few medieval documents recording land transactions in Willen give the names of individual furlongs (Westminster Abbey Muniments, Busby Mss), but none of the medieval names survived the enclosure of the fields in the mid seventeenth century to appear on later maps.

The earliest reference to the names of the great fields in the parish is a glebe terrier of 1639 (Bodleian, Willis Mss 189b) which gives the names of three open fields; *North Field*, *Middle or West Field* and *South Field*. The glebe terrier also refers to the *Out Meadow*, which can be seen on a map (Fig. 73) of the estate of Dr Richard Busby, dated c.1690 (Westminster Abbey Muniments).

Parts of the parish were enclosed in the sixteenth century (Leadam 1897, 177) and the remainder was enclosed by the Nicholl family in about 1650 (Lipscomb 1847, 408). The 1690 estate map shows the parish shortly after the enclosure.

OTHER LANDSCAPE FEATURES

The Grand Union Canal passed through the southern part of the parish, but had no effect upon the village itself. The M1 motorway runs north-west to south-east across the parish in a deep cutting on the north side of the village.

Figure 72: Willen medieval field system.

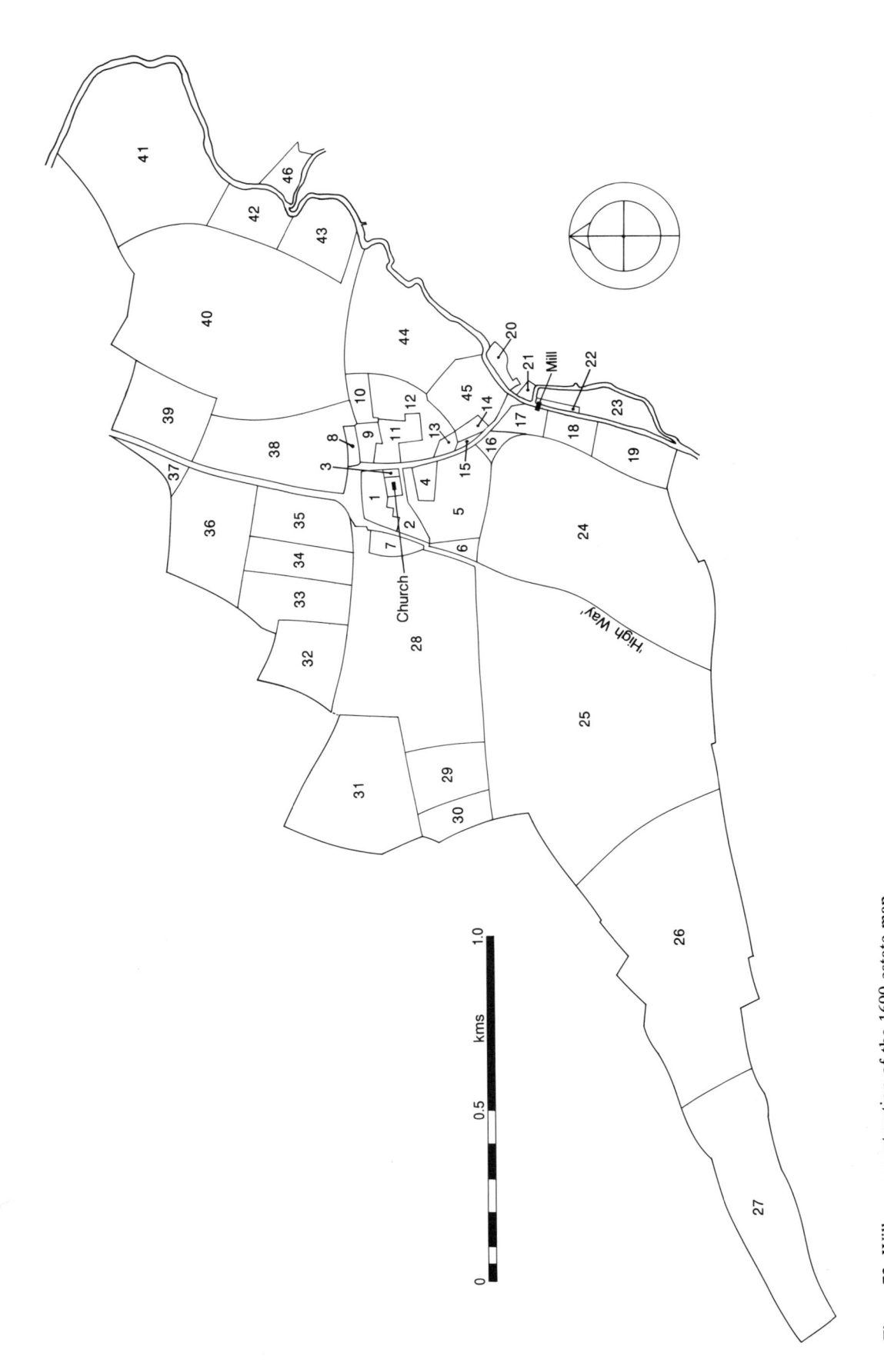

Figure 73: Willen; reconstruction of the 1690 estate map.

No.	Name	Tenant	Acres	Roods	Poles
1	Mr Hurn Sampson's homestead	HS	2	1	32
2	Grove and yard	GC/JK	3	0	26
3	Frail's (homestead)	?F	0	0	26
4	Greater Orchard	GC/JK	1	0	32
5	Conygree	GC/JK	9	1	37
6	Millers Leys	RC	1	2	32
7	Vicarage	JW	1	2	37
8	Widow Dudley's (homestead)	WD	1	1	0
9	Chapman's Little (Close)	GC	1	1	21
10	John Kilpin's second holding	JK	2	2	37
11	John Kilpin's first holding	JK	2	0	18
12	Ram Closes	JW	7	1	32
13	Lesser Orchard	JW	0	1	32
14	Widow Parrot's (homestead)	WP	0	3	8
15	Chad's (homestead)	TC	0	0	34
16	John Wise's homestead	JW	0	2	3
17	Miller's Close	RC	2	0	13
18	Bayly Close	GC/JK	2	2	37
19	Out Meadow	GC/JK	7	0	3
20	Miller's Holm	RC	1	0	24
21	Willow Plot	RC	0	1	16
22	Mill Dams	–	0	1	29
23	Mill Holmes	JW	4	2	0
24	Lower Ground	GC/JK	64	0	13
25	Great Ground	JK	100	2	34
26	Well Hill	HS	68	2	16
27	The Downs	GK	30	3	30
28	Offields	JK	47	2	13
29	New Close	JK	8	2	29
30	Frailes Close	?F	4	1	30
31	Furs Ground	HS	25	3	32
32	The Hole	JK	11	0	35
33	Cox's Great Close *	RC	9	3	16
34	Chad's Close *	TC	7	1	24
35	Chapman's Close *	GC	10	1	35
36	John Wise's Great Close *	JW	17	0	2
37	John Wise's Little Close *	JW	1	3	0
38	Glebeland	JS	18	1	8
39	Calves Close	GC	12	1	16
40	Great Whitson Pasture	GC	70	0	0
41	Great Meadow	GC/HS/JK	43	2	6
42	Little Whitson Close	JK/TC	7	2	19
43	Little Whitson Pasture	HS	9	0	21
44	Great Ash Croft	JK	20	3	38
45	Little Ashcroft	JW	6	0	32
46	The Hook	–	1	2	6
–	Church Yard	–	0	1	18
	'The Content of the Whole Lordship'		654	0	35

LANDOWNERS:
GC   George Chapman   WD   Widow Dudley   WP   Widow Parrot
RC   Richard Cox   ?F   ? Frail   JS   John Sampson
TC   Thomas Chad   JK   John Kilpin   HS   Hurn Sampson
   JW   Joseph Wise

* These fields all marked as 'Sanders his fields'.

KEY TO FIG. 73: Field names, landowners and acreages in Willen parish, 1690.

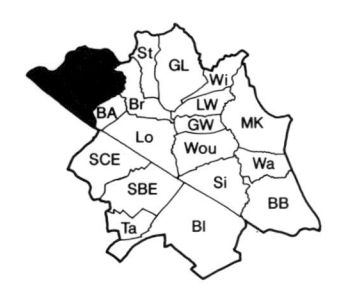

WOLVERTON

INTRODUCTION

The parish of Wolverton occupied the north-west corner of the city, and covered almost 941 ha (Fig. 74). The geology in the north of the parish consists of Jurassic deposits, including outcrops of Blisworth limestone. The central and southern parts of the parish contain a wide band of gravel of unknown age and Oxford and Boulder clays, while in the Ouse valley along the northern and eastern edges of the parish there is alluvium and terrace gravels. In general there are lighter well-drained soils in the north and heavier clay soils in the south of the parish.

The highest part of the parish is in the south, where the ground rises to more than 91 m OD. From this point the ground slopes gently southwards to Stacey Brook, which flows eastwards from Watling Street to join Bradwell Brook, which in turn drains northwards to the Ouse. The limestone outcrop in the north of the parish provided a source of local building stone, which was quarried from Roman times through to the nineteenth century.

The medieval village was situated in the north of the parish and occupied a prominent position overlooking the Ouse valley, at a height of just over 84 m OD. The earthworks of the motte and bailey castle remain on the east side of the church in the centre of the former village, on one of the most impressive defensive sites in north Buckinghamshire. From the top of the motte or the nearby church tower there is an unbroken view northwards across the Ouse towards Haversham, Castlethorpe and Cosgrove.

The western boundary of the parish ran northwards along Watling Street to the bridge over the River Ouse. The northern and eastern boundary followed the Ouse to the point where Bradwell Brook ran into the river. The boundary then turned to the south to follow the brook, finally turning west to follow Stacey Brook to Watling Street.

The parish to the south of Wolverton was Bradwell Abbey, which comprised the land given in the twelfth century by Meinfelin, lord of Wolverton, for the establishment of the priory. It is likely that this land was formerly part of Wolverton or Little Loughton.

The market town of Stony Stratford (Plate 33) was established on Watling Street between the crossroads at its intersection with the Buckingham to Newport Pagnell (Oxford to Cambridge) road and the bridge over the Ouse. The actual date of the town's establishment is uncertain, but it was already in existence in the late twelfth century (Britnell 1977, 451).

The village of Wolverton was situated approximately 1 km to the east of Watling Street, on the road to Newport Pagnell. In the centre of the village the road forked, one branch running northwards through the east end of the village and down to the meadows by the Ouse, whilst the other continued along the south side of the valley, crossing Bradwell Brook at the medieval bridge, (known as the *Stanbruge*, which gave its name to adjacent furlongs in the early thirteenth century [Jenkins 1952, No. 129]), from whence it continued to Stantonbury and Newport Pagnell.

At the point where the road forked in the village a triangular green was established, and from this a third road ran south to Bradwell Abbey and Loughton beyond. In the centre of the parish this road intersected with an east-west route called *Rugeway* (Ridgeway) in the early thirteenth century (Jenkins 1952, No. 129) and in modern times 'Green Lane' which ran from the *Stanbruge* westwards across the parish, but did not go as far as Watling Street, and appears to have been only an internal parish trackway serving the fields. Its route can be clearly traced through the medieval furlongs (Fig. 77) and it ended against a north-south headland. However, in the post-medieval period it linked with *Gib Lane*, which was named after the gallows which were situated south of Stony Stratford on Watling Street (Fig. 76), and which led to Watling Street and on to Calverton. A sixteenth-century court roll refers to *Ardwell Lane* (PRO, C116, No. 18) which may be an earlier or alternative name for *Gib Lane*. This route led to *Ardwell Fields*, which are shown on the 1742 map

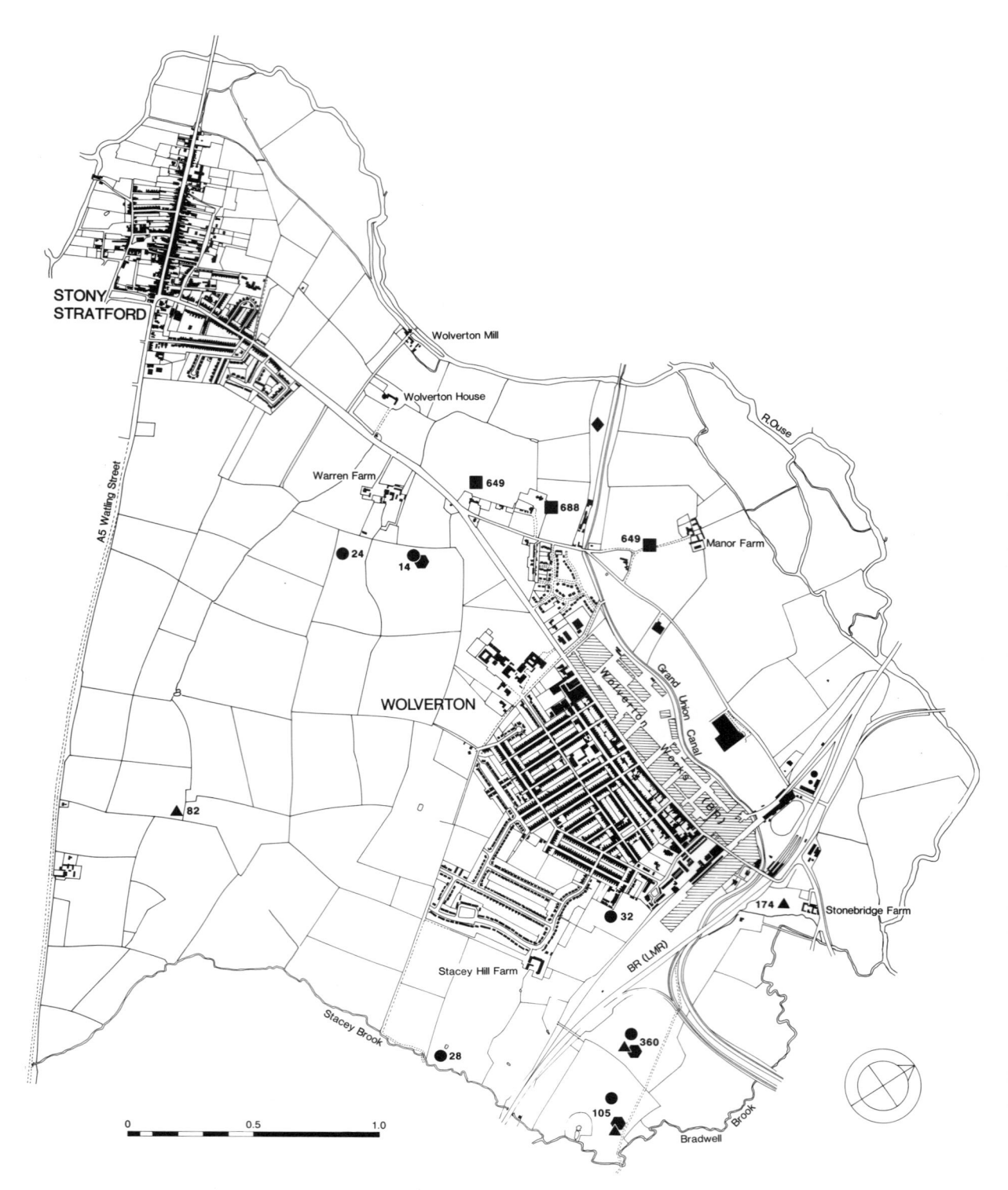

Figure 74: Wolverton parish in 1967, showing major archaeological sites.

(Fig. 75) to be between Ridgeway and Gib Lane. In fact, the map shows a dotted link between the two lanes, suggesting that the ridge-and-furrow in the area was out of use and the land put down to pasture at that time.

The name *Portwey* occurs in the early thirteenth century (Jenkins 1952, No. 129) and this may refer to the road to Stony Stratford, the nearest market town, since in the fifteenth century a grant of land refers to a furlong adjacent to Watling Street *supre le Portweye*.

Although numerous documents have been checked, the only other road names found were *Le Mylneway* (Millway) and *Le Brodeway* (Broadway). Both are mentioned many times in the medieval period. Millway led to one of the mills, but the location of Broadway is unknown.

ARCHAEOLOGY

The limestone outcrops and the sand and gravel deposits on the south bank of the Ouse presented a favourable area for settlement and agriculture from prehistoric times. Sites in the parish dating from the Bronze Age to the Saxon period occur along this ridge.

A quantity of Mesolithic flints have been found in the Bradwell Brook valley, particularly in the area around Bancroft. Stacey Bushes, a late Neolithic to early Bronze Age site (MK28) excavated in 1974, provided one of the earliest examples of settlement activity in this part of the Midlands (Green and Sofranoff 1985). At Warren Farm the excavation of two Bronze Age round barrows (MK14, MK24) provided evidence of settlement close by. A similar site was partly examined on the southern edge of Wolverton in the grounds of the Moon Street school (MK32).

Excavations at Blue Bridge between 1983 and 1985, in advance of development, revealed late Bronze Age and Iron Age farmsteads, as well as late Iron Age activity including a cremation cemetery, an impressive second-century Roman mausoleum, a fourth-century rural shrine and associated inhumation burials (MK360).

Some 300 m to the south, in the Bradwell Brook valley, excavations were carried out in the 1970s and 1980s on the site of the Bancroft Roman villa (MK105). This extensive site was established in the late first century as successor to the Blue Bridge site, and consisted of a stone farm-house and outbuildings, farmyard and walled vegetable gardens alongside a cobbled trackway leading from Watling Street. Following a fire in the late second century the site was largely abandoned, and not re-occupied until the late third century, when a new house was built partly overlying the ruins of the first. By the mid fourth century this house (Fig. 7) had aquired a formal walled garden and a kitchen garden, the former centred on an impressive stone-built fishpond, and flanked by an octagonal summer-house and a small but well-appointed cottage. The whole complex was enclosed by a ditch. Occupation at Bancroft continued into the fifth century.

The area containing Bancroft villa now forms part of the city's parks system, and the site of the later house and formal garden has been laid out for public display. The results of the Blue Bridge and Bancroft excavations are being published as a single volume (Zeepvat and Williams forthcoming).

Evidence of early Saxon activity has been found at both the villa and the mausoleum sites, but little has been found elsewhere in the parish. Several burials, thought perhaps to be of Saxon date, were found in 1956 when the McCorquodale factory at the west end of the modern town was extended (Green 1957).

At Wolverton Turn near Warren Farm, some 300 m south of the parish church, a middle Saxon settlement was located during the excavation of the Bronze Age round barrows (MK14). In addition, late Saxon coinage and metalwork has been found near the church and the northern end of the medieval village. In view of these finds it is likely that there was extensive occupation in the mid to late Saxon period in this area of the parish.

The earliest version of the name of the village occurs in the Domesday survey, when it was spelt *Wlverintone*, which probably dates from the late eigth or ninth century, and can be translated as 'Wulfhere's Tun', meaning the estate of which Wulfhere, probably a thegn, holds the overlordship (Gelling, above). At the time of the Domesday survey both Wolverton and Little Loughton were held by Mainou le Breton as part of his barony of Wolverton, and the possibility that they had formed an earlier Roman or Saxon estate has been considered. The evidence to support this Roman estate theory is very tenuous, and is based on the fact that the boundaries of the proposed land unit were all natural ones, apart from Watling Street. If this were the case, then the identification of Bancroft villa as the centre of the estate with the lesser farmstead at Wymbush as an outlying farm is an attractive model. However, such a hypothesis cannot be in any way proved.

The suggestion that there was a Saxon estate is also very tenuous, for in 1066 before Mainou held these lands they were held separately; Wolverton by three Saxon thanes, and Loughton by only one.

Plate 33: Stony Stratford and Watling Street, 1979. *(MKAU)*

However, the amount and quality of the middle and late Saxon finds from the area of the later village of Wolverton suggest that there was an important settlement here.

THE MEDIEVAL AND LATER VILLAGE

The site of the village of Wolverton is the best surviving example of a deserted medieval village in Milton Keynes. Only the parish church and the eighteenth-century Rectory, together with several cottages of similar date, have survived. The plan of the village earthworks (Fig. 75) shows that it was a linear settlement, extending from the mill on the Ouse at the west end for a distance of some 1.5 km to the Grange (now Manor Farm) in the east. In the centre of the village was the church, a motte-and-bailey castle and the manor house. The construction of the Grand Junction Canal separated the eastern end of Wolverton and the Grange from the rest of the village.

The earthworks south-west of and below the castle (Plate 34) are extensive and their quality suggests that most, if not all the buildings in the village were largely stone-founded. The distinctive platforms adjacent to the sunken road are characteristic of other limestone village sites, such as Great Linford. There are no extant references to the materials actually used for the houses, but a document of *c*.1250 refers to the grant of a certain wall (*murum*) between two properties in the east end of the village (Jenkins 1952, No. 144).

From the church a sunken roadway on average 10 m wide and 1.2 m deep runs westward through the earthworks, veering slightly to the north, towards the meadows and the watermill beyond. On the south side of the road the earthworks, particularly in the area to the south of the church, have been disturbed by the Rectory gardens and post-medieval farm buildings, but at the west end of the road at least three house sites within croft boundaries survive.

On the north of the road a more regular pattern of crofts survives, with a back lane beyond which are long closes containing ridge-and-furrow, confirming that as at Great Linford they represent early enclosure of former ploughed furlongs. The closes are bounded by substantial earth banks some 10 m across, which may have protected them from flooding by the nearby river.

On the east side of Holy Trinity church are the earthworks of the motte-and-bailey castle, which was of Norman origin. It is assumed that the castle was built by Meinfelin, baron of Wolverton, or his son Hamo in the late eleventh or early twelfth century.

The motte ditch was affected by the rebuilding of the church in the early years of the nineteenth century (*c*.1810–15). The accounts for the rebuilding and repair of the medieval church record that the churchyard was levelled and the motte ditch filled in where it bounded the churchyard (Bodleian, Radcliffe Mss C17). The only surviving traces of the ditch are on the north side, where it is a six-metre-wide, steep-sided ditch which currently contains a limestone wall.

The motte is approximately 50 m in diameter at its base, with steeply sloping sides rising to approximately 5 m above the ground level in the churchyard. It has recently been cleared of small bushes and scrub, leaving only several large trees, making it more visible and accessible than it has been for many years. The top is flat and 20 m in diameter, at a height of 78 m OD.

The bailey surrounding the motte is sub-rectangular, 220×90 m, and aligned north-west to south-east. The northern and eastern boundaries of the bailey are quite clear, forming a marked break across the field, with a possible entrance on the north-east side which has been destroyed by a post-medieval quarry pit.

North of the bailey, several flat areas intersected with ditches may represent further outer works or later medieval activity on the site. However, some of the earthworks may be a result of later activities, and in particular there are two good examples of quarry pits for limestone, possibly for the construction of the manor house.

The site of the medieval manor house was described in the eighteeenth century as being 'near a large mound thrown up east of the church' (BL Add. Mss 5839, 429), and the most likely site for it is to the south of the motte, north-east of the driveway in front of the rectory.

There must have been a substantial Norman manor house of which no record survives, unless it is the capital messuage with a court and garden described in the mid thirteenth century (VCH 1927, 505). There are also references to the meadow below the garden in the early thirteenth century (Jenkins 1952, No. 129).

The manor house demolished by the Radcliffe Trustees in 1725 was a sixteenth-century building which had been built by the Longville family during their ownership of the manor. The existing Rectory, built about 1730, incorporates stonework from the demolished manor house, notably the main door surround (VCH 1927, 505).

The earthworks of the eastern end of the village (Plate 35) were cut off from the main part by the construction of the canal, and there was

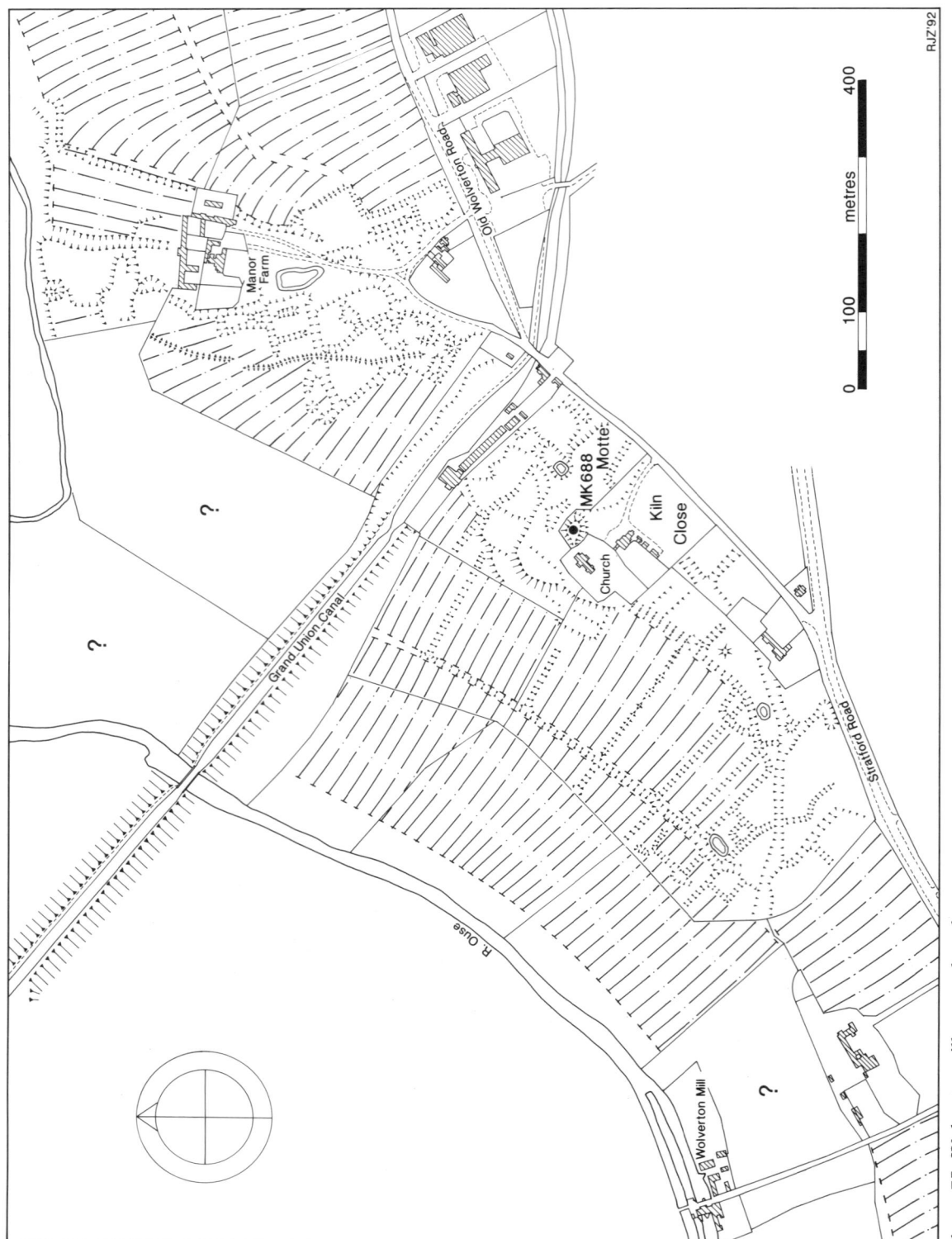

Figure 75: Wolverton village earthworks.

Plate 34: Wolverton village earthworks, church and motte. (© *British Crown Copyright 1993/MOD reproduced with the permission of the Controller of Her Britannic Majesty's Stationery Office*)

disturbance on both sides of the canal further obscuring the earthworks, particularly in the area north of the bailey.

North of the canal, the village road forked. The southern road remains as Old Wolverton Road, and the northern road as a raised track running through the eastern end of the village to Manor Farm. The latter is a substantial stone complex, dating from the late eighteenth to early nineteenth century, possibly occupying the site of a medieval grange, as suggested by adjacent field names (Fig. 76). The farmhouse, gardens and cattle yards are situated on a broad flat platform on an outcrop of Blisworth limestone overlooking the Ouse valley, with open views to the north and east. North of the farm the road continues as a deeply-cut sunken way running down towards a minor channel of the Ouse. The field on both sides of this road contained ridge-and-furrow, and that on the west has been disturbed by random limestone quarrying. There is a suggestion that there was a watermill on the Ouse at the bottom of this field in the eighteenth century (Sheahan 1862, 645). The channel there would have been large enough to operate a small watermill, and the bridging point over the river may be the site of the destroyed mill, but there are no surviving earthworks.

Returning to the centre of the village, a triangular green lay in the angle of the road fork, east of the church and castle. On the north side of this green was a road which ran south through the parish, leading to Bradwell Abbey and Loughton. North of the green there were several crofts and house sites, and running northwards from the north corner of the green up to the medieval grange was a wide open rectangular area, dominated by a large oval pond almost 50 m long. On the east side of this open area was a small close and a possible croft, whilst on the west were at least five crofts, and a sunken road running into and cutting through the ridge and furrow behind the crofts. The earthworks here were disturbed in the post-medieval period by quarrying, and by the movement of animals and farm machinery. There is also a bank over 350 m in length which probably covers the remains of a stone wall enclosing a park-like area in front of Manor Farm.

Unfortunately, even though the site is a scheduled Ancient Monument, recent agricultural pressure to plough the western side of the site has destroyed some of these earthworks. Until 1983 the large closes on the northern and eastern sides of Manor Farm contained some of the finest examples of ridge-and-furrow in Milton Keynes, but have since been ploughed out. However, the surviving village earthworks at Wolverton are well-preserved, and apart from recent damage at the western end of the site they represent the best limestone village earthworks in the city.

The desertion of the village at Wolverton was connected with early enclosures in the parish by the Longville family, who rebuilt the manor house in the mid sixteenth century and extended the medieval park. The field names recorded on the 1742 map (Hyde 1945, 13) confirm that the house sites, crofts and closes all became part of this park. The development of the market town of Stony Stratford in the west of the parish, which would have acted as an alternative source of labour, may have attracted people away from the village, or provided a useful place for the Longvilles to remove them to.

In the eighteenth and nineteenth centuries Wolverton consisted of several outlying farms and a few cottages remaining to the south-west of the church. Hyde lists seven main agricultural holdings; Manor Farm, Warren Farm, Stonebridge Farm, Stacey Hill and Old Stacey Farms, Brickkiln Farm and Wolverton House (Hyde 1945, 17). All of these except Old Stacey Farm survived until the development of Milton Keynes.

THE FIELD SYSTEM

There is no surviving pre-enclosure map of the parish, but that published by Hyde (1943, 13) was based on a map of 1742, since lost. Hyde's map, reconstructed in Fig. 76, shows the fields after enclosure. Few of the field names given can be related to the medieval furlong names recorded in the numerous manorial documents deposited by the Radcliffe Trustees in the Bodleian Library, Oxford. In fact, only two can be positively located, namely *Greenlefurlong* in 1332 (Bodleian, Radcliffe Doc. 99) which is *Great Greenleys* in 1742, and *Fulewell Slade* in 1235–70 (Bodleian, Radcliffe Doc. 44) which is *Fullers Slade* in 1742. Another furlong, *Stanbruge*, mentioned in the early thirteenth century (Jenkins 1952, No. 129) must have been beside to the Stonebridge which carried the Newport road over Bradwell Brook.

In the early thirteenth century only *East* and a *West Field* are mentioned in a grant of land in the parish, so it is likely that a two-field system was in operation at that time (Jenkins 1952, No. 129). Whether the parish developed a three-field system is uncertain, since there are no extant documents with the names of three fields.

There are references to the enclosure of land within the parish from the early sixteenth century onwards. For example, in 1501 Sir John Longville enlarged his park by inclosing *Barre Close*, which lay immediately to the south-east of the village (Leadam 1897, 182). Further enclosure was

Plate 35: Wolverton; village earthworks around Manor Farm. *(Cambridge University Collection of Air Photographs copyright reserved)*

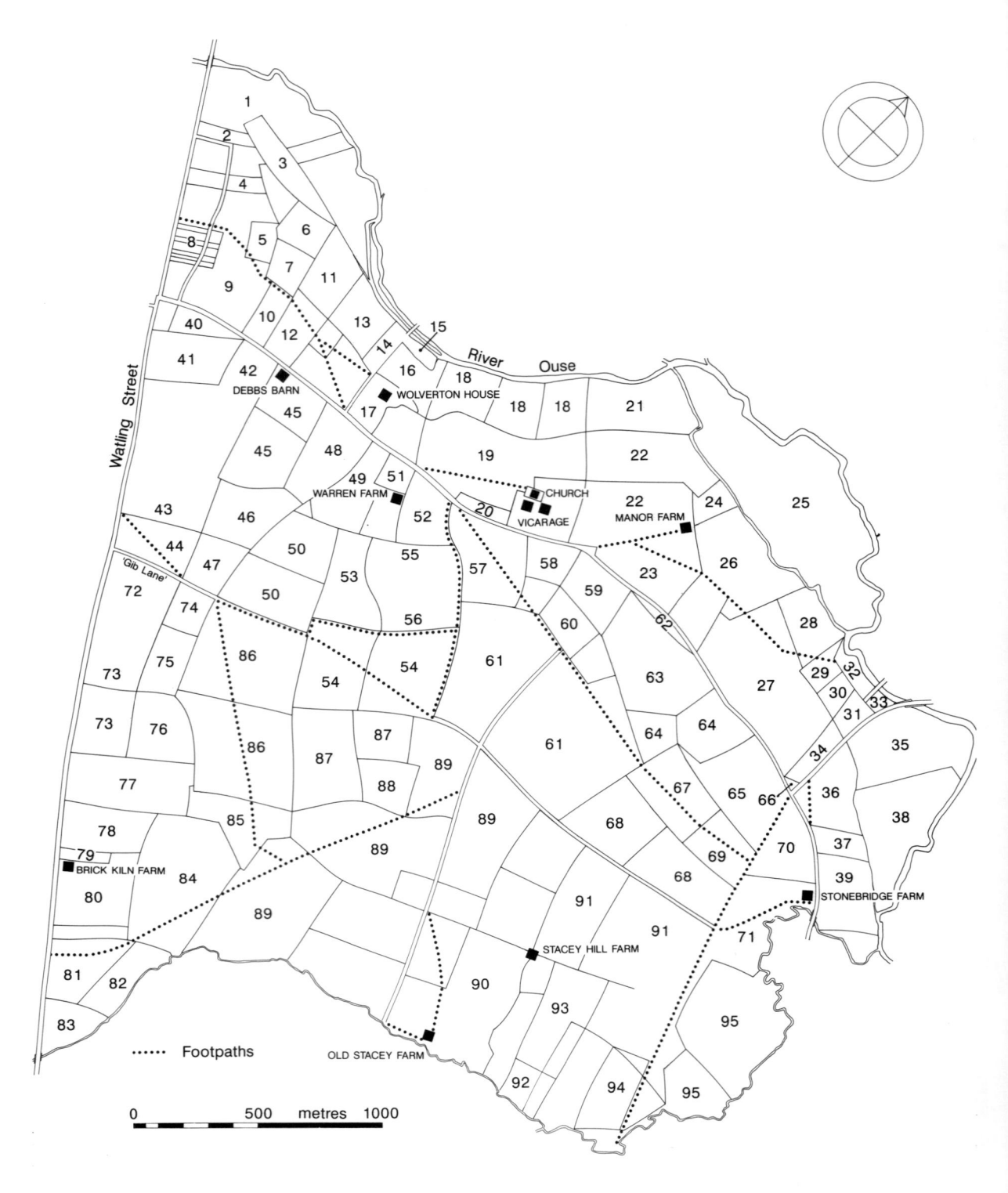

Figure 76: Wolverton; reconstruction of the 1742 estate map.

1	West Moor	33	Mill Mead Holm	65	Lower Slade Ground
2	Home Close	34	Mill Mead Ground	66	Mobs Pightlett
3	Midsomer Plot	35	Nash Meadow	67	Rogers Holm
4	Toridge Hook Close	36	Mill Mead Ground	68	Shrub Field
5	Lamas Close	37	Mill Mead Plot	69	Rogers Holm
6	Home Ryland	38	Nash Meadow	70	Post Hill Ground
7	Little Ryland	39	Gravel Pit Close	71	Post Hill Ground
8	Town Closes	40	Garden Close	72	Gib Lane Field
9	Town Lands	41	Town Lands	73	Greenleys
10	Ryland	42	Woodstock Close	74	Seven Acres
11	Lower Ryland	43	Galley Hill	75	Ten Acres
12	Upper Ryland	44	Half Mile Field	76	Fifteen Acres
13	Far Ryland	45	Lockwits Ground	77	Front Grindley
14	Mill Holm	46	Great Half Mile Close	78	Carters Ley
15	Bradford Close	47	Half Mile Close	79	Brunleys Pightlett
16	East Moor	48	The Warren	80	Brick Close
17	Home Close	49	Long Hill	81	Walks
18	Ludkins Closes	50	Fullers Slade	82	Home Close
19	Low Park	51	Clover Close	83	Two Mile Ash
20	Kiln Close	52	Black Hill	84	Pit Field
21	Park Meadow	53	Little Pool Ground	85	Little Grindley
22	High Park	54	Ardwell Fields	86	Great Greenleys
23	Home Park	55	Ardwell Sheep Rails	87	Parsons Piece
24	The Grange	56	Gravel Pit Close	88	The Meadow
25	Colts Holm and Linces	57	Barr Piece	89	Hodge Furze
26	Great Dickens	58	Barr Close	90	Stacey Bushes
27	The Severidge	59	Mortar Pitts	91	Three Bush Field
28	Upper Hey	60	Fiddlers Butts	92	Ox Yard
29	Kents Hook	61	Harrow Field	93	The Grove
30	Debbs Hook	62	Upper Slade	94	Lough Close
31	Mill Mead Reaches	63	Radcliffe Close	95	Brook Field
32	Lower Hook	64	Deans Closes		

KEY TO FIG. 76: Field names in Wolverton in 1742.

carried out by the Longvilles in the sixteenth century, and in 1580 the people of Stony Stratford were so concerned that they appealed to the Queen through the Lord Chancellor (PRO Chan. Proc. Eliz. W23, No. 25). The following is a summary of their complaints against the Longvilles:

1. That they had lost their common rights in the fields called *Nastangland*, *Stacey Bushes* and another to the east of Stacey Bushes, *Furzes* and a field on the east side of Ardwell. These fields, amounting to some 210 acres, had been enclosed by Sir John Longville in about 1526.

2. That Sir John's son Thomas had enclosed a field called the *Diggins* but "knowing that he had done manifest injury to the freeholders had caused the field to be again laid open and common". However, after his death his brother Arthur again enclosed it, but also repented and the field was opened again. Arthur was also said to have kept *Nastangland* and *Stacey Bushes* enclosed, but to have made a deathbed request that his wife and

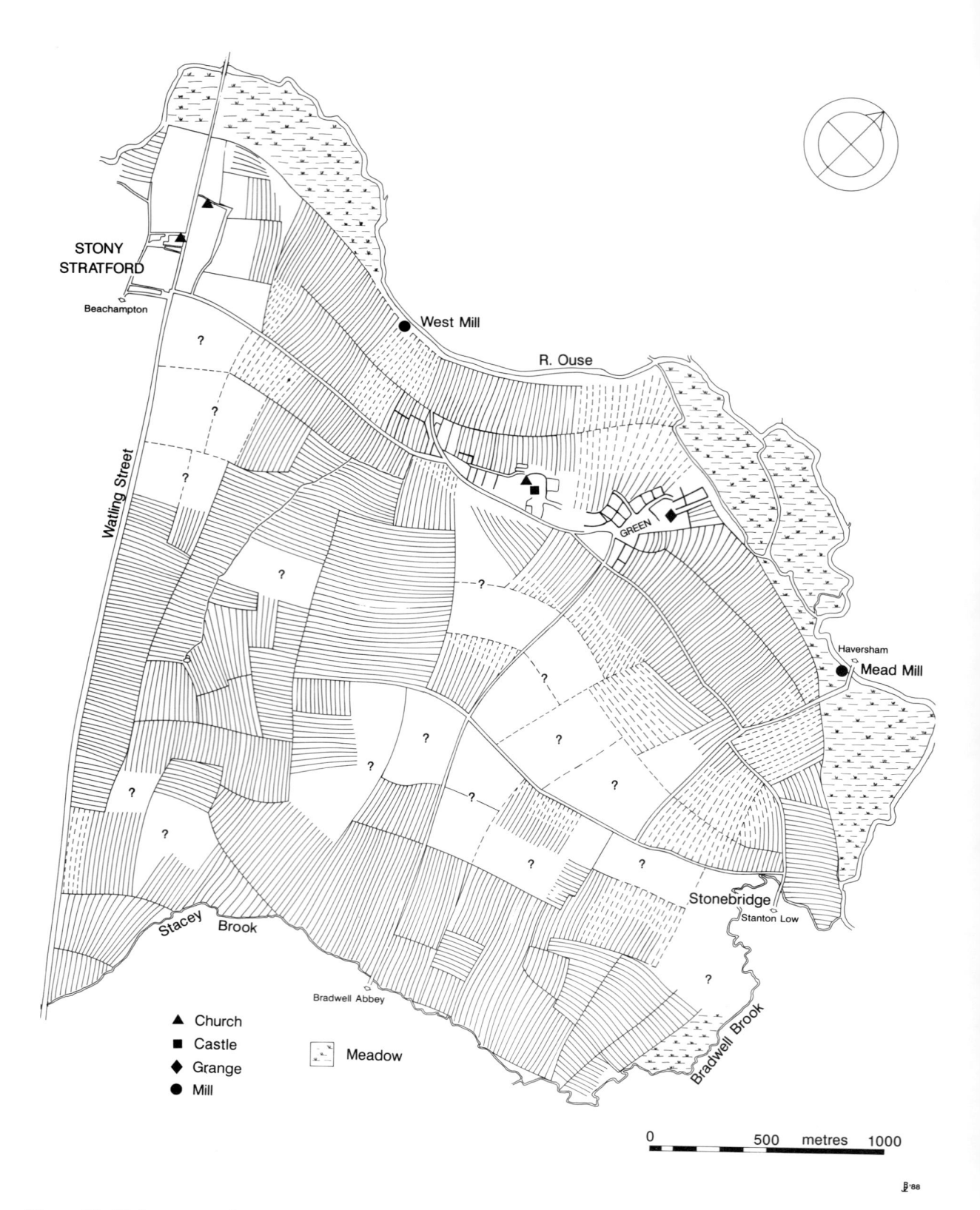

Figure 77: Wolverton medieval field system.

certain others open the fields again. However, Henry Longville, the son and heir of Arthur, continued to keep the lands enclosed, as a result of which the freeholders and inhabitants of Stony Stratford were deprived of yearly pasture for two hundred beasts and a thousand sheep.

They also claimed that Henry Longville kept many more beasts on the fields than his ancestors had done, and that between 1575 and 1580 he had "stored such a great number and multitude of coneys (rabbits) in Ardwell and the next enclosure, that the said coneys do yearly spoil and destroy the corn and grass of your said orators growing upon eighty acres of ground in Ardwell field".

The townspeople broke down Sir Henry's fences "in a most quiet manner and in convenient places", and put their cattle into the fields. This resulted in Sir Henry hiring unknown or poor persons to drive the cattle out, with threats to beat the owners and to kill their cattle.

Furthermore, Sir Henry was said to have rebuilt the West Mill in about 1570 and:

". . . raised up the banks of the river leading to the same mill to so great a height that the river doth drown and utterly spoil and destroy thirty acres of the Queen Majesty's your said orators, so that every acre of meadow called the West Meadows, containing fifty-five acres, which formerly bore five or six loads of hay, will bear very little hay, and that little nothing worth. And further your said orators, their servants and labourers, are enforced to wade very deep when they do mow the same meadows, and to bring the grass forth in their arms, for no cart is able to come thither for it, neither by the wetness of the ground can the hay be made there. And besides the said thirty acres of common which were heretofore very beneficial for the keeping of ploughing cattle, milking kine and other beasts after the first crop was taken away, is now become little or nothing worth, for that ground is become so moorish and so full of mire that no cattle is able to enter and feed".

The result of their complaints is unknown, but it is interesting that all the complainents were from Stony Stratford, suggesting perhaps that the old village of Wolverton was already depopulated.

The parish was enclosed finally in the mid seventeenth century by Sir Edward Longville (VCH 1927, 505). There are many documents in the Bodleian Library relating to the financial difficulties of the Longville family, and the resultant sale and enclosure of their land in Wolverton. In particular, one complaint which expressed the feelings of the people of the area at the time could easily have been referring to the disturbance of the countryside created by the building of Milton Keynes. The complaint was made by Symon Bennett, lord of neighbouring Beachampton and Calverton, who claimed that:

". . . in the said town and fields of Wolverton Sir John Longville had put and divided the land into many small and little closes and ploughed up the grass or pasture thereof and by ditches or otherwise had obscured and confounded the ancient and former ridges, throws, furrows, balks, heads and the order and condition of the said fields, grounds, commons and open ground so that he was not able to find out or discern the said former lands, meadows and leyes".
(Bodleian, Radcliffe Mss DD.b.3, Fol. 322).

Many of the names of fields recorded in seventeenth-century documents suggest that enclosure had largely taken place, although few of them can be placed on the 1742 map. This suggests that there was a considerable reorganisation of land in the late seventeenth century.

The meadowland adjacent to the Ouse ran for 5 km from the bridge at Old Stratford to the junction with Bradwell Brook in the east of the parish. From the ridge-and-furrow map it can be seen that much of it was ploughed, and that it was probably not always meadowland.

There are numerous documentary references to the meadows of Wolverton. The earliest found is in a document of *c*.1200, which mentions "the meadow below the garden" and must refer to meadow below and north of the site of the manor house and its gardens (Jenkins 1952, No. 129). The same document refers to the East meadow above *Norlong*, which may have been the name for part of the river at that time. There is also a reference to the meadows and headlands below *Le Park* in 1252 (Bodleian, Radcliffe Mss 655). Documents of the fifteenth and sixteenth centuries often refer to meadows which can be placed on the 1742 map.

The meadows, like the village, seem to have been divided into an east and west end, the East meadow, *Estmede*, being mentioned in *c*.1235–50 and the West meadow, *Westmede*, in *c*.1264 (Bodleian, Radcliffe Mss 52 and 340 respectively). The *Lowefurlong* mentioned in 1383 (Bodleian, Radcliffe Mss 124) may well be the in the field at the west end of the village, called the Low Park in 1742.

Few areas of good meadowland survive in Milton Keynes, but the meadows at Wolverton contain a wide variety of typical meadow flora such as yellow rattle, common sorrel and creeping buttercup. Their location within the city's linear parks system should ensure their survival as an open space, but their environment will be threatened by the increasing use of the parks as a recreational resource.

OTHER LANDSCAPE FEATURES

MILLS

There were two mill sites in the parish. One still remains, and the other, which was near the western boundary of the parish, was destroyed when Wolverton railway embankment was constructed. Both mills were working in the eleventh century, and were recorded in the Domesday survey. The mills were often referred to in documents as the East Mill and the West Mill. The former was called the *Tule mill* in 1465 (Bodleian, Radcliffe Mss 500), but was shown as the *Meade mill* on the 1742 map.

FISHERIES

Bradwell Priory held the Mead Mill in the early thirteenth century, and they also had a fishery between it and the *Stanebruge* (VCH 1927, 506). Wolverton Mill is on the site of the West Mill, which was referred to in 1252 when John son of Alan of Wolverton granted the mill to his son Richard, together with free fishing in the waters of Wolverton, except in the fishponds and the millpool (Bodleian, Radcliffe Mss D340 and D655). These documents are of further interest in that they state that Richard could fish with six *burroches* (basket traps) and one *botur* (net). Stone weights, thought to be from fishing basket traps, have frequently been dredged from the Ouse, but these documents are the first confirmation that such traps were used locally (Mynard 1979).

PARK

There seems to have been a park at Wolverton as early as the mid thirteenth century, when certain meadows and headlands were said to be "under the park" (Bodleian, Radcliffe Mss. R655). In 1383 there are references to *Le Parkfeld* (*ibid.*, R124), and *Le Park Meadows* are mentioned twice in the fifteenth century (*ibid.*, R146 and R494). In 1501 Sir John Longville had enlarged his park by enclosing *Barre Close* (Leadam 1897, 182). The 1742 map shows that most of the site of the medieval village was included in three large fields called *High Park* and *Low Park*, from which it is clear that the village had already been depopulated.

CANAL

The Grand Junction (now the Grand Union) Canal, which was opened for traffic in 1800, passes through the north-eastern corner of the parish. When first constructed the canal crossed the Ouse on the level via a series of nine wooden locks, and the earthworks of these can still be seen on the west side of the present canal between Cosgrove lock and the 'Galleon' public house. The locks were replaced in 1805 by a stone three-arched aqueduct, which collapsed in 1808, causing considerable flooding of the valley below. As a temporary measure a timber structure was erected within a few months, but this was replaced in 1811 by the present iron aqueduct, known locally as the *Iron Trunk*, which has withstood the test of time and is now a scheduled Ancient Monument. The construction of the canal considerably changed the landscape of the parish, particularly the erection of the massive embankment carrying it to the aqueduct. A wharf was constructed at Old Wolverton where the Newport Pagnell to Stony Stratford road crossed the canal, one mile from Stony Stratford. Stony Stratford was served by a wharf at Old Stratford, on the Buckingham branch of the canal.

RAILWAY

Situated approximately mid-way between London and Birmingham, Wolverton was chosen as the site for both a station and workshops for the construction and maintenance of engines and carriages when the London and Birmingham Railway was constructed. The building of the line necessitated another major embankment and bridge over the Ouse, the course of which was slightly altered during the works, obliterating the site of the Mead Mill. The railway, along with Wolverton Works and the first Wolverton station, were opened in 1838.

A new town to house the railway workers was soon established to the south of the works, and the Stony Stratford to Newport Pagnell road was re-routed to pass through the it. The old road remained to become known as Old Wolverton Road, and is still in use today. The land for the development of Wolverton was acquired from the Radcliffe Trustees, who at one stage became alarmed by the pressures of development and refused to part with any more land at Wolverton, forcing the railway company to look elsewhere and leading to the creation of New Bradwell (see parish essay).

The town of Wolverton contained a number of buildings and features of architectural and industrial interest, some of which have been destroyed in recent years, but discussion of these lies outside the scope of this survey.

TRAMWAY

A steam-powered tramway operated between Wolverton and Stony Stratford from 1887 to 1926, and the line was extended to Deanshanger in 1888 and 1889. Much of the steel track of the old line still survives under the wide grass verge on the north side of the road between Wolverton and Stony Stratford, to the east of the A5 yover. When the first Stony Stratford bypass was constructed in 1973, part of the line was excavated by the Archaeology Unit and removed to the Stacey Hill Museum, where one of the tram coaches, rescued from a farm at Shenley Church End, has since been put back onto a section of the track.

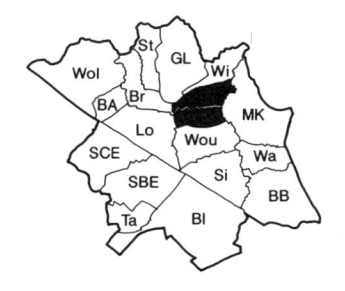

WOOLSTONES

INTRODUCTION

The parishes of Great and Little Woolstone (Fig. 78) were originally one Late Saxon land unit which became divided into two holdings, both of which acquired parish status. The introductory and general discussions of these parishes are therefore combined.

The Woolstones were situated on the west bank of the Ouzel between Willen and Woughton on the Green. Great Woolstone covered some 208 ha and Little Woolstone 252 ha. The highest point, 107 m OD, is at the western end of the parishes adjacent to Bradwell Common, from which the land slopes gently down to the Ouzel valley in the east.

The underlying geology is largely Oxford and Boulder clays, and there being no major streams the land drained through minor ditches eastwards to the river. First and second terrace gravels occur in the river valley.

The boundary between the two parishes followed the boundaries of established furlongs and must have been later than the field systems of which they were part. The eastern boundary of the two parishes was the Ouzel and the north and south boundaries ran from it at right angles. The northern boundary with Willen followed an early route leading up to Secklow Mound, the meeting place of the Saxon Secklow hundred. The southern boundary followed an almost straight line from the river up to the higher ground of Bradwell Common.

The Domesday survey listed woodland capable of supporting a hundred pigs in what is now Great Woolstone. The location of this woodland is uncertain, but must have been in the west of the parish.

The main road through the parishes was the north to south route from Newport Pagnell to Fenny Stratford, although the original line of this road north of the village to Willen is uncertain. The pre-city road cut across ridge and furrow and the medieval route probably ran around headlands, taking a route nearer the river and arriving at Willen close to the moated site and the mill. An east-west route from Milton Keynes village crossed the Ouzel at Little Woolstone Mill and continued through the village westwards to join the route along the northern parish boundary. This road eventually led to Great Linford, and in that parish it followed the boundaries of the medieval headlands rather than taking a direct route to the village.

ARCHAEOLOGY

No evidence for prehistoric settlement has so far been discovered in the Woolstones, but a few flint flakes have been found in the vicinity of Little Woolstone church. Excavation of a Roman site (MK109) in Little Woolstone parish revealed evidence of domestic occupation and field ditches but not of buildings. (Mynard 1987, 79–82). A few sherds of Roman pottery were recovered during the excavation of Little Woolstone church.

Saxon pottery was found when the sportsfield to the south of Little Woolstone church was levelled, and this may indicate the site of the middle to late Saxon settlement. The excavations within Holy Trinity Church also produced a few fragments of late Saxon pottery.

THE MEDIEVAL AND LATER VILLAGES

GREAT WOOLSTONE

The village of Great Woolstone was situated on the eastern side of the parish on the Newport Pagnell to Fenny Stratford road. It was a linear village with houses, church and manor stretching for a distance of almost 500 m along the road. The church, standing at the southern end of the village on the east side of the road, was adjacent to a moated site and a medieval fishery (MK 656). There are also village earthworks in the form of croft boundaries to the north of the church (Fig. 79).

The remaining parts of a ditch, now destroyed, on the north and west sides of the garden of the 'Cross

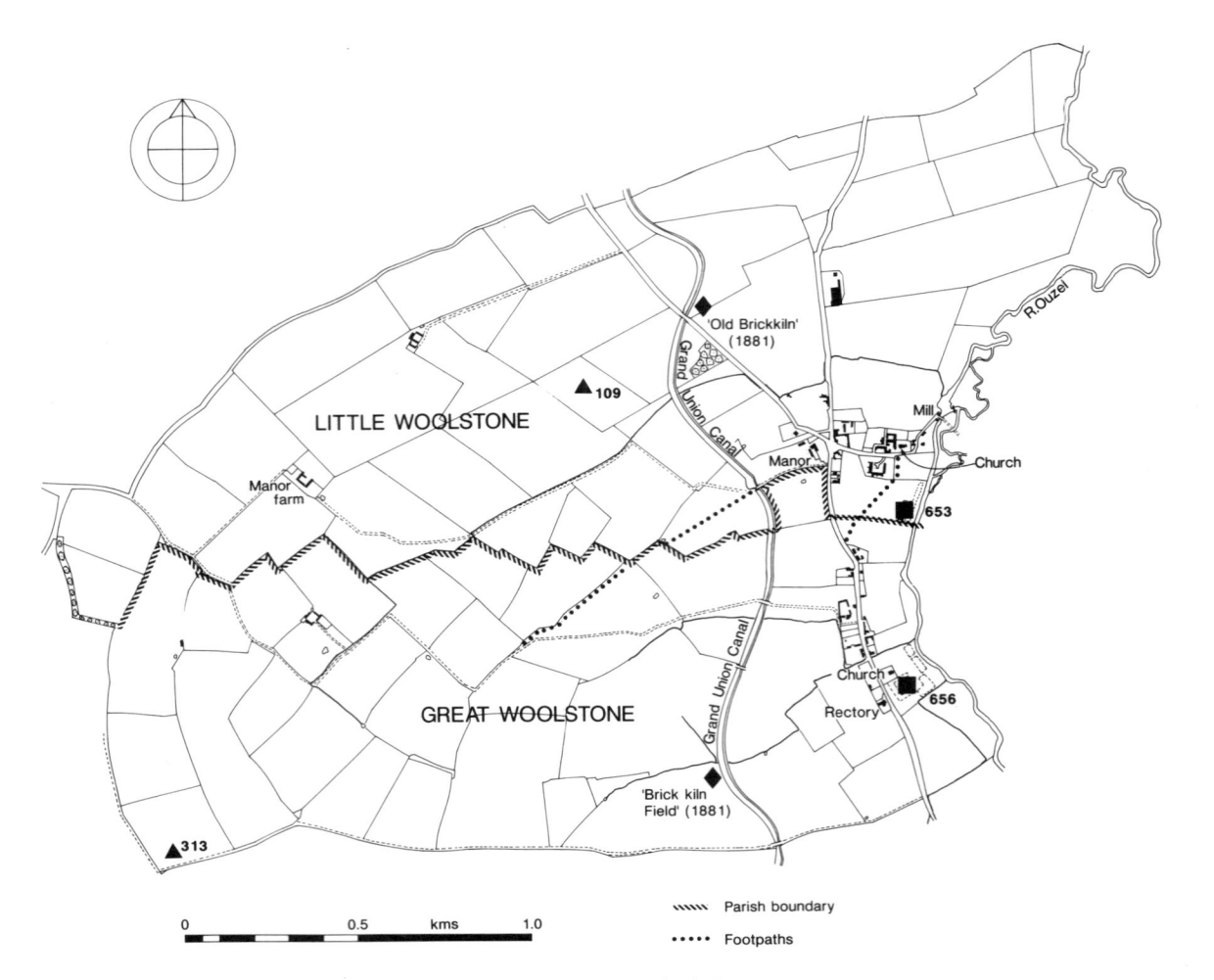

Figure 78: The Woolstones in 1967, showing major archaeological sites.

Keys' public house (MK703) were thought to be part of a moat, but it is more likely that this was a drainage ditch which continued on the east side of the road to the river. There were also medieval house sites, much reduced by modern ploughing, in the fields north of the 'Cross Keys', extending as far as Little Woolstone manor.

South of Holy Trinity church are the earthworks of the manorial moat, originally some 70 m sq. They are now almost completely levelled, particularly on the east side, but traces of the south and west sides are represented by a shallow ditch averaging 6m wide and 0.2 m deep. The western ditch may have continued northwards between the churchyard and the road, and is shown as a pond on the 1881 OS map. In 1926 the churchyard was extended westwards. The petition for consecration of the additional land described it as:

". . . a piece of land formerly the site of an old pond which has been enclosed and incorporated with the present churchyard for a period of over twelve years, situate on the west side of the churchyard and measuring 135 feet north to south and 36 feet east to west".

(Bodleian, Mss Oxford Diocese 1675–6).

The ponds of the medieval fishery, which with the moat are a Scheduled Ancient Monument, are contained within the field to the east of the church and the moat. They remain in reasonable condition, even though there has been some disturbance caused by gravel quarrying, backfilling and natural silting.

The largest pond is the southernmost, which is rectangular, some 60×25 m and 1 m in depth, and aligned at right angles to the river. This pond, which floods regularly every winter, is known locally as the 'Jack Pond'. To the north is an L-shaped pond, with a rectangular southern arm measuring 24×5 m, and a northern arm 20×6 m. This pond may have been fed with water through a break in the north bank of the larger pond to the south. There are two small ponds, one to the east and one to the north of the L-shaped pond, and north of these two long narrow ponds with internal subdivisions lie along the west bank of the river.

At the southern end of the site there are slight traces of another pond, which was shown on the 1881 edition of the OS map as a rectangular pond about 65×11 m, aligned with the river.

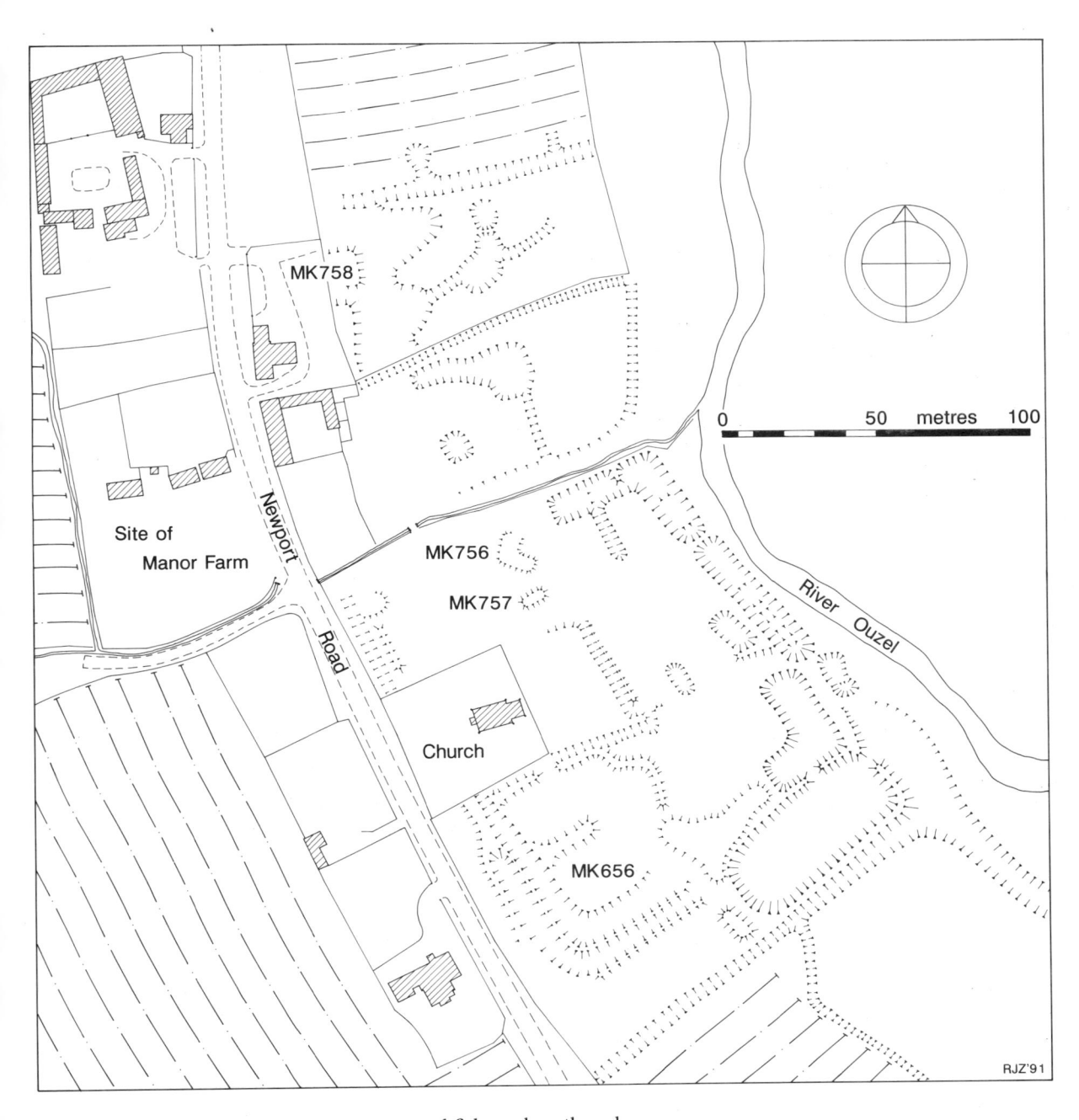

Figure 79: Great Woolstone; village, moat and fishpond earthworks.

To the east of the present churchyard a ditch marks the northern limit of the medieval churchyard, which extended for a distance of 80 m back from the present road. To the north of the church, within the same field, there are several indistinct earthworks which may be the remains of a croft. North of the field are two rectangular crofts, each 120×50 m, running from the road towards the river. The boundaries of the crofts survive as ditches behind the modern properties fronting the road. Within each croft there are several small pits, the result of random gravel quarrying.

The present church was built in 1832–3 on the same site as the medieval church. The only record of the old church is a description by Browne Willis, who visited it early in the eighteenth century and wrote that the church was "a small mean fabric consisting of a nave and chancel, with a leaded roof and a wooden turret with two windows and three bells" (Bodleian, Willis Mss 100, 191). The church, now the Rosebery Music Room, was re-ordered by the Development Corporation in 1976, at which time the font was broken and buried beneath the floor of the church and a late medieval pew removed for safe keeping.

This is now in the care of the County Museum at Aylesbury.

The post-medieval village consisted of Manor Farmhouse, which may have dated from the sixteenth century, Hill Farmhouse, an impressive building of c.1720, a fine nineteenth-century Rectory by Butterfield, and several seventeenth-century cottages, including the 'Cross Keys' public house. Manor Farmhouse, the sixteenth or seventeenth-century successor to the medieval manor house, was demolished without record in the 1960s. This building, situated on the west side of the road opposite Hill Farm and the church, was inaccurately identified as Rectory Farmhouse in the guide to the historic buildings of the area (Woodfield 1986, 62).

The earliest known map of the parish is the enclosure map of 1797 (BAS 325/39) which shows the area of the church and fishponds before the re-building of the church in 1837.

LITTLE WOOLSTONE

The village of Little Woolstone developed at the crossroads at the junction of the Fenny Stratford to Newport Pagnell road and the the road from Milton Keynes to Secklow and Great Linford. The village was largely on Mill Lane, the Milton Keynes road, between the crossroads and the mill, although there were also medieval house sites to the south and north of the crossroads (Fig. 80). Those to the south were mainly in the field to the south of Mill Lane and the church, and east of the village hall and the former school. When this field was levelled and made into a sports field medieval and post-medieval pottery and other artefacts were found. North of the crossroads in the triangular green-like area were several croft boundaries, and on the east side of the road medieval house sites (MK 759) were destroyed during construction work.

In the field south of Mill Lane a small moat survives on the west bank of the Ouzel. This moat (MK 653) is beside the mill leat and upstream of the mill, as were many other Ouzel valley moats, and it may have served as a fishpond or horticultural feature rather than a homestead moat.

The major buildings in the village were the church, the mill and the mill house, Church Farmhouse and the manor house. The church was re-ordered in 1982, and the opportunity was then taken to excavate beneath the modern floor levels. The results confirmed that the earliest church on the site dated from at least the eleventh century (Croft, forthcoming). Church Farmhouse, to the west of the church, dates from the late sixteenth century, and the manor house, south-west of the crossroads, is a seventeenth-century building, presumably occupying the site of the medieval manor. The mill, a timber-framed building, was demolished c.1940 (Woodfield 1986, 650). The mill house was a substantial building dating from the seventeenth century, the ground floor being of stone with a timber-framed upper storey. This building became disused earlier this century, and the upper floor soon became ruinous, but it was not finally demolished until the 1960s.

It is unfortunate that the Woolstones lost several important buildings in the decade before the development of Milton Keynes. Had they survived, they would have been appreciated and retained as part of the City's building heritage.

THE FIELD SYSTEM

The ridge-and-furrow maps for the two parishes have been combined (Fig. 81). All of the land in the parishes, apart from the low-lying meadowland, was ploughed during the medieval period. There are few extant medieval documents recording the field names in either parish, but a glebe terrier of 1607 for Little Woolstone refers to lands in three fields, *Upper*, *Middle* and *Nether* (Bodleian, Willis Mss 100, 201). The position of these fields is fairly obvious, with the Upper Field in the west of the parish, the Nether Field in the east towards the meadows, and the Middle Field in the centre. There is no similar information for Great Woolstone.

Part of Great Woolstone was enclosed by private agreement in 1675, but the parish was not formally enclosed until 1796 (VCH 1927, 510). Little Woolstone had been enclosed a few years earlier by an Act of Parliament dated 1791 (*ibid.*, 512).

OTHER LANDSCAPE FEATURES

The Grand Junction Canal was constructed through both parishes, cutting the villages of from the fields to the west and requiring the provision of four bridges. At the crossroads in Little Woolstone the 'Barge Inn' was constructed in the early nineteenth century to serve the canal traffic.

Two small brickworks, one in each parish, appear on the 1881 OS map. In Little Woolstone the site was on the north side of the junction of the canal and the road to Great Linford, and is marked as "Old Brickkiln". The site in Great Woolstone was near the southern end of the parish on the west bank of the canal, and was probably still working since buildings are shown and the site is labelled "Kiln and Brick Field".

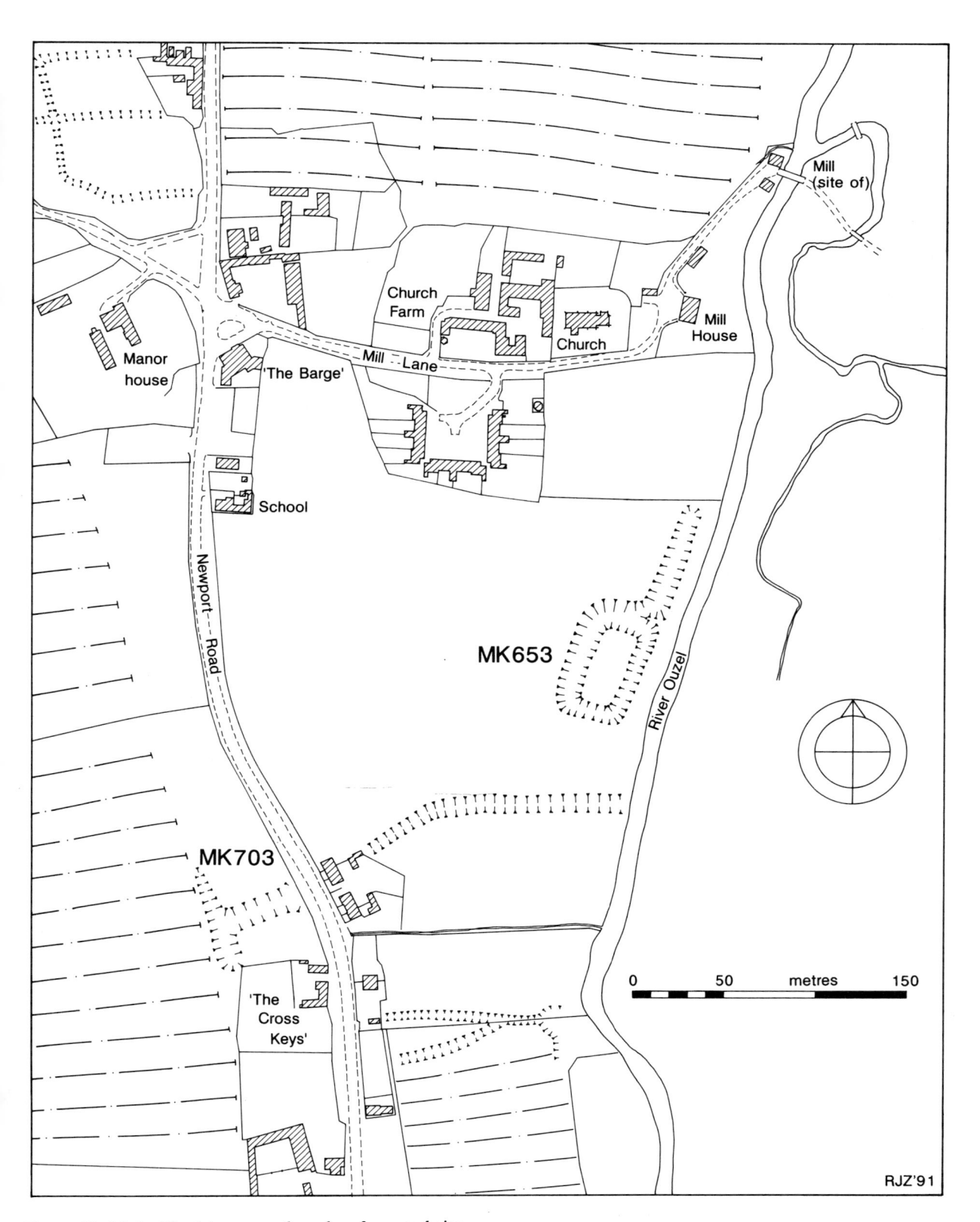

Figure 80: Little Woolstone; earthworks of moated site.

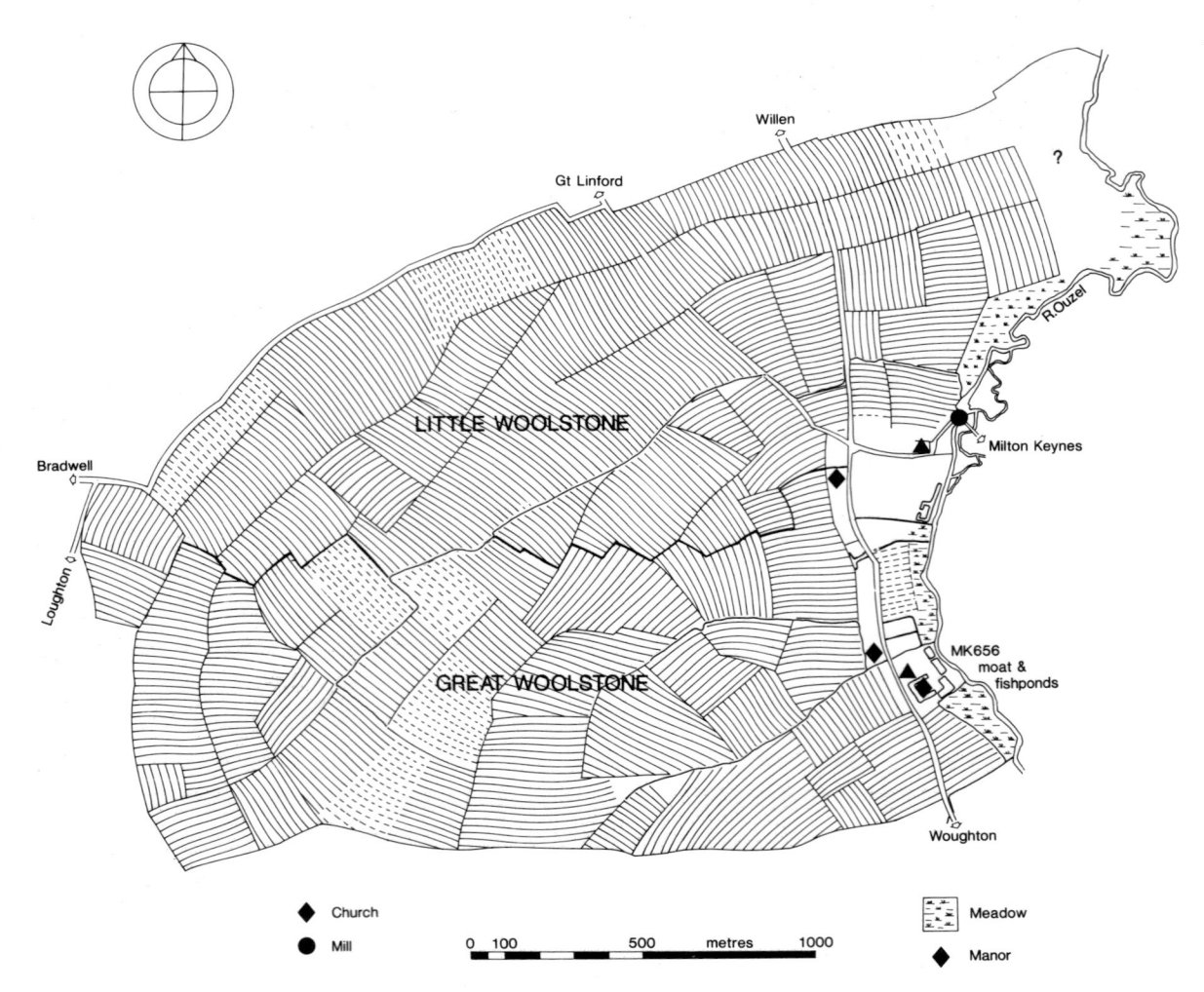

Figure 81: The Woolstones; medieval field systems.

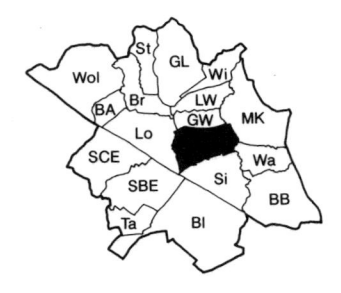

WOUGHTON ON THE GREEN

INTRODUCTION

The parish of Woughton on the Green, covering some 495 ha, was in a central position within the city on the western side of the Ouzel (Fig. 82). In the eastern part of the parish in the river valley there are drift deposits of alluvium and gravels with some head deposits. Boulder clay covers the rest of the parish, and at the western end this overlies deposits of Oxford clay. This underlying geology resulted in the formation of ill-drained heavy clay soils, except in the valley.

The land slopes gently from west to east, the highest point, about 105 m OD, being in the western end of the parish, in the area formerly known as 'Woughton Covert'. The village, situated towards the eastern end of the parish, overlooked the valley from a prominent position at a height of 76 m OD.

The Ouzel formed the eastern parish boundary, from which the northern boundary with Great Woolstone ran at right angles in an almost straight line. The southern boundary with Simpson also left the Ouzel at a right angle, but both it and the western boundary with Loughton contained dog-leg sections where they skirted medieval furlongs, suggesting that there had been agreed revision of the boundary.

The parish, rectangular in shape, was on an east-west alignment, and the main through route ran from Watling Street northwards up the western parish boundary, then turned eastwards to run through the centre of the parish and the village, down to a ford over the Ouzel and on to Milton Keynes village. Between the village and the Ouzel this road was called *Meadows Way* at the time of the enclosure in 1769 (BuCRO IR 103). The north-south route from Fenny Stratford to Newport Pagnell, which was the *Portway* in the sixteenth century (BuCRO ST 143), ran into the village from Simpson and turned left at the 'T' junction by the church, continuing to the west for a short distance before turning to the north and passing into Great Woolstone parish. This road was also known as *Blecham* and *Blechele Way* as it ran south from the village towards Bletchley, and *Woolson Way* as it ran northwards to the Woolstones. A road from Walton crossed the Ouzel at *Monkston's Bridge* and joined the Fenny Stratford road south of the village. This bridge was still in use in the eighteenth century (BL Add. Mss 5839, 223). Towards the western end of the parish a road left the east-west route and ran northwards around the furlongs, passing Secklow mound on its way to Great Linford. Several other minor routes linked the village with its fields, and one of these, called *Ridgeway* in the sixteenth century (BuCRO ST 143), ran parallel with and on the north side of the east-west route for much of its course through the parish.

ARCHAEOLOGY

As in Simpson and the Woolstones, only a few prehistoric flints have been found in the parish. In the north-west corner a small Belgic to Roman settlement (MK297) was excavated in 1973–75 (Mynard 1987, 90–97). There are no Saxon finds from the parish apart from three sherds of pottery (MK553) which were found during fieldwalking at the western end.

THE MEDIEVAL AND LATER VILLAGE

Woughton on the Green is one of the finest examples of a deserted medieval village in the city, and is a scheduled Ancient Monument. The name of the village recorded in the Domesday survey, *Ulchetone*, probably derives from the *tun* or estate of *Weoca* and dates from the late eighth or ninth century.

The village, situated towards the eastern end of the parish, was a linear development along the east-west route. It was a substantial settlement, with the church and principal manor at its centre and the moated site of a second manor at the west end. Between this moat and the church, what is now an extensive rectangular green was crossed by three parallel roads. The southern road has medieval crofts on its southern side, some of which contain houses dating from the sixteenth century. The central road, called *Churchway* in the

Figure 82: Woughton on the Green in 1967, showing major archaeological sites.

eighteenth century (BuCRO IR 103), has house sites on either side, particularly at the east end towards the church. Beyond the northern road several small closes containing ridge-and-furrow were called *Old Inclosures* in 1769, when the formal enclosure of the parish took place (*op. cit.*).

East of the church and the manor the village crofts continued on both sides of the road, *Meadows Lane*, down to the ford across the Ouzel, and the site of the medieval mill called *Voxmill* in 1346 (Bodleian, Radcliffe Mss 443).

The earthworks of the medieval village are well-preserved, particularly to the east of the church, down to the Ouzel (Fig. 83). Their quality has resulted from the fact that they became grassland after the house sites were abandoned, and have never been ploughed.

The earthworks are decribed from east to west, commencing at the Ouzel. The road from the ford survived as perhaps the best-preserved sunken road in Milton Keynes until the construction of the modern footbridge by Milton Keynes Development Corporation, undertaken without Scheduled Monument Consent or even prior consultation with the Archaeology Unit. On the way up to the centre of the village (Plate 36) the road is on average 10–15 m wide and up to 1.5 m deep.

On the north side of the road are eight crofts clearly defined by boundary ditches 5–10 m wide and up to 1 m deep. The crofts are of various sizes, all are rectangular and with the exception of the two easternmost all have their longest axis at right angles to the road. None of the crofts contain ridge-and-furrow, confirming that they are contemporary with or earlier than the establishment of the furlongs to the north. The westernmost croft, to the north of the manor site, still contains a cottage.

South of the road and north of the church, the site of the medieval manor house is occupied by the Woughton House Hotel, formerly Woughton House. To the east of this a large close extends along the south side of the road, but is separated from the meadowland and the river by a medieval furlong containing ridge-and-furrow.

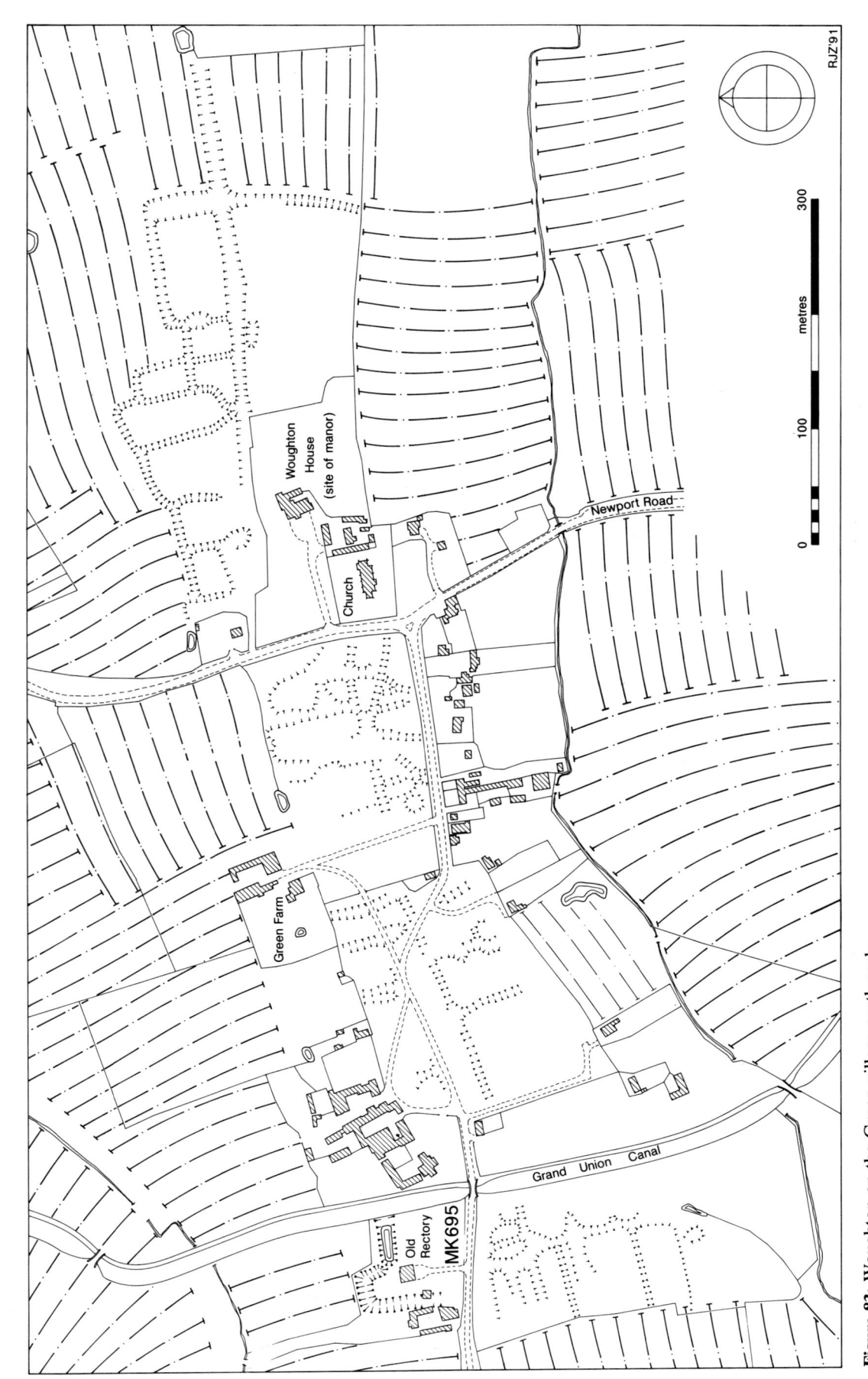

Figure 83: Woughton on the Green village earthworks.

Plate 36: Woughton; earthworks east of Woughton House, c.1960. (© *British Crown Copyright 1993/MOD reproduced with the permission of the Controller of Her Britannic Majesty's Stationery Office*)

To the west of the church and the manor, Meadows Lane continues as the northern boundary of the village green (Plate 37), and beyond to the western end of the village, which was separated from the main body of the village by the construction of the Grand Junction Canal. On the north side of Meadows Lane are several closes and the site of the post-enclosure Green Farm, demolished 1971, while to the west of this is the site of the second manor.

The nature of the village green is uncertain, as it contains earthworks which have been disturbed by modern farm tracks and associated erosion. A sunken road runs from the church across the green to the west end of the village, and this can be identified with *Church Way*, mentioned in the enclosure award of 1769 (BuCRO IR 103). On either side of Church Way, particularly at the east end, the earthworks resemble disturbed house platforms and croft boundaries, but their precise purpose and date connot be ascertained without excavation. However, it seems likely that there were houses on the green in the eighteenth century, when there was a dispute over the ownership of certain houses which had been built on waste land within the manor (BuCRO D/B 94). It is likely that this waste land occupied all or part of the green, since the records of manorial courts held in 1723 refer to a house occupied by William Yates which had been built on the waste of the manor, and in 1741 record that Yates had "inc-

Plate 37: Woughton; earthworks on and east of the green, c.1960. *(Cambridge University Collection of Air Photographs copyright reserved)*

roached upon the waste of this manor by erecting a hovel on the green near a certain lane called Herris Lane" (*op. cit.*). The location of this lane is uncertain.

The west end of the green towards the canal contains few earthworks, because it was partly levelled earlier this century to create an informal sportsfield for the village. Beyond the canal a north-south sunken way marks the western limit of the green, beyond which three crofts were excavated in 1973 in advance of the construction of Woughton Marina. The excavation revealed a fourteenth-century house with a detached kitchen on the southern croft, and a seventeenth-century cottage to the north (Mynard forthcoming). In 1985, when the area was totally stripped of topsoil during the construction of the marina, the sites of three more houses were found.

At the north-west corner of the green, a moated site (MK695), now a scheduled Ancient Monument, is the site of the second manor in the village. The manor house was rebuilt to the east in the sixteenth century, and the moat was cut off from it by the construction of the canal. The rectory occupied the site within the moat in the early seventeenth century (BuCRO ST 143), and the present house became known as the Old Rectory after the erection of the nineteenth-century rectory at the southern end of the village.

The moat was rectangular, 80×60 m, with a small extension 30 m sq. projecting north from the north-west corner. The moat ditch on the east side was on the line of the canal; the southern ditch and the south-east corner have been filled in and the only visible ditch is around the northern extension and part of the north arm, which remains as a pond. The surviving parts suggest that the ditch was on average 15 m wide.

The oldest houses in the village, dating from the sixteenth century, are the manor house on the north side of the green and Cottage Farmhouse to the south, while several others date from the seventeenth, eighteenth and nineteenth centuries.

The date of the desertion of the house sites represented by the earthworks is uncertain. Excavation at the west end of the green confirmed that one building had gone out of use in the late fourteenth to fifteenth century, and that others survived into the eighteenth century. The proceedings of a manorial court held in 1723 recorded the rents paid by tenants of various properties, and a marginal note stated "NB. As the Cottages are all down these payments have long since ceased" (BuCRO D.B.94).

THE FIELD SYSTEM

The earliest extant document which gives names of the fields and furlongs is a glebe terrier of 1612 (BuCRO ST 143). The parish had a three-field system at that time, and the names of the fields were *Middle*, *North* and *South* (Fig. 84). The precise boundaries of these fields are uncertain, but their location can be deduced from the names of the adjacent parishes and roads mentioned in the description of the location of the furlongs within them. The North Field was to the north of the main east-west route, the Middle Field was in the south-west corner of the parish and the South Field occupied the land south of the village and Chadds Lane, which runs from the south-west corner of the green. The terrier also gives the names of many of the furlongs, but without a more recent field-name map with which to compare them they are impossible to locate.

It is likely that most of the small closes around the village core and green were enclosed towards the end of the medieval period, because the parish is included in the list of parishes where some enclosure had already been carried out, which was com-

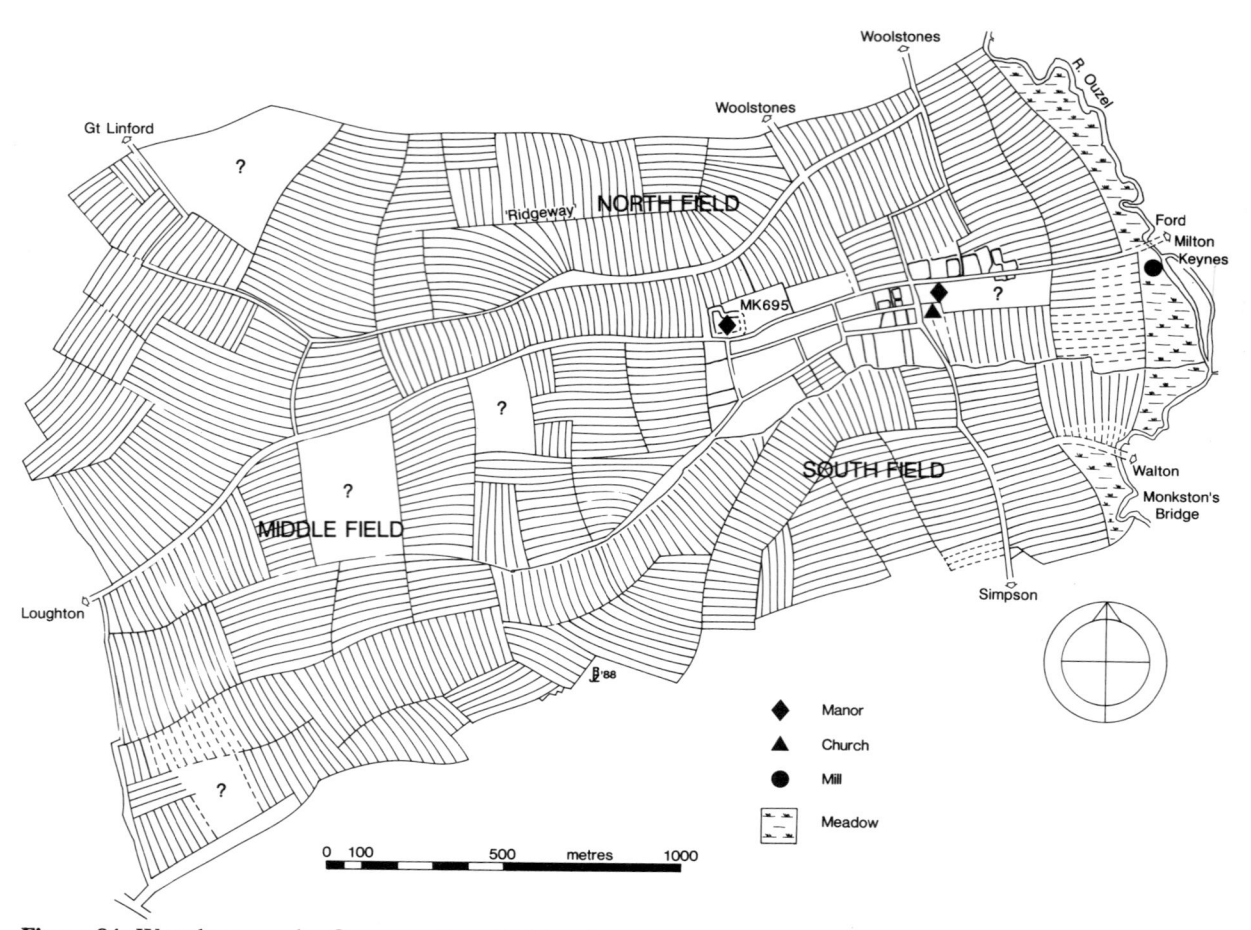

Figure 84: Woughton on the Green medieval field system.

piled by Wolsey's Commissioners in 1517 (Leadam 1897, 179). The parish was formally enclosed by an Act of Parliament in 1768 (BuCRO IR.103).

Before the development of the city, land use in the parish was fairly mixed, with several areas of post-enclosure pasture in the Ouzel Valley preserving ridge-and-furrow. During the 1960s, progressive farming resulted in the removal of many of the enclosure hedges in the western part of the parish, creating an open landscape. One area became known locally as "The Prairie", echoing the large hedgeless fields often found in East Anglia.

Virtually no woodland was shown on the 1881 OS map, and *Woughton Covert* appears to be a relatively modern plantation, used as a game covert during the nineteenth century.

OTHER LANDSCAPE FEATURES

CANAL

The Grand Union Canal runs north to south through the parish. Its route, close to the western end of the old village, separated the Old Rectory moat and the earthworks south of it from the rest of the village, taking for part of its course the eastern arm of the moat. Apart from the general disruption associated with its construction and the need to erect four bridges to enable the villagers to get to their fields in the west of the parish, the canal probably brought little change to the village.

RAILWAY

The former London and North Western Railway crosses the south-western corner of the parish in a deep cutting, and the line is crossed by a bridge linking the parish with Watling Street.

WATERMILL

The earliest reference to a watermill in the parish is in 1346, when Thomas de Kanee, rector of Woughton, granted several properties, some land and "Free fishing in Woketon (Woughton) waters and free milling in *Voxmill*" (Bodleian, Radcliffe Mss, deed 443). No other references to this mill are known, but a likely site for it is on the Ouzel where the silted-up channel of the former mill leat can be seen just upstream of the ford, where Meadows Lane crossed the river.

BIBLIOGRAPHY

ABBREVIATIONS:

BedsCRO	Bedfordshire County Records Office.	*Cal.Close*	Calendars of Close Rolls, HMSO 1892–1927.
Bodleian	Bodleian Library, Oxford.	*Cal.Fine*	Calendars of Fine Rolls, HMSO 1920–31.
Book of Fees	HMSO, 3 vols, 1920–31.	*Cal.Pat*	Calendars of Patent Rolls, HMSO 1894–1916.
BL	British Library.	*HertsCRO*	Hertfordshire County Records Office.
BAS	Buckinghamshire Archaeological Society.	*LRS*	Lincoln Record Society.
BCM	Buckinghamshire County Museum.	*LCRO*	Lincolnshire Records Office.
BuCRO	Buckinghamshire County Records Office.	*NCRO*	Northamptonshire County Records Office.
BRS	Buckinghamshire Records Society.	*OxonCRO*	Oxfordshire County Records Office.
Cal.Chart	Calendars of Charter Rolls, HMSO 1908–16.		

PUBLICATIONS:

Adkins, R.A. and Mynard, D.C., 1978. 'Neolithic axes from the Milton Keynes area of the Upper Ouse Valley', *Rec. Buckinghamshire* **20.4**, 630–35.

Adkins, R.A. and Petchey, M.R., 1984. 'Secklow Hundred mound and other meeting mounds in England', *Archaeol. J.* **141**, 243–51.

Baines, A.H.J., 1986. 'The origins of the borough of Newport Pagnell' *Rec.Buckinghamshire* **28**, 128–137.

Baines, E., Mynard, D.C. and Zeepvat, R.J., forthcoming. *A history of Bradwell Abbey*.

Benthall, Rev. J., 1888. *A paper written to Buckinghamshire Archaeology Society* (unpublished).

Bradbrook, W., 1924. 'The medieval court rolls of Fenny Stratford and Etone (Bletchley)', *Rec. Buckinghamshire* **11.6**, 289–314.

Branigan, K., 1987. *The Catuvellauni*. Alan Sutton (Gloucester).

Britnell, R.H., 1977. 'The origins of Stony Stratford', *Rec. Buckinghamshire* **20**, 451–53.

BCM 1980. *Gazetteer of Buckinghamshire brickyards, 1800–1980*. Buckinghamshire County Museum (Aylesbury).

Cantor, L.M., 1982. *The English Medieval landscape* (London).

Casey, J. (ed.), 1979. *The end of Roman Britain*, Brit. Archaeol. Rep. 71 (Oxford).

Chibnall, A.C., 1965. *Sherington, fiefs and fields of a Buckinghamshire village*. Philimore (Cambridge).

Chibnall, A.C., 1979. *Beyond Sherington*. Philimore (Cambridge).

Chibnall, A.C., 1950. *Lay subsidy rolls*. Buckinghamshire Rec. Soc. **8**.

Cocks A.H., 1897. *The church bells of Buckinghamshire, their inscriptions, founders, uses and traditions* (London).

Cornwall, J., 1959. 'An Elizabethan census', *Rec. Buckinghamshire* **16**, 258–73.

Croft, R.A., forthcoming. 'Excavations at Woolstone Church', *in* Mynard, forthcoming.

Edmondson, G.P. and Thorne, A.T., 1989. 'A late medieval tile-kiln at Shenley Church End, Milton Keynes, Buckinghamshire', *Rec. Buckinghamshire* **31**, 78–87.

Elvey, G.R., 1968. *Luffield Priory charters, part 1*. Northants. Rec. Soc. (Northampton).

Faulkner, A.H., 1972. *The Grand Junction Canal*. David and Charles (Newton Abbott).

Gelling, M., 1974. 'Some notes on Warwickshire place-names', *Trans. Birmingham Warwickshire Archaeol. Soc.* **86**, 59–79.

Gelling, M., 1978. *Signposts to the past* (London).

Gelling, M., 1984. *Place-names in the landscape* (London).

Gerard, J., 1985. *Gerard's Herbal*, ed. Marcus Woodward, Bracken Books (London).

Gibbs, R., 1879. *Buckinghamshire: a record of local occurrences and general events chronologically arranged*, vol. 2 (Aylesbury).

Giggins, B.L., 1983. *A brief history of the site of Valentin, Ord and Nagle's factory in Fenny Stratford*. Unpublished manuscript; copy in MKAU archive.

Green, C., 1957. 'Review of finds 1957', *Wolverton Dist. Archaeol. Soc. Newsletter* **2**, 5.

Green, H.S., 1971. ' A handaxe from Stantonbury, and further notes on handaxes from the valleys of the Ouse and Ouzel in North Buckinghamshire', *Rec. Buckinghamshire* **19.1**, 89–91.

Green, H.S., 1974. 'Early Bronze Age burial, territory and population in Milton Keynes, Buckinghamshire, and the Great Ouse Valley',*Archaeol. J.* **131**, 75–139.

Green, H.S. and Sofranoff, S., 1985. 'A Neolithic settlement at Stacey Bushes, Milton Keynes', *Rec. Buckinghamshire* **27**, 10–37.

Hanmer, Lord J., 1877. *Memorials of the parish and family of Hanmer in Flintshire.* Published privately (London).

Harris, M.P., 1968. 'Newport Pagnell's iron bridge', *Wolverton Dist. Archaeol. Soc. Journ.* **1**, 60–63.

Horton, A., Shephard-Thorn, E.R. and Thurrell, R.G., 1974. *The geology of the new town of Milton Keynes.* Report of Institute of Geological Sciences **74/16**, HMSO (London).

Hughes, M.W., 1940. *A calendar of the Feet of Fines for the county of Buckinghamshire, 7 Richard I to 44 Henry III.* Buckinghamshire Rec. Soc. (Aylesbury)

Hyde, F.E., 1945. *Wolverton. A short history of its economic and social development* (Wolverton).

Ivens, R.J. et al., forthcoming. *Westbury and Tattenhoe.* Buckinghamshire Archaeol. Soc. Monog. Ser. **8** (Aylesbury).

Jenkins, J.G., 1936. 'An early coroner's roll for Buckinghamshire', *Rec. Buckinghamshire* **13.3**, 163–85.

Jenkins, J.G., 1942. *Calendar of the Roll of the Justices of Eyre.* Buckinghamshire Rec. Soc. **6**.

Jenkins, J.G., 1952. *The Cartulary of Snelshall Priory*, Buckinghamshire Record Soc. **9**.

Jenkins, J.G., 1953. *The dragon of Whaddon; being an account of the life and work of Browne Willis, 1682–1760.* Bucks. Free Press (High Wycombe).

Jones, M.E., 1979. 'Climate, nutrition and disease: a hypothesis of Romano-British population', *in* Casey, 231–51.

Kennett, D.H., 1969. 'The New Bradwell late Bronze Age hoard', *Northampton Mus. Art Gall. J.* **6**, 2–7.

Leadam, I.S., 1897. *The Domesday of inclosures, 1517–1518, vol. 2.* Royal Hist. Soc. (London)

Leleux, R., 1976. *A regional history of the railways of Great Britain. Volume 9; the East Midlands.* David and Charles (Newton Abbott).

Lipscomb, G., 1847. *The history and antiquities of the county of Buckingham.* (London).

Markham, Sir F., 1973. *History of Milton Keynes and district, vol. 1.* (Luton).

Mawer and Stenton 1925. *The place-names of Buckinghamshire*, English Place-Name Society, vol. **2** (Cambridge).

Millard, L., 1965. 'Some palaeoliths from the Bletchley district', *Rec. Buckinghamshire* **17.5**, 336–42.

Millard, L., 1967. 'Some medieval pottery from north Bucks.', *Rec. Buckinghamshire* **18.2**, 109–24.

Ministry of Agriculture, Fisheries and Food, 1961. *Agricultural land classification map of England and Wales*, Sheet 146 (London).

Morris, J., 1978. *Buckinghamshire Domesday Book.* Philimore 'history from the sources' series (Chichester).

Mynard, D.C., 1971. 'Rescue excavations at the deserted medieval village of Stantonbury, Bucks.', *Rec. Buckinghamshire* **19.1**, 17–41.

Mynard, D.C., 1974. 'Excavations at Bradwell Priory 1968–1973', *Milton Keynes J. Archaeol. Hist.* **3**, 31–66.

Mynard, D.C., 1979. 'Stone weights from the rivers Great Ouse, Ouzel, Nene and Tove', Rec. Buckinghamshire **21**, 11–28.

Mynard, D.C. (ed.), 1987. *Roman Milton Keynes.* Buckinghamshire Archaeol. Soc. Monog. Ser. **1** (Aylesbury).

Mynard, D.C., forthcoming. *Medieval village excavations in Milton Keynes.* Buckinghamshire Archaeol. Soc. Monog. Ser. **6** (Aylesbury).

Mynard, D.C. and Woodfield, C., 1977. 'A Roman site at Walton, Milton Keynes', *Rec. Buckinghamshire* **20**, 351–83.

Mynard, D.C. and Zeepvat, R.J., 1992. *Great Linford.* Buckinghamshire Archaeol. Soc. Monog. Ser. **3** (Aylesbury).

Neal, D.S., 1987. 'Excavations at Magiovinium, Buckinghamshire, 1978–80', *Rec. Buckinghamshire* **29**, 1–124.

Niblett, B.R.K., 1974. 'Excavations at Bradwell Abbey Barn, 1971', *Rec. Buckinghamshire* **19.4**, 483–500.

Petchey, M.R. and Giggins, B.L., 1983. 'The excavation of a late seventeenth-century water-mill at Caldecotte, Bow Brickhill, Bucks.', *Post-Medieval Archaeol.* **17**, 65–94.

Pettit, P.A.J., 1965. *The royal forests of Northamptonshire 1558 – 1714.* Northamptonshire Rec. Soc. **23**.

Rackham, O., 1976. *Trees and woodland in the British landscape.* (London).

Rackham, O., 1980. *Ancient woodland, its history, vegetation and uses in England.* (London).

Roberts, B.K., 1982. *Village plans.* Shire Archaeology **27** (Princes Risborough).

Roberts, B.K., 1987. *The making of the English village.* (London).

Rowley, T. (ed.), 1981. *The origins of open field agriculture.* (London).

RCHM, 1914. *An inventory of the historical monuments in Buckinghamshire, volume 2.* (London).

RCHM, 1982. *An inventory of historical monuments in the county of Northampton; volume 4, archaeological sites in south-west Northamptonshire.* (London).

Sheahan, J.J., 1862. *History and topography of Buckinghamshire.* (Chicheley).

Simco, A., 1984. *Survey of Bedfordshire: The Roman period.* (Bedford and London).

Simpson, B., 1981. *The Oxford to Cambridge Railway. Volume 1; Oxford – Bletchley.* (Oxford).

Simpson, B., 1983. *The Oxford to Cambridge Railway. Volume 2; Bletchley – Cambridge.* (Oxford).

Stokes, F.G. (ed.), 1931. *The Bletchley diary of the Rev. William Cole, 1765-7.*

Tate, W.E., 1946. *Handlist of Bucks enclosure awards.* Buckinghamshire County Council (Aylesbury).

Taylor, C.C., 1975. 'Roman settlement in the Nene Valley: the impact of recent archaeology', *in* Fowler, 107.

Tull, G.K., 1972. 'The Hockcliffe – Two Mile Ash Turnpike, 1790–1807', *Milton Keynes J. Archaeol. Hist.* **1**.

Viatores, 1964. *Roman roads in the south east Midlands.* (London).

VCH, 1905. *The Victoria history of the counties of England: Buckingham*, vol. **1**. (London).

VCH, 1927. *The Victoria history of the counties of England: Buckingham*, vol. **4**. (London).

Waugh, H., Mynard, D.C. and Cain, R., 1974. 'Some Iron Age pottery from mid and north Bucks, with a gazetteer of associated sites and finds', *Rec. Buckinghamshire* **19.4**, 373–419.

Williams, R.J., 1980. 'Fieldwork', *Counc. Brit. Archaeol. Group 9 Newsletter* **10**, 77.

Williams, R.J., 1981. 'Fieldwork', *Counc. Brit. Archaeol. Group 9 Newsletter* **11**, 67–68.

Williams, R.J., 1986. 'Late Bronze Age house in Milton Keynes', *Rescue News* **40**, 1.

Williams, R.J., 1993. *Pennyland and Hartigans*. Buckinghamshire Archaeol. Soc. Monog. Ser. **4** (Aylesbury).

Williams, R.J., forthcoming. 'MK353 Ouzel valley flint scatters, *in* Zeepvat *et al*.

Williams, R.J. and Hart, P.J., forthcoming. 'A late Iron Age site at Furzton, Milton Keynes'.

Williams, R.J., Hart, P.J. and Williams, A.Ll., forthcoming. *Wavendon Gate*. Buckinghamshire Archaeol. Soc. Monog. Ser. **10** (Aylesbury).

Woodfield, C., 1977. 'A Roman military site at Magiovinium?', *Rec. Buckinghamshire* **20.3**, 384–99.

Woodfield, C, 1989. 'A Roman site at Stanton Low, on the Great Ouse, Buckinghamshire', *Archaeol. J.* **146**, 135–278.

Woodfield, P., 1986. *A guide to the historic buildings of Milton Keynes*. Milton Keynes Development Corporation (Milton Keynes).

Zeepvat, R.J., 1988. 'Another Roman building at Wymbush?', *Rec. Buckinghamshire* **30**, 111–16.

Zeepvat, R.J., 1990. *Walton Hall*. Unpublished, MKAU archives.

Zeepvat, R.J., 1991. *Roman Milton Keynes*. Milton Keynes Archaeology Unit (Milton Keynes).

Zeepvat, R.J., Roberts, J.C. and King, N.A., forthcoming. *Caldecotte*. Buckinghamshire Archaeol. Soc. Monog. Ser. **9** (Aylesbury).

Zeepvat, R.J. and Williams, R.J., forthcoming. *Bancroft*. Buckinghamshire Archaeol. Soc. Monog. Ser. **7** (Aylesbury).